ASK
THE BIBLE

ASK THE BIBLE

by R. T. BROOKS

GRAMERCY PUBLISHING COMPANY
New York

*To the late Martin Self who initiated this project
and to his widow Anke Self who carried it through*

This 1989 edition is published by Gramercy Publishing
Company, distributed by Outlet Book Company, Inc.,
a Random House Company, 225 Park Avenue South,
New York, New York 10003, by arrangement with
The Stonesong Press, Inc.

Printed and Bound in the United States of America

LIBRARY OF CONGRESS CATALOGING-IN-PUBLICATION DATA

Brooks, R. T.
  Ask the Bible.

  Includes index.
  1. Christian life—Biblical teaching.   I. Title.
BS680.C47B76   1989   248.4   88-32838

ISBN 0-517-67695-8
10 9 8 7 6 5 4 3

CONTENTS

ASK THE BIBLE: PREFACE

If you ask the Bible about the issue uppermost in your mind, it does not give you the answer to your problem packaged, custom-built, or gift-wrapped. It does, however, offer you the light and the tools you need to shape your own solution. The end product is both biblical and personal. In fact, you probably will not be able to tell where the biblical contribution ends and your own reflections take over. That, at any rate, has been my experience in working on this book, and I offer neither more nor less to any who may read it.

Most of the words that appear in alphabetical order at the tops of the following pages were chosen for me rather than by me. Martin Self, before his death, selected them because they encapsulate the issues that concern thinking people today. My job was first to find some biblical readings that are relevant to each issue, and then to write a brief introduction to help release the meaning of those biblical passages into the circumstances of our time. These introductions look first at the Old Testament, then at the New Testament, then at the world of the 1980s.

In this book the columns of biblical quotation are all in the familiar version known as King James's, but in the case of the poetic Old Testament books such as Psalms, Job, and Proverbs the lines have been divided in such a way as to bring out the parallelism which is the basic characteristic of Hebrew poetry. Such passages can readily be identified here by the fact that the type is a little smaller and there are no verse numberings against the text.

All other quotations, whether from the Old Testament or the New, are reproduced just as they would be found in a normal Bible. Since the verses have been specially selected for their aptness to each particular subject, a quotation may begin in the middle of a passage or direct speech without naming the speaker. Or it may use a pronoun instead of a person's name. Or it may begin with a word such as "and" or "for" which clearly links it to earlier verses not quoted here.

None of this should cause a lot of difficulty. If a speech is identified as coming from Matthew, Mark, Luke or John, it is safe to assume that the speaker is Jesus—and "he" will be Jesus too. If a quotation is said to come from one of Paul's letters such as Romans or Corinthians, it is safe to assume that the pronoun "I" refers to Paul. And so on. In all cases the passage will become clear if read as a whole.

Because a variety of verses have been chosen for their special relevance, the verse numbers beside the text may not run consecutively—they may not all even refer to the same chapter. However, the chapter and verse references given at the head of each quotation will make it easy to trace any verse to its original context if (as is much to be desired) you should wish to see a particular text in its full setting.

Inevitably, both the selections and the introductory comments are those of just one very fallible Bible reader, but my aim was to let the Bible speak for itself. I tried not to take to it any preconceptions about the nature of its inspiration, about the answers it ought to give, about the way passages have been understood in this tradition or in that. I may have failed, but I was trying to read the Bible biblically.

This does not mean that I think we get the help we need by transporting ourselves back into biblical times and staying there. The authors of the Bible wrote in response to a vision of God granted to them in the circumstances of their day. We have to stand in their shoes so as to see something of their vision, but then we have to respond to their message in the circumstances of our day. I would ask readers to set themselves, as I did, the task described by Professor James D. Smart when he tells us to "wrestle with the words of these ancient witnesses until the walls of the centuries become thin and they tell us in *our* day what they knew so well in their day. They knew God."*

---

*Smart, *The Interpretation of Scripture* (London: SCM, 1961). James D. Smart is Professor of Biblical Interpretation, Union Theological Seminary, New York.

ADULTERY

On this subject the Bible both lays down the law and transcends the law. It issues commandments and prohibitions, but it also goes beyond them to something more inward. It does not withdraw the commands or the prohibitions, but it does reveal through them a better and more positive way than that of the man or woman who merely refrains from breaking an outward code of conduct.

The Old Testament begins by invoking law to deal with the matter. It allowed polygamous marriage and was not much bothered by sexual relations that did not involve another man's wife. If intercourse took place between a married woman and any man other than her husband, however, both parties were in principle liable to the death penalty. The law was even more severe for women than for men. A married man could make love to an unmarried woman without penalty, but a married woman was bound absolutely to her husband.

In practice the law was broken—by David and Bathsheba, for example. Their story was told, however, not to condone the offense, but to make clear that even the greatest of Old Testament kings and heroes was not above the law, though his penitence did secure some remission of the penalty. (The fact that David went on from committing adultery to arranging the death of Bathsheba's husband made matters worse, but that is irrelevant here.)

Some of the later prophets opened up the subject from a different angle. They regarded the people of Israel as having behaved toward God the way an unfaithful wife behaves toward her husband. Israel was bound to God by covenant—married to him, as it were—and had not been true to that union. Some of the prophets hoped and believed that God would remake the covenant in a new and more inward form. This theological hope could not but reflect back on human relationships: if God did not treat adultery as unforgivable, should a human husband do so? One prophet, Hosea, even felt that he was himself called to take a promiscuous woman as his wife, and apparently to take her back again after her infidelity.

In the New Testament Jesus is in some ways even more demanding than the legalists. He extends the ancient prohibition to include lust—adultery in the heart. Such an extension, however, makes the rigor of the law unenforceable. According to a story omitted from some of the oldest manuscripts of the Gospel of John (but included here), Jesus showed that to be so when an adulterous woman was brought to him. More important, his extension of the commandment pushed the whole issue inward. Adultery now concerns not just the body but the whole personality.

Not that the body is unimportant. It is, says the New Testament, the temple of the Spirit. Outward and inward must correspond.

1

To regard casual adultery as a light matter is to treat the outward and the inward as easily separable. They are not. The bonds formed by sexual relationships are real bonds. They go deep into the personality. Breaking them hurts. The Bible's high and demanding view of marriage is not an expression of sour frustration. It springs from a deep appreciation of all that is involved in the coming together of men and women.

The Bible is just as discouraging to those who are eager to adopt condemnatory attitudes, however. It seems to imply that those who enjoy the scandal while condemning the offense may themselves be offending quite as seriously. The real answer is not to condemn but to make clear that adultery is ruled out, not in order to restrict human freedom, but in order to promote human happiness.

The true fulfillment of human sexuality demands personal commitment as well as physical enjoyment. The body is exalted, not humiliated, by being made the vehicle of moral law and of spiritual love. If adultery is of the heart, so too is fidelity. The absence of misconduct is something; the presence of love is much more.

ADULTERY

OLD TESTAMENT

Exodus 20:14

14 Thou shalt not commit adultery.

Leviticus 20:10

10 And the man that committeth adultery with another man's wife, even he that committeth adultery with his neighbour's wife, the adulterer and the adulteress shall surely be put to death.

2 Samuel 11:2–4; 12:1–7

2 And it came to pass in an eveningtide, that David arose from off his bed, and walked upon the roof of the king's house: and from the roof he saw a woman washing herself; and the woman was very beautiful to look upon.

3 And David sent and inquired after the woman. And one said, Is not this Bathsheba, the daughter of Eliam, the wife of Uriah the Hittite?

4 And David sent messengers, and took her; and she came in unto him, and he lay with her. . . .

1 And the Lord sent Nathan unto David. And he came unto him, and said unto him, There were two men in one city; the one rich, and the other poor.

2 The rich man had exceeding many flocks and herds:

3 But the poor man had nothing, save one little ewe lamb, which he had bought and nourished up: and it grew up together with him, and with his children; it did eat of his own meat, and drank of his own cup, and lay in his bosom, and was unto him as a daughter.

Remorse – Some never discover it!

4 And there came a traveller unto the rich man, and he spared to take of his own flock and of his own herd, to dress for the wayfaring man that was come unto him; but took the poor man's lamb, and dressed it for the man that was come to him.

5 And David's anger was greatly kindled against the man; and he said to Nathan, As the Lord liveth, the man that hath done this thing shall surely die:

6 And he shall restore the lamb fourfold, because he did this thing, and because he had no pity.

7 And Nathan said to David, Thou art the man.

Hosea 3:1

1 Then said the Lord unto me, Go yet, love a woman beloved of her friend, yet an adulteress, according to the love of the Lord toward the children of Israel, who look to other gods.

NEW TESTAMENT

Matthew 5:27–28

27 Ye have heard that it was said by them of old time, Thou shalt not commit adultery:

28 But I say unto you, That whosoever looketh on a woman to lust after her hath committed adultery with her already in his heart.

John 8:3–11

3 And the scribes and Pharisees brought unto him a woman taken in adultery; and when they had set her in the midst,

4 They say unto him, Master, this woman was taken in adultery, in the very act.

5 Now Moses in the law commanded us, that such should be stoned: but what sayest thou?

6 This they said, tempting him, that they might have to accuse him. But Jesus stooped down, and with his finger wrote on the ground, as though he heard them not.

7 So when they continued asking him, he lifted up himself, and said unto them, He that is without sin among you, let him first cast a stone at her.

8 And again he stooped down, and wrote on the ground.

9 And they which heard it, being convicted by their own conscience, went out one by one, beginning at the eldest, even unto the last: and Jesus was left alone, and the woman standing in the midst.

10 When Jesus had lifted up himself, and saw none but the woman, he said unto her, Woman, where are those thine accusers? hath no man condemned thee?

11 She said, No man, Lord. And Jesus said unto her, Neither do I condemn thee: go, and sin no more.

Mark 7:21–23

21 For from within, out of the hearts of men, proceed evil thoughts, adulteries, fornications, murders,

22 Thefts, covetousness, wickedness, deceit, lasciviousness, an evil eye, blasphemy, pride, foolishness:

23 All these evil things come from within, and defile the man.

1 Corinthians 6:18–19

18 Flee fornication. Every sin that a man doeth is without the body; but he that committeth fornication sinneth against his own body.

19 What? know ye not that your body is the temple of the Holy Ghost which is in you, which ye have of God, and ye are not your own?

AGGRESSION

The word "aggression" does not occur in the Bible, but the thing does. Present-day knowledge confirms that it was bound to do so. We live in a world of conflicting interests. There is a limited amount of space; there are limited resources. One man's pay raise is another man's price increase. As soon as interests conflict, one person is tempted to kick another out of the way. Whoever takes the initiative in doing so is an aggressor. And once admitted to the human scene, aggressiveness tends to take on a life of its own. Even when there is no real conflict of interests, an individual or a group or a nation can be aggressive just for the hell of it. Or we can act aggressively against an innocent party to revenge ourselves for having been the victims of aggression by some other, stronger person.

It has always been so. The Bible both recognizes and challenges this reality.

The Old Testament demonstrates the deep-rootedness of aggression by ascribing it to the first child of Adam and Eve. Cain's murder of his brother, Abel, is seen by some to reflect the conflict of interests between the settled agriculturist and the nomadic herdsman. It certainly symbolizes the potential for violence in the human race, and with the release of that potential comes the disruption of human brotherhood. "How do I know where Abel is?" says Cain. "Am I his keeper?"

From there the tale of violence goes on, but in spite of much glorying in military victory the Old Testament writers see aggression as the disruption of an underlying order that exists in the purpose of God and is to be brought to realization through his people. Until that time comes, God champions the victim of aggression.

The New Testament calls for a person not only to renounce aggression but also to refuse even to counter it. Yet the Christian is certainly not required to be a doormat on which the world can wipe its feet. Jesus speaks of his own work as an attack by the kingdom of God on a stronghold occupied and defended by the power of evil. What is more, his work will result in the disruption of families and the overturning of the established order.

Nevertheless, the kingdom that Jesus brings is a peaceable one, as his followers make clear in the letters they write to one another. They are to be purged of the mark of Cain. Their spiritual weapons are to be turned against those very forces that work in humanity beneath the level of conscious will—that aggressiveness which has acquired a life of its own.

So the aggression in us needs to be modified. The deep forcefulness in it is to be redeemed rather than destroyed. It has to change its orientation so that it looks out on the world and sees, not a battlefield of competing self-interests, but a potentially brotherly community invaded and disrupted by that which has no right to occupy the human scene at all. Cain's question was meant to be rhetorical, but it can be answered. The appropriate reply to "Am I my brother's keeper?" is "No, but you *are* his brother."

AGGRESSION

OLD TESTAMENT

Genesis 4:2, 8–12

2 And Abel was a keeper of sheep, but Cain was a tiller of the ground.

8 And Cain talked with Abel his brother: and it came to pass, when they were in the field, that Cain rose up against Abel his brother, and slew him.

9 And the Lord said unto Cain, Where is Abel thy brother? And he said, I know not: Am I my brother's keeper?

10 And he said, What hast thou done? the voice of thy brother's blood crieth unto me from the ground.

11 And now art thou cursed from the earth, which hath opened her mouth to receive thy brother's blood from thy hand;

12 When thou tillest the ground, it shall not henceforth yield unto thee her strength; a fugitive and a vagabond shalt thou be in the earth.

Psalm 140:1–2, 12–13

Deliver me, O Lord, from the evil man:
Preserve me from the violent man;
Which imagine mischiefs in their heart;
Continually are they gathered together
 for war.
I know that the Lord will maintain the
 cause of the afflicted,
And the right of the poor.
Surely the righteous shall give thanks unto
 thy name:
The upright shall dwell in thy presence.

Isaiah 2:4

4 And he shall judge among the nations, and shall rebuke many people: and they shall beat their swords into ploughshares, and their spears into pruninghooks: nation shall not lift up sword against nation, neither shall they learn war any more.

NEW TESTAMENT

Matthew 5:39

39 But I say unto you, That ye re-

sist not evil: but whosoever shall smite thee on thy right cheek, turn to him the other also.

Luke 11:21–22, 20

21 When a strong man armed keepeth his palace, his goods are in peace:

22 But when a stronger than he shall come upon him, and overcome him, he taketh from him all his armour wherein he trusted, and divideth his spoils.

20 But if I with the finger of God cast out devils, no doubt the kingdom of God is come upon you.

Matthew 10:34–36

34 Think not that I am come to send peace on earth: I came not to send peace, but a sword.

35 For I am come to set a man at variance against his father, and the daughter against her mother, and the daughter in law against her mother in law.

36 And a man's foes shall be they of his own household.

1 John 3:10–12

10 Whosoever doeth not righteous-

ness is not of God, neither he that loveth not his brother.

11 For this is the message that ye heard from the beginning, that we should love one another.

12 Not as Cain, who was of that wicked one, and slew his brother.

Ephesians 6:10–15

10 Finally, my brethren, be strong in the Lord, and in the power of his might.

11 Put on the whole armour of God, that ye may be able to stand against the wiles of the devil.

12 For we wrestle not against flesh and blood, but against principalities, against powers, against the rulers of the darkness of this world, against spiritual wickedness in high places.

13 Wherefore take unto you the whole armour of God, that ye may be able to withstand in the evil day, and having done all, to stand.

14 Stand therefore, having your loins girt about with truth, and having on the breastplate of righteousness;

15 And your feet shod with the preparation of the gospel of peace.

AMBITION

The Old Testament cuts ordinary ambitions down to size grimly and effectively by pointing out that they all end in the grave. Such realism might seem to deprive life of any goal worth aiming at, but it does not. It has two far more positive effects.

One effect is that it teaches a proper appreciation of the passing moment as a time of fulfillment. Ordinary ambition tends to devalue today. To the crudely ambitious man or woman, today is just a stage on the road to the fulfillment of ambition tomorrow. Not so to the individual who has looked at tomorrow (or the day after, perhaps) as clearly as the psalmist did. Such a person values the present moment.

So did the writer of Ecclesiastes, and his is a particularly interesting case because he speaks as one who not only has been ambitious but has also fulfilled his ambitions. He reports that this achievement did not mean a thing, except— and this is his way of saluting the passing moment—that the work itself was a delight. A reward was to be found in the pursuit of the goal that could not be found in the achievement of it.

This leads to the second positive effect: ambition can disregard death if its goal transcends death, and it does that if it is determined by imperishable values.

Ambition is not a matter of merely extending worldly values beyond the grave. In the New Testament two of the original apostles are criticized for doing just that. (One of the Gospels says it was rather their mother who did it, but this does not affect the wrongness of the ambition.) Their desire was to be one up on the others in the kingdom to come. Theirs was an ambition dominated by conventional images of power and glory, projected into eternity. Jesus not only repudiated this ambition; he also reversed it. The bottom rung of the ladder became in his account the top one, the one to aspire to if you were ambitious. Ambition is not excluded: it is just stood on its head.

Jesus himself does not appear in the New Testament as a man without ambition in some senses of the word, but his ambition involved pursuing imperishable values and heavenly goals here and now rather than seeking the fulfillment of meaner ambitions either here or hereafter. He is plainly reaching for the greatest imaginable prize—in fact for an unimaginable prize. So the ambitions of those with more measurable goals were revealed as the tawdry things they were.

Paul, too, is a prize-seeker. His ambition reaches to the skies. But under the influence of Jesus he reverses his values. He has looked at the ledger in which he keeps account of his ambitions and has simply switched the debit and credit signs.

The Bible does not so much denounce ambition as outbid it. It says in effect that the value of the success which beckons to the ambitious man or woman of the twentieth century is too low. Earthly success merely requires one to excel as compared with others—in wealth, or in power, or in sexual attractiveness, or in some other easily measured achievement. But this is a very little league to be so concerned about. The Bible envisages more exalted and less perishable goals. Given the right ones, it allows us to be unashamedly determined to achieve.

And the passing moment is enhanced rather than devalued by being related to the timeless objective. The reversed ladder of ambition reaches down into every day. Those who seek to climb it are not aiming to do better than others; instead, they are trying to do supremely well. They are trying to do everything supremely well, because every present action gains in significance from being immediately related to the ultimate glory.

This biblical attitude has many consequences. The athlete, for example, wants to be at peak form rather than to have the opposition break a leg. The artist wants to be true to his or her own vision rather than to get better notices than others. Those in business want to be efficient rather than to bankrupt their competitors. These are the temporal ambitions of those committed to transcendent values.

AMBITION

OLD TESTAMENT

Psalm 39:4–7

Lord, make me to know mine end,
And the measure of my days, what it is;
That I may know how frail I am.
Behold, thou hast made my days as an handbreadth;
And mine age is as nothing before thee;
Verily every man at his best state is altogether vanity.
Surely every man walketh in a vain shew:
Surely they are disquieted in vain:
He heapeth up riches, and knoweth not who shall gather them.
And now, Lord, what wait I for?
My hope is in thee.

Ecclesiastes 2:4–11; 3:22

4 I made me great works; I builded me houses; I planted me vineyards:

5 I made me gardens and orchards, and I planted trees in them of all kind of fruits:

6 I made me pools of water, to water therewith the wood that bringeth forth trees:

7 I got me servants and maidens, and had servants born in my house;

also I had great possessions of great and small cattle above all that were in Jerusalem before me:

8 I gathered me also silver and gold, and the peculiar treasure of kings and of the provinces: I gat me men singers and women singers, and the delights of the sons of men, as musical instruments, and that of all sorts.

9 So I was great, and increased more than all that were before me in Jerusalem: also my wisdom remained with me.

10 And whatsoever mine eyes desired I kept not from them, I withheld not my heart from any joy; for my heart rejoiced in all my labour: and this was my portion of all my labour.

11 Then I looked on all the works that my hands had wrought, and on the labour that I had laboured to do: and, behold, all was vanity and vexation of spirit, and there was no profit under the sun.

22 Wherefore I perceive that there is nothing better, than that a man should rejoice in his own works; for that is his portion: for who shall bring him to see what shall be after him?

NEW TESTAMENT

Mark 10:35–38, 41–45

35 And James and John, the sons of Zebedee, come unto him, saying, Master, we would that thou shouldest do for us whatsoever we shall desire.

36 And he said unto them, What would ye that I should do for you?

37 They said unto him, Grant unto us that we may sit, one on thy right hand, and the other on thy left hand, in thy glory.

38 But Jesus said unto them, Ye know not what ye ask.

41 And when the ten heard it, they began to be much displeased with James and John.

42 But Jesus called them to him, and saith unto them, Ye know that they which are accounted to rule over the Gentiles exercise lordship over them; and their great ones exercise authority upon them.

43 But so shall it not be among you: but whosoever will be great among you, shall be your minister:

44 And whosoever of you will be the chiefest, shall be servant of all.

45 For even the Son of man came not to be ministered unto, but to minister, and to give his life a ransom for many.

Philippians 3:7–12

7 But what things were gain to me, those I counted loss for Christ.

8 Yea doubtless, and I count all things but loss for the excellency of the knowledge of Christ Jesus my Lord: for whom I have suffered the loss of all things, and do count them but dung, that I may win Christ,

9 And be found in him, not having mine own righteousness, which is of the law, but that which is through the faith of Christ, the righteousness which is of God by faith:

10 That I may know him, and the power of his resurrection, and the fellowship of his sufferings, being made conformable unto his death;

11 If by any means I might attain unto the resurrection of the dead.

12 Not as though I had already attained, either were already perfect: but I follow after. . . .

James 3:14, 16

14 But if ye have bitter envying and strife in your hearts, glory not, and lie not against the truth.

16 For where envying and strife is, there is confusion and every evil work.

ANGER

The Old Testament speaks clearly about anger in God. His anger is never unprovoked, can always be appeased by repentance and is quenched more quickly than it is kindled, but it flames out against iniquity as naturally as fire responds to a draft of wind. Human anger can be equally justified, but it rarely is. The writers of the Old Testament express a healthy suspicion of human pretensions to divine wrath. Far from being a copy of God's anger, human anger can be aroused precisely by God's *not* acting angrily.

The story of Jonah is the parable of a man who was angry with God for not being angry enough. Like teacher's pet in the classroom, he did not want the bad boys returned to favor. In his case the bad boys are the wicked, pagan people of Nineveh, while he himself represents the people of God. In the climax of the story God shows Jonah that his petulance has led him to get things entirely out of proportion.

In the New Testament Jesus speaks of anger as the inward equivalent of murder, but he himself is angry when a man's suffering is used to bait a Sabbatarian trap. His anger, however, was mixed with sorrow. It could drive Jesus to act, as when he drove the profiteers from the temple precincts, but his anger was allied to love and not to hate.

The followers of Jesus continued the Old Testament belief in the anger of God as a fact of nature, but as an anger directed against wrong itself rather than against the wrongdoer. God's anger was entirely compatible with his maintaining a loving and merciful relationship to the sinner. As to human anger, the New Testament writers warned against the dangerous assumption that it was likely to be an echo or instrument of the righteous anger of God. Paul quoted Psalm 4:4, in which the psalmist assumes that a man will experience anger and only warns him not to let it lead him into doing wrong. Paul himself added the psychologically sound advice not to sleep on it.

So anger is not altogether a bad thing. A world filled with injustice and oppression is not one to be lived in with an ever-smiling face. Anger that is fueled by compassion and directed against wrong can be a powerful engine for advance. But once it gets out of hand, less and less provocation will ignite more and more anger. And what provokes it is increasingly likely to be what pricks our own ego rather than what oppresses our fellow man.

The trouble with anger is that it is apt to destroy all sense of proportion. The affront to my petty dignity, for example, rather than the offense against justice and love makes me see red, and it is this self-centered petulance that I like to mistake for righteous indignation. A true perspective on the world's ills might increase rather than diminish the total force of the anger in any of us, but it would be a better directed and healthier emotion.

Even then it would be well to cultivate the ability to put anger aside at the close of the day. Given a just cause, anger may have to be taken up afresh in the morning, but it should not be cherished through the night. When anger simmers on out of conscious control a mist arises from it and one's vision becomes clouded. Even when I am asleep, an unsleeping concern for justice remains alive in the world. We do not need to fan its fire all the time. We can let it go for a few hours so that tomorrow we will be the better able to serve wrath and forgiveness, both of which are expressions of love.

ANGER

OLD TESTAMENT

Isaiah 54:7–8

7 For a small moment have I forsaken thee; but with great mercies will I gather thee.

8 In a little wrath I hid my face from thee for a moment; but with everlasting kindness will I have mercy on thee, saith the Lord thy Redeemer.

Jonah 3:10–4:11

10 And God saw their works, that they turned from their evil way; and God repented of the evil, that he had said that he would do unto them; and he did it not.

1 But it displeased Jonah exceedingly, and he was very angry.

2 And he prayed unto the Lord, and said, I pray thee, O Lord, was not this my saying, when I was yet in my country? Therefore I fled before unto Tarshish: for I knew that thou art a gracious God, and merciful, slow to anger, and of great kindness, and repentest thee of the evil.

3 Therefore now, O Lord, take, I beseech thee, my life from me; for it is better for me to die than to live.

4 Then said the Lord, Doest thou well to be angry?

5 So Jonah went out of the city, and sat on the east side of the city, and

there made him a booth, and sat under it in the shadow, till he might see what would become of the city.

6 And the Lord God prepared a gourd, and made it to come up over Jonah, that it might be a shadow over his head, to deliver him from his grief. So Jonah was exceeding glad of the gourd.

7 But God prepared a worm when the morning rose the next day, and it smote the gourd that it withered.

8 And it came to pass, when the sun did arise, that God prepared a vehement east wind; and the sun beat upon the head of Jonah, that he fainted, and wished in himself to die, and said, It is better for me to die than to live.

9 And God said to Jonah, Doest thou well to be angry for the gourd? And he said, I do well to be angry, even unto death.

10 Then said the Lord, Thou hast had pity on the gourd, for the which thou hast not laboured, neither madest it grow; which came up in a night, and perished in a night:

11 And should not I spare Nineveh, that great city, wherein are more than sixscore thousand persons that cannot discern between their right hand and their left hand; and also much cattle?

NEW TESTAMENT

Matthew 5:21–22

21 Ye have heard that it was said by them of old time, Thou shalt not kill; and whosoever shall kill shall be in danger of the judgment:

22 But I say unto you, That whosoever is angry with his brother without a cause shall be in danger of the judgment.

Mark 3:1–6

1 And he entered again into the synagogue; and there was a man there which had a withered hand

2 And they watched him, whether he would heal him on the sabbath day; that they might accuse him.

3 And he saith unto the man which had the withered hand, Stand forth.

4 And he saith unto them, Is it lawful to do good on the sabbath days, or to do evil? to save life, or to kill? But they held their peace.

5 And when he had looked round about on them with anger, being grieved for the hardness of their hearts, he saith unto the man, Stretch forth thine hand. And he stretched it out: and his hand was restored whole as the other.

6 And the Pharisees went forth, and straightway took counsel with the Herodians against him, how they might destroy him.

Romans 1:18

18 For the wrath of God is revealed from heaven against all ungodliness and unrighteousness of men, who hold the truth in unrighteousness.

James 1:19–20

19 Wherefore, my beloved brethren, let every man be swift to hear, slow to speak, slow to wrath:

20 For the wrath of man worketh not the righteousness of God.

Ephesians 4:26–27

26 Be ye angry, and sin not: let not the sun go down upon your wrath:

27 Neither give place to the devil.

ANXIETY

The worried writer of Psalm 77 sings a worried song. His anxieties are only increased when he compares his present feelings with the more buoyant mood of earlier years. As his sleepless night drags on, he finds no relief or comfort. He feels as anxious as ever until at last he turns beyond feelings and looks outside his own experience to see the solid evidence of divine care in the history of Israel long ago. That objective point of reference steadies him and restores his sense of proportion.

Anxiety is not just worry; it is *needless* worry. It is worry looking for a cause rather than arising from one. Daniel in the lions' den might be said to have had sufficient grounds for anxiety, but grounds are not what anxiety thrives on. The Persian king who was tricked into putting Daniel in with the lions was the one who had a sleepless night, not knowing whether Daniel's God was equal to the situation.

In the Sermon on the Mount Jesus draws the worried man's attention away from himself and fastens it instead on the external evidence of God's care. Jesus recognizes a legitimate concern with each day's worries, but he rules out a fruitless preoccupation with unreal troubles and with future situations that will be helped not at all by being made the focus of anxiety.

Paul regards Jesus himself as the outside object in which we can find sufficient evidence of God's care.

Anxiety is so much a feature of our time that whole industries have grown up to deal with it. Some offer chemicals to dull the anxiety, while others offer psychological ways of coming to terms with it. Some treatments work; some do not. All of them together have not succeeded in wiping the worried look from the face of mankind.

In the Museum of Modern Art, in New York, there is a painting by Edvard Munch entitled *Anxiety*. It shows a number of people under a lowering sky, and each person is looking fixedly ahead. These people give never a glance at one another or at their immediate environment. The picture seems to say that anxiety is a self-isolating fixation on possibilities yet to be realized. Munch was quite capable of painting realistic faces, but none of these characters has one. Anxiety is not a realistic state of mind.

The alternative to anxiety is not complacency or optimism but realism. Look around. There are other people with whom we can share whatever may come from that threatening sky. There are flowers in the fields and birds in the sky (and not only in Galilee). For all its difficulties, life has a way of asserting itself triumphantly. The objective evidence is there outside us, if only we can turn our attention in that direction and away from the nameless fears and irrational anxieties within ourselves.

To look with love at the things and people around us seems almost too easy a cure for anxiety, given that we live in a world in which appalling things can and do happen. Yet it is precisely this outward-looking attitude that opens people to a therapy which can reach down a long way beneath the deep, irrational roots of anxiety.

ANXIETY

OLD TESTAMENT

Psalm 77:1–12

I cried unto God with my voice,
Even unto God with my voice; and he
  gave ear unto me.
In the day of my trouble I sought the
  Lord:
My sore ran in the night, and ceased not:
My soul refused to be comforted.
I remembered God, and was troubled:
I complained, and my spirit was over-
  whelmed.
Thou holdest mine eyes waking:
I am so troubled that I cannot speak.
I have considered the days of old,
The years of ancient times.
I call to remembrance my song in the
  night:
I commune with mine own heart:
And my spirit made diligent search.
Will the Lord cast off for ever?
And will he be favourable no more?
Is his mercy clean gone for ever?
Doth his promise fail for evermore?
Hath God forgotten to be gracious?
Hath he in anger shut up his tender
  mercies?
And I said, This is my infirmity:
But I will remember the years of the right
  hand of the most High.
I will remember the works of the Lord:
Surely I will remember thy wonders of
  old.
I will meditate also of all thy work,
And talk of thy doings.

Daniel 6:17–22

17 And a stone was brought, and
laid upon the mouth of the den; and
the king sealed it with his own signet,
and with the signet of his lords; that
the purpose might not be changed
concerning Daniel.

18 Then the king went to his palace, and passed the night fasting: neither were instruments of music brought
before him: and his sleep went from
him.

19 Then the king arose very early
in the morning, and went in haste unto
the den of lions.

20 And when he came to the den,
he cried with a lamentable voice unto
Daniel: and the king spake and said to
Daniel, O Daniel, servant of the living God, is thy God, whom thou serv-
est continually, able to deliver thee from
the lions?

21 Then said Daniel unto the king,
O king, live for ever.

22 My God hath sent his angel, and
hath shut the lions' mouths, that they
have not hurt me: forasmuch as before
him innocency was found in me.

NEW TESTAMENT

Matthew 6:25–34

25 Therefore I say unto you, Take
no thought for your life, what ye shall
eat, or what ye shall drink; nor yet for
your body, what ye shall put on. Is not
the life more than meat, and the body
than raiment?

26 Behold the fowls of the air: for
they sow not, neither do they reap,
nor gather into barns; yet your heavenly Father feedeth them. Are ye not
much better than they?

27 Which of you by taking thought
can add one cubit unto his stature?

28 And why take ye thought for raiment? Consider the lilies of the field, how they grow; they toil not, neither do they spin:

29 And yet I say unto you, That even Solomon in all his glory was not arrayed like one of these.

30 Wherefore, if God so clothe the grass of the field, which today is, and to-morrow is cast into the oven, shall he not much more clothe you, O ye of little faith?

31 Therefore take no thought, saying, What shall we eat? or, What shall we drink? or, Wherewithal shall we be clothed?

32 (For after all these things do the Gentiles seek:) for your heavenly Father knoweth that ye have need of all these things.

33 But seek ye first the kingdom of God, and his righteousness; and all these things shall be added unto you.

34 Take therefore no thought for the morrow: for the morrow shall take thought for the things of itself. Sufficient unto the day is the evil thereof.

Philippians 4:6–7

6 Be careful for nothing; but in every thing by prayer and supplication with thanksgiving let your requests be made known unto God.

7 And the peace of God, which passeth all understanding, shall keep your hearts and minds through Christ Jesus.

AUTHORITY

The Old Testament certainly speaks of a society in which some teach and others listen, some give orders and others obey them. But the ruler's power is only provisional. It is subject to his serving the divine purpose. A ruler who steps out of line will find that true authority passes him by and rests on a rival. So the people of Israel always had the responsibility of recognizing where true authority resided. They had to discern the true king, the true teacher, the true prophet as distinct from those who merely inhabited a position and claimed its power.

Sometimes the process of discerning where true authority was to be found was a slow and fumbling one. Samuel, for example, had to identify a new king after genuine authority had passed away from Saul. Only in the least likely of Jesse's sons did he recognize the true charisma of kingship.

In New Testament times people noticed that Jesus exercised an authority unique to himself, not one derived from official channels. Consequently his authority was recognized only by some. On the one hand, a centurion, claiming as an army officer a professional ability to recognize authority when he met it, understood perfectly. On the other hand, the priests and elders, anxious about inherited and institutional authority, could only ask, "By what authority are you acting? Who gave you this authority?"

Jesus is reported to have answered that question from beyond death, when he spoke to his followers and claimed for himself the authority that is not only above all other but within all other as well.

The New Testament, however, retains the Old Testament's respect for the legitimate—that is to say, the provisional—authority of rulers. Paul taught submission to the institutions of the state so long as the state was an instrument of justice, but both Paul and his master went to death rather than submit to the excessive demands of those in high positions.

Those who repudiate the very idea of authority on the ground that they must be responsible for their own lives have not thought very clearly about either authority or responsibility. Far from being opposed to each other, authority and responsibility cannot live apart. Certainly a bogus authoritarianism takes responsibility away from others, but biblical authority is not like that. It is flanked by responsibility on either side. It has to be responsibly discerned, and unless it is to pass away it has to be responsibly exercised.

In our time the young are said particularly to resent, resist, and reject authority. If they mean the because-I-say-so type, then they have a point. But they overstate their case if they repudiate authority as such. Nor do they actually succeed in doing it. In practice they usually do defer to some authoritative model when shaping their life-style and values. Even if they resist traditional and institutional authority, most young people submit meekly enough to what is called peer pressure. This means simply that one's own social and age group provides the authoritative model that one feels bound to obey.

The Bible tells us that we all need to learn how to recognize true authority and distinguish it from false. It says that we should look for the ultimate source of authority within and behind each authority figure who claims our obedience. True authority is closely related to the authority of truth. To deny a fact would be the ultimate rejection of legitimate authority. Conversely, to recognize legitimate authority in another human being or in a human institution is to see that somewhere beyond is a truth which that man, that woman, or that institution serves. Those who have authority are those who are under authority.

Perhaps it would help if this were made more visible. Even the young might have more respect for authority if they saw their elders as men and women who were themselves subject to transcendent authority—not just as links in an unending chain of command, but as responsible servants of most high truth.

AUTHORITY

OLD TESTAMENT

1 Samuel 13:13–14

13 And Samuel said to Saul, Thou hast done foolishly: thou hast not kept the commandment of the Lord thy God, which he commanded thee: for now would the Lord have established thy kingdom upon Israel for ever.

14 But now thy kingdom shall not continue: the Lord hath sought him a man after his own heart, and the Lord hath commanded him to be captain over his people, because thou hast not kept that which the Lord commanded thee.

1 Samuel 16:4–12

4 And Samuel did that which the Lord spake, and came to Bethlehem. And the elders of the town trembled at his coming, and said, Comest thou peaceably?

5 And he said, Peaceably: I am come to sacrifice unto the Lord: sanctify yourselves, and come with me to the sacrifice. And he sanctified Jesse and his sons, and called them to the sacrifice.

6 And it came to pass, when they were come, that he looked on Eliab, and said, Surely the Lord's anointed is before him.

7 But the Lord said unto Samuel, Look not on his countenance, or on the height of his stature; because I have refused him: for the Lord seeth not as man seeth; for man looketh on the outward appearance, but the Lord looketh on the heart.

8 Then Jesse called Abinadab, and made him pass before Samuel. And he said, neither hath the Lord chosen this.

9 Then Jesse made Shammah to pass by. And he said, Neither has the Lord chosen this.

10 Again, Jesse made seven of his sons to pass before Samuel. And Samuel said unto Jesse, The Lord hath not chosen these.

11 And Samuel said unto Jesse, Are here all thy children? And he said, There remaineth yet the youngest, and, behold, he keepeth the sheep. And Samuel said unto Jesse, Send and fetch him: for we will not sit down till he come hither.

12 And he sent, and brought him in. Now he was ruddy, and withal of a beautiful countenance, and goodly to look to. And the Lord said, Arise, anoint him: for this is he.

NEW TESTAMENT

Mark 1:21–22

21 And they went into Capernaum; and straightway on the sabbath day he entered into the synagogue, and taught.

22 And they were astonished at his doctrine: for he taught them as one that had authority, and not as the scribes.

Matthew 8:5–10

5 And when Jesus was entered into

Capernaum there came unto him a centurion, beseeching him,

6 And saying, Lord, my servant lieth at home sick of the palsy, grievously tormented.

7 And Jesus saith unto him, I will come and heal him.

8 The centurion answered and said, Lord, I am not worthy that thou shouldest come under my roof: but speak the word only, and my servant shall be healed.

9 For I am a man under authority, having soldiers under me: and I say to this man, Go, and he goeth; and to another, Come, and he cometh; and to my servant, Do this, and he doeth it.

10 When Jesus heard it, he marvelled, and said to them that followed, Verily I say unto you, I have not found so great faith, no, not in Israel.

Matthew 21:23

23 And when he was come into the temple, the chief priests and the elders of the people came unto him as he was teaching, and said, By what authority doest thou these things? and who gave thee this authority?

Matthew 28:18 (after the resurrection of Jesus)

18 And Jesus came and spake unto them, saying, All power is given unto me in heaven and in earth.

Romans 13:1

1 Let every soul be subject unto the higher powers. For there is no power but of God: the powers that be are ordained of God.

BEAUTY

The entire Old Testament is the work of people who appreciated the beauty of words. Such books as Job and the Psalms are the work of people who appreciated the beauty of nature as well. The Jerusalem temple was the work of people who appreciated beauty in art. The Song of Solomon is the work of a writer who appreciated the beauty of a woman in the eyes of her lover and the beauty of a man in the eyes of the beloved. But the Old Testament is not interested in mere aesthetics.

Over all created beauty it sets the divine glory. Beauty might be regarded as a spillover of the divine glory—but one that was never allowed to obscure it, replace it, or be separated from it. In fact, God and beauty are so inseparable that even the passionate love poetry of the Song of Solomon appears to have been included on the ground that God must be the ultimate if not the immediate object of such adoration. He alone could be the source of such beauty in man, in woman, and in nature.

So beauty belongs to the religion of the Old Testament, but only in the context of a true faith. Its presence or its absence was not in itself sufficient evidence of the presence or absence of the holy. An idol could be beautiful, but its beauty was a deceptive covering that hid corruption. The servant of God could be ugly, made hideous by vicarious suffering, but this ugliness was the deceptive covering that masked the true glory.

The New Testament takes up the word "glory" and links it to the person of Jesus. He is the splendor of God manifested on earth. The divine glory is there in him whether he stands on a hillside preaching about the flowers, or whether he hangs on a cross crying out in dereliction. Only in the visionary experience of the Transfiguration was it granted to a select few to see that divine beauty outwardly and visibly expressed—and those who saw it were so shaken by the experience that Peter began at once to talk nonsense.

Among his followers, however, even those who had never seen Jesus at all in an outward sense were able to speak of having been given "the light of the knowledge of the glory of God in the face of Jesus Christ" (2 Corinthians 4:6).

Still today beauty is a pointer to the transcendent, and still today it is an ambiguous one. On the one hand, it points the individual beyond himself. In relation to the rest of the world the artist may be as arrogant as a pagan god and as self-centered as a greedy child, but in relation to his art he is called to be as humble as a worshiper. He may relate to beauty, but it is greater than he; he may participate in it, but it is outside him; he may serve it, but he cannot master it. There are those for whom great art is the only remaining pointer to a whole order of transcendent values.

This beauty is not merely pleasing, however. There is a beauty that points to nothing beyond itself, and there is a way of relating to beauty that gets no further than the aesthetic. And on the other hand there is an ugliness that points through the absence of beauty toward its fulfillment. Look at Grünewald's painting of the crucifixion, the one that forms a central part of the Isenheim altarpiece at Colmar. On a bow-shaped cross hangs a scarred body with hands like skewered claws. Is it beautiful? Certainly not. And yet it is. There is a beauty within and beyond the hideous figure. There is glory.

The world needs to recover a vision of glory—one that speaks of transcendent beauty, transcendent value and significance, and that is manifest in and through the things of this world—even, sometimes, the ugly things of this world.

BEAUTY

OLD TESTAMENT

1 Chronicles 16:23–29

Sing unto the Lord, all the earth;
Shew forth from day to day his salvation.

Declare his glory among the heathen;
His marvellous works among all nations.
For great is the Lord, and greatly to be
    praised:
He also is to be feared above all gods.

For all the gods of the people are idols:
But the Lord made the heavens.
Glory and honour are in his presence;
Strength and gladness are in his place.
Give unto the Lord, ye kindreds of the
people,
Give unto the Lord glory and strength.
Give unto the Lord the glory due unto
his name:
Bring an offering, and come before him:
Worship the Lord in the beauty of
holiness.

Psalm 27:4

One thing have I desired of the Lord,
that will I seek after;
That I may dwell in the house of the
Lord all the days of my life,
To behold the beauty of the Lord, and to
enquire in his temple.

Psalm 50:2

Out of Zion, the perfection of beauty,
God hath shined.

Song of Songs 2:10–13

My beloved spake, and said unto me,
Rise up, my love, my fair one, and come
away.
For, lo, the winter is past,
The rain is over and gone;
The flowers appear on the earth;
The time of the singing of birds is come,
And the voice of the turtle is heard in
our land;
The fig tree putteth forth her green figs,
And the vines with the tender grape
Give a good smell.
Arise, my love, my fair one, and come
away.

Isaiah 53:2–3

2 He hath no form nor comeliness;
and when we shall see him, there is
no beauty that we should desire him.

3 He is despised and rejected of
men; a man of sorrows, and acquainted with grief: and we hid as it
were our faces from him; he was despised, and we esteemed him not.

NEW TESTAMENT

John 1:14

14 And the Word was made flesh,
and dwelt among us, (and we beheld
his glory, the glory as of the only begotten of the Father,) full of grace and
truth.

Luke 9:28–36

28 And it came to pass about an
eight days after these sayings, he took
Peter and John and James, and went
up into a mountain to pray.

29 And as he prayed, the fashion of
his countenance was altered, and his
raiment was white and glistering.

30 And, behold, there talked with
him two men, which were Moses and
Elias:

31 Who appeared in glory, and spake
of his decease which he should accomplish at Jerusalem.

32 But Peter and they that were with
him were heavy with sleep: and when
they were awake, they saw his glory,
and the two men that stood with him.

33 And it came to pass, as they departed from him, Peter said unto
Jesus, Master, it is good for us to be
here: and let us make three tabernacles; one for thee, and one for Moses,
and one for Elias: not knowing what
he said.

34 While he thus spake, there came

a cloud, and overshadowed them: and they feared as they entered into the cloud.

35 And there came a voice out of the cloud, saying, This is my beloved Son: hear him.

36 And when the voice was past, Jesus was found alone.

BIRTH

From an Old Testament point of view the ultimate malediction was to curse (as Job did at one point) the day of one's birth, and the ultimate cynicism was to prefer (as the writer of Ecclesiastes did at one point) not having been born to living and dying. Statements such as those made by Job and the writer of Ecclesiastes were intended to be shocking, and they were. They depend for their effect on the Old Testament's central emphasis on the joy of birth. Giving birth was a painful and dangerous business to the women of that time (as Eve, the representative woman, had been warned it would be), but the gain in life made the pain worthwhile, even if the mother had to pay the ultimate price for it, as did beloved Rachel. The positive nature of birth was greater than the negative nature of death. The safe delivery of a child—especially, it must be admitted, of a male child— was a matter for rejoicing and for the paying of thankful dues to God, the giver of life.

So directly was God the giver of life that the psalmist could contemplate with wonder the way God had assembled the embryo that was to become the psalmist himself. To be known before one could know was to be known to the core, and the psalmist was assured when he contemplated the mystery of birth that in just this way was he known to God. Indeed, the mystery of birth was such that whoever had contemplated it might even face with some confidence the dark mystery of death.

The New Testament, having celebrated the birth of John the Baptist and of Jesus, takes up the thought that the birth we know may be an image of a birth we await. New life, here or hereafter, is a logical extension of possibilities inherent in birth itself. Nicodemus is asked to see that, having been born once, there is nothing to prevent his being born again to a richer, more spirit-filled life. All the disciples are told to think of the coming death of Jesus as they would think of the pangs of birth, and to look beyond it to joy. The followers of Jesus spoke more than once of his resurrection in terms of his being "the firstborn from the dead" (e.g., Colossians 1:18).

In such passages the writers are not using birth as a mere illustration of something else; they are pointing to a real connection between knowable experience and that experience which can be grasped only through faith. They are arguing that a God who has once created a living, conscious human being is

21

capable of yet further acts of life-giving. Their hope of spiritual regeneration and of resurrection was related to what they saw happening in natural birth, because birth as they saw it was not just the selfish gene reproducing itself but the emergence into the world of the image of God.

Of course, the writers of the Bible had none of our modern knowledge of biology, our understanding of DNA, our ability to fertilize an ovum outside the womb or to prevent its being fertilized inside the womb, our ability to undertake genetic engineering. The genetic engineer will find not one of his or her problems so much as contemplated in the Bible. But the Bible can profoundly affect the way in which we approach and handle this modern knowledge.

On the one hand, the biblical attitude could never be reconciled with the use of biology to tear the mystery from birth and to make the process one that serves the immediate self-interest of those with the knowledge to manipulate it. On the other hand, the Bible would allow and encourage us to see the new knowledge as a reason for an increase of wonder and an enhanced reverence for life. It would prompt us to seek ever larger and more humane purposes that biology might serve. To harness science to a biblical sense of mystery might be to strengthen rather than weaken it.

Meanwhile, ordinary men and women can continue to find in the birth of a child one of those experiences that seem to reduce to gossamer the veil between the existence we know so well and a transcendent order of reality too often hidden from us. The coming into being of a self-conscious person, capable of love, of poetry, of self-sacrifice, is an experience that still points beyond itself.

BIRTH

OLD TESTAMENT

Job 3:1–4

After this opened Job his mouth, and cursed his day. And Job spake, and said,
Let the day perish wherein I was born,
And the night in which it was said, There is a man child conceived.
Let that day be darkness;
Let not God regard it from above,
Neither let the light shine upon it.

Ecclesiastes 4:2–3

2 Wherefore I praised the dead which are already dead more than the living which are yet alive.

3 Yea, better is he than both they, which hath not yet been, who hath not seen the evil work that is done under the sun.

Psalm 139:14, 13, 15–18

I will praise thee; for I am fearfully and wonderfully made:
Marvellous are thy works;
And that my soul knoweth right well.
For thou hast possessed my reins:
Thou hast covered me in my mother's womb.

My substance was not hid from thee,
When I was made in secret,
And curiously wrought in the lowest parts
of the earth.
Thine eyes did see my substance, yet being
unperfect;
And in thy book all my members were
written,
Which in continuance were fashioned,
When as yet there was none of them.
How precious also are thy thoughts unto
me, O God!
How great is the sum of them!
If I should count them, they are more in
number than the sand:
When I awake, I am still with thee.

NEW TESTAMENT

Luke 1:57–58

57 Now Elisabeth's full time came that she should be delivered; and she brought forth a son.

58 And her neighbours and her cousins heard how the Lord had shewed great mercy upon her; and they rejoiced with her.

Luke 2:4–7

4 And Joseph also went up from Galilee, out of the city of Nazareth, into Judæa, unto the city of David, which is called Bethlehem; (because he was of the house and lineage of David:)

5 To be taxed with Mary his espoused wife, being great with child.

6 And so it was, that, while they were there, the days were accomplished that she should be delivered.

7 And she brought forth her first-born son, and wrapped him in swaddling clothes, and laid him in a manger; because there was no room for them in the inn.

John 3:3–8

3 Jesus answered and said unto him, Verily, verily, I say unto thee, Except a man be born again, he cannot see the kingdom of God.

4 Nicodemus saith unto him, How can a man be born when he is old? can he enter the second time into his mother's womb, and be born?

5 Jesus answered, Verily, verily, I say unto thee, Except a man be born of water and of the Spirit, he cannot enter into the kingdom of God.

6 That which is born of the flesh is flesh; and that which is born of the Spirit is spirit.

7 Marvel not that I said unto thee, Ye must be born again.

8 The wind bloweth where it listeth, and thou hearest the sound thereof, but canst not tell whence it cometh, and whither it goeth: so is every one that is born of the Spirit.

John 16:21–22

21 A woman when she is in travail hath sorrow, because her hour is come: but as soon as she is delivered of the child, she remembereth no more the anguish, for joy that a man is born into the world.

22 And ye now therefore have sorrow: but I will see you again, and your heart shall rejoice, and your joy no man taketh from you.

BLESSING

To count your blessings is to take note of the things you have to be happy about. That kind of blessing is to be found in this book under Happiness. Here we are concerned with the act of blessing, with the verb "to bless."

The Old Testament story of Jacob and Esau depends for its force on the irrevocable power of the act of blessing. Jacob and Esau were twins, but the notoriously hairy Esau was slightly the elder and his father's favorite. He was "a cunning hunter, a man of the field." Unlike his brother, Jacob was "a plain man, dwelling in tents." Their father Isaac did not care so much for Jacob, but their mother Rebekah preferred him to Esau. That is why she schemed to deflect the old man's dying blessing. With that blessing went the leadership of the tribe. It was more than a last will and testament. A will can be changed, but the blessing could not be revoked even though the deception was uncovered within hours. The power of the blessing had been released; it was already in motion. The Old Testament sees it as running on through all the course of subsequent history.

It all ties in with the biblical belief in the power of the word, especially the word of God. This is what created the world in the first place and what makes God's will effective at every stage. To bless, to speak good in the name of God, is to participate in that creative power. The blessing is a force of nature. A fictional but highly convincing account of patriarchal blessing set in a much later period can be found in John Steinbeck's *To a God Unknown*.

In the New Testament Gospels Jesus blesses children, food, and his disciples. He also tells them to bless others, including those who curse them. The blessing, however, is not irresistible. The shalom, the blessing of peace, for example, rests on the man of peace and may be rejected. Even then, however, it has life and power in itself. The rejected blessing rebounds on the one who gave it.

Clearly blessings were to Jesus much more than good wishes. Through a blessing, a child or a piece of bread, a cup of wine or a man or woman could be touched by an active force for good. They could be drawn into line with the movement of the purpose of God. According to Luke, it is in the very act of blessing that the risen Jesus ends a sequence of appearances to his disciples.

Many in the twentieth century regard blessings as just formal rituals in church or synagogue. To some, "Bless you" is either a slightly chic way of saying thank you or a conventional way of acknowledging a sneeze. Certainly it is no longer easy (unless you are inclined to believe in magic) to picture a divine force so mighty as to change the course of life for generations, yet so fallible as to be deflected by a bit of trickery that makes use of the skin of a goat. Such a force would be expected to work, if at all, in the deep levels of personality well beyond the reach of such deceptions.

That such forces do play upon us is a biblical belief that modern men and women might well include in their world view. We all know that a human being can be profoundly influenced by being loved. And we know that the individual is never an isolated human being: all kinds of forces have beaten upon his unconscious and subconscious mind; all kinds of forces are still shaping his character and his course in life. It is quite possible to think of all these forces as contained within a single movement, a power for good that we can release toward each other (as in blessing) or turn from each other (as in cursing).

This differs from magic if only in demanding love as its channel. It is not a force to be captured and manipulated by human cunning. Magic, in fact, flourishes precisely when this deeper belief weakens. Astrologers, fortune-tellers, witch doctors of all kinds prosper when ordinary people lose the belief in their own power to bless—that is, to direct toward one another in love a power of good that has creative force.

BLESSING

OLD TESTAMENT

Genesis 27:1–23

1 And it came to pass, that when Isaac was old, and his eyes were dim, so that he could not see, he called Esau his eldest son, and said unto him, My son: and he said unto him, Behold, here am I.

2 And he said, Behold now, I am old, I know not the day of my death:

3 Now therefore take, I pray thee, thy weapons, thy quiver and thy bow, and go out to the field, and take me some venison;

4 And make me savoury meat, such as I love, and bring it to me, that I may eat; that my soul may bless thee before I die.

5 And Rebekah heard when Isaac spake to Esau his son. And Esau went to the field to hunt for venison, and to bring it.

6 And Rebekah spake unto Jacob her son, saying, Behold, I heard thy father speak unto Esau thy brother, saying,

7 Bring me venison, and make me savoury meat, that I may eat, and bless thee before the Lord before my death.

8 Now therefore, my son, obey my voice according to that which I command thee.

9 Go now to the flock, and fetch me from thence two good kids of the goats; and I will make them savoury meat for thy father, such as he loveth:

10 And thou shalt bring it to thy father, that he may eat, and that he may bless thee before his death.

11 And Jacob said to Rebekah his mother, Behold, Esau my brother is a hairy man, and I am a smooth man:

12 My father peradventure will feel me, and I shall seem to him as a deceiver; and I shall bring a curse upon me, and not a blessing.

13 And his mother said unto him, Upon me be thy curse, my son: only obey my voice, and go fetch me them.

14 And he went, and fetched, and brought them to his mother: and his mother made savoury meat, such as his father loved.

15 And Rebekah took goodly raiment of her eldest son Esau, which were with her in the house, and put them upon Jacob her younger son:

16 And she put the skins of the kids of the goats upon his hands, and upon the smooth of his neck:

17 And she gave the savoury meat and the bread, which she had prepared, into the hand of her son Jacob.

18 And he came unto his father, and said, My father: and he said, Here am I; who art thou, my son?

19 And Jacob said unto his father, I am Esau thy firstborn; I have done according as thou badest me: arise, I pray thee, sit and eat of my venison, that thy soul may bless me.

20 And Isaac said unto his son, How is it that thou hast found it so quickly, my son? And he said, Because the Lord thy God brought it to me.

21 And Isaac said unto Jacob, Come near, I pray thee, that I may feel thee, my son, whether thou be my very son Esau or not.

22 And Jacob went near unto Isaac his father; and he felt him, and said, The voice is Jacob's voice, but the hands are the hands of Esau.

23 And he discerned him not, because his hands were hairy, as his brother Esau's hands: so he blessed him.

NEW TESTAMENT

Mark 10:13–16

13 And they brought young children to him, that he should touch them: and his disciples rebuked those that brought them.

14 But when Jesus saw it, he was much displeased, and said unto them, Suffer the little children to come unto me, and forbid them not: for of such is the kingdom of God.

15 Verily I say unto you, Whosoever shall not receive the kingdom of God as a little child, he shall not enter therein.

16 And he took them up in his arms, put his hands upon them, and blessed them.

Luke 6:27–28

27 But I say unto you which hear, Love your enemies, do good to them which hate you,

28 Bless them that curse you, and pray for them which despitefully use you.

Luke 10:1, 5–6

1 After these things the Lord appointed other seventy also, and sent them two and two before his face into every city and place, whither he himself would come. Therefore said he unto them,

5 And into whatsoever house ye enter, first say, Peace be to this house.

6 And if the son of peace be there, your peace shall rest upon it: if not, it shall turn to you again.

Luke 24:50–51

50 And he led them out as far as to Bethany, and he lifted up his hands, and blessed them.

51 And it came to pass, while he blessed them, he was parted from them, and carried up into heaven.

BODY

The human being (represented by Adam) is a spirit-filled body. All human beings (represented by Noah and his sons) are commanded to live a bodily life—eating, drinking, and procreating in obedience to God. They are bearers of God's image, not just on the spiritual side of their nature but as whole men and women, and this wholeness includes that part of them which they have in common with the animals. In a body of flesh and blood—and blood, to the Hebrew way of thinking, was the very life of man and beast—they are to live as God's image and God's agent.

The Old Testament, seeing man as embodied spirit, has no great interest in his possible future as a disembodied spirit. From an Old Testament point of view the death of the body means the death of the person and the end of all real relationship with God. The common view is that the spirits of the dead are in a soundless, sightless place called sheol. From there God can be neither served nor worshiped. Service and worship are positive actions, and such activities demand a body.

Even the Teacher of Ecclesiastes, though he speaks of the spirit as returning to God, sees nothing of value in that. This is what gives such melancholy splendor to his account of the body's decline, when the senses fade, when the limbs ("the keepers of the house") grow shaky, the teeth ("the grinders") few, the eyes ("the windows") dim. The sadness of such a passage is the reverse of the Old Testament's happy affirmation of the glory and religious significance of life in the body.

The New Testament reaffirms the positive and counters the negative by its belief in the resurrection of the body. The resurrected body need not be a physical one—indeed, Paul insists in 1 Corinthians 15 that it is not—but the personality must always have some means of expressing itself, and that is the essential purpose that a body serves.

In fact, the body as we know it can already be spoken of as a temple. In the New Testament the word "temple" is used in reference to both the body of Jesus and the bodies of his imperfect Corinthian followers ("Don't you know that your body is a temple of the Holy Spirit?" 1 Corinthians 6:19). All the books of the New Testament are dominated by the thought of the bodily presence of God in the person of Jesus Christ.

This incarnation has made possible a fresh encounter between God and man, a renewal of the divine image. Humanity in its bodily life is incorporated into union with God in the person of Christ. Paul does recognize the possibility of a mystical experience in which the body is left behind (2 Corinthians 12:2), but makes much more of the need to see that the body is kept a fitting habitation for the Spirit of God. Every aspect of bodily life, as in the Old Testament, is involved: sexual morality, attitudes toward food and drink, ideas on health and sickness.

To treat the human body as a mere machine to be kept running by medical engineering is to misunderstand what it is and does. In the biblical view the body is essentially an instrument of personality, a means of self-expression and of interpersonal communication. One of the classic expressions of rapturous appreciation of the body and of its senses is the poem "Thanksgivings for the Body" by the seventeenth-century mystic Thomas Traherne. He could write in this way precisely because he was a mystic. His spirituality, far from diminishing his appreciation of the body, immeasurably heightened his enjoyment of each of the five senses.

There are many ways of misunderstanding and misusing the body. You can indulge its appetites in the belief that the body is all there is of you. You can fuss over your body in the belief that it has no purpose but survival. You can deny your body in the belief that it is the enemy of your spirit. From a biblical point of view all these attitudes are erroneous.

Body and spirit are united, and the former is the articulation of the latter. We make the most of our bodies when we reach out through them to and beyond one another. The care of the body is more akin to the tuning of a musical instrument than it is to the servicing of a car, and the art of living in the body is more like playing that instrument in harmony with all life than it is like serving the body as a master or fighting it as an enemy.

BODY

OLD TESTAMENT

Genesis 2:4–7

4 These are the generations of the heavens and of the earth when they were created, in the day that the Lord God made the earth and the heavens,

5 And every plant of the field before it was in the earth, and every herb of the field before it grew: for the Lord God had not caused it to rain upon the earth, and there was not a man to till the ground.

6 But there went up a mist from the earth, and watered the whole face of the ground.

7 And the Lord God formed man of the dust of the ground, and breathed into his nostrils the breath of life; and man became a living soul.

Genesis 9:1–7

1 And God blessed Noah and his sons, and said unto them, Be fruitful, and multiply, and replenish the earth.

2 And the fear of you and the dread of you shall be upon every beast of the earth, and upon every fowl of the air, upon all that moveth upon the earth, and upon all the fishes of the sea; into your hand are they delivered.

3 Every moving thing that liveth shall be meat for you; even as the green herb have I given you all things.

4 But flesh with the life thereof, which is the blood thereof, shall ye not eat.

5 And surely your blood of your lives will I require; at the hand of every beast will I require it, and at the hand of man; at the hand of every man's brother will I require the life of man.

6 Whoso sheddeth man's blood, by man shall his blood be shed: for in the image of God made he man.

7 And you, be ye fruitful, and multiply; bring forth abundantly in the earth, and multiply therein.

Ecclesiastes 12:1–7

1 Remember now thy Creator in the days of thy youth, while the evil days come not, nor the years draw nigh, when thou shalt say, I have no pleasure in them;

2 While the sun, or the light, or the moon; or the stars, be not darkened, nor the clouds return after the rain:

3 In the day when the keepers of the house shall tremble, and the strong men shall bow themselves, and the grinders cease because they are few, and those that look out of the windows be darkened,

4 And the doors shall be shut in the streets, when the sound of the grinding is low, and he shall rise up at the voice of the bird, and all the daughters of music shall be brought low;

5 Also when they shall be afraid of that which is high, and fears shall be in the way, and the almond tree shall flourish, and the grasshopper shall be a burden, and desire shall fail: because man goeth to his long home, and the mourners go about the streets:

6 Or ever the silver cord be loosed, or the golden bowl be broken, or the pitcher be broken at the fountain, or the wheel broken at the cistern.

7 Then shall the dust return to the earth as it was: and the spirit shall return unto God who gave it.

NEW TESTAMENT

John 2:19–21

19 Jesus answered and said unto them, Destroy this temple, and in three days I will raise it up.

20 Then said the Jews, Forty and six years was this temple in building, and wilt thou rear it up in three days?

21 But he spake of the temple of his body.

Colossians 2:9

9 For in him dwelleth all the fullness of the Godhead bodily.

1 Corinthians 6:13–15

13 Now the body is not for fornication, but for the Lord; and the Lord for the body.

14 And God hath both raised up the Lord, and will also raise up us by his own power.

15 Know ye not that your bodies are the members of Christ?

BROTHERHOOD

The Old Testament distinguishes the physical fact of brotherhood as kinship from the practice of brotherliness as a personal relationship. It recognizes that the latter can occasionally exist without the former ("there is a friend that sticketh closer than a brother," Proverbs 18:24). The former very often exists without the latter (as with Cain and Abel). The story of Joseph and his brethren is the story of the spiritual relationship slowly evolving from the physical one.

As is often true in polygamous societies, these "brothers" did not all have the same mother, but they were regarded as full brothers nonetheless because they were all legitimate sons of Jacob. Joseph became the object of the other brothers' jealousy, so they faked his death and sold him into slavery. Many years later they were starving as a result of a series of bad harvests. They knew that there was food in Egypt, however, so all of them except Benjamin (who, like Joseph, was Rachel's son) were sent to beg supplies from Pharaoh's agent. He was, of course, their unrecognized brother Joseph.

Joseph will not reveal himself until he has evidence that there is now a true sense of brotherhood among them. He meets their immediate needs, but tells them that next time *all* the brothers must come. When this happens, he rigs a charge against Benjamin and proposes to detain him. It is then that Judah delivers the speech quoted here.

What Judah says, with much polite circumlocution, is that he will take his brother's place and bear the punishment due to him. This is the essence of real brotherhood. Joseph is at last assured that a relationship of love, not just of blood, now exists. So he reveals himself.

The New Testament writers, like some of their Old Testament predecessors, were concerned with making the spiritual relationship of brotherhood a wider and more inclusive one than the physical, but they were also interested in brotherhood in the literal sense. There were biological brothers among the twelve apostles of Jesus, and Peter, the leading member of the group, had been introduced by his own brother.

Jesus himself extended the meaning of the relationship in a way that must have hurt his own kin. But he was extending and deepening the notion of the fatherhood of God, and this inevitably involved stretching the idea of brotherhood beyond what was readily acceptable to his own family or even to his own nation. It was not as if the deepened and extended pattern of relationships was readily discernible on the surface. It was hidden, even—or especially—from the wise. It had to be revealed or discovered. It had to be spoken of forcefully so that it could be seen by Jesus' hearers and achieved among his followers.

The way was hard, but before long the word "brother" became the standard term for a fellow Christian, regardless of parentage, nationality, or social class. This brotherhood was rooted in the belief that each of them was an adopted child of God. The mark of brotherhood was love, and the shape of that mark was the death of Jesus.

Sentimentalists imagine that brotherhood exists as a fact and will naturally be felt and acted upon. Within the biological family the fact of brotherhood is real, but sibling rivalry seems to be as natural as brotherly love. And it can be vicious. Within the wider family of humanity, some measure of kinship is also a fact, and within the community of those who believe in God as their Father, spiritual brotherhood is at least an accepted doctrine, but in these realms, too, human beings seem to have little natural aptitude for brotherliness.

The truth is that brotherhood, whether in the narrow sense or the wider one, needs to be seen before it can be achieved. It begins as a deliberate and disciplined way of looking at people. Instead of seeing others from behind the palisades of an enclosure designed to preserve "me" from "them," we have to learn to see them as offspring of a common stock, sharers of a common home, and (in the long term) partners in a common destiny. When this concept has really sunk in so that we feel other men's unity with us (and enjoy their differences from us), then we can begin to live in brotherhood spontaneously and instinctively. But it will not do to leave the attainment of brotherhood to nature, either in the home or in the world at large.

BROTHERHOOD

OLD TESTAMENT

Genesis 44:18–45:1

18 Then Judah came near unto him, and said, Oh my lord, let thy servant, I pray thee, speak a word in my lord's ears, and let not thine anger burn against thy servant: for thou art even as Pharaoh.

19 My lord asked his servants, saying, Have ye a father, or a brother?

20 And we said unto my lord, We have a father, an old man, and a child of his old age, a little one; and his brother is dead, and he alone is left of his mother, and his father loveth him.

21 And thou saidst unto thy servants, Bring him down unto me, that I may set mine eyes upon him.

22 And we said unto my lord, The lad cannot leave his father: for if he should leave his father, his father would die.

23 And thou saidst unto thy servants, Except your youngest brother come down with you, ye shall see my face no more.

24 And it came to pass when we came up unto thy servant my father, we told him the words of my lord.

25 And our father said, Go again, and buy us a little food.

26 And we said, We cannot go down: if our youngest brother be with us, then will we go down: for we may not see the man's face, except our youngest brother be with us.

27 And thy servant my father said

unto us, Ye know that my wife bare me two sons:

28 And the one went out from me, and I said, Surely he is torn in pieces; and I saw him not since:

29 And if ye take this also from me, and mischief befall him, ye shall bring down my gray hairs with sorrow to the grave.

30 Now therefore when I come to thy servant my father, and the lad be not with us; seeing that his life is bound up in the lad's life;

31 It shall come to pass, when he seeth that the lad is not with us, that he will die: and thy servants shall bring down the gray hairs of thy servant our father with sorrow to the grave.

32 For thy servant became surety for the lad unto my father, saying, If I bring him not unto thee, then I shall bear the blame to my father for ever.

33 Now therefore, I pray thee, let thy servant abide instead of the lad a bondman to my lord; and let the lad go up with his brethren.

34 For how shall I go up to my father, and the lad be not with me? lest peradventure I see the evil that shall come on my father.

1 Then Joseph could not refrain himself before all them that stood by him; and he cried, Cause every man to go out from me. And there stood no man with him, while Joseph made himself known unto his brethren.

NEW TESTAMENT

John 1:40–42

40 One of the two which heard John speak, and followed him, was Andrew, Simon Peter's brother.

41 He first findeth his own brother Simon, and saith unto him, We have found the Messias, which is, being interpreted, the Christ.

42 And he brought him to Jesus.

Luke 8:19–21

19 Then came to him his mother and his brethren, and could not come at him for the press.

20 And it was told him by certain which said, Thy mother and thy brethren stand without, desiring to see thee.

21 And he answered and said unto them, My mother and my brethren are these which hear the word of God, and do it.

Luke 10:21–22

21 In that hour Jesus rejoiced in spirit, and said, I thank thee, O Father, Lord of heaven and earth, that thou hast hid these things from the wise and prudent, and hath revealed them unto babes: even so, Father; for so it seemed good in thy sight.

22 All things are delivered to me of my Father: and no man knoweth who the Son is, but the Father; and who the Father is, but the Son, and he to whom the Son will reveal him.

1 John 3:14–18

14 We know that we have passed from death unto life, because we love the brethren. He that loveth not his brother abideth in death.

15 Whosoever hateth his brother is

a murderer: and ye know that no murderer hath eternal life abiding in him.

16 Hereby perceive we the love of
God, because he laid down his life for
us: and we ought to lay down our lives
for the brethren.

17 But whoso hath this world's good,

and seeth his brother have need, and
shutteth up his bowels of compassion
from him, how dwelleth the love of
God in him?

18 My little children, let us not love
in word, neither in tongue; but in deed
and in truth.

CALLING

The Old Testament is full of people answering the call of God. Some were not
very keen to answer it, but none seemed to have much difficulty in knowing
what it was. Perhaps they later recalled the experience with greater clarity than it
had at the time. Often the voice of God is described as being audible to normal
hearing and as speaking in the common tongue. Yet the variety of callings spoken
of in the Old Testament suggests that there were in fact many ways in which a
vocation could be made known.

Abram (later called Abraham) was directed to begin a migration that was to
have, and is still having, momentous significance in the history of mankind.
That was a calling—one that had to be embraced by faith and without ever
seeing its outcome. ("By faith Abraham, when he was called to go out into a
place which he should after receive for an inheritance, obeyed; and went out not
knowing whither he went," Hebrews 11:8). Bezaleel was an inspired craftsman in
metal, stone, and wood. That, too, was a divine calling—one that presumably
became known through the discovery of a natural aptitude and that could be
tested over and over again as each new piece of work came to hand. Jeremiah
was required to be a prophet and was prepared for the job before he had a chance
to reveal any other aptitudes at all. That was a calling too—one that the prophet
himself regretted and perhaps even resented. The whole people of Israel was
nominated the people of God. That, yet again, was a calling—a corporate one.
The variety of callings was endless. The variety of ways in which the calling was
made known must have been almost equally limitless.

These callings have one factor is common, however. In every instance a
human life is made to fulfill a God-given purpose, and in every instance the
God-given purpose is the vital qualification for the job. Human frailty does not
stand in the way when God calls.

For some in the New Testament the divine call was made audible by the voice
of Jesus, but those who came to the Christian way at a later date were also said
to have been called—called to be saints, what is more, although they were well
known (especially in Corinth) to be an ordinary cross-section of sinful humanity.

Answering the call involved the whole life of each believer, but in a variety of ways. Some changed their jobs; some did not. Some left their homes; some did not. Again, however, there is a common factor: each is believed to have an assigned place. In the divine economy a vacancy may exist; something in the human spirit rises up and prompts a man or a woman to move into that vacant place as its natural and destined occupant. This, says the New Testament, is the work of the spirit of God through the ministry of Jesus.

The modern tendency to think of vocation only where religion, medicine, or teaching is involved is a much narrower interpretation than the biblical one (see Work). A biblical approach would involve not only seeing all kinds of work as callings but also seeing the whole course of a person's life in that way—work, leisure, family life, personal relationships . . . everything. It is not just a matter of what a human being is called to do but of what he or she is called to be. The very identity of each individual is involved. Freedom does not consist of unqualified self-determination but of the freedom to respond or not respond to a challenge, an invitation from the beyond.

Some still speak of their calling as if a divine voice had issued audible instructions, but when questioned they usually reveal that the experience was a subtler one. It is the world around us that articulates the challenge to us. To get the message we must first see the world as a purposeful place. A meaningless pattern of random events would leave little room for vocation, but most people are aware of some design to which human life at least *ought* to conform. Within this design certain spaces are waiting to be occupied. Purposes need to be fulfilled, jobs to be done, ideas to be stated, experiences to be had. Our environment is full of such spiritual vacancies.

And within us there is that which wants to respond, to move into such a vacancy—one with our name on it—and to fill it with all that we are. In this larger sense the search for a vocation is the search for a whole way of life that will enable us to be what we were born to be.

CALLING

OLD TESTAMENT

Genesis 12:1–4

1 Now the Lord had said unto Abram, Get thee out of thy country, and from thy kindred, and from thy father's house, unto a land that I will shew thee:

2 And I will make of thee a great nation, and I will bless thee, and make thy name great; and thou shalt be a blessing:

3 And I will bless them that bless thee, and curse him that curseth thee: and in thee shall all families of the earth be blessed.

4 So Abram departed, as the Lord had spoken unto him; and Lot went

with him: and Abram was seventy and five years old when he departed out of Haran.

Exodus 35:30–33

30 And Moses said unto the children of Israel, See, the Lord hath called by name Bezaleel the son of Uri, the son of Hur, of the tribe of Judah;

31 And he hath filled him with the spirit of God, in wisdom, in understanding, and in knowledge, and in all manner of workmanship;

32 And to devise curious works, to work in gold, and in silver, and in brass,

33 And in the cutting of stones to set them, and in carving of wood, to make any manner of cunning work.

Jeremiah 1:4–7

4 Then the word of the Lord came unto me, saying,

5 Before I formed thee in the belly, I knew thee; and before thou camest forth out of the womb I sanctified thee, and I ordained thee a prophet unto the nations.

6 Then said I, Ah, Lord God! behold, I cannot speak: for I am a child.

7 But the Lord said unto me, Say not, I am a child: for thou shalt go to all that I shall send thee, and whatsoever I command thee thou shalt speak.

Isaiah 43:1

1 But now thus saith the Lord that created thee, O Jacob, and he that formed thee, O Israel, Fear not: for I have redeemed thee, I have called thee by thy name; thou art mine.

NEW TESTAMENT

Mark 1:16–20

16 Now as he walked by the sea of Galilee, he saw Simon and Andrew his brother casting a net into the sea: for they were fishers.

17 And Jesus said unto them, Come ye after me, and I will make you to become fishers of men.

18 And straightway they forsook their nets, and followed him.

19 And when he had gone a little farther thence, he saw James the son of Zebedee, and John his brother, who also were in the ship mending their nets.

20 And straightway he called them: and they left their father Zebedee in the ship with the hired servants, and went after him.

1 Corinthians 1:1–2, 26–29

1 Paul, called to be an apostle of Jesus Christ through the will of God, and Sosthenes our brother,

2 Unto the church of God which is at Corinth, to them that are sanctified in Christ Jesus, called to be saints.

26 For ye see your calling, brethren, how that not many wise men after the flesh, not many mighty, not many noble, are called:

27 But God hath chosen the foolish things of the world to confound the wise; and God hath chosen the weak things of the world to confound the things which are mighty;

28 And base things of the world, and things which are despised, hath God chosen, yea, and things which

are not, to bring to nought things that are:

29 That no flesh should glory in his presence.

Romans 1:1,7; 12:6–8

1 Paul, a servant of Jesus Christ, called to be an apostle, separated unto the gospel of God . . .

7 To all that be in Rome, beloved of God, called to be saints. . . .

6 Having then gifts differing according to the grace that is given to us, whether prophecy, let us prophesy according to the proportion of faith;

7 Or ministry, let us wait on our ministering: or he that teacheth, on teaching;

8 Or he that exhorteth, on exhortation: he that giveth, let him do it with simplicity; he that ruleth, with diligence; he that sheweth mercy, with cheerfulness.

CHILDREN

In the Old Testament children are regarded as a blessing, barrenness as a curse. The prudent psalmist seemed to look on children as to some extent a form of insurance, but there was more to it than that. In the absence of any real belief in personal life after death, a man's future place in the world depended on his children. So did the future of his tribe, his nation, and his religion. And the child, even while still a child, could be the agent of God's purpose and the bearer of his word. The boy Samuel was an example of this.

The Old Testament has plenty to say about the upbringing of children (see Discipline and Teaching), but more important than that is its deep appreciation of the child's value in himself or herself. Each child is a fresh creation in the image of God the Creator, a direct gift from God.

The New Testament story of the birth of Jesus has something in common with the Old Testament story of the birth of Samuel, and Jesus, too, makes a notable appearance in God's house, the temple. Again the story emphasizes the child's capacity to hear and understand the word of God, though the stories of both Jesus and Samuel set this experience within a context of discipline and of respect for elders.

Later Jesus was to make childhood significant in a way that some have regarded as one of the most original features of his teaching. He took a child, placed him in the middle of a group of disciples, and told them to take the child as an example. An example of what? Not, if Jesus knew children, of goodness or meekness or innocence. The significant word in the sayings of Jesus about children is the verb "to receive." When he was brought a number of children and blessed them (see Blessing), he said, "Whosoever shall not receive the kingdom of God as a little child, he shall not enter therein."

Children are model receivers. They make it a way of life freely to accept love and care and every form of giving. They consider it natural to be loved and provided for. They may give love in return, but it never occurs to them that they must love first, or first deserve to be loved. They live by grace. In this respect they are models. All that Paul was later to say about salvation by grace alone rather than by works was anticipated in the form of an acted parable when Jesus took a child and told his followers that they were looking at the only way into the kingdom of God.

Today our most common question about children is a bit like that of the animal trainer: "How can we teach them, train them, domesticate them?" In view of the dangerous characteristics of the human animal, this is a natural and important question. The Bible has some answers to it, but it is more concerned with answering a different question, one that adults are sometimes reluctant to ask where children are concerned: What can we learn from them? Perhaps if we asked this question first, the original question would be raised in a different context and would receive different answers.

The answer to the question about what we have to learn from children has little to do with whether they are good or bad. It is not moral behavior that we shall study in them, but the behavior of a being with an instinctively right attitude toward life itself. The child gulps life in with eager enthusiasm, accepts it as a gift rather than as a reward, expects love—and will be seriously injured if deprived of it.

Perhaps one of the gravest things an adult can do to a child is to suppress the trust in grace that is at the heart of life. "Be good or mommy and daddy won't love you" is a monstrous assertion. Mommy and daddy may well be angry, but their anger can express love as clearly as their kindness does. And that love must be given freely and unconditionally.

The Bible in no way diminishes our proper adult concern for children as dependents. Adults must carry heavy responsibilities, especially in a world where many children are unloved and many more think they are because they are unfed. Yet one thing must have priority even over the inescapable task of providing for the world's children—and that is enjoying them.

CHILDREN

OLD TESTAMENT

Psalm 127:3–5

Lo, children are an heritage of the Lord:
And the fruit of the womb is his reward.
As arrows are in the hand of a mighty
man;

So are children of the youth.
Happy is the man that hath his quiver
full of them.

1 Samuel 3:1–10

1 And the child Samuel ministered unto the Lord before Eli. And the word

of the Lord was precious in those days; there was no open vision.

2 And it came to pass at that time, when Eli was laid down in his place, and his eyes began to wax dim, that he could not see;

3 And ere the lamp of God went out in the temple of the Lord, where the ark of God was, and Samuel was laid down to sleep;

4 That the Lord called Samuel: and he answered, Here am I.

5 And he ran unto Eli, and said, Here am I; for thou calledst me. And he said, I called not; lie down again. And he went and lay down.

6 And the Lord called yet again, Samuel. And Samuel arose and went to Eli, and said, Here am I; for thou didst call me. And he answered, I called not, my son; lie down again.

7 Now Samuel did not yet know the Lord, neither was the word of the Lord yet revealed unto him.

8 And the Lord called Samuel again the third time. And he arose and went to Eli, and said, Here am I; for thou didst call me. And Eli perceived that the Lord had called the child.

9 Therefore Eli said unto Samuel, Go, lie down: and it shall be, if he call thee, that thou shalt say, Speak, Lord; for thy servant heareth. So Samuel went and lay down in his place.

10 And the Lord came, and stood, and called as at other times, Samuel, Samuel. Then Samuel answered, Speak; for thy servant heareth.

NEW TESTAMENT
Luke 2:40–52

40 And the child grew, and waxed strong in spirit, filled with wisdom: and the grace of God was upon him.

41 Now his parents went to Jerusalem every year at the feast of the passover.

42 And when he was twelve years old, they went up to Jerusalem after the custom of the feast.

43 And when they had fulfilled the days, as they returned, the child Jesus tarried behind in Jerusalem; and Joseph and his mother knew not of it.

44 But they, supposing him to have been in the company, went a day's journey; and they sought him among their kinsfolk and acquaintance.

45 And when they found him not, they turned back again to Jerusalem, seeking him.

46 And it came to pass, that after three days they found him in the temple, sitting in the midst of the doctors, both hearing them, and asking them questions.

47 And all that heard him were astonished at his understanding and answers.

48 And when they saw him, they were amazed: and his mother said unto him, Son, why hast thou thus dealt with us? behold, thy father and I have sought thee sorrowing.

49 And he said unto them, How is it that ye sought me? wist ye not that I must be about my Father's business?

50 And they understood not the saying which he spake unto them.

51 And he went down with them, and came to Nazareth, and was subject unto them: but his mother kept all these sayings in her heart.

52 And Jesus increased in wisdom and stature, and in favour with God and man.

Matthew 18: 1–6

1 At the same time came the disciples unto Jesus, saying, Who is the greatest in the kingdom of heaven?

2 And Jesus called a little child unto him, and set him in the midst of them,

3 And said, Verily I say unto you, Except ye be converted, and become as little children, ye shall not enter into the kingdom of heaven.

4 Whosoever therefore shall humble himself as this little child, the same is greatest in the kingdom of heaven.

5 And whoso shall receive one such little child in my name receiveth me.

6 But whoso shall offend one of these little ones which believe in me, it were better for him that a millstone were hanged about his neck, and that he were drowned in the depth of the sea.

COMMITMENT

The Old Testament view of commitment is rooted in that work's dominant theme, the idea of covenant, which is supremely represented by the covenant binding God and his people to each other. This relationship involved a commitment that made demands on every aspect of human life: sacred and secular, individual and corporate, familial and political. When Josiah found a book of laws that had been neglected, he led the people in a solemn act of recommitment to all that was involved in being a covenanted nation.

The system built on this foundation was not a rigid one, however. Josiah's law book said, as most people would, that you are more committed when you make a formal promise or take an oath than you would otherwise be. Given an explicit commitment, you are not free to withdraw just because it would be to your own advantage to do so. Psalm 15 salutes the man who keeps his promise even when it hurts. That is the kind of person who gets close to God, says the psalmist.

The Old Testament is well aware of human fallibility. It knows that covenants do get broken. Above all the covenant between God and Israel has been broken by the Israelites. They have been unfaithful to their religious commitment, and they have been unfaithful to their commitments to one another. Because commitments of both kinds have been underwritten by God, he is entitled to exact retribution on both counts. But he is not a God who exacts the last penny of his claim upon others. Indeed, the prophet Jeremiah sees his God as one who offers a new and more inward covenant that will achieve the commitment of the heart.

The New Testament is inclined to start from this more inward kind of commitment and to say that outward obligations will be met as a natural outcome of it rather than as an imposed requirement. Like the Old Testament, it is both demanding and flexible. In many respects it is the more demanding of the two.

For Jesus, a simple yes or no is as firm a commitment as a solemn oath. Yet he does not allow even a solemn oath to be so binding as to excuse the neglect of a simple human responsibility. The point of "Corban" would seem to be that, once a piece of property was in this way formally promised to God, it could not be used for anything else, not even to relieve the poverty of a destitute parent. Jesus would have none of this honoring of the letter of commitment while being false to the personal relationships that commitments are designed to serve.

Indeed he spoke of his own death as sealing the promised new covenant ("testament" in the old translation)—new, that is, in quality as well as in time. This was the supreme example of the rebuilding of an inward relationship on the ruins of a broken commitment.

Those who would like to add a secret clause to every agreement—an unspoken "so long as it is convenient"—will find no encouragement here. Commitments are for keeps, and society must do its best to make them stick. Marriages, business contracts, and political treaties are all examples of what the Bible would regard as covenants that bind us together. To treat them as just so many scraps of paper is to dissolve the fabric of human society.

But a formal commitment is the outward manifestation of something more inward: a personal relationship. The commitment is designed to articulate the relationship, to define it, to publish it, and so to protect and preserve it. But the agreement exists for the sake of the relationship, not the relationship for the agreement. Society must uphold the published terms of the commitment, but the Bible requires individual human beings to go deeper. They must be concerned with the relationship itself.

There are those who will boast of having kept the explicit terms of a covenant when they have ruined the relationship behind it. "I've always been true to you," says the shrewish wife or the insensitive husband. Presumably this person means that he or she has avoided adultery, but that is not enough. To be true to the covenant of marriage is to foster and enrich the marriage relationship. There is more in a commitment than meets the lawyer's eye.

COMMITMENT

OLD TESTAMENT

2 Kings 23:1-3

1 And the king sent, and they gathered unto him all the elders of Judah and of Jerusalem.

2 And the king went up into the house of the Lord, and all the men of Judah and all the inhabitants of Jerusalem with him, and the priests, and the prophets, and all the people, both small and great: and he read in their ears all the words of the book of the covenant which was found in the house of the Lord.

3 And the king stood by a pillar,

and made a covenant before the Lord, to walk after the Lord, and to keep his commandments and his testimonies and his statutes with all their heart and all their soul, to perform the words of this covenant that were written in this book. And all the people stood to the covenant.

Deuteronomy 23:21–23

21 When thou shalt vow a vow unto the Lord thy God, thou shalt not slack to pay it: for the Lord thy God will surely require it of thee; and it would be sin in thee.

22 But if thou shalt forbear to vow, it shall be no sin in thee.

23 That which is gone out of thy lips thou shalt keep and perform; even a freewill offering, according as thou hast vowed unto the Lord thy God, which thou hast promised with thy mouth.

Psalm 15:1–2, 4

Lord, who shall abide in thy tabernacle?
Who shall dwell in thy holy hill?
He that walketh uprightly, and worketh righteousness,
He that sweareth to his own hurt, and changeth not.

Jeremiah 31:31–33

31 Behold, the days come, saith the Lord, and I will make a new covenant with the house of Israel, and with the house of Judah:

32 Not according to the covenant that I made with their fathers in the day that I took them by the hand to bring them out of the land of Egypt; which my covenant they brake, al-though I was an husband unto them, saith the Lord:

33 But this shall be the covenant that I will make with the house of Israel; After those days, saith the Lord, I will put my law in their inward parts, and write it in their hearts; and will be their God, and they shall be my people.

NEW TESTAMENT

Matthew 5:33–37

33 Again, ye have heard that it hath been said by them of old time, Thou shalt not forswear thyself, but shalt perform unto the Lord thine oaths:

34 But I say unto you, Swear not at all; neither by heaven; for it is God's throne:

35 Nor by the earth; for it is his footstool: neither by Jerusalem; for it is the city of the great King.

36 Neither shalt thou swear by thy head, because thou canst not make one hair white or black.

37 But let your communication be, Yea, yea; Nay, nay: for whatsoever is more than these cometh of evil.

Mark 7:9–13

9 And he said unto them, Full well ye reject the commandment of God, that ye may keep your own tradition.

10 For Moses said, Honour thy father and thy mother; and, Whoso curseth father or mother, let him die the death:

11 But ye say, If a man shall say to his father or mother, It is Corban, that is to say, a gift, by whatsoever thou mightest be profited by me; he shall be free.

12 And ye suffer him no more to do aught for his father or his mother;

13 Making the word of God of none effect through your tradition, which ye have delivered: and many such like things do ye.

Luke 22:20

20 Likewise [Jesus took] also the cup after supper, saying, This cup is the new testament in my blood, which is shed for you.

2 Corinthians 3:6

6 Who also hath made us able ministers of the new testament; not of the letter, but of the spirit: for the letter killeth, but the spirit giveth life.

COMMUNICATION

The Old Testament regards communication as just about the most fundamental thing in the universe. It speaks of "the word"—a symbol of interpersonal communication in all its forms—as the basic principle of creation. The world itself is formed by God's word. The universe is itself a communication. It exists as a statement, and man is designed to receive the statement and reply to it. Job, in his suffering, could not get the message that the world was delivering. He knew it was not the simple moral that his friends professed to find in things, but he could not make out what it was. Yet he could not regard his experience as meaningless. Somehow it must communicate to him a statement of the mind of God. So he boldly challenged God to open a dialogue with him. Communication between God and man was essential, and the whole dramatic story of Old Testament prophecy consists of just such a dialogue as Job demanded.

As to communication among human beings, its failure is symbolized in the story of Babel. The Hebrew way of saying that what has happened falls within the providence of God is to say that God intended it and brought it about. "Go to," says the God of the Hebrews. "Let us go down and confound their language that they may not understand one another's speech." The English way of putting it would be to say that the world is a Babel of noncommunication, and that given humanity's pretentiousness and God's demand, that is bound to be the case.

The New Testament neatly reverses the story of Babel in its story of Pentecost. What happened bears some resemblance to the well-known phenomenon of "speaking with tongues," but Luke's story in Acts is that the people heard the preaching of the apostles in their own languages, not in an unfamiliar tongue. The long history of human noncommunication has been turned around by the power of the Spirit.

When speaking in an unknown language does take place, Paul insists that it must be interpreted. Communication is all. Indeed the whole work of Jesus can be understood as communication through incarnation. The broken syllables of prophecy have been joined together into a coherent statement in the person of Jesus.

All this places our modern problems of communication in a sublime context. The human being appears to be so constructed that he cannot function except within a network of signals that he can receive and transmit. "I just can't get through to him" is the ultimate admission of defeat. Until that obstacle is overcome, no other problems can be solved. This applies between parents and children, between estranged lovers, between therapist and patient, between employer and worker, between nation and nation. There is no limit to the problems that must remain insoluble until communication is established.

Those who work on communication theory, those who teach the use of language, and those who create nonverbal forms of communication (artists, for example) are all working at the very roots of our humanity. Work of such significance is bound to involve dangers as well as blessings. Probably the greatest dangers are associated with the mass communication media and with the search for shortcuts. The advertiser may want to get a message across quickly and widely by bypassing the critical faculties of those for whom the message is intended. The demagogue will want a form of communication that will offer instant control of the masses. Experts in communication could sell their souls to such masters.

The Bible would forbid them to do so on the ground that the power to communicate and to receive communication is a sacred thing to be preserved inviolate in every human being. And the whole personality must be involved: head and heart together. One should neither speak off the top of one's head nor receive communications merely emotionally. The lines of communication must be joined to the whole person. We are to value communication as we value life itself, because for us it *is* life itself. Whoever cheapens it is destroying humanity.

COMMUNICATION

OLD TESTAMENT

Psalm 33:6, 8–9

By the word of the Lord were the heavens made;
And all the host of them by the breath of his mouth.
Let all the earth fear the Lord:
Let all the inhabitants of the world stand in awe of him.

For he spake, and it was done;
He commanded, and it stood fast.

Job 13:3, 15, 20–22

Surely I would speak to the Almighty,
And I desire to reason with God.
Though he slay me, yet will I trust in him:
But I will maintain mine own ways before him.
Only do not two things unto me:
Then will I not hide myself from thee.

Withdraw thine hand far from me:
And let not thy dread make me afraid.
Then call thou, and I will answer:
Or let me speak, and answer thou me.

Genesis 11:1–9

1 And the whole earth was of one language, and of one speech.

2 And it came to pass, as they journeyed from the east, that they found a plain in the land of Shinar, and they dwelt there.

3 And they said one to another, Go to, let us make brick, and burn them throughly. And they had brick for stone, and slime had they for mortar.

4 And they said, Go to, let us build us a city and a tower, whose top may reach unto heaven; and let us make us a name, lest we be scattered abroad upon the face of the whole earth.

5 And the Lord came down to see the city and the tower, which the children of men builded.

6 And the Lord said, Behold, the people is one, and they have all one language; and this they begin to do: and now nothing will be restrained from them, which they have imagined to do.

7 Go to, let us go down, and there confound their language, that they may not understand one another's speech.

8 So the Lord scattered them abroad from thence upon the face of all the earth: and they left off to build the city.

9 Therefore is the name of it called Babel; because the Lord did there confound the language of all the earth: and from thence did the Lord scatter them abroad upon the face of all the earth.

NEW TESTAMENT

Acts 2:1–12

1 And when the day of Pentecost was fully come, they were all with one accord in one place.

2 And suddenly there came a sound from heaven as of a rushing mighty wind, and it filled all the house where they were sitting.

3 And there appeared unto them cloven tongues like as of fire, and it sat upon each of them.

4 And they were all filled with the Holy Ghost, and began to speak with other tongues, as the Spirit gave them utterance.

5 And there were dwelling at Jerusalem Jews, devout men, out of every nation under heaven.

6 Now when this was noised abroad, the multitude came together, and were confounded, because that every man heard them speak in his own language.

7 And they were all amazed and marvelled, saying one to another, Behold, are not all these which speak Galilæans?

8 And how hear we every man in our own tongue, wherein we were born?

9 Parthians and Medes, and Elamites, and the dwellers in Mesopotamia, and in Judæa, and Cappadocia, in Pontus, and Asia,

10 Phrygia, and Pamphylia, in Egypt, and in the parts of Libya about Cyrene, and strangers of Rome, Jews and proselytes,

11 Cretes and Arabians, we do hear them speak in our tongues the wonderful works of God.

12 And they were all amazed, and were in doubt, saying one to another, What meaneth this?

1 Corinthians 14:9, 13, 18–19

9 So likewise ye, except ye utter by the tongue words easy to be understood, how shall it be known what is spoken? for ye shall speak into the air.

13 Wherefore let him that speaketh in an unknown tongue pray that he may interpret.

18 I thank my God, I speak with tongues more than ye all:

19 Yet in the church I had rather speak five words with my understanding, that by my voice I might teach others also, than ten thousand words in an unknown tongue.

Hebrews 1:1–3

1 God, who at sundry times and in divers manners spake in time past unto the fathers by the prophets,

2 Hath in these last days spoken unto us by his Son, whom he hath appointed heir of all things, by whom also he made the worlds;

3 Who being the brightness of his glory, and the express image of his person, and upholding all things by the word of his power, when he had by himself purged our sins, sat down on the right hand of the Majesty on high.

COMPETITION

The Old Testament recognizes many forms of competitive rivalry. Between strangers it was not condemned. Between members of the same community, however, and especially between members of the same family, competition had to be restrained. Abraham (known earlier as Abram) felt that he had to withdraw from a situation that made him a competitor with Lot for limited pasture. Generously he allowed Lot to make the choice and himself accepted the poorer ground.

Later the law of Jubilee severely restricted the power of one competitor to prevail over another of the same nation. Every fifty years the losers in economic competition were given a fresh start and the winners pulled back. The man who had been forced to sell his land could return to it and take possession of it. The man who had been forced to work for others was freed from his commitment. Non-Israelites did not fully participate in these benefits, but it was thought to be unwise to make prevailing over others, even foreigners, the criterion for success. Wisdom itself was a truer goal. A man should measure himself against perfection rather than against competitors as frail as himself.

Jesus' parable of workers in a vineyard is a story *of* economics, but not *about* economics. It is aimed at those who want God to limit his love according to each individual's merit. It says that God is never less than just but always more than generous. But this message, aimed at the heart of the debate between moralism and the Gospel, does have implications in the area of economics and competition. If we live by grace so that our whole standing in the world is an expression of God's generosity rather than of our merit, then there cannot be many fields in which it makes sense to measure rival achievements one against the other. To rate ourselves against other people is to adopt a false standard. Love will not allow us to use our neighbor's comparative failure as the measure of our success.

The Bible's concern is to contain competition within what is good for community. In the years since the Bible was written human community has become much wider and more interdependent. Now we are all involved in the prosperity of the whole worldwide community. To subjugate any rival group is to disturb the balance on which everyone's well-being depends. Competition can be healthy only if it provides, as the Old Testament does, for the care and self-respect of those who are less successful in it. And that now means anywhere in the world.

But perhaps the best way to restrain competition where it would be destructive is to divert it into other channels where it cannot hurt anyone. There is little point in chastising ourselves because we have competitive feelings. They are ingrained in us. A better strategy is to have fun with them where they do little or no harm—in sports, for instance.

The Bible does not deny that the best way to evaluate your running is to measure it against that of another runner. In such fields competition can have its fling. What the Bible does dispute is that the best way to assess the quality of your life is to measure it against somebody else's life. The Bible would vigorously deny that the best way to measure your success is to count the number of people you have passed by and humiliated on your way to wherever you have got.

It is said of one television mogul, "For him it was not enough to succeed; the others had to fail." From a biblical point of view he (if correctly described) had got it all wrong. He needed better standards against which to measure himself. Even a business corporation should be able to work out noncompetitive criteria such as quality, efficiency, and growth rate. Trade unions should be able to find ways of evaluating their members' work without just pointing to some other group that has achieved a greater increase in wages.

Above all, the individual needs to be aware of his own unique significance and to aim at filling his own special place, without reference to other people and their places. Except in games and similar frivolities, he does not need to be looking over his shoulder at what the rest are doing.

COMPETITION

OLD TESTAMENT

Genesis 13:1–12

1 And Abram went up out of Egypt, he, and his wife, and all that he had, and Lot with him, into the south.

2 And Abram was very rich in cattle, in silver, and in gold.

46

3 And he went on his journeys from the south even to Beth–el, unto the place where his tent had been at the beginning, between Beth–el and Hai;

4 Unto the place of the altar, which he had made there at the first: and there Abram called on the name of the Lord.

5 And Lot also, which went with Abram, had flocks, and herds, and tents.

6 And the land was not able to bear them, that they might dwell together: for their substance was great, so that they could not dwell together.

7 And there was a strife between the herdmen of Abram's cattle and the herdmen of Lot's cattle: and the Canaanite and the Perizzite dwelled then in the land.

8 And Abram said unto Lot, Let there be no strife, I pray thee, between me and thee, and between my herdmen and thy herdmen; for we be brethren.

9 Is not the whole land before thee? separate thyself, I pray thee, from me: if thou wilt take the left hand, then I will go to the right; or if thou depart to the right hand, then I will go to the left.

10 And Lot lifted up his eyes, and beheld all the plain of Jordan, that it was well watered every where, before the Lord destroyed Sodom and Gomorrah, even as the garden of the Lord, like the land of Egypt, as thou comest unto Zoar.

11 Then Lot chose him all the plain of Jordan; and Lot journeyed east: and they separated themselves the one from the other.

12 Abram dwelled in the land of Canaan, and Lot dwelled in the cities of the plain, and pitched his tent toward Sodom.

Leviticus 25:25–26, 28, 39–41

25 If thy brother be waxen poor, and hath sold away some of his possession,

26 And if the man have none to redeem it . . .

28 . . . then that which is sold shall remain in the hand of him that hath bought it until the year of jubile: and in the jubile it shall go out, and he shall return unto his possession.

39 And if thy brother that dwelleth by thee be waxen poor, and be sold unto thee; thou shalt not compel him to serve as a bondservant:

40 But as an hired servant, and as a sojourner, he shall be with thee, and shall serve thee unto the year of jubile:

41 And then shall he depart from thee, both he and his children with him, and shall return unto his own family, and unto the possession of his fathers shall he return.

NEW TESTAMENT

Matthew 20:1–15

1 For the kingdom of heaven is like unto a man that is an householder, which went out early in the morning to hire labourers into his vineyard.

2 And when he had agreed with the labourers for a penny a day, he sent them into his vineyard.

3 And he went out about the third hour, and saw others standing idle in the marketplace,

4 And said unto them; Go ye also into the vineyard, and whatsoever is right I will give you. And they went their way.

5 Again he went out about the sixth and ninth hour, and did likewise.

6 And about the eleventh hour he went out, and found others standing idle, and saith unto them, Why stand ye here all the day idle?

7 They say unto him, Because no man hath hired us. He saith unto them, Go ye also into the vineyard; and whatsoever is right, that shall ye receive.

8 So when even was come, the lord of the vineyard saith unto his steward, Call the labourers, and give them their hire, beginning from the last unto the first.

9 And when they came that were hired about the eleventh hour, they received every man a penny.

10 But when the first came, they supposed that they should have received more; and they likewise received every man a penny.

11 And when they had received it, they murmured against the goodman of the house,

12 Saying, These last have wrought but one hour, and thou hast made them equal unto us, which have borne the burden and heat of the day.

13 But he answered one of them, and said, Friend, I do thee no wrong: didst not thou agree with me for a penny?

14 Take that thine is, and go thy way: I will give unto this last, even as unto thee.

15 Is it not lawful for me to do what I will with mine own? Is thine eye evil, because I am good?

Romans 13:10

10 Love worketh no ill to his neighbour.

CONFIDENCE

One great Old Testament figure—Moses, no less—is said to have been lacking in confidence. But what he lacked was *self*-confidence, and that was irrelevant. The real question was whether he had confidence in God.

This became the characteristic, even proverbial, Old Testament position. "Confidence" essentially meant "confidence *in*." Supremely it was confidence in God, in his laws, in his providence, in his prophets and his people. Isaiah believed that, in the political tumult of his time, Israel's security lay in its behaving with quiet confidence. Trust in arms and horses was misplaced confidence.

Biblical confidence is not a feeling—certainly not a feeling of complacency. It is a relationship of trust. What matters is that this trust should be well founded so that confidence will remain unshaken. Its orientation is outward.

This is dramatized in a New Testament story about Peter. As long as he kept his attention on Jesus, he could walk on the water. Once he looked around and saw himself in relation to the storm instead of in relation to his master, he sank.

At this point Peter exemplified lack of confidence. The New Testament, however, shows him not only *lacking* confidence but also *falsely* confident and *truly* confident—the whole gamut. The false confidence was, as usual, self-confidence. He was sure that he had in him what it takes to follow his leader to prison or to death. He was wrong. And yet eventually he did both those things. The difference was in his own orientation. The true confidence reflected a relationship of trust to God in Christ. He no longer reckoned on his own resources as the determining factor. If suffering came he had only to commit himself to God and go on doing what was right. No problem.

"Loss of nerve" is the modern term for lack of confidence, and there is said to be a lot of it about. It afflicts whole nations and civilizations as well as individuals. Fearing that their ability is unequal to the demands of the times, nations and civilizations fail to perform to the level of their actual ability. But a nation or a civilization can also make the mistake of turning its attention inward rather than outward, seeking the grounds for confidence where they are not to be found in any case. A nation can measure its gross national product and add up its balance of payments and work out the relative strength of its armed forces as if nothing else were involved. If the figures come out badly, the community will lose confidence. If they come out well, it will gain false confidence. True confidence can arise only if the nation orients itself toward the values that endure, however armies and economies fluctuate. A firm commitment to justice and to freedom and to equity is the true source of security. The confidence that flows from it is a confidence in those values rather than in the nation itself, but any nation with that sort of confidence would be itself a confident nation.

Something very similar is true of individuals. Self-confident people are falsely confident. Very probably they know it and are only blustering to cover up their own sense of inadequacy. A relationship of trust, given and received, would knit them into a more stable order of things. A much quieter confidence based on that stability could lead to more effective action.

To pursue confidence as a self-contained feeling of adequacy is to pursue a will-o'-the-wisp. To identify and trust that which is secure and unchanging is to find confidence without even looking for it.

CONFIDENCE

OLD TESTAMENT

Exodus 4:10–16

10 And Moses said unto the Lord, O my Lord, I am not eloquent, nei-

ther heretofore, nor since thou hast spoken unto thy servant: but I am slow of speech, and of a slow tongue.

11 And the Lord said unto him, Who hath made man's mouth? or who

maketh the dumb, or deaf, or the seeing, or the blind? have not I the Lord?

12 Now therefore go, and I will be with thy mouth, and teach thee what thou shalt say.

13 And he said, O my Lord, send, I pray thee, by the hand of him whom thou wilt send.

14 And the anger of the Lord was kindled against Moses, and he said, Is not Aaron the Levite thy brother? I know that he can speak well. And also, behold, he cometh forth to meet thee: and when he seeth thee, he will be glad in his heart.

15 And thou shalt speak unto him, and put words in his mouth: and I will be with thy mouth, and with his mouth, and will teach you what ye shall do.

16 And he shall be thy spokesman unto the people: and he shall be, even he shall be to thee instead of a mouth, and thou shalt be to him instead of God.

Proverbs 3:25–26

Be not afraid of sudden fear,
Neither of the desolation of the wicked, when it cometh.
For the Lord shall be thy confidence,
And shall keep thy foot from being taken.

Isaiah 30:15–17

15 For thus saith the Lord God, the Holy One of Israel; In returning and rest shall ye be saved; in quietness and in confidence shall be your strength: and ye would not.

16 But ye said, No; for we will flee upon horses; therefore shall ye flee: and,

We will ride upon the swift; therefore shall they that pursue you be swift.

17 One thousand shall flee at the rebuke of one; at the rebuke of five shall ye flee: till ye be left as a beacon upon the top of a mountain, and as an ensign on an hill.

NEW TESTAMENT

Matthew 14:22–31

22 And straightway Jesus constrained his disciples to get into a ship, and to go before him unto the other side, while he sent the multitudes away.

23 And when he had sent the multitudes away, he went up into a mountain apart to pray: and when the evening was come, he was there alone.

24 But the ship was now in the midst of the sea, tossed with waves: for the wind was contrary.

25 And in the fourth watch of the night Jesus went unto them, walking on the sea.

26 And when the disciples saw him walking on the sea, they were troubled, saying, It is a spirit; and they cried out for fear.

27 But straightway Jesus spake unto them, saying, Be of good cheer; it is I; be not afraid.

28 And Peter answered him and said, Lord, if it be thou, bid me come unto thee on the water.

29 And he said, Come. And when Peter was come down out of the ship, he walked on the water, to go to Jesus.

30 But when he saw the wind boisterous, he was afraid; and beginning to sink, he cried, saying, Lord, save me.

31 And immediately Jesus stretched forth his hand, and caught him, and said unto him, O thou of little faith, wherefore didst thou doubt?

Luke 22:31–34

31 And the Lord said, Simon, Simon, behold, Satan hath desired *to* have you, that he may sift you as wheat:

32 But I have prayed for thee, that thy faith fail not: and when thou art converted, strengthen thy brethren.

33 And he said unto him, Lord, I am ready to go with thee, both into prison, and to death.

34 And he said, I tell thee, Peter, the cock shall not crow this day, before that thou shalt thrice deny that thou knowest me.

1 Peter 4:19

19 Wherefore let them that suffer according to the will of God commit the keeping of their souls to him in well-doing, as unto a faithful Creator.

CONSCIENCE

The Old Testament does not leave it to our inner conscience to find out the difference between right and wrong. It tells us the difference. Its emphasis is on the objectivity of the moral law. The later prophets spoke of having the law written on men's hearts, but most of the Old Testament is concerned with having it written on tablets of stone and in books of law. It does not follow, however, that in this period the human conscience had no function. Even if the content of the right was presented in black and white, there was still a need for something within the individual to respond.

The effect is nicely illustrated in the contrasted stories of two kings, Josiah and Jehoiakim. Each was presented with a document that stated the right course for him and his people. Josiah's document was a lost law book that turned up when he was having some much-needed repairs done on the temple. In Jehoiakim's story the document was a scroll containing the prophecies of Jeremiah. Each king had the document read to him. Josiah tore his clothes as a symbol of penitence and ordered action to be taken at once. Jehoiakim cut off pieces of the scroll as they were read and dropped them into the fire. That is the difference made by the presence or absence of a sensitive conscience.

Increasingly, prophets such as Jeremiah and Ezekiel turned their attention to this inward area. They saw the need for a spirit that would respond to the right when it was made known—would perhaps even know the right for itself.

In the New Testament Jesus speaks of an inner light and promises an indwelling Spirit. What he had been saying outwardly in men's ears was to be repeated inwardly by the Spirit. What had been an imposed law enforced by sanctions was to become a natural way of life motivated by love. Conscience was to come of age.

Paul wrote from experience of the fulfillment of these promises, but he remembered the divided heart of which Ezekiel had spoken. He knew how conscience can manifest itself as just a guilty conscience, one part of a man or woman condemning another part for not doing what is clearly seen to be right. Paul contrasts with that the condition of the man who has been inwardly renewed by the Spirit so that he can both discover and do the will of God.

Not that he always will. But the verdict of conscience is no longer final. There is a way forward from its condemnation. Our hearts may condemn us, says John, "but God is greater than our hearts."

It is too often assumed that the noun "conscience" must always take the adjective "guilty." The whole idea of conscience tends to gather negative associations. Conscience is that which says, "No, you must not"—or more often, "No, you should not have." It is a source of both guilt and depression.

This is to belittle the conscience. Paradoxically, the way to enlarge the scope of the conscience is to recognize its limitations. It is neither the sole arbiter of good and evil nor the court beyond which there is no appeal. It is subordinate to the objective realities of a moral order that knows not only good and evil but also forgiveness. Within that context it can function positively as well as negatively. It is a magnet that is attracted by the good and repelled by the bad.

Conscience, being subordinate, needs education and development. The difference between right and wrong does actually exist outside us. What is inside us needs to be taught about that reality. And it can be. It can learn from experience and from the wisdom of the past, from written codes and spoken prophecies, from the example of the good and the visions of the inspired. It needs to be exposed to all these influences in the course of its education, and then consulted increasingly often.

The educated conscience writes sound laws in the human heart and strengthens in us an instinct to fulfill them. The healthy conscience (a redeemed version of the guilty one) not only rejects what is bad but reaches out in love and longing toward all that is good and beautiful and true.

CONSCIENCE

OLD TESTAMENT

2 Kings 22:8, 10–13

8 And Hilkiah the high priest said unto Shaphan the scribe, I have found the book of the law in the house of the Lord. And Hilkiah gave the book to Shaphan, and he read it.

10 And Shaphan the scribe shewed the king, saying Hilkiah the priest hath delivered me a book. And Shaphan read it before the king.

11 And it came to pass, when the king had heard the words of the book of the law, that he rent his clothes.

12 And the king commanded Hil-

kiah the priest, and Ahikam the son of Shaphan, and Achbor the son of Michaiah, and Shaphan the scribe, and Asahiah a servant of the king's, saying,

13 Go ye, inquire of the Lord for me, and for the people, and for all Judah, concerning the words of this book that is found: for great is the wrath of the Lord that is kindled against us, because our fathers have not hearkened unto the words of this book, to do according unto all that which is written concerning us.

Jeremiah 36:4–6, 8, 21–26

4 Then Jeremiah called Baruch the son of Neriah: and Baruch wrote from the mouth of Jeremiah all the words of the Lord, which he had spoken unto him, upon a roll of a book.

5 And Jeremiah commanded Baruch, saying, I am shut up; I cannot go into the house of the Lord:

6 Therefore go thou, and read in the roll, which thou hast written from my mouth, the words of the Lord in the ears of the people in the Lord's house upon the fasting day: and also thou shalt read them in the ears of all Judah that come out of their cities.

8 And Baruch the son of Neriah did according to all that Jeremiah the prophet commanded him, reading in the book the words of the Lord in the Lord's house.

21 So the king sent Jehudi to fetch the roll: and he took it out of Elishama the scribe's chamber. And Jehudi read it in the ears of the king, and in the ears of all the princes which stood beside the king.

22 Now the king sat in the winterhouse in the ninth month: and there was a fire on the hearth burning before him.

23 And it came to pass, that when Jehudi had read three or four leaves, he cut it with the penknife, and cast it into the fire that was on the hearth, until all the roll was consumed in the fire that was on the hearth.

24 Yet they were not afraid, nor rent their garments, neither the king, nor any of his servants that heard all these words.

25 Nevertheless Elnathan and Delaiah and Gemariah had made intercession to the king that he would not burn the roll: but he would not hear them.

26 But the king commanded Jerahmeel the son of Hammelech, and Saraiah the son of Azriel, and Shelemiah the son of Abdeel, to take Baruch the scribe and Jeremiah the prophet: but the Lord hid them.

Ezekiel 11:14, 19–20

14 Again the word of the Lord came unto me, saying,

19 And I will give them one heart, and I will put a new spirit within you; and I will take the stony heart out of their flesh, and will give them an heart of flesh:

20 That they may walk in my statutes, and keep mine ordinances, and do them.

NEW TESTAMENT

Matthew 6:22–23

22 The light of the body is the eye: if therefore thine eye be single, thy whole body shall be full of light.

23 But if thine eye be evil, thy whole body shall be full of darkness. If therefore the light that is in thee be darkness, how great is that darkness!

John 14:23–26

23 Jesus answered and said unto him, If a man love me, he will keep my words: and my Father will love him, and we will come unto him, and make our abode with him.

24 He that loveth me not keepeth not my sayings: and the word which ye hear is not mine, but the Father's which sent me.

25 These things have I spoken unto you, being yet present with you.

26 But the Comforter, which is the Holy Ghost, whom the Father will send in my name, he shall teach you all things, and bring all things to your remembrance, whatsoever I have said unto you.

Romans 7:18–19; 8:2; 12:1–2

18 For I know that in me (that is, in my flesh,) dwelleth no good thing:

for to will is present with me; but how to perform that which is good I find not.

19 For the good that I would I do not: but the evil which I would not, that I do.

2 For the law of the Spirit of life in Christ Jesus hath made me free from the law of sin and death.

1 I beseech you therefore, brethren, by the mercies of God, that ye present your bodies a living sacrifice, holy, acceptable unto God, which is your reasonable service.

2 And be not conformed to this world: but be ye transformed by the renewing of your mind, that ye may prove what is that good, and acceptable, and perfect, will of God.

1 John 3:19–20

19 And hereby we know that we are of the truth, and shall assure our hearts before him.

20 For if our heart condemn us, God is greater than our heart, and knoweth all things.

CORRUPTION

The Old Testament story of Naboth's vineyard is a classic tale of corruption. King Ahab is the rising man and, as yet, a well-meaning one. He finds a relatively modest desire frustrated by a much smaller man's old-fashioned belief that his family must not be separated from its inherited land. Ahab's wife, the model of a tycoon's consort, mocks her husband for being so feeble. Then she procures the death of Naboth and (as we are told in a later Old Testament book) of his sons, so that the freehold of Naboth's land, being uninherited, passes to the crown. In the very act of taking possession Ahab is shown the reality of the transaction: he has, after a fashion, obtained the land, but he has sold himself.

In New Testament terms he has gained not the whole world but a desirable piece of it, and he has lost his soul—his integrity and his identity as a person.

One character in the New Testament had the bad luck to give his name to the dictionary-makers as representative of the corrupt practice of buying a privileged position in the church. During the many centuries in which such purchases could be made, the practice was called "simony," after Simon Magus. Again it is a story of the corruption of the best being the worst. As an ordinary charlatan magician Simon could have lived in comfort and died forgotten. But he got converted. He saw the strong power of the Spirit. He coveted a role like that of the apostles, and he turned to the old, mundane shortcut of using money as a way to the new, transcendent authority. That made him infamous forever, as he would never have been but for his being drawn out of magic and into Christianity.

Peter's "Thy money perish with thee" was a significant remark. Simon's corruption had joined him as a person to the things that are perishable. The process of decay carries matter and spirit down together when they are linked. But that process can be reversed. Peter's next words, immediately following those quoted here, are: "Repent of this thy wickedness, and pray, God, if perhaps the thought of thine heart may be forgiven thee." A New Testament letter that bears Peter's name speaks of participating in a divine nature that ousts the corrupt one. It goes on to indicate that grasping this life by faith initiates a process of growth through goodness which is exactly like the process of decay through corruption, except that it moves in the opposite direction: "add to your faith, virtue; and to virtue, knowledge; and to knowledge, temperance; and to temperance, patience; and to patience, godliness; and to godliness, brotherly kindness; and to brotherly kindness, charity."

It is interesting that the word "corruption" is used to denote both moral misbehavior and the process of natural decay. Corruption can be observed in a great man misusing his power, or in a dead body mouldering in the grave. According to the Bible the connection between the two is not just linguistic.

And this is helpful. Denouncing corruption is easy—like being against sin. But corruption remains insidiously attractive so long as it looks to be only a shortcut to a great prize. Much better to realize that it will be a tainted prize and will taste like dust in the mouth. There are no corrupt means to the achievement of enduring good. Corruption is just another word for death.

If that is so, the way to turn from corruption is to turn toward life—toward life as it truly is. The natural process of decay leading toward death, once reversed, becomes a natural process of growth leading toward life. The Bible counters moral corruption not so much with condemnation as with affirmation—the affirmation of the good life, and the affirmation of it not as a turning away from the material things that dazzle the corrupt but as a way of using them well and creatively. Against the specious attraction of using corrupt means to attain tainted goals it sets the possibility of integrity as a union of body and soul, of temporal and eternal, of material and spiritual. Faith and love fastened on such goals do make a difference. It seems likely that right conduct owes more to seeing the good in a true light than it does to any amount of moral condemnation.

CORRUPTION

OLD TESTAMENT

1 Kings 21:1–4, 7–11, 15–20

1 And it came to pass after these things, that Naboth the Jezreelite had a vineyard, which was in Jezreel, hard by the palace of Ahab king of Samaria.

2 And Ahab spake unto Naboth, saying, Give me thy vineyard, that I may have it for a garden of herbs, because it is near unto my house: and I will give thee for it a better vineyard than it; or, if it seem good to thee, I will give thee the worth of it in money.

3 And Naboth said to Ahab, The Lord forbid it me, that I should give the inheritance of my fathers unto thee.

4 And Ahab came into his house heavy and displeased because of the word which Naboth the Jezreelite had spoken to him: for he had said, I will not give thee the inheritance of my fathers. And he laid him down upon his bed, and turned away his face, and would eat no bread.

7 And Jezebel his wife said unto him, Dost thou now govern the kingdom of Israel? arise, and eat bread, and let thine heart be merry: I will give thee the vineyard of Naboth the Jezreelite.

8 So she wrote letters in Ahab's name, and sealed them with his seal, and sent the letters unto the elders and to the nobles that were in his city, dwelling with Naboth.

9 And she wrote in the letters, saying, Proclaim a fast, and set Naboth on high among the people:

10 And set two men, sons of Belial, before him, to bear witness against him, saying, Thou didst blaspheme God and the king. And then carry him out, and stone him, that he may die.

11 And the men of his city, even the elders and the nobles who were the inhabitants in his city, did as Jezebel had sent unto them, and as it was written in the letters which she had sent unto them.

15 And it came to pass, when Jezebel heard that Naboth was stoned, and was dead, that Jezebel said to Ahab, Arise, take possession of the vineyard of Naboth the Jezreelite, which he refused to give thee for money: for Naboth is not alive, but dead.

16 And it came to pass, when Ahab heard that Naboth was dead, that Ahab rose up to go down to the vineyard of Naboth the Jezreelite, to take possession of it.

17 And the word of the Lord came to Elijah the Tishbite, saying,

18 Arise, go down to meet Ahab king of Israel, which is in Samaria: behold, he is in the vineyard of Na-

both, whither he is gone down to possess it.

19 And thou shalt speak unto him, saying, Thus saith the Lord, Hast thou killed, and also taken possession? And thou shalt speak unto him, saying, Thus saith the Lord, In the place where dogs licked the blood of Naboth shall dogs lick thy blood, even thine.

20 And Ahab said to Elijah, hast thou found me, O mine enemy? And he answered, I have found thee; because thou hast sold thyself to work evil in the sight of the Lord.

NEW TESTAMENT

Mark 8:36–37

36 For what shall it profit a man, if he shall gain the whole world, and lose his own soul?

37 Or what shall a man give in exchange for his soul?

Acts 8:5, 9–21

5 Then Philip went down to the city of Samaria, and preached Christ unto them.

9 But there was a certain man, called Simon, which beforetime in the same city used sorcery, and bewitched the people of Samaria, giving out that himself was some great one:

10 To whom they all gave heed, from the least to the greatest, saying, This man is the great power of God.

11 And to him they had regard, because that of long time he had bewitched them with sorceries.

12 But when they believed Philip preaching the things concerning the kingdom of God, and the name of Jesus

Christ, they were baptized, both men and women.

13 Then Simon himself believed also: and when he was baptized, he continued with Philip, and wondered, beholding the miracles and signs which were done.

14 Now when the apostles which were at Jerusalem heard that Samaria had received the word of God, they sent unto them Peter and John:

15 Who, when they were come down, prayed for them, that they might receive the Holy Ghost:

16 (For as yet he was fallen upon none of them: only they were baptized in the name of the Lord Jesus.)

17 Then laid they their hands on them, and they received the Holy Ghost.

18 And when Simon saw that through laying on of the apostles' hands the Holy Ghost was given, he offered them money,

19 Saying, Give me also this power, that on whomsoever I lay hands, he may receive the Holy Ghost.

20 But Peter said unto him, Thy money perish with thee, because thou hast thought that the gift of God may be purchased with money.

21 Thou hast neither part nor lot in this matter: for thy heart is not right in the sight of God.

2 Peter 1:4

4 Whereby are given unto us exceeding great and precious promises: that by these ye might be partakers of the divine nature, having escaped the corruption that is in the world through lust.

COURAGE

The classic Old Testament picture of courage can be found in the story of the contest between the stripling David and the giant Goliath—Goliath in massive armor, David armed only with his shepherd's weapon and his belief that the Lord was being insulted and that the Lord's people must be vindicated. As the story-teller narrates the tale, it is this approach even more than the outcome that is significant.

Yet the divine rightness of his cause and the assurance of ultimate divine victory do not detract from David's human courage. He was a volunteer. He did not have to put himself forward as Israel's champion. He did not even belong to the army. He was just visiting his soldier brothers. And assurance of ultimate divine victory carries with it no guarantee of immediate success for the Lord's fighting representative. So when David's sling sent that smooth stone straight into Goliath's forehead, David became the all-time symbol of true grit.

The New Testament account of Jesus' journey to Jerusalem also provides an example of courage in the face of avoidable danger. Even his disciples, trailing along at some distance behind Jesus, were aware of the risk, although they had shown themselves much less clear-eyed than he was about the likely outcome. It would have been so easy for Jesus to find plausible reasons for not going. There were so many things to do elsewhere: sick people to be healed, crowds to be preached to. But he was the Son of Man, the representative and embodiment of God's new order. He was under a moral obligation to present himself at the religious center of the community and to its spiritual leaders. Constrained by that necessity he made the journey. The moral necessity was more important than the physical danger.

So it was to Paul. Only once was he provoked into listing the dangers he had faced and the hardships he had endured. Far more often he spoke of the cause that constrained him, and that he served for love and with joy. Even the rough times he could face with delight, because the situations that would have been too much for a mere human being became demonstrations of the power that was working with him and in him.

Two conditions must exist before courage can be exercised. One is danger. Inevitably half of what needs to be said about courage appears in the entry for Fear. When there is nothing to be afraid of, there is nothing to be brave about. The thing feared may not be a physical danger. It may be only a fear of social embarrassment. It may be a psychological phobia centering on crowds, or snakes, or spiders, or darkness. Any kind of dread will provide the first condition for courage.

The second condition—and this is what distinguishes courage from fool-hardiness—is a cause worth facing danger for. This is where the biblical emphasis falls. There is nothing to be said for recklessly jeopardizing one's life and health. The moral compulsion needs to be there, even if it is only a compulsion to see the view from the top of the mountain or to find out if you are capable of sailing around the world single-handed. The good mountaineer and the good yachtsman minimize their risks as much as possible. They do not court danger as such and in itself.

Some have said that the modern world needs to find the moral equivalents of war—that is, the activities that demand as much courage as war does but are creative rather than destructive. Such causes are not really hard to find. There are enough injustices waiting to be righted, and enough needs waiting to be met, and enough unacceptable truths waiting to be spoken—enough moral issues and complex dangers to provide us all with good occasion for the exercise of high courage. And morally it is all the better if these causes call to us as volunteers rather than as conscripts.

A society in which nobody volunteered to take any risks would be a society in danger of stagnation. It would also have to be one with so few beliefs and such shallow values that no cause seemed worth dying for.

COURAGE

OLD TESTAMENT

1 Samuel 17:4–10, 24, 26, 31–33, 37, 40–42, 45

4 And there went out a champion out of the camp of the Philistines, named Goliath, of Gath, whose height was six cubits and a span.

5 And he had an helmet of brass upon his head, and he was armed with a coat of mail; and the weight of the coat was five thousand shekels of brass.

6 And he had greaves of brass upon his legs, and a target of brass between his shoulders.

7 And the staff of his spear was like a weaver's beam; and his spear's head weighed six hundred shekels of iron: and one bearing a shield went before him.

8 And he stood and cried unto the armies of Israel, and said unto them, Why are ye come out to set your battle in array? am not I a Philistine, and ye servants to Saul? choose you a man for you, and let him come down to me.

9 If he be able to fight with me, and to kill me, then will we be your servants: but if I prevail against him, and kill him, then shall ye be our servants, and serve us.

10 And the Philistine said, I defy the armies of Israel this day; give me a man, that we may fight together.

24 And all the men of Israel, when they saw the man, fled from him, and were sore afraid.

26 And David spake to the men that stood by him, saying, What shall be done to the man that killeth this Phil-

istine, and taketh away the reproach from Israel? for who is this uncircumcised Philistine, that he should defy the armies of the living God?

31 And when the words were heard which David spake, they rehearsed them before Saul: and he sent for him.

32 And David said to Saul, Let no man's heart fail because of him; thy servant will go and fight with this Philistine.

33 And Saul said to David, Thou art not able to go against this Philistine to fight with him: for thou art but a youth, and he a man of war from his youth.

37 David said moreover, The Lord that delivered me out of the paw of the lion, and out of the paw of the bear, he will deliver me out of the hand of this Philistine. And Saul said unto David, Go, and the Lord be with thee.

40 And he took his staff in his hand, and chose him five smooth stones out of the brook, and put them in a shepherd's bag which he had, even in a scrip; and his sling was in his hand: and he drew near to the Philistine.

41 And the Philistine came on and drew near unto David; and the man that bare the shield went before him.

42 And when the Philistine looked about, and saw David, he disdained him: for he was but a youth, and ruddy, and of a fair countenance.

45 Then said David to the Philistine, Thou comest to me with a sword, and with a spear, and with a shield: but I come to thee in the name of the Lord of hosts, the God of the armies of Israel, whom thou hast defied.

NEW TESTAMENT

Mark 10:32–34

32 And they were in the way going up to Jerusalem; and Jesus went before them: and they were amazed; and as they followed, they were afraid. And he took again the twelve, and began to tell them what things should happen unto him,

33 Saying, Behold, we go up to Jerusalem; and the Son of man shall be delivered unto the chief priests, and unto the scribes; and they shall condemn him to death, and shall deliver him to the Gentiles:

34 And they shall mock him, and shall scourge him, and shall spit upon him, and shall kill him: and the third day he shall rise again.

2 Corinthians 11:21, 23–27, 30; 12:9–10

21 Howbeit whereinsoever any is bold, (I speak foolishly,) I am bold also.

23 Are they ministers of Christ? (I speak as a fool) I am more; in labours more abundant, in stripes above measure, in prisons more frequent, in deaths oft.

24 Of the Jews five times received I forty stripes save one.

25 Thrice was I beaten with rods, once was I stoned, thrice I suffered shipwreck, a night and a day I have been in the deep;

26 In journeyings often, in perils of waters, in perils of robbers, in perils by mine own countrymen, in perils by the heathen, in perils in the city, in perils in the wilderness, in perils in

the sea, in perils among false brethren;

27 In weariness and painfulness, in watchings often, in hunger and thirst, in fastings often, in cold and nakedness.

30 If I must needs glory, I will glory of the things which concern mine infirmities.

9 . . . that the power of Christ may rest upon me.

10 Therefore I take pleasure in infirmities, in reproaches, in necessities, in persecutions, in distresses for Christ's sake: for when I am weak, then am I strong.

CREATION

God is described in the opening chapter of the Bible as making the world out of nothing by the sheer power of his thought, his word. He is also described as delighting in the task. He not only makes things; he contemplates them when they are made and relishes their goodness. And he makes them capable of themselves bringing forth and multiplying so that the work of creating goes on with the created themselves participating in it.

God's act of creation out of nothing is beyond the reach of human beings, but their subordinate creative role does enable them to feel some sense of kinship between their activity and God's. Although the story of Noah is really about the rather different issue of the role of the independent human being in a moral universe, it nevertheless allows itself a small digression to interest itself in Noah's creative role as a boat builder. After we read about Noah carrying out all those instructions on triple-decking and double-caulking, we half expect to hear that he, too, stood back to contemplate his work and "saw that it was good."

According to the Old Testament it is possible to learn something about God even by watching a manufacturer at work. That is why Jeremiah was sent down to the potter's house. There he learned not to assume that what God has fashioned will remain unaltered even if it turns out wrong. God, like the potter, is a continuous creator and can modify his creation.

Jesus (a carpenter) spoke of himself as a workman engaged in God's creative work, and he used the earth and the human body as his media for both physical and spiritual reconstruction. The special relevance of this passage to this subject is in its underlying picture of a Creator whose work is ongoing and continuous but requires man's active participation.

Paul (a tentmaker), when he got to Athens, found the creative arts even of a pagan world speaking of the Creator, though they testified to an unknown God. Paul seeks to remedy their ignorance by speaking of God as the active source of all created things, therefore different from them and yet expressed in them. The apostle recognizes that a poet (what the Scots call, significantly, a "maker") can show himself specially sensitive to this relationship between Creator and creation.

Paul's letters insist that Christians must continue to maintain the fabric of the world, working with their hands and being fruitful. Behind this plea was Paul's vision of the Christian as one who has been united with the creative power that shapes and sustains the very universe (see Environment, Nature, Universe, and World).

Human power to do things to the creation has immensely increased since the Bible was written. It is now humanly possible for the human race to shape or break the world in very quick time. This capability is new. But that it is up to human beings to shape the world, and within their power to fail in doing so, is no new belief. The Bible assigned human beings that role from the beginning, and taught that, in performing it well, they come near to fulfilling their own true nature. The artist, the artisan, and the parent ("procreator" equals "pro-creator") are not merely securing their own line or surviving as individuals: they are involved with that in nature which continuously sustains and renews the life of the world.

This essentially mystical view of the activity of making is easier to relate to the work of poet or potter than it is to that of the man or woman on an assembly line, but if the factory worker could see the end product as a fresh contribution to the richness of the creation—one to which the worker had made a responsible contribution—the work might be more highly valued. It might even be better done.

A child almost always discovers the wonder of taking on the God-like role of creator. A first wobbly drawing on a crumpled piece of paper, handed to an admiring and grateful parent, gives the child an exalted sense of having enriched the world by his or her own act. For that sense of creative significance to be extinguished is one of the saddest things that can happen to a human being. But happen it does.

CREATION

OLD TESTAMENT

Genesis 1:20–22

20 And God said, Let the waters bring forth abundantly the moving creature that hath life, and fowl that may fly above the earth in the open firmament of heaven.

21 And God created great whales, and every living creature that moveth, which the waters brought forth abun-dantly, after their kind, and every winged fowl after his kind: and God saw that it was good.

22 And God blessed them, saying, Be fruitful, and multiply, and fill the waters in the seas, and let fowl multiply in the earth.

Genesis 6:14–16

14 Make thee an ark of gopher wood; rooms shalt thou make in the

ark, and shalt pitch it within and without with pitch.

15 And this is the fashion which thou shalt make it of: The length of the ark shall be three hundred cubits, the breadth of it fifty cubits, and the height of it thirty cubits.

16 A window shalt thou make to the ark, and in a cubit shalt thou finish it above; and the door of the ark shalt thou set in the side thereof; with lower, second, and third stories shalt thou make it.

Jeremiah 18:1–6

1 The word which came to Jeremiah from the Lord, saying,

2 Arise, and go down to the potter's house, and there I will cause thee to hear my words.

3 Then I went down to the potter's house, and, behold, he wrought a work on the wheels.

4 And the vessel that he made of clay was marred in the hand of the potter: so he made it again another vessel, as seemed good to the potter to make it.

5 Then the word of the Lord came to me, saying,

6 O house of Israel, cannot I do with you as this potter? saith the Lord. Behold, as the clay is in the potter's hand, so are ye in mine hand, O house of Israel.

NEW TESTAMENT

John 9:1–7

1 And as Jesus passed by, he saw a man which was blind from his birth.

2 And his disciples asked him, saying, Master, who did sin, this man, or his parents, that he was born blind?

3 Jesus answered, Neither hath this man sinned, nor his parents: but that the works of God should be made manifest in him.

4 I must work the works of him that sent me, while it is day: the night cometh, when no man can work.

5 As long as I am in the world, I am the light of the world.

6 When he had thus spoken, he spat on the ground, and made clay of the spittle, and he anointed the eyes of the blind man with the clay,

7 And said unto him, Go, wash in the pool of Siloam, (which is by interpretation, Sent.) He went his way therefore, and washed, and came seeing.

Acts 17:22–28

22 Then Paul stood in the midst of Mars' hill, and said, Ye men of Athens, I perceive that in all things ye are too superstitious.

23 For as I passed by, and beheld your devotions, I found an altar with this inscription, To the Unknown God. Whom therefore ye ignorantly worship, him declare I unto you.

24 God that made the world and all things therein, seeing that he is Lord of heaven and earth, dwelleth not in temples made with hands;

25 Neither is worshipped with men's hands, as though he needed any thing, seeing he giveth to all life, and breath, and all things;

26 And hath made of one blood all nations of men for to dwell on all the face of the earth, and hath determined

the times before appointed, and the bounds of their habitation;

27 That they should seek the Lord, if haply they might feel after him, and find him, though he be not far from every one of us:

28 For in him we live, and move, and have our being; as certain also of your own poets have said, For we are also his offspring.

Colossians 1:9–10, 13–17

9 For this cause we also, since the day we heard it, do not cease to pray for you, and to desire that ye might be filled with the knowledge of his will in all wisdom and spiritual understanding;

10 That ye might walk worthy of the Lord unto all pleasing, being fruitful in every good work, and increasing in the knowledge of God,

13 Who hath delivered us from the power of darkness, and hath translated us into the kingdom of his dear Son:

14 In whom we have redemption through his blood, even the forgiveness of sins:

15 Who is the image of the invisible God, the firstborn of every creature:

16 For by him were all things created, that are in heaven, and that are in earth, visible and invisible, whether they be thrones, or dominions, or principalities, or powers: all things were created by him, and for him:

17 And he is before all things, and by him all things consist.

CRIME

The Old Testament makes no real distinction between crime and sin. In Israel all laws were God's laws, so a social offense such as theft and a religious offense such as idolatry were condemned by the same code. Anything said about the one would apply to the other. This, of course, is not to say that every offense merited the same punishment (see Punishment), but every crime or sin merited the same approach. And that approach was both stern and merciful.

Several principles emerge:

1. The offense must be acknowledged for what it is. You may sympathize with a criminal, but you must still judge him. There is to be no condoning, no cover-up. On incitement to idolatry the Book of Deuteronomy carries this to such lengths that we can be sure we are reading a statement of principle rather than a code of practice.

2. Many offenses are self-punishing. Crime disrupts the harmony of things in a way that brings inevitable retribution. A Greek might have called it nemesis, and a modern might call it natural, but the Bible calls it the wrath of God. It is

significant that when Cain says, "My punishment is greater than I can bear," the Hebrew word for "punishment" really means "iniquity." The offense and its consequences are so closely linked as to be indistinguishable one from the other. Moreover the soil itself, by the law of its nature, imposes the penalty.

3. A man may punish another for an offense against the person, but the punishment must be no greater than the crime. The law of "an eye for an eye" was probably a limiting statute. It meant *only* an eye for an eye, not a vendetta.

4. Whenever possible one must provide a way back for the offender. For a civil offense a due confession of guilt and a properly apportioned act of restitution ended the matter. The offender was taken back into the community of Israel.

In the New Testament, Zacchæus was one from whom such restitution was thought to be due, because he would have bought the tax concession from the Romans outright and then kept all the taxes he could raise. Influenced by Jesus he offered restitution far in excess of the Old Testament minimum, and when Jesus immediately spoke of Zacchæus as a son of Abraham he was probably asking that Zacchæus be immediately taken back into the community of Israel.

However, by this time church and state were no longer the same thing. To some extent sin and crime now fell under different jurisdictions. Jesus himself was tried by a Jewish court (the church) for blasphemy, but he was condemned by the Roman governor (the state) on an unproven charge of sedition and was consequently crucified between two criminals. One of the two acknowledged that Jesus' case was quite different from theirs, but the common bond between Christ and criminals was established—especially as in his own extremity he accepted the penitence of one of them.

Paul was not surprised to find thieves among his own converts. He simply instructed them to change their trade and to switch from taking to giving.

So the Bible is not soft on crime, but it does make clear that we have not done all that needs to be done about it when we have detected it and punished it. For one thing there is the matter of an open way back from crime into full membership in the community. That route is not kept open without considerable effort, and it is important to note that the Bible regards restitution as a feature of this path.

There is also the biblical idea that behind crime is sin, and beyond sin is forgiveness. The criminal law of any state, if it is just, is related to the underlying moral law built into the nature of man. Why does a lawbreaker disobey the law? At bottom because he shares with the law-abiding person and the law enforcement authority a common egoism that inclines him to seek his own advantage at the expense of others. On seeing a lawbreaker led to execution, John Bradford said, "But for the grace of God there goes John Bradford." That is a sound approach. It will lead no community to disregard criminality, but it will lead people to take a sensitive and constructive attitude toward the criminal.

CRIME

OLD TESTAMENT

Proverbs 6:30–31

Men do not despise a thief, if he steal
To satisfy his soul when he is hungry;
But if he be found, he shall restore
  sevenfold;
He shall give all the substance of his
  house.

Deuteronomy 13:6, 8–9

6 If thy brother, the son of thy mother, or thy son, or thy daughter, or the wife of thy bosom, or thy friend, which is as thine own soul, entice thee secretly, saying, Let us go and serve other gods,

8 Thou shalt not consent unto him, nor hearken unto him; neither shall thine eye pity him, neither shalt thou spare, neither shalt thou conceal him:

9 But thou shalt surely kill him.

Genesis 4:10–13

10 And he said, What hast thou done? the voice of thy brother's blood crieth unto me from the ground.

11 And now art thou cursed from the earth, which hath opened her mouth to receive thy brother's blood from thy hand;

12 When thou tillest the ground, it shall not henceforth yield unto thee her strength; a fugitive and a vagabond shalt thou be in the earth.

13 And Cain said unto the Lord, My punishment is greater than I can bear.

Leviticus 6:1–7; 24:19–20

1 And the Lord spake unto Moses, saying,

2 If a soul sin, and commit a trespass against the Lord, and lie unto his neighbour in that which was delivered him to keep, or in fellowship, or in a thing taken away by violence, or hath deceived his neighbour;

3 Or have found that which was lost, and lieth concerning it, and sweareth falsely; in any of all these that a man doeth, sinning therein:

4 Then it shall be, because he hath sinned, and is guilty, that he shall restore that which he took violently away, or the thing which he hath deceitfully gotten, or that which was delivered him to keep, or the lost thing which he found,

5 Or all that about which he hath sworn falsely; he shall even restore it in the principal, and shall add the fifth part more thereto, and give it unto him to whom it appertaineth, in the day of his trespass offering.

6 And he shall bring his trespass offering unto the Lord, a ram without blemish out of the flock, with thy estimation, for a trespass offering, unto the priest:

7 And the priest shall make an atonement for him before the Lord: and it shall be forgiven him for any thing of all that he hath done in trespassing therein.

19 And if a man cause a blemish in his neighbour; as he hath done, so shall it be done to him;

20 Breach for breach, eye for eye, tooth for tooth: as he hath caused a blemish in a man, so shall it be done to him again.

NEW TESTAMENT

Luke 19:2–9

2 And, behold, there was a man named Zacchæus, which was the chief among the publicans, and he was rich.

3 And he sought to see Jesus who he was; and could not for the press, because he was little of stature.

4 And he ran before, and climbed up into a sycomore tree to see him: for he was to pass that way.

5 And when Jesus came to the place, he looked up, and saw him, and said unto him, Zacchæus, make haste, and come down; for to-day I must abide at thy house.

6 And he made haste, and came down, and received him joyfully.

7 And when they saw it, they all murmured, saying, That he was gone to be guest with a man that is a sinner.

8 And Zacchæus stood, and said unto the Lord; Behold, Lord, the half of my goods I give to the poor; and if I have taken any thing from any man by false accusation, I restore him fourfold.

9 And Jesus said unto him, This day is salvation come to this house, forsomuch as he also is a son of Abraham.

Luke 23:32, 39–43

32 And there were also two other, malefactors, led with him to be put to death.

39 And one of the malefactors which were hanged railed on him, saying, If thou be Christ, save thyself and us.

40 But the other answering rebuked him, saying, Dost not thou fear God, seeing thou art in the same condemnation?

41 And we indeed justly; for we receive the due reward of our deeds: but this man hath done nothing amiss.

42 And he said unto Jesus, Lord, remember me when thou comest into thy kingdom.

43 And Jesus said unto him, Verily I say unto thee, To-day shalt thou be with me in paradise.

Ephesians 4:28

28 Let him that stole steal no more: but rather let him labour, working with his hands the thing which is good, that he may have to give to him that needeth.

DEATH

There is a great deal of slaughter in the Old Testament, but somehow death is never deprived of its dignity and significance. In those days death was not hidden from sight or dismissed from the mind, and few died alone. Not even a child could be unaware of death as inseparable from life.

Moses was one of the exceptions to the rule, in that he did die away from human companionship—not, however, until he had provided the perfect example of the pathos of death by gazing on the promised land he was never to enter.

That "never" is characteristic of Old Testament accounts of death. The dead go to their fathers, but not to God. The living are actively involved, together with God, in the real business of life. The dead are not. Yet their departure to sheol, the place of shades, can be the more heroic for being final.

Only occasionally does the Old Testament look with any hope beyond the moment of death, and even then (as in Isaiah) it is not too clear whether the hoped-for resurrection is not just an image of a reborn Israel. Job in his hopelessness longs for a return from the grave to a living encounter with his God, but he does not believe that such a thing could happen.

By the time Jesus was born, many had arrived at a belief in the resurrection of the dead, but the act of dying remained significant. Jesus' own death was said to have been marked by the dimming of the sun and the rending of the temple veil, the curtain that screened off the very holiest part of the temple. His followers celebrated this moment as marking the completion and perfection of his identification with man and of his self-offering to God. As such it joined the human to the divine. Death opened the way to life.

Death remained "the last enemy" (a phrase of Paul's), but it was now an experience shared with a living Christ. It no longer involved separation from God—or from other human beings. Within a very few years of the death of Jesus, Stephen was able to lay down his life in the same spirit of love, forgiveness, and trust.

It is often said that death, rather than sex, is now the subject about which society goes into a conspiracy of silence. Certainly a modern child in the prosperous West is less likely than a biblical child was to witness human death at first hand. Watching hundreds of actors "fall down dead" on the television screen is likely to have increased rather than diminished the unreality of the subject in the child's mind. Probably few would want to return to an earlier generation's custom of having children brought into contact with the corpse of a dead relative, but some of the Bible's realism about the natural event of death might be healthier than a nervous hiding away of the truth, or even a discreet veiling of it behind such euphemisms as "passing on."

Many adults say that they have no fear of death but do dread the process of dying. Of these some believe in life after death and some do not: the fear of dying can be present in either case. A part of that fear can be dispelled by the assurance of modern medicine that the experience is rarely painful and usually peaceful. But having to face with courage anything so final remains a huge demand.

And the Bible does not take away that sense of finality, not even by its ultimate belief in resurrection life. Whatever is to come, death closes the account of life as we have known it. It might be thought that this matters least to those whose estimate of life is a low one. The opposite is true. The way to make the closure of this life's account most acceptable is the biblical way of living fully and richly until death comes. The greatly afflicted may welcome death as a lesser evil, but the greatly blessed look on it as a friend. Saint Francis, for instance, approaches death singing. He sings the splendor of brother sun and sister earth and of all that belongs to this life, but he also sings with affection and gratitude of "our Sister, Bodily Death."

DEATH

OLD TESTAMENT

Deuteronomy 34:1, 4–6

1 And Moses went up from the plains of Moab unto the mountain of Nebo, to the top of Pisgah, that is over against Jericho. And the Lord shewed him all the land of Gilead, unto Dan,

4 And the Lord said unto him, This is the land which I sware unto Abraham, unto Isaac, and unto Jacob, saying, I will give it unto thy seed: I have caused thee to see it with thine eyes, but thou shalt not go over thither.

5 So Moses the servant of the Lord died there in the land of Moab, according to the word of the Lord.

6 And he buried him in a valley in the land of Moab, over against Beth–peor: but no man knoweth of his sepulchre unto this day.

1 Samuel 31:3–6

3 And the battle went sore against Saul, and the archer hit him; and he was sore wounded of the archers.

4 Then said Saul unto his armourbearer, Draw thy sword, and thrust me through therewith; lest these uncircumcised come and thrust me through,

and abuse me. But his armour-bearer would not; for he was sore afraid. Therefore Saul took a sword, and fell upon it.

5 And when his armour-bearer saw that Saul was dead, he fell likewise upon his sword, and died with him.

6 So Saul died, and his three sons, and his armour-bearer, and all his men, that same day together.

Job 14:7, 10–14

For there is hope of a tree, if it be cut
   down, that it will sprout again,
And that the tender branch thereof will
   not cease.
But man dieth, and wasteth away:
Yea, man giveth up the ghost, and where
   is he?
As the waters fail from the sea,
And the flood decayeth and drieth up:
So man lieth down, and riseth not:
Till the heavens be no more, they shall
   not awake,
Nor be raised out of their sleep.

Isaiah 26:19

19 Thy dead men shall live, together with my dead body shall they arise. Awake and sing, ye that dwell in dust: for thy dew is as the dew of herbs, and the earth shall cast out the dead.

NEW TESTAMENT

Luke 23:44–46

44 And it was about the sixth hour, and there was a darkness over all the earth until the ninth hour.

45 And the sun was darkened, and the veil of the temple was rent in the midst.

46 And when Jesus had cried with a loud voice, he said, Father, into thy hands I commend my spirit: and having said thus, he gave up the ghost.

Hebrews 2:9–10

9 But we see Jesus, who was made a little lower than the angels for the suffering of death, crowned with glory and honour; that he by the grace of God should taste death for every man.

10 For it became him, for whom are all things, and by whom are all things, in bringing many sons unto glory, to make the captain of their salvation perfect through sufferings.

Romans 14:7–9

7 For none of us liveth to himself, and no man dieth to himself.

8 For whether we live, we live unto the Lord; and whether we die, we die unto the Lord: whether we live therefore, or die, we are the Lord's.

9 For to this end Christ both died, and rose, and revived, that he might be Lord both of the dead and living.

Acts 7:55–60

55 But he, being full of the Holy Ghost, looked up stedfastly into heaven, and saw the glory of God, and Jesus standing on the right hand of God,

56 And said, Behold, I see the heavens opened, and the Son of man standing on the right hand of God.

57 Then they cried out with a loud voice, and stopped their ears, and ran upon him with one accord,

58 And cast him out of the city, and stoned him: and the witnesses laid down their clothes at a young man's feet, whose name was Saul.

59 And they stoned Stephen, calling upon God, and saying, Lord Jesus, receive my spirit.

60 And he kneeled down, and cried with a loud voice, Lord, lay not this sin to their charge. And when he had said this, he fell asleep.

DEPRESSION

In biblical times a person's moods were sharply distinguished from the person. The black depression was an evil spirit—a visitant. Saul's evil spirit was said to be from God, because everything that happened, good and bad alike, was believed to be within the providence of God, and the Hebrew way of expressing this was to say that it was *from* God. No one was thereby discouraged from trying to drive the evil away again; Saul, for example, did so with music.

Not that this always worked. After the passage quoted here, the story goes on to tell how Saul grew jealous of David and tried to pin him to the wall with a spear instead of allowing the music of the harp to have its pacifying effect. Such are the varying fortunes of the therapist!

The Psalm, the *de profundis*, offers a firmer lifeline. Many passing through the dark night of the soul have used it. The psalmist calls from out of the depths, but he is aware of a power outside his interior darkness. Light does at least exist. His God is there and can be appealed to. What is more (and perhaps this comes as a surprise to some), God's attitude is not judgmental: the light is not concerned with passing judgment on the psalmist's darkness.

The New Testament continues to speak of evil spirits as the cause of mental and physical illness. Jesus cures an epileptic boy, a demented man who has isolated himself among the rocks, a woman whose whole way of life was out of true, and in each case the cure is described in terms of the casting out of devils. But Jesus says that casting out is not enough. One needs a positive good to occupy the space left by displaced evil, for without this good the end result may be a worsening rather than an improvement.

Paul writes as a man who has been down in the depths among the roots of depression. He speaks of the helplessness of one who can see and approve what is right, but who finds some stronger force attaching him to what is not. Like the psalmist he gives thanks for the knowledge of a power outside his own divided and distracted personality. But this knowledge is no instant cure. To be troubled, perplexed, and weighed down is no sin. Human frailty remains, though it both contains and is contained by the lasting reality of light and peace. The coexistence of light and darkness is accepted. What is ruled out for the Christian is both despair and complacency—the despair that says, "There is no such thing as light or peace," and the complacency that says, "There is no such thing anymore as darkness or death."

In nineteenth-century London a depressed patient visited a prosperous doctor. The doctor did not recognize depression as an illness. He said to his patient, "You need taking out of yourself. You need to be entertained. Go and watch Grimaldi the clown."

The man sighed. "I am Grimaldi the clown," he said.

That story epitomizes the problem. Depression is not the only illness we feel we could cure if only we had not got it. It attacks us at the very center from which our remedial action would begin. If we could get outside it, we could deal with it.

The biblical notion of a world full of evil spirits anxious to find a home in human lives may be an unacceptable diagnosis, but it has one feature that could be assimilated to modern knowledge and that might be helpful. That feature is the sharp distinction it makes between the man himself and his affliction. He is not to be identified with his depression. It is something he has, but not something he is. It is detachable, alien even. When it is taken away from him, he is

71

still himself. In fact, he is more than ever himself. But he will need some positive replacement to occupy the attention he previously gave to his misery.

Everyone is unhappy at times. Depression is different from unhappiness, however: it is more deep-seated, more continuous, more all-consuming. It is an illness and is therefore the business of the medical profession. But there is a measure of help in the biblical reminder that the inner darkness does not eclipse all light. Light and peace do exist. They are the ultimate reality. And there is, if required, forgiveness.

DEPRESSION

OLD TESTAMENT

1 Samuel 16:14–23

14 But the spirit of the Lord departed from Saul, and an evil spirit from the Lord troubled him.

15 And Saul's servants said unto him, Behold now, an evil spirit from God troubleth thee.

16 Let our lord now command thy servants, which are before thee, to seek out a man, who is a cunning player on an harp: and it shall come to pass, when the evil spirit from God is upon thee, that he shall play with his hand, and thou shalt be well.

17 And Saul said unto his servants, Provide me now a man that can play well, and bring him to me.

18 Then answered one of the servants, and said, Behold, I have seen a son of Jesse the Bethlehemite, that is cunning in playing, and a mighty valiant man, and a man of war, and prudent in matters, and a comely person, and the Lord is with him.

19 Wherefore Saul sent messengers unto Jesse, and said, Send me David thy son, which is with the sheep.

20 And Jesse took an ass laden with bread, and a bottle of wine, and a kid, and sent them by David his son unto Saul.

21 And David came to Saul, and stood before him: and he loved him greatly; and he became his armourbearer.

22 And Saul sent to Jesse, saying, Let David, I pray thee, stand before me; for he hath found favour in my sight.

23 And it came to pass, when the evil spirit from God was upon Saul, that David took an harp, and played with his hand: so Saul was refreshed, and was well, and the evil spirit departed from him.

Psalm 130:1–6

Out of the depths have I cried unto thee,
  O Lord.
Lord, hear my voice:
Let thine ears be attentive
To the voice of my supplications.
If thou, Lord, shouldest mark iniquities,
O Lord, who shall stand?
But there is forgiveness with thee,
That thou mayest be feared.
I wait for the Lord, my soul doth wait,
  and in his word do I hope.
My soul waiteth for the Lord

More than they that watch for the morning:

I say, more than they that watch for the morning.

NEW TESTAMENT

Matthew 12:43–45

43 When the unclean spirit is gone out of a man, he walketh through dry places, seeking rest, and findeth none.

44 Then he saith, I will return into my house from whence I came out; and when he is come, he findeth it empty, swept, and garnished.

45 Then goeth he, and taketh with himself seven other spirits more wicked than himself, and they enter in and dwell there: and the last state of that man is worse than the first.

Romans 7:21–25

21 I find then a law, that, when I would do good, evil is present with me.

22 For I delight in the law of God after the inward man:

23 But I see another law in my members, warring against the law of my mind, and bringing me into captivity to the law of sin which is in my members.

24 O wretched man that I am! who shall deliver me from the body of this death?

25 I thank God through Jesus Christ our Lord.

2 Corinthians 4:6–10

6 For God, who commanded the light to shine out of darkness, hath shined in our hearts, to give the light of the knowledge of the glory of God in the face of Jesus Christ.

7 But we have this treasure in earthen vessels, that the excellency of the power may be of God, and not of us.

8 We are troubled on every side, yet not distressed; we are perplexed, but not in despair;

9 Persecuted, but not forsaken; cast down, but not destroyed;

10 Always bearing about in the body the dying of the Lord Jesus, that the life also of Jesus might be made manifest in our body.

John 14:27

27 Peace I leave with you, my peace I give unto you: not as the world giveth, give I unto you. Let not your heart be troubled, neither let it be afraid.

Mark 15:34

34 And at the ninth hour Jesus cried with a loud voice, saying, Eloi, Eloi, lama sabachthani? which is, being interpreted, My God, my God, why hast thou forsaken me?

DESIRE

The adult in the Old Testament is expected to be the bearer of many strong passions and desires, but not to be their slave. Eve is condemned not for desiring the forbidden fruit but for taking it. Part of her punishment—an inevitable part, though it is described as if it were imposed arbitrarily—is that desire and its consequences become that much harder to handle from then on.

The Book of Proverbs, too, is more concerned to control desire than to eliminate it. There are proverbs that speak out for the satisfying of a good desire, and there are proverbs that pronounce doom on the satisfying of a false desire. Discrimination is all. In the same way the many dietetic laws of Israel sanctioned and yet controlled the satisfaction of physical hunger. What was true of the desire for food was true also of sexual desire: people were both to delight in it and to discipline it. Within the terms set by divine law, even the raptures of the Song of Solomon are sanctified.

Early sections of the Old Testament speak as if God himself obtained some sensory satisfaction from animal sacrifices ("The Lord smelled a sweet savour," Genesis 8:21), but the later prophets spoke of God's desires in moral terms as a hunger for mercy and justice. They and the psalmists spoke too of moral and spiritual desires in human beings as an extension of their physical ones. The worshiper's desire for God reached out toward God's desire for the image of his own justice and mercy in the worshiper.

The New Testament takes this further. It speaks of a union between the divine and the human so close that men and women can be filled with God's spirit and therefore desire what God desires as naturally as they breathe. This was expected not to put an end to physical desire but to sanctify and discipline it. In fact it made the true fulfillment of desire possible. Unredeemed desires are at war not only with the Spirit but with each other as well. Frustration is inevitable.

Much of the New Testament was written for people living in cities where the undisciplined indulgence of desire was ruining many lives. It was inevitable that more should be said about the control of the lusts of the flesh than about their true value. Yet Jesus was described as enjoying the desirable things of life, and his followers kept up a running battle with any who regarded the body and its desires as intrinsically evil. Nothing, they said, is undesirable in itself. The test is whether it can be received with thanks to God. By that test, corrupt desire was distinguished from true. And both kinds could be found in the physical or in the spiritual aspects of human nature.

From a moral and religious point of view there is not much to choose between the desires of the mind (for fame, success, power) and the desires of the body (for food, sex, possessions). Both kinds of craving need to be kept healthy by being disciplined. They are neither to be indulged nor to be denied simply on the ground that we find them pleasurable. Give free rein to your desires and you will be trampled to death in the stampede. Try to eliminate desire and you will drive it from one hiding place to another—perhaps from the body to the mind. Hold out before it the things that are most truly and deeply desirable and you have a chance of educating your urges so that they pull you forward like horses in harness.

One part of this training consists of learning to desire things realistically—that is, for what they are rather than for what they pretend to be. Status symbols, virility symbols, and all such fantasies go down before the Bible's realistic attitude toward human craving.

The Bible also recognizes that a good desire can be the ground on which to build an even better one. In this we are helped by the fact that desire is not as easily satisfied as we suppose. A new hunger is born within each satisfaction, and it can be a hunger for something larger and deeper. In this respect satisfying a desire has an oddly similar effect to denying it. What some have learned by denying themselves, say, sexual satisfaction, others have learned by having it and reaching through it and beyond it.

DESIRE

OLD TESTAMENT

Genesis 3:16 (part of God's judgment on Eve)

16 Thy desire shall be to thy husband, and he shall rule over thee.

Proverbs 13:12, 19

Hope deferred maketh the heart sick:
But when the desire cometh, it is a tree of life.
The desire accomplished is sweet to the soul:
But it is abomination to fools to depart from evil.

Deuteronomy 12:20–23

20 When the Lord thy God shall enlarge thy border, as he hath promised thee, and thou shalt say, I will eat flesh, because thy soul longeth to eat flesh; thou mayest eat flesh, whatsoever thy soul lusteth after.

21 If the place which the Lord thy God hath chosen to put his name there be too far from thee, then thou shalt kill of thy herd and of thy flock, which the Lord hath given thee, as I have commanded thee, and thou shalt eat in thy gates whatsoever thy soul lusteth after.

22 Even as the roebuck and the hart is eaten, so thou shalt eat them: the unclean and the clean shall eat of them alike.

23 Only be sure that thou eat not the blood: for the blood is the life; and thou mayest not eat the life with the flesh.

Song of Songs 7:6–10

How fair and how pleasant art thou,
O love, for delights!
This thy stature is like to a palm tree,
And thy breasts to clusters of grapes.
I said, I will go up to the palm tree,
I will take hold of the boughs thereof:
Now also thy breasts shall be as clusters
of the vine,
And the smell of thy nose like apples;
And the roof of thy mouth like the best
wine
For my beloved, that goeth down sweetly,
Causing the lips of those that are asleep
to speak.

I am my beloved's,
And his desire is toward me.

Psalm 63:1

O God, thou art my God; early will I
seek thee:
My soul thirsteth for thee, my flesh longeth for thee.

Hosea 6:6

6 For I desired mercy, and not
sacrifice; and the knowledge of God
more than burnt offerings.

NEW TESTAMENT

Matthew 11:18–19

18 For John came neither eating nor
drinking, and they say, He hath a devil.
19 The Son of man came eating
and drinking, and they say, Behold a
man gluttonous, and a winebibber, a
friend of publicans and sinners. But
wisdom is justified of her children.

1 Timothy 4:1–5

1 Now the Spirit speaketh ex-
pressly, that in the latter times some
shall depart from the faith. . . . Forbidding to marry, and commanding to
abstain from meats, which God hath
created to be received with thanksgiving of them which believe and know
the truth.
4 For every creature of God is good,
and nothing to be refused, if it be received with thanksgiving:
5 For it is sanctified by the word of
God and prayer.

James 4:1–3

1 From whence come wars and
fightings among you? come they not
hence, even of your lusts that war in
your members?
2 Ye lust, and have not: ye kill, and
desire to have, and cannot obtain: ye
fight and war, yet ye have not, because
ye ask not.
3 Ye ask, and receive not, because
ye ask amiss, that ye may consume it
upon your lusts.

Galatians 5:16–17

16 This I say then, Walk in the
Spirit, and ye shall not fulfil the lust
of the flesh.
17 For the flesh lusteth against the
Spirit, and the Spirit against the flesh:
and these are contrary the one to the
other: so that ye cannot do the things
that ye would.

1 Corinthians 12:31

31 But covet earnestly the best gifts.

DISASTER

The Hebrew way of explaining why something bad or something good happens
is to say that God intended it to happen. In Mark's Gospel (4:12) Jesus says,
quoting Isaiah, that he speaks to people in parables "lest at any time they should
be converted, and their sins be forgiven them." Did he really tell stories in order

to prevent people from being converted? Presumably not, but the result has to be described as if it were his intention. It is a feature of the Hebrew language that derives from a sense of the driving purpose of God present in all things.

So disasters are described in the Old Testament as if God planned them all. The fundamental belief, however, is not that everything falls out just as God would wish, but that every contingency is contained within God's plan. All events happen in the providence of God, not in the sense that he has ordained their happening, but in the sense that he has provided for their happening. Disaster is allowed for, not sent.

Thus the psalmist sees flood and earthquake as neither sent to him nor kept from him, but as places where the hand of God still holds him. Even the story of Noah's ark ends with God's deciding never again to use universal disaster as a punishment for sin.

Many Old Testament writers did in fact speak of disaster as sent by God to punish sin, but this view is challenged in the great dialogues of the Book of Job. These poems are sandwiched between a prologue and an epilogue, both written in prose, that tell the story of a man who suffers an unparalleled succession of disasters. These disasters are actually the work of Satan acting, by divine permission, to test Job. The poor man's friends offer the conventional explanation: disaster is a punishment for sin. Job denies this. He cannot understand what has happened, and he pleads with God to justify it, but he is quite certain that his disastrous experience has not been matched to his deserts. He will not endorse a doctrine that is contrary to observable fact.

Jesus also saw that nature does not discriminate between good and bad and that disasters are not directed to the specially wicked. But he shared the psalmist's belief that all events are in the hand of God. Not a sparrow falls to the ground "without your Father" (Matthew 10:29). This need not mean that it falls—any more than the tower at Siloam did—by special arrangement with the Almighty, but only that its fall is contained within God's loving purpose (see Providence).

Jesus faced even the calamity of his own crucifixion by speaking of it as something brought about by man but made possible by God. (It seems more likely that "from above" would mean from God than from Caesar.) In the New Testament the distinction between man-made disaster and natural disaster is not all that significant, since God was believed to accept responsibility for both. To the followers of Jesus, however, the crucifixion was the disaster of all disasters. Reflecting on it, they came to believe that there is a divine purpose at work that will not be impeded by the worst that can happen. Indeed, this divine purpose can use the worst that can happen for its own good ends. Disaster does not cease to be disastrous, but neither does it have the last word.

Once we have disposed of the idea of disaster as punishment, we are free to ask whether we would ever become what we are meant to be if we lived in an accident-free world—a world presumably without heroism, without self-sacrifice, without ever a rescue to be performed or a wound to be bound up. It is easy to admire the man or woman who says, "If I were running the world, I would see to it that innocent people did not get hurt the way they do now." But it is also possible to reply, "Yes, but you have evolved as a human being with this admirably sympathetic nature precisely in the world we have got, not in the world you would design. Are you sure that your proposed order would produce better human beings and not just better vegetables?".

Anyway, like Job we have to build our understanding of things around this accident-prone world as it is. We cannot start with a theory and impose it on the facts.

DISASTER

OLD TESTAMENT

Isaiah 45:7

7 I form the light, and create darkness: I make peace, and create evil: I the Lord do all these things.

Genesis 8:18–21

18 And Noah went forth, and his sons, and his wife, and his sons' wives with him:

19 Every beast, every creeping thing, and every fowl, and whatsoever creepeth upon the earth, after their kinds, went forth out of the ark.

20 And Noah builded an altar unto the Lord; and took of every clean beast, and of every clean fowl, and offered burnt offerings on the altar.

21 And the Lord smelled a sweet savour; and the Lord said in his heart, I will not again curse the ground any more for man's sake; for the imagination of man's heart is evil from his youth; neither will I again smite any more every thing living, as I have done.

Psalm 46:1–3

God is our refuge and strength,
A very present help in trouble.
Therefore will not we fear, though the earth be removed,
And though the mountains be carried into the midst of the sea;
Though the waters thereof roar and be troubled,
Though the mountains shake with the swelling thereof.

Job 1:8–12

8 And the Lord said unto Satan, Hast thou considered my servant Job, that there is none like him in the earth, a perfect and an upright man, one that feareth God, and escheweth evil?

9 Then Satan answered the Lord, and said, Doth Job fear God for nought?

10 Hast not thou made an hedge about him, and about his house, and about all that he hath on every side? thou has blessed the work of his hands, and his substance is increased in the land.

11 But put forth thine hand now, and touch all that he hath, and he will curse thee to thy face.

12 And the Lord said unto Satan, Behold, all that he hath is in thy power.

Job 6:4; 9: 21–24

For the arrows of the Almighty are within me,
The poison whereof drinketh up my spirit:
The terrors of God do set themselves in array against me.
Though I were perfect, yet would I not know my soul:
I would despise my life.
This is one thing, therefore I said it,
He destroyeth the perfect and the wicked.
If the scourge slay suddenly,
He will laugh at the trial of the innocent.
The earth is given into the hand of the wicked:
He covereth the faces of the judges thereof;
If not, where, and who is he?

NEW TESTAMENT

Luke 13:4–5; Matthew 5:45

4 Or those eighteen, upon whom the tower in Siloam fell, and slew them, think ye that they were sinners above all men that dwelt in Jerusalem?

5 I tell you, Nay: but, except ye repent, ye shall all likewise perish.

45 Your Father which is in heaven. . . . maketh his sun to rise on the evil and on the good, and sendeth rain on the just and on the unjust.

John 19:10–11

10 Then saith Pilate unto him, Speakest thou not unto me? knowest thou not that I have power to crucify thee, and have power to release thee?

11 Jesus answered, Thou couldest have no power at all against me, except it were given thee from above: therefore he that delivered me unto thee hath the greater sin.

Romans 8:35, 37–39

35 Who shall separate us from the love of Christ? shall tribulation, or distress, or persecution, or famine, or nakedness, or peril, or sword?

37 Nay, in all these things we are more than conquerors through him that loved us.

38 For I am persuaded, that neither death, nor life, nor angels, nor principalities, nor powers, nor things present, nor things to come,

39 Nor height, nor depth, nor any other creature, shall be able to separate us from the love of God, which is in Christ Jesus our Lord.

DISCIPLINE

Old Testament Israel was most certainly a disciplined society. Its tumultuous and often tragic history was believed to be a discipline imposed by God, and the individual Israelite was expected to be no less severe in disciplining those under him. To assign the death penalty as the punishment for an undisciplined son, though the law was doubtless an expression of principle rather than practice, was to state the case for family discipline with unsurpassable firmness, not to say savagery.

Yet discipline was believed to be one of the faces of love. It had to express the law of God, not the feelings of the disciplinarian. In the Psalms discipline is both dreaded and sung of as a blessing. But then a psalmist, being a musician, was aware of a deeper and subtler kind of discipline: that of his art—his "discipline," in the academic sense. The temple singers—appointed, significantly, by the king and the army officers—experienced discipline at two levels. At one level they sang to order. They submitted to rigorous training by their seniors, who themselves were subject to the discipline of the king. At a deeper level, however, the singers were also under the discipline of the music. The demands and laws of music controlled them all, and this fact was symbolized by juniors and seniors alike drawing lots when duties were assigned.

Discipline in the New Testament is made the clearer for speakers of English by the similarity between the word "discipline" and the word "disciple." A disciple is one who learns and practices alongside the teacher. Both are caught up in a common activity, and the demand made by that activity is the real source of discipline. To be a disciple of Jesus could be a discipline heavy enough to be described, literally or metaphorically, as taking up a cross. People were warned not to undertake such a responsibility unless they loved the work more than themselves or their families—a warning expressed in the strong Hebraic idiom by speaking of "hating" self and family.

There was no masochism about this work. Hardship was not to be sought for its own sake. It was simply the cost of living in the kingdom while living also in the world, a discipline resulting from love and embraced with joy. In the later books of the New Testament the writers can speak from experience of turning inescapable hardships into gracious disciplines, and of using discipline as a means of entry into spiritual communion.

Discipline itself needs to be disciplined. Random punishments—which often express the frustration of a parent, a teacher, or a superior rather than a measured training incentive—have nothing at all to do with discipline in the biblical sense. True discipline is always related to an end that constrains both the one being disciplined and the one doing the disciplining, and both parties should be made aware of that end. The members of an orchestra will respect the discipline imposed on them by the conductor if they are aware that he himself is disciplined by the music.

Children or young people sometimes reject discipline because they are deaf to the "music" behind it. The discipline looks to them like an end in itself. They see the "conductor" (i.e., the teacher, the lawgiver, the authority figure) as just a man waving his arms and demanding obedience for its own sake—or his own sake.

A truly disciplined, law-abiding society is not one in which the punishments are so severe that no one dares to step out of line. It is one in which the music of social harmony is sufficiently clear to impose its own restraints and to give valid sanction to whatever punishments and controls are needed. It is not so much a question of getting people to submit to a discipline as a matter of getting them to identify with a discipline inherent in the nature of things.

DISCIPLINE

OLD TESTAMENT

Deuteronomy 8:2, 5

2 And thou shalt remember all the way which the Lord thy God led thee these forty years in the wilderness, to humble thee, and to prove thee, to know what was in thine heart, whether thou wouldest keep his commandments, or no.

5 Thou shalt also consider in thine heart, that, as a man chasteneth his son, so the Lord thy God chasteneth thee.

Proverbs 3:11–12; 13:24; 19:18; 22:15

My son, despise not the chastening of the Lord;
Neither be weary of his correction:
For whom the Lord loveth he correcteth;
Even as a father the son in whom he delighteth.
He that spareth his rod hateth his son:
But he that loveth him chasteneth him betimes.
Chasten thy son while there is hope,
And let not thy soul spare for his crying.
Foolishness is bound in the heart of a child;
But the rod of correction shall drive it far from him.

Deuteronomy 21:18–21

18 If a man have a stubborn and rebellious son, which will not obey the voice of his father, or the voice of his mother, and that, when they have chastened him, will not hearken unto them:

19 Then shall his father and his mother lay hold on him, and bring him out unto the elders of his city, and unto the gate of his place;

20 And they shall say unto the elders of his city, This our son is stubborn and rebellious, he will not obey our voice; he is a glutton, and a drunkard.

21 And all the men of his city shall stone him with stones, that he die: so shalt thou put evil away from among you; and all Israel shall hear, and fear.

Psalm 38:1; 94:12

O Lord, rebuke me not in thy wrath:
Neither chasten me in thy hot displeasure.
Blessed is the man whom thou chastenest, O Lord,
And teachest him out of thy law.

1 Chronicles 25:1, 6–8

1 Moreover David and the captains of the host separated to the service of

the sons of Asaph, and of Heman, and of Jeduthun, who should prophesy with harps, with psalteries, and with cymbals.

6 All these were under the hands of their father for song in the house of the Lord, with cymbals, psalteries, and harps, for the service of the house of God, according to the king's order to Asaph, Jeduthun, and Heman.

7 So the number of them, with their brethren that were instructed in the songs of the Lord, even all that were cunning, was two hundred fourscore and eight.

8 And they cast lots, ward against ward, as well the small as the great, the teacher as the scholar.

NEW TESTAMENT

Luke 14:25–27

25 And there went great multitudes with him: and he turned, and said unto them,

26 If any man come to me, and hate not his father, and mother, and wife, and children, and brethren, and sisters, yea, and his own life also, he cannot be my disciple.

27 And whosoever doth not bear his cross, and come after me, cannot be my disciple.

Hebrews 12:4–11

4 Ye have not yet resisted unto blood, striving against sin.

5 And ye have forgotten the exhortation which speaketh unto you as unto children, My son, despise not thou the chastening of the Lord, nor faint when thou art rebuked of him:

6 For whom the Lord loveth he chasteneth, and scourgeth every son whom he receiveth.

7 If ye endure chastening, God dealeth with you as with sons; for what son is he whom the father chasteneth not?

8 But if ye be without chastisement, whereof all are partakers, then are ye bastards, and not sons.

9 Furthermore we have had fathers of our flesh which corrected us, and we gave them reverence: shall we not much rather be in subjection unto the Father of spirits, and live?

10 For they verily for a few days chastened us after their own pleasure; but he for our profit, that we might be partakers of his holiness.

11 Now no chastening for the present seemeth to be joyous, but grievous: nevertheless afterward it yieldeth the peaceable fruit of righteousness unto them which are exercised thereby.

Revelation 3:19–20 (a message to the church in Laodicea)

19 As many as I love, I rebuke and chasten: be zealous therefore, and repent.

20 Behold, I stand at the door, and knock: if any man hear my voice, and open the door, I will come in to him, and will sup with him, and he with me.

DIVORCE

The Old Testament permits a man to divorce his wife, but does not allow a wife to divorce her husband. The divorced wife is free to marry again, but she cannot remarry her first husband if she has had a second. Deuteronomy states what is legal, however, not what is desirable.

The prophets see God as one who himself transcends such legal standards. Jeremiah is one of those who recognize a parallel between a husband's union with his wife and God's union with his people. So God's feelings about divorce from his people reveal much about what a husband might feel about divorce from his wife. And God hates it. Jeremiah urges the southern kingdom of Judah to learn from the northern kingdom of Israel, long since divorced from the Lord for infidelity, yet now invited back. The direct reference is to the sin of idolatry and to rejection by God, but the analogy used brings into view the subject of human marriage and divorce and the possibility of reconciliation between estranged husbands and wives (see Adultery).

Malachi, on the other hand, refers directly to marriage breakdown, and he reports that God loathes it.

Jesus clearly regarded divorce as failure—as never more than a permitted concession to human frailty. It is less clear whether Jesus forbade it to his own followers in all circumstances (as indicated in Mark and Luke) or whether he added "except for infidelity" (as in Matthew). Has the concession dropped out of the text of Mark and Luke, or was it added to the text of Matthew? Who can say? The point remains, however, that Jesus did not want his followers to govern their conduct by such minimal standards. They were to reach toward the fulfillment of the original intention of marriage, not look for legal avenues of escape from it.

Nevertheless, Paul was asked by his friends in Corinth to lay down some guidelines for the Christian community there. He told them that, if both husband and wife were believers, the saying of Jesus bound them to stay together. When one partner was not, then the believing husband or wife might have to accept divorce—but only on the initiative of the unbeliever.

Such decisions appear to have been forced from Paul rather against his will. More eagerly he spoke, as does the Old Testament, about the union of God with man as the model of union between husband and wife—and indeed between other parties as well. He spoke particularly of the relationship between Christ and the church as normative (see Marriage). Seen in this light, no division can be regarded as irreconcilable. The passage from Ephesians quoted here was not directly about husbands and wives at all; it was about Jews and Gentiles. Its principles, however, were those that Paul applied to the subject of division and reconciliation wherever it arose between Jews and Gentiles, slaves and masters, husbands and wives. The Christian concern was not with legally permitted separation so much as with transcendent unity. God intends union, not division, and where division has occurred, God's reconciling action is available to overcome it.

A husband and wife contemplating divorce will not find their decision made for them by the Bible. That would be true even if the Bible's verdict on the permissibility of divorce were clearer than it is. They would have to ask not only "Does the Bible permit us to divorce?" but also "Do we have what the Bible regards as a marriage?" The Bible does make clear to them, however, that their parting cannot be accepted lightly just because they have experienced a change of heart or a change of circumstances. The marriage union is something much more fundamental than a legal bond. It is rooted in the very nature of man and woman. It transcends a host of differences—including, says Paul, differences in religion.

The Bible does recognize that human beings and institutions are mortal, however. Perhaps, if a man and woman can show that their marriage is actually dead, they might be able to argue that giving it a decent burial would be in line with biblical principles. But the Bible portrays life as going on a long way under the surface of things. Its primary concern is with resurrection and reconciliation, not death and division.

DIVORCE

OLD TESTAMENT

Deuteronomy 24:1–4

1 When a man hath taken a wife, and married her, and it come to pass that she find no favour in his eyes, because he hath found some uncleanness in her: then let him write her a bill of divorcement, and give it in her hand, and send her out of his house.

2 And when she is departed out of his house, she may go and be another man's wife.

3 And if the latter husband hate her, and write her a bill of divorcement, and giveth it in her hand, and sendeth her out of his house; or if the latter husband die, which took her to be his wife;

4 Her former husband, which sent her away, may not take her again to be his wife, after that she is defiled; for that is abomination before the Lord.

Jeremiah 3:8, 11–12

8 And I saw, when for all the causes whereby backsliding Israel committed adultery I had put her away, and given her a bill of divorce; yet her treacherous sister Judah feared not, but went and played the harlot also.

11 And the Lord said unto me, The backsliding Israel hath justified herself more than treacherous Judah.

12 Go and proclaim these words toward the north, and say, Return, thou backsliding Israel, saith the Lord; and I will not cause mine anger to fall upon

you: for I am merciful, saith the Lord, and I will not keep anger for ever.

Malachi 2:13–16

13 And this have ye done again, covering the altar of the Lord with tears, with weeping, and with crying out, insomuch that he regardeth not the offering any more, or receiveth it with good will at your hand.

14 Yet ye say, Wherefore? Because the Lord hath been witness between thee and the wife of thy youth, against whom thou hast dealt treacherously: yet is she thy companion, and the wife of thy covenant.

15 And did not he make one? Yet had he the residue of the spirit. And wherefore one? That he might seek a godly seed. Therefore take heed to your spirit, and let none deal treacherously against the wife of his youth.

16 For the Lord, the God of Israel, saith that he hateth putting away.

NEW TESTAMENT

Mark 10:2–12

2 And the Pharisees came to him, and asked him, Is it lawful for a man to put away his wife? tempting him.

3 And he answered and said unto them, What did Moses command you?

4 And they said, Moses suffered to write a bill of divorcement, and to put her away.

5 And Jesus answered and said unto them, For the hardness of your heart he wrote you this precept.

6 But from the beginning of the creation God made them male and female.

7 For this cause shall a man leave his father and mother, and cleave to his wife;

8 And they twain shall be one flesh: so then they are no more twain, but one flesh.

9 What therefore God hath joined together, let not man put asunder.

10 And in the house his disciples asked him again of the same matter.

11 And he saith unto them, Whosoever shall put away his wife, and marry another, committeth adultery against her.

12 And if a woman shall put away her husband, and be married to another, she committeth adultery.

1 Corinthians 7:10–15

10 And unto the married I command, yet not I, but the Lord, Let not the wife depart from her husband:

11 But and if she depart, let her remain unmarried, or be reconciled to her husband: and let not the husband put away his wife.

12 But to the rest speak I, not the Lord: If any brother hath a wife that believeth not, and she be pleased to dwell with him, let him not put her away.

13 And the woman which hath an husband that believeth not, and if he be pleased to dwell with her, let her not leave him.

14 For the unbelieving husband is sanctified by the wife, and the unbelieving wife is sanctified by the husband: else were your children unclean; but now are they holy.

15 But if the unbelieving depart, let him depart. A brother or a sister is

not under bondage in such cases: but God hath called us to peace.

Ephesians 2:14–15

14 For he is our peace, who hath made both one, and hath broken down the middle wall of partition between us;

15 Having abolished in his flesh the enmity, even the law of commandments contained in ordinances; for to make in himself of twain one new man, so making peace.

DUTY

When David rebuked Abner for not taking better care of Saul, all that he said was based on three closely entwined beliefs: that both David and Abner owed a duty to Saul; that to be false to that duty was an offense worthy of death; that it was a duty derived from the mystical charisma of kingship. The fact that Saul acknowledged no reciprocal responsibility toward David—and was in fact trying to kill him—made no difference. Saul, as king, was "the Lord's anointed." The duty owed him was therefore unconditional. It was a religious obligation as well as a political one.

Usually the Old Testament treated duties and responsibilities as reciprocal, but the underpinning of civic duty by religious sanction was always a consideration. Duties arose from the corporate nature of Israel as God's people. To neglect one's duty was an offense against God as well as against the law. Moreover, as Ezekiel recognized, anyone who failed to do his duty could be held responsible for the consequences of that failure not only in his own life but in the lives of others. The idea of duty springs from a strong sense of community.

The writers of the New Testament make it clear that simply doing one's duty is not enough—not even if one does it with the scrupulosity of the scribes and Pharisees. The Gospels insist that God deals with people not in terms of strict justice but with unbounded generosity. It follows that in their dealings with one another people should naturally exceed what duty obligates them to do. A citizen might be obligated to carry official baggage for a distance of one mile, but Jesus recommended carrying it two miles. That way the service became voluntary and not forced. In his parable of the dutiful servant, Jesus (using the standard rather than the ideal relationship between master and servant) struck at any system of morality that sees the fulfillment of legal obligations as sufficient.

The result was not anarchy. The New Testament principle of love encouraged people to go far beyond the call of duty, but not to fall short of it. Paul moved in a world where civic duty was owed to irreligious powers such as Caesar in Rome or the heathen magistrates of a Greek city. All the same he regarded it as a religious duty to perform such legal duties to the full. No reversion to a legalistic spirit was involved because love enabled believers to fulfill and overfulfill all such duties without even thinking of them as painful obligations. This was particularly true within the Christian community, precisely because it *was* a community. The lesser forms of community (such as the Roman Empire) engendered duties; the greater forms of community (such as the church, the body of Christ) engendered even heavier obligations but was animated by a spirit that enabled believers to carry them readily and joyfully.

Duty, therefore, is not always the "stern daughter of the voice of God" that Wordsworth spoke of. The Bible would not dissent from its being the offspring of the voice of God, but the Bible sees duty as just one aspect of a kindly face. It does not have to be stern. Those who reject their obligations on the ground that duties are inhibiting and life-denying may well be shrinking rather than expanding their own personalities. What they are really demanding is to be cut off from community, and that is no road to fullness of life. Wherever there is community, there are duties. The way to rob them of their sternness and heaviness is to outbid them. Love of the community may involve going a second mile, but neither the second mile nor the first one is felt to be an imposition.

If the citizens of any society become restless about the performance of their civic duties, that society may feel bound to increase the strength of its police and the rigor of its sanctions, but the Bible suggests that the society should first ask two questions: What has happened to the life of this society to make duty to it so unpalatable? Why do the people not love the community enough to meet its obligations willingly? It may be found that some citizens do not value their society because that society does not appear to value them. Without this reciprocal appreciation duty loses its moral force.

DUTY

OLD TESTAMENT

1 Samuel 26:7–16 (King Saul is hunting for David, whom he wishes to kill)

7 So David and Abishai came to the people by night: and, behold, Saul lay sleeping within the trench, and his spear stuck in the ground at his bolster: but Abner and the people lay round about him.

8 Then said Abishai to David, God hath delivered thine enemy into thine hand this day: now therefore let me smite him, I pray thee, with the spear even to the earth at once, and I will not smite him the second time.

9 And David said to Abishai, Destroy him not: for who can stretch forth his hand against the Lord's anointed, and be guiltless?

10 David said furthermore, As the Lord liveth, the Lord shall smite him; or his day shall come to die; or he shall descend into battle, and perish.

11 The Lord forbid that I should stretch forth mine hand against the

Lord's anointed: but, I pray thee, take thou now the spear that is at his bolster, and the cruse of water, and let us go.

12 So David took the spear and the cruse of water from Saul's bolster; and they gat them away, and no man saw it, nor knew it, neither awaked: for they were all asleep; because a deep sleep from the Lord was fallen upon them.

13 Then David went over to the other side, and stood on the top of an hill afar off; a great space being between them:

14 And David cried to the people, and to Abner the son of Ner, saying, Answerest thou not, Abner? Then Abner answered and said, Who art thou that criest to the king?

15 And David said to Abner, Art not thou a valiant man? and who is like to thee in Israel? wherefore then hast thou not kept thy lord the king? for there came one of the people in to destroy the king thy lord.

16 This thing is not good that thou hast done. As the Lord liveth, ye are worthy to die, because ye have not kept your master, the Lord's anointed. And now see where the king's spear is, and the cruse of water that was at his bolster.

Ezekiel 33:1–4, 6–7

1 Again the word of the Lord came unto me, saying,

2 Son of man, speak to the children of thy people, and say unto them, When I bring the sword upon a land, if the people of the land take a man of their coasts, and set him for their watchman:

3 If when he seeth the sword come upon the land, he blow the trumpet, and warn the people;

4 Then whosoever heareth the sound of the trumpet, and taketh not warning; if the sword come, and take him away, his blood shall be upon his own head.

6 But if the watchman see the sword come, and blow not the trumpet, and the people be not warned; if the sword come, and take any person from among them, he is taken away in his iniquity; but his blood will I require at the watchman's hand.

7 So thou, O son of man, I have set thee a watchman unto the house of Israel; therefore thou shalt hear the word at my mouth, and warn them from me.

NEW TESTAMENT

Matthew 5:20, 41

20 For I say unto you, That except your righteousness shall exceed the righteousness of the scribes and Pharisees, ye shall in no case enter into the kingdom of heaven.

41 And whosoever shall compel thee to go a mile, go with him twain.

Luke 17:7–10

7 But which of you, having a servant ploughing or feeding cattle, will say unto him by and by, when he is come from the field, Go and sit down to meat?

8 And will not rather say unto him, Make ready wherewith I may sup, and gird thyself, and serve me, till I have eaten and drunken; and afterward thou shalt eat and drink?

9 Doth he thank that servant because he did the things that were commanded him? I trow not.

10 So likewise ye, when ye shall have done all those things which are commanded you, say, We are unprofitable servants: we have done that which was our duty to do.

Romans 13:7–9

7 Render therefore to all their dues: tribute to whom tribute is due; custom to whom custom; fear to whom fear; honour to whom honour.

8 Owe no man any thing, but to love one another: for he that loveth another hath fulfilled the law.

9 For this, Thou shalt not commit adultery, Thou shalt not kill, Thou shalt not steal, Thou shalt not bear false witness, Thou shalt not covet; and if there be any other commandment, it is briefly comprehended in this saying, namely, Thou shalt love thy neighbour as thyself.

ENCOURAGEMENT

Encouragement in the Old Testament does not consist of saying, "Go on, you can do it!" It is more likely to say, "Be still, and know that I am God" (Psalm 46:10). Its assurance is that good causes are sustained by a more than human power. Yet this leads neither to an enervating fatalism nor to a disbelief in the significance of human effort. The point is that within the strong tide of the divine purpose it is necessary for us to swim hard. We will need all our strength and all our courage. Moreover, we will be swimming against strong currents. The assurance of divine power is meant to encourage human effort, not to discourage it. So Moses must encourage Joshua to be strong, not because God's purposes are shaky but because they are certain. Joshua may pitch his expectations infinitely high, so long as they are bounded by the purposes of God.

For Joshua the path led to military leadership, but the Old Testament is equally encouraging to those whose calling is a lonely, unpopular, and uncomfortable one. Many of the prophets doubted their adequacy for such work, but the Spirit of God caused them to stand up as men and to do what needed to be done regardless of consequences. Success was not promised.

If need be, individuals must encourage themselves. Job's somewhat mystifying but deeply moving affirmation of confidence was wrung from him in his loneliness as he found himself alienated from his friends and deep in incomprehensible suffering. It was an assurance that truth and purity could not ultimately be frustrated.

The New Testament speaks with equal confidence of an invisible power that can be trusted to make up what is lacking in human strength and wisdom, so long as such wisdom and strength as human beings have are fully extended. The

Gospel of John gives a unique place to Jesus, and yet it encourages his followers to believe that they can do as much or more than he himself did—always provided that it is "in his name" (that is to say, within the boundaries of his purpose). The disciples are encouraged to rise to the height of their destiny, not to the (much lower) height of their ambitions.

In New Testament times the effect of this encouragement was astonishing. The "little flock" to which the hidden resources of the kingdom had been given simply diverted the course of history. The world was turned upside down by those whom it regarded as nonentities. As the church grew and got organized, a young man such as Timothy could find himself a minister exercising responsible leadership in a community that successfully challenged the values and beliefs of the age. And he was encouraged (at a time when the young were not usually given such encouragement) to claim the full stature of his calling, and that meant not only acting with confidence but also encouraging confidence in others.

The Bible affirms that the strongest forces at work in the universe are on the side of true humanity. They are not on the side of our selfish ambitions (or even, perhaps, our unselfish ambitions), they do not deliver us from affliction, and they do not relieve us of responsibility. They are for us, however, and not against us. They are for us in all that is most significant about us. All that the Bible says for our encouragement is summed up in the name originally proposed for a child to be born in Isaiah's time and later applied to the infant Jesus. The name is Emmanuel, which means "God with us."

According to the Bible the encouragement we should give to one another is an extension of the same principle. There are two common ways of discouraging people from fulfilling their own potential. One is to give them so much help that they never develop any confidence in their ability to do things themselves. The other is to stand so far back that they are given no appreciation of what their potential might be. The biblical way is to reveal the possibilities in everybody without taking responsibility from anybody.

ENCOURAGEMENT

OLD TESTAMENT

Deuteronomy 3:27–28; Joshua 1:1, 5–7

27 Get thee up into the top of Pisgah, and lift up thine eyes westward, and northward, and southward, and eastward, and behold it with thine eyes: for thou shalt not go over this Jordan.

28 But charge Joshua, and encourage him, and strengthen him: for he shall go over before this people, and he shall cause them to inherit the land which thou shalt see.

1 Now after the death of Moses the servant of the Lord it came to pass,

that the Lord spake unto Joshua the son of Nun, Moses' minister, saying,

5 . . . as I was with Moses, so I will be with thee: I will not fail thee, nor forsake thee.

6 Be strong and of a good courage: for unto this people shalt thou divide for an inheritance the land, which I sware unto their fathers to give them.

7 Only be thou strong and very courageous, that thou mayest observe to do according to all the law, which Moses my servant commanded thee: turn not from it to the right hand or to the left, that thou mayest prosper whithersoever thou goest.

Ezekiel 1:28–2:3,6–7

28 This was the appearance of the likeness of the glory of the Lord. And when I saw it I fell upon my face, and I heard a voice of one that spake.

1 And he said unto me, Son of man, stand upon thy feet, and I will speak unto thee.

2 And the spirit entered into me when he spake unto me, and set me upon my feet, that I heard him that spake unto me.

3 And he said unto me, Son of man, I send thee to the children of Israel, to a rebellious nation that hath rebelled against me: they and their fathers have transgressed against me, even unto this very day.

6 And thou, son of man, be not afraid of them, neither be afraid of their words, though briers and thorns be with thee, and thou dost dwell among scorpions: be not afraid of their words, nor be dismayed at their looks, though they be a rebellious house.

7 And thou shalt speak my words unto them, whether they will hear or whether they will forbear.

Job 19:25–27

For I know that my redeemer liveth,
And that he shall stand at the latter day upon the earth:
And though after my skin worms destroy this body,
Yet in my flesh shall I see God:
Whom I shall see for myself,
And mine eyes shall behold, and not another.

NEW TESTAMENT

Luke 12:32

32 Fear not, little flock; for it is your Father's good pleasure to give you the kingdom.

Matthew 10:16–20

16 Behold, I send you forth as sheep in the midst of wolves: be ye therefore wise as serpents, and harmless as doves.

17 But beware of men: for they will deliver you up to the councils, and they will scourge you in their synagogues;

18 And ye shall be brought before governors and kings for my sake, for a testimony against them and the Gentiles.

19 But when they deliver you up, take no thought how or what ye shall speak: for it shall be given you in that same hour what ye shall speak.

20 For it is not ye that speak, but the Spirit of your Father which speaketh in you.

John 14:10–14

10 The words that I speak unto you I speak not of myself: but the Father that dwelleth in me, he doeth the works.

11 Believe me that I am in the Father, and the Father in me: or else believe me for the very works' sake.

12 Verily, verily, I say unto you, He that believeth on me, the works that I do shall he do also; and greater works than these shall he do; because I go unto my Father.

13 And whatsoever ye shall ask in my name, that will I do, that the Father may be glorified in the Son.

14 If ye shall ask any thing in my name, I will do it.

1 Timothy 4:12–16

12 Let no man despise thy youth; but be thou an example of the believers, in word, in conversation, in charity, in spirit, in faith, in purity.

13 Till I come, give attendance to reading, to exhortation, to doctrine.

14 Neglect not the gift that is in thee, which was given thee by prophecy, with the laying on of the hands of the presbytery.

15 Meditate upon these things; give thyself wholly to them; that thy profiting may appear to all.

16 Take heed unto thyself, and unto the doctrine; continue in them: for in doing this thou shalt both save thyself, and them that hear thee.

ENEMIES

The Old Testament is not initially very loving toward enemies. The religious zeal needed to shape a nation that would be specially responsive to the revelation of God had as its early accompaniment an intolerant determination to destroy the national and religious enemy. Inevitably this was expressed as a belief that God wanted the adversary destroyed.

Later, however, the enemy came to be seen as the instrument of God. Sometimes he was thought of as just a stick in the Lord's hand for beating some sense into God's childish people, but sometimes God's concern with the enemy was a good deal closer than that. Cyrus, a foreign king, was referred to in the Book of Isaiah as the Lord's shepherd (44:28) and even as the Lord's anointed (45:1)— that is, his Messiah or Christ.

At the interpersonal level the Book of Proverbs warned people against letting hatred shape their attitude toward an adversary. As at the international level, God was said to be involved on both sides of the division and to have his own ways of dealing with the offending party.

The New Testament takes up this same line of development: enemies are to be loved. This was not only Jesus' teaching but his practice as well, as the story of his arrest makes clear. He, too, derived his attitude toward the enemy from his understanding of God. The passage quoted here about loving one's enemy goes on to say "that ye may be the children of your Father which is in heaven." The Father is himself one who loves and does good to those who are opposed to him. This is a law built into the very nature of things ("He maketh his sun to rise on the evil and on the good, and sendeth rain on the just and on the unjust"). Thus it behooves men and women to go along with it.

Paul's idea of a peaceable attitude toward opponents draws on quotations from both Deuteronomy and Proverbs, but he too recommends approaching the enemy by way of God. The enemy is to be seen as one who is himself in God's hands and subject to God's loving discipline. Paul knew what he was talking about: he had himself been an opponent and persecutor of Christians, and he had received the treatment he recommends—blessing, not cursing.

In our culture the word "enemy" most often denotes a national adversary, but personal, ethnic, and class enmities, and enmities of many other kinds are still with us. No general rule will resolve all these problems—neither a universal application of unresisting pacifism nor a universal application of unremitting force. A variety of treatments is called for, but each of them begins with something like the biblical view that God is active on both sides. In secular terms this means recognizing a certain kinship with our enemies, a fundamental brotherhood. Whether the enemy is to be resisted with force or with unarmed love, he must first be understood. What the situation looks like through his eyes, how it feels from within his skin—this is essential information, and it is information that can come only through the exercise of love and imagination.

However, Marshall McLuhan says (in *Understanding Media*) that "in the electric age we wear all mankind as our skin." Perhaps we do have a better chance to get into other people's shoes, feel from within their skin, see through their eyes. Whether we use that chance to diminish enmity or to increase it may depend on our vision of the world. See it as an array of separated factions and enmity will only be exacerbated by our new awareness of each other. See it biblically as a world of underlying unity and enmity can be transcended.

ENEMIES

OLD TESTAMENT

1 Samuel 15:2–3, 7–11 (Samuel speaking to Saul)

2 Thus saith the Lord of hosts, I remember that which Amalek did to Israel, how he laid wait for him in the way, when he came up from Egypt.

3 Now go and smite Amalek and utterly destroy all that they have, and spare them not; but slay both man and woman, infant and suckling, ox and sheep, camel and ass.

7 And Saul smote the Amalekites from Havilah until thou comest to Shur, that is over against Egypt.

8 And he took Agag the king of the Amalekites alive, and utterly destroyed all the people with the edge of the sword.

9 But Saul and the people spared Agag, and the best of the sheep, and of the oxen, and of the fatlings, and the lambs, and all that was good, and would not utterly destroy them: but every thing that was vile and refuse, that they destroyed utterly.

10 Then came the word of the Lord unto Samuel, saying,

11 It repenteth me that I have set up Saul to be king: for he is turned back from following me, and hath not performed my commandments. And it grieved Samuel; and he cried unto the Lord all night.

Nehemiah 9:26–28 (Israelite history recalled in prayer to God)

26 Nevertheless they were disobedient, and rebelled against thee, and cast thy law behind their backs, and slew thy prophets which testified against them to turn them to thee, and they wrought great provocations.

27 Therefore thou deliveredst them into the hand of their enemies, who vexed them: and in the time of their trouble, when they cried unto thee, thou heardest them from heaven; and according to thy manifold mercies thou gavest them saviours, who saved them out of the hand of their enemies.

28 But after they had rest, they did evil again before thee: therefore leftest thou them in the hand of their enemies, so that they had the dominion over them: yet when they returned, and cried unto thee, thou heardest them from heaven; and many times didst thou deliver them according to thy mercies.

Proverbs 24:17–18; 25:21–22

Rejoice not when thine enemy falleth,
And let not thine heart be glad when he stumbleth:
Lest the Lord see it, and it displease him,
And he turn away his wrath from him.
If thine enemy be hungry, give him bread to eat;
And if he be thirsty, give him water to drink:
For thou shalt heap coals of fire upon his head,
And the Lord shall reward thee.

NEW TESTAMENT

Matthew 5:43–44

43 Ye have heard that it hath been said, Thou shalt love thy neighbour, and hate thine enemy.

44 But I say unto you, Love your enemies, bless them that curse you, do good to them that hate you, and pray for them which despitefully use you, and persecute you.

Matthew 26:47–52 (in the Garden of Gethsemane)

47 And while he yet spake, lo, Judas, one of the twelve, came, and with him a great multitude with swords and staves, from the chief priests and elders of the people.

48 Now he that betrayed him gave them a sign, saying, Whomsoever I shall kiss, that same is he: hold him fast.

49 And forthwith he came to Jesus, and said, Hail, master; and kissed him.

50 And Jesus said unto him, Friend, wherefore art thou come? Then came

they, and laid hands on Jesus, and took him.

51 And, behold, one of them which were with Jesus stretched out his hand, and drew his sword, and struck a servant of the high priest's, and smote off his ear.

52 Then said Jesus unto him, Put up again thy sword into his place: for all they that take the sword shall perish with the sword.

Romans 12:14, 17–21

14 Bless them which persecute you: bless, and curse not.

17 Recompense to no man evil for evil. Provide things honest in the sight of all men.

18 If it be possible, as much as lieth in you, live peaceably with all men.

19 Dearly beloved, avenge not yourselves, but rather give place unto wrath: for it is written, Vengeance is mine; I will repay, saith the Lord.

20 Therefore if thine enemy hunger, feed him; if he thirst, give him drink: for in so doing thou shalt heap coals of fire on his head.

21 Be not overcome of evil, but overcome evil with good.

ENVIRONMENT

Genesis has been accused of teaching human beings arrogance in relation to their environment because they are told to rule over it and subdue it. They are just as clearly told, however, that they themselves are under the rule of God and that his laws run right through the creation. A less selective reading suggests that we must subdue nature to God's will and in God's way, never ignoring its built-in laws and balances. Moreover, Genesis shows the human race as part of nature, created with it and for it. Arrogance is uncalled for.

Indeed, Old Testament law required the environment to be respected as a kind of equal under God. Just as human beings are entitled to a Sabbath rest, so is the land, though in years instead of days. This not only secured a fallow period for the soil but also engendered the feeling that both the human being (Adam) and the ground (adamah) shared kinship with the holy.

So close was the triangular relationship among humanity, God, and nature that when a plague of locusts devastated the land, the prophet Joel could see it only as the consequence of a religious offense to be corrected by prayer and fasting. This view was challenged elsewhere in the Old Testament (see Disaster), but there remained a sense of the intimate connection between the life of nature and the life of man. The psalmist rolled human beings and natural forces together in one great bundle. In his exhortation to praise the Lord, he addresses the "kings of the earth and all people" in exact parallelism with mountains, trees, beasts, and birds.

To Jesus, humanity and the environment were so much in the same position that God's bounty in nature was sufficient reason for expecting equal generosity (in fact, "much more") to be shown to men and women. The sense of continuity between humanity and nature is still there in the New Testament.

To his followers Jesus' trust in the environment sometimes seemed excessive. They complained because he slept while they were caught in a storm on the lake. As soon as they awakened him, Jesus stilled the storm. The story seems to repeat what Genesis said: man, the true man, is lord of the environment to exactly the same degree as he is subject to the Creator. The helplessness of the disciples when left to themselves was a failure of faith and obedience.

Being faithful and obedient did not save Paul from shipwreck, but it did enable him to see the life of creation in general and of man in particular as part of the same process. Together they had experienced futility; together they would experience redemption. ("Creature" here means "creation.")

George Fox, founder of the Society of Friends, spoke of having "unity with the creation." That is a mystical type of perception, but one with very practical consequences of which the world is now more urgently in need. It was a momentous day indeed when man became strong enough to inflict a mortal wound on his environment and to upset the balance of nature on this planet irrevocably. And this momentous day fell in our time. Plenty of local damage had been done before, but people now young are the first ever to be born into an age when they could make this earth incapable of sustaining human life. The tender sense of unity with and responsibility for the creation is both biblical and necessary.

The practical attitude that this sense of unity engenders is neither that of the simple-lifer nor that of the technological tyrant. The environment is neither to be left alone to go its own sweet (or sour) way nor to be manhandled into yielding the maximum number of immediate material conveniences. It is to be controlled, but only in the interests of becoming its true self. It is to be disciplined in accordance with its own laws. It is to be lovingly nursed with a deep understanding of and concern for its health.

ENVIRONMENT

OLD TESTAMENT

Genesis 1:28 *(after the creation of mankind)*

28 And God blessed them, and God said unto them, Be fruitful, and multiply, and replenish the earth, and subdue it: and have dominion over the fish of the sea, and over the fowl of the air, and over every living thing that moveth upon the earth.

Leviticus 25:1–5

1 And the Lord spake unto Moses in mount Sinai, saying,

2 Speak unto the children of Israel,

and say unto them, When ye come into the land which I give you, then shall the land keep a sabbath unto the Lord.

3 Six years thou shalt sow thy field, and six years thou shalt prune thy vineyard, and gather in the fruit thereof;

4 But in the seventh year shall be a sabbath of rest unto the land, a sabbath for the Lord: thou shalt neither sow thy field, nor prune thy vineyard.

5 That which groweth of its own accord of thy harvest thou shalt not reap, neither gather the grapes of thy vine undressed: for it is a year of rest unto the land.

Joel 1:4, 13–14

4 That which the palmerworm hath left hath the locust eaten; and that which the locust hath left hath the cankerworm eaten; and that which the cankerworm hath left hath the caterpillar eaten.

13 Gird yourselves, and lament, ye priests: howl, ye ministers of the altar: come, lie all night in sackcloth, ye ministers of my God: for the meat offering and the drink offering is withholden from the house of your God.

14 Sanctify ye a fast, call a solemn assembly, gather the elders and all the inhabitants of the land into the house of the Lord your God, and cry unto the Lord.

Psalm 148:7–13

Praise the Lord from the earth,
Ye dragons, and all deeps:
Fire, and hail; snow, and vapours;
Stormy wind fulfilling his word:
Mountains, and all hills;

Fruitful trees, and all cedars:
Beasts, and all cattle;
Creeping things, and flying fowl:
Kings of the earth, and all people;
Princes, and all judges of the earth;
Both young men, and maidens;
Old men, and children:
Let them praise the name of the Lord.

NEW TESTAMENT

Matthew 6:28–30

28 And why take ye thought for raiment? Consider the lilies of the field, how they grow; they toil not, neither do they spin:

29 And yet I say unto you, That even Solomon in all his glory was not arrayed like one of these.

30 Wherefore, if God so clothe the grass of the field, which today is, and to-morrow is cast into the oven, shall he not much more clothe you, O ye of little faith?

Mark 4:37–41

37 And there arose a great storm of wind, and the waves beat into the ship, so that it was now full.

38 And he was in the hinder part of the ship, asleep on a pillow: and they awake him, and say unto him, Master, carest thou not that we perish?

39 And he arose, and rebuked the wind, and said unto the sea, Peace, be still. And the wind ceased, and there was a great calm.

40 And he said unto them, Why are ye so fearful? how is it that ye have no faith?

41 And they feared exceedingly, and said one to another, What manner of

man is this, that even the wind and the sea obey him?

Romans 8:19–21

19 For the earnest expectation of the creature waiteth for the manifestation of the sons of God. \

20 For the creature was made subject to vanity, not willingly, but by reason of him who hath subjected the same in hope,

21 Because the creature itself also shall be delivered from the bondage of corruption into the glorious liberty of the children of God.

ENVY

Those who translate the Bible into English, like most speakers of English, tend to regard the words "envy" and "jealousy" as more or less interchangeable. Strictly, however, there is a distinction between them. Properly speaking we are jealous about what we have got and envious about what we have not got. Some witty purist claimed that both characteristics were demonstrated by a motorist's wife when she sat in the front passenger seat and said, "This seat belt has been tightened: who is she?" The poor woman was jealous of an imagined rival for her husband's affections, and at the same time envious of the other woman's slimness.

As between envy and jealousy the Old Testament takes much the sterner view of envy. Envy is plainly shown to be a socially destructive force, but it is also clear that it can focus on something much more trivial than what is really at stake. Joseph's brothers, for instance, may have expressed envy of his coat of many colors, but their real envy was of the paternal affection in which they did not fully share.

Such ambiguities arise because people usually hide their envy. The last of the Ten Commandments stands apart from the rest. Where others have forbidden an outward act such as murder or theft, this one forbids an inward disposition: covetousness, or envy. Part of the remedy for envy is to identify it for what it is— and to identify its true causes as distinct from its trivial manifestations. But a feeling is not easily corrected by commandment. A false desire such as envy can be finally displaced only by a stronger and better desire such as love. The biblical passages that most effectively dispose of envy are those which do not even mention it. The man who approaches the temple with the desires expressed in Psalm 42 is not going to be too troubled by his fellow worshiper's new shoes.

Jesus also put envy in its place without mentioning it: "What is a man profited, if he shall gain the whole world, and lose his own soul?" (Matthew 16:26). He who is envious of others' possessions damages his true self by placing his heart elsewhere. If he were to have his wish, the transaction would represent a net loss.

But envy was never more concisely exemplified than in the parable of the

Prodigal Son. Of the three main characters in the story the least interesting is the prodigal himself; the rake's progress is, after all, a familiar story. The father's forgiving generosity is much more noteworthy and the elder brother's envy much nearer to the target of the story. No doubt his attitude was intended to symbolize Israel's temptation to exclusivity and self-righteousness, but the power of the story lies in the ease with which most of us can see our own envy mirrored in that of the elder brother—and in this case it was not provoked by lack of paternal love.

The Bible makes it clear that only a radical shift of conventional values will prevent envy from gnawing away at human life. Certainly it cannot be bought off with a supply of coveted objects. Most of us who live in the Western Hemisphere have what the people of the Third World would regard as untold wealth, but this alone does not stop us from envying our neighbor, who may own a house with a swimming pool—or two pools. The remedy for envy is to value the self for something other than its possessions or its material success—not only to rank being above doing, as some current philosophy advises, but to rank both above having.

Paradoxically, this unenvious attitude toward possessions actually increases their value. They become the ground on which we meet with others to enjoy them. What envy does is, first, to make us pine for what we have not got and, then, to make us build a fence around what we have got. Within that fence we sit imprisoned—our hearts set on what is outside it and ourselves alone inside it.

ENVY

OLD TESTAMENT

Genesis 37:3–4

3 Now Israel loved Joseph more than all his children, because he was the son of his old age: and he made him a coat of many colours.

4 And when his brethren saw that their father loved him more than all his brethren, they hated him, and could not speak peaceably unto him.

Exodus 20:17

17 Thou shalt not covet thy neighbour's house, thou shalt not covet thy neighbour's wife, nor his manservant, nor his maidservant, nor his ox, nor his ass, nor any thing that is thy neighbour's.

Proverbs 23:17

Let not thine heart envy sinners:
But be thou in fear of the Lord all the
day long.

Psalm 42:1–2

As the hart panteth after the water brooks,
So panteth my soul after thee, O God.
My soul thirsteth for God, for the living
God;

When shall I come and appear before God?

NEW TESTAMENT

Luke 15:11–32

11 And he said, A certain man had two sons:

12 And the younger of them said to his father, Father, give me the portion of goods that falleth to me. And he divided unto them his living.

13 And not many days after the younger son gathered all together, and took his journey into a far country, and there wasted his substance with riotous living.

14 And when he had spent all, there arose a mighty famine in that land; and he began to be in want.

15 And he went and joined himself to a citizen of that country; and he sent him into his fields to feed swine.

16 And he would fain have filled his belly with the husks that the swine did eat: and no man gave unto him.

17 And when he came to himself, he said, How many hired servants of my father's have bread enough and to spare, and I perish with hunger!

18 I will arise and go to my father, and will say unto him, Father, I have sinned against heaven, and before thee,

19 And am no more worthy to be called thy son: make me as one of thy hired servants.

20 And he arose, and came to his father. But when he was yet a great way off, his father saw him, and had compassion, and ran, and fell on his neck, and kissed him.

21 And the son said unto him, Father, I have sinned against heaven, and in thy sight, and am no more worthy to be called thy son.

22 But the father said to his servants, Bring forth the best robe, and put it on him; and put a ring on his hand, and shoes on his feet:

23 And bring hither the fatted calf, and kill it; and let us eat, and be merry:

24 For this my son was dead, and is alive again; he was lost, and is found. And they began to be merry.

25 Now his elder son was in the field: and as he came and drew nigh to the house, he heard music and dancing.

26 And he called one of the servants, and asked what these things meant.

27 And he said unto him, Thy brother is come; and thy father hath killed the fatted calf, because he hath received him safe and sound.

28 And he was angry, and would not go in: therefore came his father out, and entreated him.

29 And he answering said to his father, Lo, these many years do I serve thee, neither transgressed I at any time thy commandment: and yet thou never gavest me a kid, that I might make merry with my friends:

30 But as soon as this thy son was come, which hath devoured thy living with harlots, thou hast killed for him the fatted calf.

31 And he said unto him, Son, thou art ever with me, and all that I have is thine.

32 It was meet that we should make merry, and be glad: for this thy brother

was dead, and is alive again; and was lost, and is found.

Matthew 27:17–18

17 Therefore when they were gathered together, Pilate said unto them, Whom will ye that I release unto you? Barabbas, or Jesus which is called Christ?

18 For he knew that for envy they had delivered him.

Galatians 5:24–26

24 And they that are Christ's have crucified the flesh with the affections and lusts.

25 If we live in the Spirit, let us also walk in the Spirit.

26 Let us not be desirous of vain glory, provoking one another, envying one another.

EVIL

In the Garden of Eden as described in Genesis the knowledge of God and the knowledge of evil grow on one and the same tree. Philosophically we might ask, How could they not? How could a knowledge of good fail to bring with it at least the potential knowledge of the privation of good, which is evil?

The Old Testament, however, is not philosophically inclined. It notes only that from the moment this potential knowledge of evil is realized, evil has a life of its own. Genesis does not speculate on the origin of that wretched snake and all it symbolizes (and later talk of a fallen angel only shifts the problem to a different area), but it does assert that evil is an objective reality that will be a continuing factor in human experience.

So evil is not entirely contained within human behavior. It is certainly active there and the Old Testament constantly detailed what it meant in practice to refrain from evil and to do good. But there is also an evil which is a concrete reality outside of man.

Even so, evil remains subordinate to good and may render it positive if reluctant service. Satan in the story of Job, for instance, is pictured as an official in God's service, one charged with sorting God-fearers from time-servers. God remains God, and evil is restricted to what God permits. Man is not required to understand evil, only to fight it.

Jesus also treated evil as an objective reality, sometimes personalizing it, as in the playful hyperbole about Satan falling from heaven at the preaching of the disciples. At the same time Jesus held people morally responsible for the evil they allowed to enter their lives and express itself in their actions. His parable of the weeds and the wheat suggests that evil must continue indefinitely to play its part in human experience, because wiping it out would involve the destruction of what is most valuable—freedom, perhaps.

The New Testament, like the Old, sees no inconsistency in describing the confrontation with evil in two different ways. At one level the encounter is a hidden struggle between God and the powers of evil, with the human personality as the ground over which the battle is fought. At another level it is our moral struggle with the temptations that beset us daily. These two are deeply connected, even though God's fight with the forces of evil has been fought to a finish whereas our struggle still goes on. At the first level Christ has secured absolute victory: evil expended its full force in the crucifixion, but good remained unbroken. Faith appropriates this victory so that all believers are a part of it, but the spoils of victory still have to be claimed in terms of ordinary daily behavior, and at this level the moral effort of resisting temptation continues. The Christian lives in two ages at once (see Future).

The "problem of evil" is to reconcile the existence of evil with the sovereignty of a good God, but clearly this is a problem only for the believer. If there is no good God, then the universe has as much right to be nasty as to be nice. It may be possible to go further: not only is evil a problem only to belief, but evil is evil only to belief. How can anything be regarded as ultimately bad unless something is transcendently good? How can that which is evil be condemned unless some superior goodness exists by whose standards the evil is found to be wanting? The very experience of evil bears testimony to the existence of good, and it seems possible to conceive only of good as the supreme and ultimate one of the two. It is, after all, possible to conceive of a perfectly straight line but not of a perfectly crooked one!

The Bible leaves no doubt that the ultimate ground of reality is good. And its writers did not arrive at this view in happy ignorance of the fact of evil. Their beliefs had always taken account of its existence and vitality. Because they were a practical people, however, they encouraged one another to fight evil and to leave others to theorize about it.

EVIL

OLD TESTAMENT

Genesis 2:15–17

15 And the Lord God took the man, and put him into the garden of Eden to dress it and to keep it.

16 And the Lord God commanded the man, saying, Of every tree of the garden thou mayest freely eat:

17 But of the tree of the knowledge of good and evil, thou shalt not eat of it: for in the day that thou eatest thereof thou shalt surely die.

Genesis 3:14–15

14 And the Lord God said unto the serpent, Because thou hast done this, thou art cursed above all cattle, and above every beast of the field; upon thy belly shalt thou go, and dust shalt thou eat all the days of thy life:

15 And I will put enmity between thee and the woman, and between thy seed and her seed; it shall bruise thy head, and thou shalt bruise his heel.

Proverbs 8:13

The fear of the Lord is to hate evil.

Job 2:1–6

1 Again there was a day when the sons of God came to present themselves before the Lord, and Satan came also among them to present himself before the Lord.

2 And the Lord said unto Satan, From whence comest thou? And Satan answered the Lord, and said, From going to and fro in the earth, and from walking up and down in it.

3 And the Lord said unto Satan, Hast thou considered my servant Job, that there is none like him in the earth, a perfect and an upright man, one that feareth God, and escheweth evil? and still he holdeth fast his integrity, although thou movedst me against him, to destroy him without cause.

4 And Satan answered the Lord, and said, Skin for skin, yea, all that a man hath will he give for his life.

5 But put forth thine hand now, and touch his bone and his flesh, and he will curse thee to thy face.

6 And the Lord said unto Satan, Behold, he is in thine hand; but save his life.

NEW TESTAMENT

Matthew 6:13 (from the Lord's Prayer)

13 And lead us not into temptation, but deliver us from evil.

Luke 10:17–20 (Jesus' disciples having been away on a mission)

17 And the seventy returned again with joy, saying, Lord, even the devils are subject unto us through thy name.

18 And he said unto them, I beheld Satan as lightning fall from heaven.

19 Behold, I give unto you power to tread on serpents and scorpions, and over all the power of the enemy: and nothing shall by any means hurt you.

20 Notwithstanding in this rejoice not, that the spirits are subject unto you; but rather rejoice, because your names are written in heaven.

Matthew 13:24–30

24 Another parable put he forth unto them, saying, The kingdom of heaven is likened unto a man which sowed good seed in his field:

25 But while men slept, his enemy came and sowed tares among the wheat, and went his way.

26 But when the blade was sprung up, and brought forth fruit, then appeared the tares also.

27 So the servants of the householder came and said unto him, Sir, didst not thou sow good seed in thy field? from whence then hath it tares?

28 He said unto them, An enemy hath done this. The servants said unto him, Wilt thou then that we go and gather them up?

29 But he said, Nay; lest while ye gather up the tares, ye root up also the wheat with them.

30 Let both grow together until the harvest: and in the time of harvest I will say to the reapers, Gather ye to-

gether first the tares, and bind them in bundles to burn them: but gather the wheat into my barn.

Colossians 2:15

15 And having spoiled principalities and powers, he made a shew of them openly, triumphing over them in it [the cross of Christ].

Ephesians 6:16

16 Above all, taking the shield of faith, wherewith ye shall be able to quench all the fiery darts of the wicked.

FAITH

Some people nowadays distinguish between belief (by which they mean ideas they hold to be true), trust (by which they mean the confidence they feel in someone else), and faith (by which they mean "believing where we cannot prove," as Tennyson put it). The Bible, however, knows nothing of these distinctions. Both the Hebrew of the Old Testament and the Greek of the New have only one word to convey what we mean by "belief," by "trust," and by "faith"—except that the biblical word never really means "believing where we cannot prove" if this means that faith disregards known fact. Biblical faith includes believing things to be true; it includes an attitude of trust toward another person; and it includes a way of seeing things visible in a context of things invisible. This last, however, is not at all the same thing as giving intellectual assent to propositions for which there is no supporting evidence. This faith is hypothesis, and its strength is proportionate to the extent to which it rings true when all known facts are looked at in its light.

So in the Old Testament the man or woman of faith is not the one who is credulous but rather the one who is faithful. Firmness is at the heart of faith, but human firmness of this kind comes from a relationship with the ever-constant God. His steadfast love is the ground of our steadfast faith—and action. Abraham (or Abram) is the pioneer of faith, not just because he accepted the truth of God's promises, but because he resolutely acted on them.

Jehoshaphat exhorted his army both to believe *in* and to believe. His story also dramatizes what is involved in faith: God's love evoking a resolute response in both weapons and worship.

The mission of Jesus opens with a challenge to believe the good news (gospel) that he brings. Since he was himself at the heart of this good news, a personal relationship was involved. Epilepsy was always described at that time as "being in the grip of an evil spirit," and it was the father of an epileptic boy who demonstrated the many-sidedness of this personal relationship. He trusted, he believed, he also trusted Jesus with his unbelief. That is faith: putting the whole self, doubts included, into the hands of another.

Paul sees faith as the very core of a right relationship with God. He finds evidence for this in the Old Testament—especially in the texts that treat faith as an entry into righteousness—but for Paul it is the coming of Jesus that has made it possible to put aside any thought of getting right with God by fulfilling his law, and to substitute a trusting relationship with God's representative. It is this union through faith that justifies—that is, puts right.

The comprehensive significance of the term "faith" as the Bible uses it is hardly recoverable. We would probably be wise to accept the variety of terms in our current vocabulary and to use a number of them to cover different aspects of the subject. For instance, when people speak of identifying with some person or cause, they may be expressing something of what the Bible would call faith. And it is true that to some degree people *are* what they identify with. To identify with righteousness is to place yourself in a position where you can be treated as righteous—at any rate by a judge who looks at your intentions rather than your achievements.

Inevitably, however, the various shades of faith do run into one another. The trusting, loving, admiring attitude of "identification with" leads to a personal relationship (see Trust), to commitment, and to action. All of these involve the formulating of ideas about what is true: believing *in* leads to believing *that* this, that, or the other is in fact true. But the believing in is always larger than the believing that, and there is room within it for change and variety in the matter of ideas. Believing can include much uncertainty and agnosticism. It can even embrace much unbelief.

FAITH

OLD TESTAMENT

Genesis 15:5–6

5 And he brought him forth abroad, and said, Look now toward heaven, and tell the stars, if thou be able to number them: and he said unto him, So shall thy seed be.

6 And he believed in the Lord; and he counted it to him for righteousness.

Habakkuk 2:4

4 The just shall live by his faith.

2 Chronicles 20:1, 15, 20–21

1 It came to pass after this also, that the children of Moab, and the children of Ammon, and with them other beside the Ammonites, came against Jehoshaphat to battle.

15 And he said, Hearken ye, all Judah, and ye inhabitants of Jerusalem, and thou king Jehoshaphat, Thus saith the Lord unto you, Be not afraid nor dismayed by reason of this great multitude; for the battle is not yours, but God's.

20 And they rose early in the morning, and went forth into the wilderness of Tekoa: and as they went forth, Jehoshaphat stood and said, Hear me, O Judah, and ye inhabitants of

Jerusalem; Believe in the Lord your God, so shall ye be established; believe his prophets, so shall ye prosper.

21 And when he had consulted with the people, he appointed singers unto the Lord, and that should praise the beauty of holiness, as they went out before the army, and to say, Praise the Lord; for his mercy endureth for ever.

Isaiah 26:1–4

1 We have a strong city; salvation will God appoint for walls and bulwarks.

2 Open ye the gates, that the righteous nation which keepeth the truth may enter in.

3 Thou wilt keep him in perfect peace, whose mind is stayed on thee: because he trusteth in thee.

4 Trust ye in the Lord for ever: for in the Lord Jehovah is everlasting strength.

NEW TESTAMENT

Mark 1:14–15

14 Now after that John was put in prison, Jesus came into Galilee, preaching the gospel of the kingdom of God,

15 And saying, The time is fulfilled, and the kingdom of God is at hand: repent ye, and believe the gospel.

Mark 9:17–24

17 And one of the multitude answered and said, Master, I have brought unto thee my son, which hath a dumb spirit;

18 And wheresoever he taketh him, he teareth him: and he foameth, and gnasheth with his teeth, and pineth away: and I spake to thy disciples that they should cast him out; and they could not.

19 He answereth him, and saith, O faithless generation, how long shall I be with you? how long shall I suffer you? bring him unto me.

20 And they brought him unto him: and when he saw him, straightway the spirit tare him; and he fell on the ground, and wallowed foaming.

21 And he asked his father, How long is it ago since this came unto him? And he said, Of a child.

22 And ofttimes it hath cast him into the fire, and into the waters, to destroy him: but if thou canst do any thing, have compassion on us, and help us.

23 Jesus said unto him, If thou canst believe, all things are possible to him that believeth.

24 And straightway the father of the child cried out, and said with tears, Lord, I believe; help thou mine unbelief.

Matthew 17:19–20

19 Then came the disciples to Jesus apart, and said, Why could we not cast him out?

20 And Jesus said unto them, Because of your unbelief: for verily I say unto you, If ye have faith as a grain of mustard seed, ye shall say unto this mountain, Remove hence to yonder place; and it shall remove; and nothing shall be impossible unto you.

Romans 1:16–17; 3:28

16 For I am not ashamed of the gospel of Christ: for it is the power of God unto salvation to every one that believeth;

17 For therein is the righteousness of God revealed from faith to faith.

28 Therefore we conclude that a man is justified by faith without the deeds of the law.

FAMILY

The Old Testament commandment was to honor both father and mother, but the father's was the dominant position. It was not an unfeeling one, however. David's lament for his rebellious son, Absalom, is as poignant as anything in literature, and Micah's warning about the hurt that can be done by those nearest to a man derives its force from the fact that friends and relatives do matter so much. These loving agonies light up the nature of Old Testament family life more clearly than do such sociological (and not at all distinctive) features as male dominance, polygamy, and the fact that the family was then a much wider unit than what is now called the nuclear family (i.e., one couple and their children).

In spite of all the hurts that arise from family life, the solidarity of the kinship group was the unquestioned basis of the good life in Israel. Israel himself (also called Jacob) went down into Egypt, we are told, to reunite the family unit that had been disrupted when Joseph was sold into slavery by his brothers (see Brotherhood). At Beersheba, near the boundary of what was regarded as his country, God assured Israel that not even the soil of the promised land mattered as much as the kinship of God's people.

Jesus accepted the Old Testament estimate of the family and set his seal on it by speaking of God as Father—his and ours. He even argued that it was possible to see in the behavior of a human father something of the attitude of God: if human fathers could be trusted to do what was best for their children, how much more trustworthy must be the divine Father.

Yet Jesus' own activity was often disruptive of family life, both his own and that of his followers. He is reported as saying, in words very like Micah's, that he had come "to set a man at variance against his father, and the daughter against her mother, and the daughter-in-law against her mother-in-law" (Matthew 10:35). When his own mother sought him out, Jesus spoke of the transcending of natural family life. Nevertheless, at his death he committed her to the care of a beloved disciple, and in so doing he used the language of family relationships.

In any case, when Jesus spoke of the transcending of family bonds, he enhanced rather than reduced their significance. His followers taught that God's fatherhood sets the pattern for all family life and that family bonds should be respected as an obligation of faith, not just of social custom.

The family in the television commercial forms a glowing circle from breakfast cereal to bedtime drink. The viewer may learn to resist the explicit message to buy this breakfast cereal or that bedtime drink, but it is not so easy to resist the implicit message that family life can and should be one continuous affectionate smile. It is not, and never was.

Life in the Bible is not a game of happy families. This is not to say that we pitch our expectations too high. In some ways the commercial image of the happy family is not exalted enough. It is trivial compared with the rich blend of creative pain and pleasure of which the Bible speaks. The family is designed to shape people for experiences that the family itself cannot provide. Its claims are sometimes to be challenged, though it will itself have provided the environment in which the will and the ability to challenge them evolved. The family is a cocoon that has to be broken open before its purpose can be fulfilled.

Paradoxically this strengthens rather than weakens the force of its obligations. Once the family is seen to be an image and foretaste of transcendent commitments, it becomes itself that much more precious, and its own commitments become at their own level that much more binding.

FAMILY

OLD TESTAMENT

Exodus 20:12

12 Honour thy father and thy mother: that thy days may be long upon the land which the Lord thy God giveth thee.

2 Samuel 18:31–33

31 And, behold, Cushi came; and Cushi said, Tidings, my lord the king: for the Lord hath avenged thee this day of all them that rose up against thee.

32 And the king said unto Cushi, Is the young man Absalom safe? And Cushi answered, The enemies of my lord the king, and all that rise against thee to do thee hurt, be as that young man is.

33 And the king was much moved, and went up to the chamber over the gate, and wept: and as he went, thus he said, O my son Absalom, my son, my son Absalom! would God I had died for thee, O Absalom, my son, my son!

Micah 7:5–6

5 Trust ye not in a friend, put ye not confidence in a guide: keep the doors of thy mouth from her that lieth in thy bosom.

6 For the son dishonoureth the father, the daughter riseth up against her mother, the daughter in law against her mother in law; a man's enemies are the men of his own house.

Genesis 46:1–7

1 And Israel took his journey with

all that he had, and came to Beer-sheba, and offered sacrifices unto the God of his father Isaac.

2 And God spake unto Israel in the visions of the night, and said, Jacob, Jacob. And he said, Here am I.

3 And he said, I am God, the God of thy father: fear not to go down into Egypt; for I will there make of thee a great nation:

4 I will go down with thee into Egypt; and I will also surely bring thee up again: and Joseph shall put his hand upon thine eyes.

5 And Jacob rose up from Beer-sheba: and the sons of Israel carried Jacob their father, and their little ones, and their wives, in the wagons which Pharaoh had sent to carry them.

6 And they took their cattle, and their goods, which they had gotten in the land of Canaan, and came into Egypt, Jacob, and all his seed with him:

7 His sons, and his sons' sons with him, his daughters, and his sons' daughters, and all his seed brought he with him into Egypt.

NEW TESTAMENT

Luke 11:2, 11–13

2 And he said unto them, When ye pray, say, Our Father . . .

11 If a son shall ask bread of any of you that is a father, will he give him a stone? or if he ask a fish, will he for a fish give him a serpent?

12 Or if he shall ask an egg, will he offer him a scorpion?

13 If ye then, being evil, know how to give good gifts unto your children: how much more shall your heavenly Father give the Holy Spirit to them that ask him?

Mark 3:31–35

31 There came then his brethren and his mother, and, standing with-out, sent unto him, calling him.

32 And the multitude sat about him, and they said unto him, Behold, thy mother and thy brethren without seek for thee.

33 And he answered them, saying, Who is my mother, or my brethren?

34 And he looked round about on them which sat about him, and said, Behold my mother and my brethren!

35 For whosoever shall do the will of God, the same is my brother, and my sister, and mother.

John 19:25–27

25 Now there stood by the cross of Jesus his mother, and his mother's sister, Mary the wife of Cleophas and Mary Magdalene.

26 When Jesus therefore saw his mother, and the disciple standing by, whom he loved, he saith unto his mother, Woman, behold thy son!

27 Then saith he to the disciple, Behold thy mother! And from that hour that disciple took her unto his own home.

Ephesians 3:14–15; 5:22, 25; 6:1,4

14 For this cause I bow my knees unto the Father of our Lord Jesus Christ,

15 Of whom the whole family in heaven and earth is named.

22 Wives, submit yourselves unto your own husbands, as unto the Lord.

25 Husbands, love your wives, even as Christ also loved the church, and gave himself for it.

1 Children, obey your parents in the Lord: for this is right.

4 And, ye fathers, provoke not your children to wrath.

FEAR

The Old Testament does speak of men without fear, but since it regards the fear of the Lord as the very foundation of wisdom and knowledge it cannot mean that these pious heroes were altogether without the experience. It does mean that they declined to be frightened by relatively small things—such as death.

Admittedly the fear of God is not the same thing as fear of a clenched fist, or of a hungry lion, or of a dizzying height, but there are connections. The fear of God at its deepest is a sense of awe and reverence before the holy, but since the men of the Old Testament believed the holy God to hold their lives in his hand at every moment, an ordinary prudent sort of fear was present as well. Indeed, the holiness of God could strike a man physically dead, and the punishments of God included many experiences that could be, and were designed to be, feared in the most natural way. The frightening list of the horrors of exile in Deuteronomy are explicitly stated to be what happens to people who disobey because they do not fear God's "glorious and fearful name" (Deuteronomy 28:58).

This God-centered fear made it possible to see all other kinds of fear in perspective. From this belief sprang the celebrated fearlessness of such folk heroes as Shadrach, Meshach, and Abednego. It enabled them to say not only "Our God whom we serve is able to deliver us, and he will deliver us" but also the much braver "but if not . . ."

"Fear not" is a repeated command in the New Testament Gospels. It is said to those with spiritual fears (such as the shepherds in the nativity story) and to those with bodily fears (such as the apostles when being sent out on a preaching mission). Not that it did much good to issue this command. Up to and immediately after the crucifixion the disciples were no examples of fearlessness. That something then made them what they had never been before is strong evidence for the truth of the resurrection of Jesus and of the gift of the Spirit.

Even then, their courage cannot properly be called fearlessness. They were fearful still, but now they went ahead just the same. Paul acknowledges being fearful to the point of despair. In another passage he lists an astonishing catalog of dangerous and painful adventures through which he has passed (2 Corinthians 11:23–27). His point is that all such natural fears can be controlled by the Spirit and outmatched by the hope that is in us all.

The New Testament suggests that if the fear of God is at bottom a proper reverence before that which is holy, then another emotion will do the job equally well: love involves perhaps an even deeper reverence than fear does, so "love casteth out fear."

There are two things to fear about fear itself. One is that it may be present in such strength as to prevent us from taking the necessary action. The other is that it may be absent. The resut, then, is likely to be even worse, for without fear to signal to us where dangers lie, we would have little chance of survival.

So what we need is not a recipe for dispelling fear, but a method for containing it within useful bounds. We must separate irrational phobias from healthy fears. The Bible affirms that its transcendent vision shows all fears in a realistic light and so enables us to have a sense of proportion about them. The wide perspective breeds neither foolhardiness nor cowardice.

Perhaps the most insistent of all fears is still that of the unknown. The Bible's position is that all that is unknown can be faced with faith and love precisely because love is concealed within the unknown. Not everyone can readily embrace this belief, but all have some experience of love as a ground of trust. On such foundations—even when they are invisible—it is possible to build an attitude that can cope with fear.

FEAR

OLD TESTAMENT

Psalm 56:3–4

What time I am afraid,
I will trust in thee.
In God I will praise his word,
In God I have put my trust; I will not fear
What flesh can do unto me.

Deuteronomy 28:65–67 (exile, the penalty for disobedience)

65 And among these nations shalt thou find no ease, neither shall the sole of thy foot have rest: but the Lord shall give thee there a trembling heart, and failing of eyes, and sorrow of mind:
66 And thy life shall hang in doubt before thee; and thou shalt fear day and night, and shalt have none assurance of thy life:
67 In the morning thou shalt say, Would God it were even! and at even thou shalt say, Would God it were morning! for the fear of thine heart wherewith thou shalt fear, and for the sight of thine eyes which thou shalt see.

Psalm 111:10; Proverbs 1:7

The fear of the Lord is the beginning of wisdom.
The fear of the Lord is the beginning of knowledge.

Daniel 3:13–18

13 Then Nebuchadnezzar in his rage and fury commanded to bring

Shadrach, Meshach, and Abednego. Then they brought these men before the king.

14 Nebuchadnezzar spake and said unto them, Is it true, O Shadrach, Meshach, and Abednego, do not ye serve my gods, nor worship the golden image which I have set up?

15 Now if ye be ready that at what time ye hear the sound of the cornet, flute, harp, sackbut, psaltery, and dulcimer, and all kinds of music, ye fall down and worship the image which I have made; well: but if ye worship not, ye shall be cast the same hour into the midst of a burning fiery furnace; and who is that God that shall deliver you out of my hands?

16 Shadrach, Meshach, and Abednego, answered and said to the king, O Nebuchadnezzar, we are not careful to answer thee in this matter.

17 If it be so, our God whom we serve is able to deliver us from the burning fiery furnace, and he will deliver us out of thine hand, O king.

18 But if not, be it known unto thee, O king, that we will not serve thy gods, nor worship the golden image which thou hast set up.

NEW TESTAMENT

Luke 2:8–12

8 And there were in the same country shepherds abiding in the field, keeping watch over their flock by night.

9 And, lo, the angel of the Lord came upon them, and the glory of the Lord shone round about them: and they were sore afraid.

10 And the angel said unto them, Fear not: for, behold, I bring you good tidings of great joy, which shall be to all people.

11 For unto you is born this day in the city of David a Saviour, which is Christ the Lord.

12 And this shall be a sign unto you; Ye shall find the babe wrapped in swaddling clothes, lying in a manger.

Matthew 8:23–27

23 And when he was entered into a ship, his disciples followed him.

24 And, behold, there arose a great tempest in the sea, insomuch that the ship was covered with the waves: but he was asleep.

25 And his disciples came to him, and awoke him, saying, Lord, save us: we perish.

26 And he saith unto them, Why are ye fearful, O ye of little faith? Then he arose, and rebuked the winds and the sea; and there was a great calm.

27 But the men marvelled, saying, What manner of man is this, that even the winds and the sea obey him!

Matthew 10:28

28 And fear not them which kill the body, but are not able to kill the soul.

2 Corinthians 1:8–10

8 For we would not, brethren, have you ignorant of our trouble which came to us in Asia, that we were pressed out of measure, above strength, insomuch that we despaired even of life:

9 But we had the sentence of death in ourselves, that we should not trust

in ourselves, but in God which raiseth the dead:

10 Who delivered us from so great a death, and doth deliver: in whom we trust that he will yet deliver us.

1 John 4:18

18 There is no fear in love; but perfect love casteth out fear. . . . He that feareth is not made perfect in love.

FOOD

Vegetarians will find little comfort in the readings on this subject. The Old Testament reflects in part the life of a nomadic, pastoral people. To them vegetarianism was not an option. The Old Testament story of the Exodus, however, is dominated by food: the ritual meal taken before leaving Egypt, which became (perhaps by way of earlier agricultural festivals) the feast of Passover; manna and quails and water supplies in the wilderness; a land flowing with milk and honey as the dreamed-of goal.

Throughout the history of Israel dietetic laws have made every meal a reminder of the bond that unites the people to one another and to God. The harvest celebrations made it clear that the people had two particular religious obligations to fulfill relating to food: they were expected to be grateful for it, and they were bound to share it.

Jesus made the feeding of the hungry a crucial test of the human being's relationship with himself (see Judgment), but he also made food a theme of prayer, a subject for miracles, and, above all, a symbol of himself: "I am the bread of life" (John 6:35). The mystical use of food strengthened rather than weakened the sense of an obligation to share it with the needy. Those who have seen the broken bread as a symbol of God's unity with men and women should be the last to ignore its importance as food for the hungry. The ever-practical James does not hesitate to state the obvious: for a hungry person, a pious word is no substitute for a loaf of bread.

Our greatest problem with food is that too many have too little. The maldistribution of food is probably greater now than it has ever been; it is certainly better known than it has ever been. The hungry now know that people in other parts of the world have plenty of food. The well-fed now know that people in other parts of the world are starving. The hungry will not, and the well-fed must not, ignore the disparity. Compared with this problem and with the necessity of finding political and economic ways of solving it, the dietetic laws of the various religions seem a trifling subject.

But the political and economic measures that are called for need motivation. Only some strong moral compulsion will bring enough resources to bear on the subject to resolve it peaceably. On this point, religion is relevant. The Bible sees food as both a bodily fuel and a spiritual sacrament. Mentioning the second of these may seem like a digression from the immediate problem. But the Bible often digresses from an immediate problem, soars into the transcendent, then bounces back to the original target from a great height and with great force. In both Testaments the concern for feeding the hungry is linked with the sacramental use of food.

Food is in fact a means of communication. We use it to say things to one another. The setting can be an ordinary family meal, or a formal dinner party, or a religious sacrament, or a national festival such as Thankgsiving. As a means of communication food often speaks louder than words. If it were equitably distributed throughout the world it would say something loud and clear—something that will never be heard if it is said in words alone.

But those who would use food as a means of communicating their goodwill must listen to this language as well as speak it. The Bible insists that we misunderstand the medium if our own hearts are not touched with a sense of gratitude. To think of food only as something we have earned or grown—or, worse, to think of it as something that has its origin in packets and tins at the supermarket—is to be deaf to its meaning. We are to think of it always as a gift—one that comes to us from a transcendent source through the mysterious and beautiful processes of organic growth.

FOOD

OLD TESTAMENT

Exodus 12:1–8

1 And the Lord spake unto Moses and Aaron in the land of Egypt, saying,

2 This month shall be unto you the beginning of months: it shall be the first month of the year to you.

3 Speak ye unto all the congregation of Israel, saying, In the tenth day of this month they shall take to them every man a lamb, according to the house of their fathers, a lamb for an house:

4 And if the household be too little for the lamb, let him and his neighbour next unto his house take it according to the number of the souls; every man according to his eating shall make your count for the lamb.

5 Your lamb shall be without blemish, a male of the first year: ye shall take it out from the sheep, or from the goats:

6 And ye shall keep it up until the fourteenth day of the same month: and the whole assembly of the congregation of Israel shall kill it in the evening.

7 And they shall take of the blood, and strike it on the two side posts and on the upper door post of the houses, wherein they shall eat it.

8 And they shall eat the flesh in that night, roast with fire, and unleav-

ened bread; and with bitter herbs they shall eat it.

Deuteronomy 24:19–21 and 26:1–4

19 When thou cuttest down thine harvest in thy field, and hast forgot a sheaf in the field, thou shalt not go again to fetch it: it shall be for the stranger, for the fatherless, and for the widow: that the Lord thy God may bless thee in all the work of thine hands.

20 When thou beatest thine olive tree, thou shalt not go over the boughs again: it shall be for the stranger, for the fatherless, and for the widow.

21 When thou gatherest the grapes of thy vineyard, thou shalt not glean it afterward: it shall be for the stranger, for the fatherless, and for the widow.

1 And it shall be, when thou art come in unto the land which the Lord thy God giveth thee for an inheritance, and possessest it, and dwellest therein;

2 That thou shalt take of the first of all the fruit of the earth, which thou shalt bring of thy land that the Lord thy God giveth thee, and shalt put it in a basket, and shalt go unto the place which the Lord thy God shall choose to place his name there.

3 And thou shalt go unto the priest that shall be in those days, and say unto him, I profess this day unto the Lord thy God, that I am come unto the country which the Lord sware unto our fathers for to give us.

4 And the priest shall take the basket out of thine hand, and set it down before the altar of the Lord thy God.

NEW TESTAMENT

Matthew 6:11 (from the Lord's Prayer)

11 Give us this day our daily bread.

Matthew 14:15–21

15 And when it was evening, his disciples came to him, saying, This is a desert place, and the time is now past; send the multitude away, that they may go into the villages, and buy themselves victuals.

16 But Jesus said unto them, They need not depart; give ye them to eat.

17 And they said unto him, We have here but five loaves, and two fishes.

18 He said, Bring them hither to me.

19 And he commanded the multitude to sit down on the grass, and took the five loaves, and the two fishes, and looking up to heaven, he blessed, and brake, and gave the loaves to his disciples, and the disciples to the multitude.

20 And they did all eat, and were filled: and they took up of the fragments that remained twelve baskets full.

21 And they that had eaten were about five thousand men, beside women and children.

Mark 14:22–24 (in Jerusalem on the night of Jesus' betrayal)

22 And as they did eat, Jesus took bread, and blessed, and brake it, and gave to them, and said, Take, eat: this is my body.

23 And he took the cup, and when

he had given thanks, he gave it to them: and they all drank of it.

24 And he said unto them, This is my blood of the new testament, which is shed for many.

Luke 24:30–31 (the risen Jesus with two disciples at Emmaus)

30 And it came to pass, as he sat at meat with them, he took bread, and blessed it, and brake, and gave to them.

31 And their eyes were opened, and they knew him.

James 2:15–16

15 If a brother or sister be naked, and destitute of daily food,

16 And one of you say unto them, Depart in peace, be ye warmed and filled; notwithstanding ye give them not those things which are needful to the body; what doth it profit?

FORGIVENESS

Forgiveness between one human being and another is not exactly an Old Testament rule, but the laws of jubilee provided for a periodic canceling of debts and obligations, and a forgiving spirit was nourished by stories of great and generous acts of pardon. Joseph, for instance, revealing himself to his brothers who had sold him into slavery, pardons them with what has been called a magnificent lie: "it was not you who sent me hither."

According to the Old Testament, forgiveness is always from God to man. It was to be sought in prescribed ways at prescribed places, especially in the temple at Jerusalem. The prayer that Solomon offers at the consecration of that temple approaches God in measured cadences that climb humbly toward God until at last Solomon feels able actually to ask something, and then—in what perhaps seems an unexpected climax to modern ears—it is contained in the single word "forgive."

The indispensable condition for divine forgiveness was, however, not the sacrifice or the ritual or the prayer in itself, but the penitence that it expressed. This was the emphasis of the prophets and the psalmists. Significantly they discovered that God's readiness to forgive increases rather than diminishes his awesomeness.

Jesus makes our forgiveness of one another inseparable from God's forgiveness of us. In his parable of the unforgiving servant (see Mercy) he hits at the human preference for a selective application of forgiveness: mercy for me, justice for him. Far from allowing this separation of divine forgiveness from human, Jesus even suggested that if a choice must be made, then reconciliation with a fellow human being has priority over reconciliation with God: "First be reconciled to thy brother, and then come and offer thy gift" at the altar (Matthew 5:24). He also used a rabbinic Hebrew phrase meaning "without limit" when asked how often forgiveness was to be granted.

In act as well as word Jesus linked forgiveness with health—that is, with wholeness in every sense. The New Testament belief is that the refusal of forgiveness creates a deep rift in the human spirit and that many forms of disease follow. After his death the followers of Jesus believed that this rift had been healed at the deepest level and that their identification with the suffering, dying Jesus had both expressed their penitence and secured their pardon.

Forgiveness is not indifference to wrongdoing. Least of all is it indifference to the wrongs of which others are the victims. Nobody may ignore the oppression of a neighbor on the ground that the oppressor has to be forgiven. On the contrary, forgiveness implies deep sensitivity to all forms of wrong. But instead of just being hurt by them, it reaches out in an active spirit of reconciliation to the wrongdoer, to the victim, and to the consequences of the wrong that has been done (see Reconciliation). This action is in harmony with the laws of life, though it is often contrary to human inclination.

So many wrongs have been done in the world that life is a logjam that only forgiveness can release. The psychological equivalents of dynamite (denunciation, condemnation, righteous indignation, and so on) can splinter some of the logs and change the pattern of the jam, but a jam it will remain. There is no way by which the tangle of overlapping moral demands and complaints can be resolved without the giving and receiving of forgiveness.

And within the logjam all of us carry not only the burden of particular offenses against our neighbor but a general sense of guilt about not being what we were meant to be. Whether forgiveness is built into the design of the universe is a question that matters deeply to everyone, no matter how few of us ask it openly or explicitly.

FORGIVENESS

OLD TESTAMENT

Genesis 45:4–5, 8

4 And Joseph said unto his brethren, Come near to me, I pray you. And they came near. And he said, I am Joseph your brother, whom ye sold into Egypt.

5 Now therefore be not grieved, nor angry with yourselves, that ye sold me hither: for God did send me before you. . . .

8 So now it was not you that sent me hither, but God.

2 Chronicles 6:18–21 (Solomon dedicates the Temple)

18 But will God in very deed dwell with men on the earth? behold, heaven and the heaven of heavens cannot contain thee; how much less this house which I have built!

19 Have respect therefore to the prayer of thy servant, and to his sup-

plication, O Lord my God, to hearken unto the cry and the prayer which thy servant prayeth before thee:

20 That thine eyes may be open upon this house day and night, upon the place whereof thou hast said that thou wouldest put thy name there; to hearken unto the prayer which thy servant prayeth toward this place.

21 Hearken therefore unto the supplications of thy servant, and of thy people Israel, which they shall make toward this place: hear thou from thy dwelling place, even from heaven; and when thou hearest, forgive.

Isaiah 55:7

7 Let the wicked forsake his way, and the unrighteous man his thoughts: and let him return unto the Lord, and he will have mercy upon him; and to our God, for he will abundantly pardon.

Psalm 51:16–17

For thou desirest not sacrifice; else would
  I give it:
Thou delightest not in burnt offering.
The sacrifices of God are a broken spirit:
A broken and a contrite heart, O God,
  thou wilt not despise.

Psalm 130:3–4

If thou, Lord, shouldest mark iniquities,
O Lord, who shall stand?
But there is forgiveness with thee,
That thou mayest be feared.

NEW TESTAMENT

Matthew 6:12, 14–15

12 And forgive us our debts, as we forgive our debtors.

14 For if ye forgive men their trespasses, your heavenly Father will also forgive you:

15 But if ye forgive not men their trespasses, neither will your Father forgive your trespasses.

Matthew 9:2–7

2 And, behold, they brought to him a man sick of the palsy, lying on a bed: and Jesus seeing their faith said unto the sick of the palsy; Son, be of good cheer; thy sins be forgiven thee.

3 And, behold, certain of the scribes said within themselves, This man blasphemeth.

4 And Jesus knowing their thoughts said, Wherefore think ye evil in your hearts?

5 For whether is easier, to say, Thy sins be forgiven thee; or to say, Arise, and walk?

6 But that ye may know that the Son of man hath power on earth to forgive sins, (then saith he to the sick of the palsy,) Arise, take up thy bed, and go unto thine house.

7 And he arose, and departed to his house.

Luke 23:33–34

33 And when they were come to the place, which is called Calvary, there they crucified him, and the malefactors, one on the right hand, and the other on the left.

34 Then said Jesus, Father, forgive them; for they know not what they do.

Ephesians 4:31–32

31 Let all bitterness, and wrath, and anger, and clamour, and evil speak-

ing, be put away from you, with all malice:

32 And be ye kind one to another, tenderhearted, forgiving one another, even as God for Christ's sake hath forgiven you.

Colossians 3:13

13 Forbearing one another, and forgiving one another, if any man have a quarrel against any: even as Christ forgave you, so also do ye.

FREEDOM

The Old Testament is dominated by the idea that God has redeemed his people from slavery in Egypt. That they should be free both as a nationality and as individuals was the natural consequence of their special history, though their freedom was always conditional upon their living within God's law.

Yet the Old Testament was not wholly against slavery. Foreign slaves were permitted, but fellow Israelites could be kept in servitude only for a limited period, unless they voluntarily renounced their right to go free. Bondage, however, always seemed something of an anomaly. It was an interim arrangement and an unsatisfactory one. Full freedom was the goal toward which the prophets saw Israel moving. They saw some sad experiences of captivity standing between Israel and freedom, but this seemed to deepen not only their love of freedom but their understanding of it as well.

The later prophets spoke of freedom in a more inward sense than is contained in the mere absence of external restraints. Freedom was not just a matter of liberating slaves or of achieving national independence. It involved being free of every kind of oppression and handicap, being free of all that restricts and inhibits human life.

This emphasis was explicitly endorsed by Jesus in his home synagogue. He read aloud a passage from Isaiah 61 which spoke of deliverance from poverty, captivity, blindness, and oppression. "Today," he said, "this prophecy is fulfilled." At an outward and political level the prophecy was not fulfilled. Inwardly and in principle, however, it was. The outward consequences would follow.

For Jesus, however, freedom means freedom only within the will of God. It is the truth that liberates. We are free to be what we truly are. It would make no sense to speak of our being free to be what we were neither made nor meant to be.

His followers affirmed their inward liberty as a matter of experience. Institutions such as slavery remained, and Christians were at the time in no position to end them. By undermining slavery in principle and in personal relationships, however, they prepared the way for its destruction. The more serious threats to their spiritual liberty came from two opposite sides: license and legalism. Some used their spiritual freedom as an excuse for permissiveness, and some used it as an opportunity to devise whole new sets of rules and regulations. Both had mistaken the nature of true freedom.

Freedom is, indeed, an easily misunderstood concept. It does not involve unconditional self-determination, since men and women are not free to choose just anything. They cannot, for instance, choose to be all flesh or all spirit, all animal or all angel. That simply is not what they are. It is contrary to the truth that sets them free.

Nor are people necessarily free just because they live in a democracy and have the right to vote. Such liberties are of great importance. We must condemn every restraint on people's freedom to be what they are and to play a responsible part in the community to which they belong. But from a biblical point of view it is naive to assume that within certain geographical frontiers men and women are free, while beyond them they are not. People can be in bondage to social habits, market forces, evil influences, or mere ignorance and sloth. "The condition upon which God hath given liberty to man is eternal vigilance," said John Curran in 1790. And it is vigilance on many fronts.

There is even a sense in which our full freedom demands that we accept some commitments and restraints. After all, it is our nature to live in community. We cannot be truly free outside it. But to live in community involves some curbing of our individual right to do as we please. And "freedom under the law" can be seen as an image of a greater freedom within the rule of God.

FREEDOM

OLD TESTAMENT

Deuteronomy 15:12–17

12 And if thy brother, an Hebrew man, or an Hebrew woman, be sold unto thee, and serve thee six years; then in the seventh year thou shalt let him go free from thee.

13 And when thou sendest him out free from thee, thou shalt not let him go away empty:

14 Thou shalt furnish him liberally out of thy flock, and out of thy floor, and out of thy winepress: of that wherewith the Lord thy God hath blessed thee thou shalt give unto him.

15 And thou shalt remember that thou wast a bondman in the land of Egypt, and the Lord thy God redeemed thee: therefore I command thee this thing to-day.

16 And it shall be, if he say unto thee, I will not go away from thee; because he loveth thee and thine house, because he is well with thee;

17 Then thou shalt take an awl, and thrust it through his ear unto the door, and he shall be thy servant for ever.

And also unto thy maidservant thou shalt do likewise.

Jeremiah 34:8–17

8 This is the word that came unto Jeremiah from the Lord, after that the king Zedekiah had made a covenant with all the people which were at Jerusalem, to proclaim liberty unto them;

9 That every man should let his manservant, and every man his maidservant, being an Hebrew or an Hebrewess, go free; that none should serve himself of them, to wit, of a Jew his brother.

10 Now when all the princes, and all the people, which had entered into the covenant, heard that every one should let his manservant, and every one his maidservant, go free, that none should serve themselves of them any more, then they obeyed, and let them go.

11 But afterward they turned, and caused the servants and the handmaids, whom they had let go free, to return, and brought them into subjection for servants and for handmaids.

12 Therefore the word of the Lord came to Jeremiah from the Lord, saying,

13 Thus saith the Lord, the God of Israel; I made a covenant with your fathers in the day that I brought them forth out of the land of Egypt, out of the house of bondmen, saying,

14 At the end of seven years let ye go every man his brother an Hebrew, which hath been sold unto thee; and when he hath served thee six years, thou shalt let him go free from thee:

but your fathers hearkened not unto me, neither inclined their ear.

15 And ye were now turned, and had done right in my sight, in proclaiming liberty every man to his neighbour; and ye had made a covenant before me in the house which is called by my name:

16 But ye turned and polluted my name, and caused every man his servant, and every man his handmaid, whom ye had set at liberty at their pleasure, to return, and brought them into subjection, to be unto you for servants and for handmaids.

17 Therefore thus saith the Lord: Ye have not hearkened unto me, in proclaiming liberty, every one to his brother, and every man to his neighbour: behold, I proclaim a liberty for you, saith the Lord, to the sword, to the pestilence, and to the famine.

NEW TESTAMENT

Luke 4:16–21

16 And he came to Nazareth, where he had been brought up: and, as his custom was, he went into the synagogue on the sabbath day, and stood up for to read.

17 And there was delivered unto him the book of the prophet Esaias. And when he had opened the book, he found the place where it was written,

18 The Spirit of the Lord is upon me, because he hath anointed me to preach the gospel to the poor; he hath sent me to heal the brokenhearted, to preach deliverance to the captives, and

121

recovering of sight to the blind, to set at liberty them that are bruised,

19 To preach the acceptable year of the Lord.

20 And he closed the book, and he gave it again to the minister, and sat down. And the eyes of all them that were in the synagogue were fastened on him.

21 And he began to say unto them, This day is this scripture fulfilled in your ears.

John 8:31–36

31 Then said Jesus to those Jews which believed on him, If ye continue in my word, then are ye my disciples indeed;

32 And ye shall know the truth, and the truth shall make you free.

33 They answered him, We be Abraham's seed, and were never in bondage to any man: how sayest thou, Ye shall be made free?

34 Jesus answered them, Verily, verily, I say unto you, Whosoever committeth sin is the servant of sin.

35 And the servant abideth not in the house for ever: but the Son abideth ever.

36 If the Son therefore shall make you free, ye shall be free indeed.

Galatians 3:28; 5:1, 13

28 There is neither Jew nor Greek, there is neither bond nor free, there is neither male nor female: for ye are all one in Christ Jesus.

1 Stand fast therefore in the liberty wherewith Christ hath made us free, and be not entangled again with the yoke of bondage.

13 Only use not liberty for an occasion to the flesh, but by love serve one another.

FRIENDSHIP

The Old Testament recognizes that friendship can be the most exalted of relationships. It speaks of Abraham as God's friend. It could not rank him higher without idolatry. Yet friendly feelings do not ensure that everything is as it should be. The Book of Proverbs says many shrewd and by no means starry-eyed things about friendship. Haman's friends only inflame his vanity and persuade him to erect the scaffold on which he himself will eventually perish. Friendship has to be a common sharing in what is good; otherwise it may just provide reinforcement for what is bad.

The Old Testament probably says most about true friendship when it is simply describing the friendships between its leading characters. Most notable is the friendship between David and Jonathan. This friendship is threatened by their being potential rivals for the kingship of Israel, but that threat is brushed aside by the strength of what they have in common: a shared life of danger and the shared values of religious patriotism.

The New Testament continues the idea of friendship grounded in a common enterprise. In John's Gospel, Jesus uses the word "friends" to describe his relationship with his followers. The word emphasizes that their role in his enterprise is a responsible one. It is a relationship of love and may be expressed in the laying down of life. That willingness to die vicariously is the measure of true friendship. False friendship, it is recognized, far from leading to the offering of life, may still lead to the taking of it.

Jesus was often criticized for not being sufficiently selective in his friendships— "a friend of publicans and sinners," they said. But he himself taught that personal relationships and hospitality should be extended far beyond the conventional limits, and far beyond the limits of reciprocity. After his death the followers of Jesus found themselves impelled in this direction. The logic of their faith compelled them to enter homes and friendship circles that they had once believed to be closed to them on religious grounds.

In many parts of the world the shrinking of the family circle has increased the importance of friendship. When people lived in an extended family of brothers, sisters, cousins, aunts, uncles, and the rest, a variety of relationships was built into their experience at all times. A family unit consisting only of one couple and their (often few) children carries a much greater weight of potential isolation and loneliness. In this situation a variety of friendships is needed to bring out the different facets of every individual's character.

But the need for friendship does not automatically provide the opportunity to make friends. Friendship forms around some nucleus of common experience or values. C. S. Lewis says that this is the reason why "those pathetic people who simply 'want friends' can never make any. . . . There would be nothing for the friendship to be *about*; and friendship must be about something."

In the biblical vision of life there is plenty for friendship to be about. Perhaps we have expected friendship to arise too easily from merely living in the same area, or having the same kind of house, or appearing to lead the same kind of life. That is not what friendship is about. Still less is it about belonging to the same social class or the same ethnic group. These are just the distinctions that the New Testament wants friendship to transcend. It needs to reach much wider and deeper. It arises most naturally between those who are exploring in the same direction in hope of finding the good life. "But there again," the Bible says in effect, "the friends will need the right idea of 'the good.' "

FRIENDSHIP

OLD TESTAMENT

Isaiah 41:8 (God addresses his people)

8 But thou, Israel, art my servant, Jacob whom I have chosen, the seed of Abraham my friend.

Proverbs 17:17; 18:24; 19:4

A friend loveth at all times,
And a brother is born for adversity.

A man that hath friends must shew himself friendly:
And there is a friend that sticketh closer than a brother.

Wealth maketh many friends;
But the poor is separated from his neighbor.

Esther 5:9–14

9 Then went Haman forth that day joyful and with a glad heart: but when Haman saw Mordecai in the king's gate, that he stood not up, nor moved for him, he was full of indignation against Mordecai.

10 Nevertheless Haman refrained himself: and when he came home, he sent and called for his friends, and Zeresh his wife.

11 And Haman told them of the glory of his riches, and the multitude of his children, and all the things wherein the king had promoted him, and how he had advanced him above the princes and servants of the king.

12 Haman said moreover, Yea, Esther the queen did let no man come in with the king unto the banquet that she had prepared but myself; and to-morrow am I invited unto her also with the king.

13 Yet all this availeth me nothing, so long as I see Mordecai the Jew sitting at the king's gate.

14 Then said Zeresh his wife and all his friends unto him, Let a gallows be made of fifty cubits high, and to-morrow speak thou unto the king that Mordecai may be hanged thereon: then go thou in merrily with the king unto the banquet. And the thing pleased Haman; and he caused the gallows to be made.

1 Samuel 18:1, 3–4

1 The soul of Jonathan was knit with the soul of David, and Jonathan loved him as his own soul.

3 Then Jonathan and David made a covenant, because he loved him as his own soul.

4 And Jonathan stripped himself of the robe that was upon him, and gave it to David, and his garments, even to his sword, and to his bow, and to his girdle.

2 Samuel 1:26 (David's lament on Jonathan's death)

26 I am distressed for thee, my brother Jonathan: very pleasant hast thou been unto me: thy love to me was wonderful, passing the love of women.

NEW TESTAMENT

John 15:12–15

12 This is my commandment, That

ye love one another, as I have loved you.

13 Greater love hath no man than this, that a man lay down his life for his friends.

14 Ye are my friends, if ye do whatsoever I command you.

15 Henceforth I call you not servants; for the servant knoweth not what his lord doeth: but I have called you friends; for all things that I have heard of my Father I have made known unto you.

Luke 14:12–14

12 Then said he also to him that bade him, When thou makest a dinner or a supper, call not thy friends, nor thy brethren, neither thy kinsmen, nor thy rich neighbours; lest they also bid thee again, and a recompence be made thee.

13 But when thou makest a feast, call the poor, the maimed, the lame, the blind:

14 And thou shalt be blessed; for they cannot recompense thee: for thou shalt be recompensed at the resurrection of the just.

Luke 21:16 (Jesus warns his disciples)

16 And ye shall be betrayed both by parents, and brethren, and kinsfolks, and friends; and some of you shall they cause to be put to death.

Acts 10:24–29

24 And the morrow after they entered into Cæsarea. And Cornelius waited for them, and had called together his kinsmen and near friends.

25 And as Peter was coming in, Cornelius met him, and fell down at his feet, and worshipped him.

26 But Peter took him up, saying, Stand up; I myself also am a man.

27 And as he talked with him, he went in, and found many that were come together.

28 And he said unto them, Ye know how that it is an unlawful thing for a man that is a Jew to keep company, or come unto one of another nation; but God hath shewed me that I should not call any man common or unclean.

29 Therefore came I unto you without gainsaying, as soon as I was sent for.

FUTURE

The Bible is a very future-oriented book. The Golden Age of the Greek imagination may have been in the past, but the Hebrew equivalent was in the future. Almost from the beginning the Old Testament points forward—forward to a promised land yet to be possessed, or beyond that to an age yet to dawn when a new world order will be established with Jerusalem as its center, the Lord as its God, and his anointed (his Messiah, his Israel) as the instrument of universal justice and peace.

The optimism of this last vision as it is presented by Isaiah and by other prophets is, however, challenged in two ways. There are those such as "the Teacher" of Ecclesiastes who can see no profit in expecting the future to be any different from the past. It could be argued that the author of Ecclesiastes was thinking of the ordinary tomorrow that arises from yesterday, whereas the prophets were speaking of a transcendent tomorrow brought about by the intervention of God, but there remains the difference between facing forward with expectation and without it.

The other challenge to optimism was harder to deal with and was made by the prophets themselves: Certainly the day of the Lord is coming, said some, but what right have you to suppose that you are fit for it or will enjoy it?

In the earliest of the New Testament Gospels (Mark) the first reported words of Jesus are "The time is fulfilled." The New Testament position is that the day of the Lord has come, but that its consummation will be delayed until people have had a chance to adjust themselves to it. Paul speaks (1 Corinthians 10:11) of his own generation as those "upon whom the ends of the world have come." Another translation is "upon whom the end [or ends] of the ages" has come. In other words, the people of Paul's time are living in both the ordinary time of Ecclesiastes and the transcended time of Isaiah. The two ages overlap.

So they do in John's Gospel. Jesus *is* the resurrection and the life. The age to come has come, the kingdom is present, the promised future is now.

Yet the consummation is still to be looked for with hope and longing. It is real but not yet manifest. Its ultimate manifestation cannot be envisaged or described in literal terms because it transcends all the experiences by which human minds and human language have been formed. The last book of the Bible and the so-called apocalyptic passages in the Gospels use traditional symbols to speak of this consummation, but the New Testament letter writers are content much of the time just to say that Christ himself is the measure of the fulfillment to which we aspire.

If our future is annihilation, there is a certain logic in the principle "Let us eat, drink, and be merry for tomorrow we die." If, on the contrary, the future life is all that matters, then there is a certain logic in saying, "Never mind what happened today; it's unimportant." A future that is not a black hole and yet does make the present significant is a very different possibility from either of these.

The Bible's enthusiasm for the future is never at the expense of the present. It does not offer pie in the sky when you die as a palliative for present deprivation or past injustice. It does the very opposite: instead of making the present insignificant, it gives today the value of eternity. Marxism also claims to be a future-oriented faith that makes the present significant, but to the Marxist every year that passes presumably shows the gap between struggle and fulfillment to be that much wider. The Christian fulfillment is both present (in the transcendent dimension) and future (in the historical dimension).

The biblical use of such words as "fullness" and "fulfillment" suggests that the future is best faced with some sense of the direction that is truly forward (see Progress) and that this sense of direction can best be derived not from crude materialism or from secular utopianism but from an understanding and foretaste of the fullness of life.

FUTURE

OLD TESTAMENT

Genesis 13:14–17

14 And the Lord said unto Abram, after that Lot was separated from him, Lift up now thine eyes, and look from the place where thou art northward, and southward, and eastward, and westward:

15 For all the land which thou seest, to thee will I give it, and to thy seed for ever.

16 And I will make thy seed as the dust of the earth: so that if a man can number the dust of the earth, then shall thy seed also be numbered.

17 Arise, walk through the land in the length of it and in the breadth of it; for I will give it unto thee.

Isaiah 2:2; 11:1–2, 9–10

2 And it shall come to pass in the last days, that the mountain of the Lord's house shall be established in the top of the mountains, and shall be exalted above the hills; and all nations shall flow unto it.

1 And there shall come forth a rod out of the stem of Jesse, and a Branch shall grow out of his roots:

2 And the spirit of the Lord shall rest upon him, the spirit of wisdom and understanding, the spirit of coun-

sel and might, the spirit of knowledge and of the fear of the Lord.

9 They shall not hurt nor destroy in all my holy mountain: for the earth shall be full of the knowledge of the Lord, as the waters cover the sea.

10 And in that day there shall be a root of Jesse, which shall stand for an ensign of the people; to it shall the Gentiles seek: and his rest shall be glorious.

Ecclesiastes 1:9

9 The thing that hath been, it is that which shall be; and that which is done is that which shall be done: and there is no new thing under the sun.

Malachi 3:1–2

1 And the Lord, whom ye seek, shall suddenly come to his temple, even the messenger of the covenant, whom ye delight in: behold, he shall come, saith the Lord of hosts.

2 But who may abide the day of his coming? and who shall stand when he appeareth?

NEW TESTAMENT

Luke 17:20–21; 21:25–28

20 And when he was demanded of the Pharisees, when the kingdom of

God should come, he answered them and said, The kingdom of God cometh not with observation:

21 Neither shall they say, Lo here! or, lo there! for, behold, the kingdom of God is within you.

25 And there shall be signs in the sun, and in the moon, and in the stars; and upon the earth distress of nations, with perplexity; the sea and the waves roaring;

26 Men's hearts failing them for fear, and for looking after those things which are coming on the earth: for the powers of heaven shall be shaken.

27 And then shall they see the Son of man coming in a cloud with power and great glory.

28 And when these things begin to come to pass, then look up, and lift up your heads; for your redemption draweth nigh.

1 Corinthians 15:22–24

22 For as in Adam all die, even so in Christ shall all be made alive.

23 But every man in his own order: Christ the firstfruits; afterward they that are Christ's at his coming.

24 Then cometh the end, when he shall have delivered up the kingdom to God, even the Father.

Colossians 1:19–20 (the ultimate supremacy of Christ)

19 For it pleased the Father that in him should all fulness dwell;

20 And, having made peace through the blood of his cross, by him to reconcile all things unto himself; by him, I say, whether they be things in earth, or things in heaven.

Revelation 21:1–4

1 And I saw a new heaven and a new earth: for the first heaven and the first earth were passed away; and there was no more sea.

2 And I John saw the holy city, new Jerusalem, coming down from God out of heaven, prepared as a bride adorned for her husband.

3 And I heard a great voice out of heaven saying, Behold, the tabernacle of God is with men, and he will dwell with them, and they shall be his people, and God himself shall be with them, and be their God.

4 And God shall wipe away all tears from their eyes; and there shall be no more death, neither sorrow, nor crying, neither shall there be any more pain: for the former things are passed away.

GENTLENESS

The Old Testament emphasizes the power and even the wrath of God, but not at the expense of his gentleness. One picture of this is provided by the shepherd. In pastoral Israel this would be no sentimental image. Sheep and their ways were too well known to be romanticized. So were shepherds. But the shepherd could not maintain his authority over his flock by roughness. That way he would lose lambs. God's concern for his people was said to be like that of a gentle shepherd.

Other symbols of divine gentleness were also used—that of the parent, for instance:

> Like as a father pitieth his children,
>   so the Lord pitieth them that fear him.
> For he knoweth our frame;
>   he remembereth that we are dust.
>   (Psalm 103:13)

Inevitably such images set a standard that men and women knew they should adopt in their dealings with one another. Psalm 103 would tell a father who had not been compassionate toward his children that he ought to have been: the divine gentleness is normative.

The end of the whole process was symbolized by the vision of a gentle age when wild beasts and children would be at peace with one another—and this was a symbol rather than a realistic expectation. Gentleness is now more than normative: it is the ultimate goal toward which creation moves.

The New Testament continues the shepherd image. Many people reject "gentle Jesus, meek and mild" as a description of the powerful figure who strides through the pages of the Gospels. Those objectors have a point. And yet there is an inescapable tenderness in the picture of Jesus, and it is revealed both in his approach to others (especially, as was unusual at the time, to women and children) and in his response to those who inflicted suffering on him.

Indeed, the tenderness of Jesus stands out strongly against his background and becomes one of the controversial features of his character. He was born when a monster in the person of Herod ruled Judea. He died when an unfeeling despot in the person of Tiberius ruled the Roman Empire and when the local rulers who examined Jesus before he was put to death were Herod's son Antipas (who had himself ordered the execution of Jesus' cousin John) and the cynical Pilate. Under such rulers the popular figures of the time were men who were tough— men like Barabbas. The gentleness of Jesus was a direct challenge to the values of the day. It won enemies as well as admirers.

Yet there emerged from this gentleness a community characterized by a new tenderness between men and women, between adults and children, between servants and masters. Their way of life was the natural product of what they believed about God.

Toughness is a strange quality to be as much in vogue as it is at present in books, in films, and on television—to say nothing of the nonfictional leaders of youth gangs and political factions. Something might be said for strength as a quality to be admired, but toughness has nothing to do with that. Strength, in fact, is more often allied to gentleness, which in turn has nothing to do with weakness. To be gentle is to be sensitive and tender toward the feelings of others. Gentleness is a sign of strength.

The biblical association of gentleness with infinite power gives transcendent authority to a way of approaching other people with a sensitive awareness of what it is like inside their skins and with a strong determination to cause no unnecessary hurt.

GENTLENESS

OLD TESTAMENT

Isaiah 40:10–11

10 Behold, the Lord God will come with strong hand, and his arm shall rule for him: behold, his reward is with him, and his work before him.

11 He shall feed his flock like a shepherd: he shall gather the lambs with his arm, and carry them in his bosom, and shall gently lead those that are with young.

Psalm 23:1–6

The Lord is my shepherd; I shall not want.
He maketh me to lie down in green pastures:
He leadeth me beside the still waters.
He restoreth my soul:
He leadeth me in the paths of righteousness for his name's sake.
Yea, though I walk through the valley of the shadow of death,
I will fear no evil: for thou art with me;
Thy rod and thy staff they comfort me.
Thou preparest a table before me in the presence of mine enemies:
Thou anointest my head with oil; my cup runneth over.
Surely goodness and mercy shall follow me all the days of my life:
And I will dwell in the house of the Lord for ever.

Isaiah 11:6–8

6 The wolf also shall dwell with the lamb, and the leopard shall lie down with the kid; and the calf and the young lion and the fatling together; and a little child shall lead them.

7 And the cow and the bear shall feed; their young ones shall lie down together: and the lion shall eat straw like the ox.

8 And the sucking child shall play on the hole of the asp, and the weaned child shall put his hand on the cockatrice's den.

NEW TESTAMENT

John 10:11–16

11 I am the good shepherd: the good shepherd giveth his life for the sheep.

12 But he that is an hireling, and not the shepherd, whose own the sheep are not, seeth the wolf coming, and leaveth the sheep, and fleeth: and the wolf catcheth them, and scattereth the sheep.

13 The hireling fleeth, because he is an hireling, and careth not for the sheep.

14 I am the good shepherd, and know my sheep, and am known of mine.

15 As the Father knoweth me, even so know I the Father: and I lay down my life for the sheep.

16 And other sheep I have, which are not of this fold: them also I must bring, and they shall hear my voice;

and there shall be one fold, and one shepherd.

Luke 23:18–21

18 And they cried out all at once, saying, Away with this man, and release unto us Barabbas:

19 (Who for a certain sedition made in the city, and for murder, was cast into prison.)

20 Pilate therefore, willing to release Jesus, spake again to them.

21 But they cried, saying, Crucify him, crucify him.

1 Peter 2:20–25

20 If, when ye do well, and suffer for it, ye take it patiently, this is acceptable with God.

21 For even hereunto were ye called: because Christ also suffered for us,

leaving us an example, that ye should follow his steps:

22 Who did no sin, neither was guile found in his mouth:

23 Who, when he was reviled, reviled not again; when he suffered, he threatened not; but committed himself to him that judgeth righteously:

24 Who his own self bare our sins in his own body on the tree, that we, being dead to sins, should live unto righteousness: by whose stripes ye were healed.

25 For ye were as sheep going astray; but are now returned unto the Shepherd and Bishop of your souls.

Titus 3:1–2

1 Put them in mind . . .

2 To speak evil of no man, to be no brawlers, but gentle, shewing all meekness unto all men.

GIVING

Jacob had reason enough to expect a frosty reception from his twin brother, Esau (see Blessing). When their nomadic paths were about to cross, Jacob began by thinking of gifts as sweeteners. These gifts were designed, with much skill in presentation, to secure him a favorable reception. Esau's waiving of any claim to them may have been no more than a gesture demanded by the courtesies of the time, but it was an important courtesy. It made the giving voluntary. It changed the presents from bribes into true gifts. They became the outward expression of a reconciliation between brothers.

This is the standard attitude of the Old Testament. Gifts are not to be bribes. They must be voluntary. They must provide a link between person and person, not just between purse and purse.

So it is with giving to God. What was done at the altar (see Sacrifice) was thought of as a way of bringing gifts to God, but the Old Testament makes clear that unless the giving is right in spirit, the gift is valueless to him. Indeed, the spirit of giving is all that is really given, since everything on earth is already

God's. Moreover, the sacrificial animal had to be unblemished because only something perfect of its kind could symbolize the link between man and God.

The New Testament's emphasis is on giving as grace—that is, as an act of pure generosity by one who is under no obligation to give at all (a characteristic of God in both Testaments). Jesus as a child is greeted with such gifts, and as a man he taught that everything is to be received as a child receives gifts. Nothing—from the flowers of the field to the forgiveness of sins and the life of the king-dom—is to be thought of as merited, earned, or bargained for.

It followed that openhanded giving had to be a way of life for those who themselves were the recipients of grace. Giving, though unconditional, is natu-rally reciprocal: "Give and it shall be given unto you; good measure, pressed down, shaken together and running over" (Luke 6:38).

All New Testament writers seem concerned with widening the significance of the gift: it always meant more than it was in itself. Paul was much involved in collecting money for the impoverished church of Jerusalem. He directed his appeal to the distant churches among which he himself worked. The tangible size of the gift mattered to him, but never as much as the significance of the giving. It was a symbol of self-giving at the donor's end, and a symbol of fellow-ship at the receiver's end. More than that, it linked them not only with each other but with God. "Every good and perfect gift," said James in another context, "is from above."

Great churches and cathedrals have been built with the "gifts" of those who thought they were buying the salvation of their souls, but we have to get rid of the whole idea of religious practices as bribes or insurance policies. And, as so often happens, this religious principle has some very practical, secular applications.

Even among friends and relatives some giving is little more than bartering. The Christmas gift whose value has been carefully calculated to equal that of the one expected from its recipient is in itself hardly a gift at all; it is more of a trade. The giving is limited to the effort that has gone into finding a present which will be appreciated by the receiver and is well matched to the giver. The cant phrase, "It's the thought that counts," is not silly. Certainly cash values have little to do with the value of a gift.

What is true at the interpersonal level is also true at the international level. An aid program that is always looking for a quid pro quo is only a bargain wearing the mask of piety. At the same time, a giving that is all one-sided can be humil-iating. Every act of generosity has to open up a relationship that is reciprocal. The gifts exchanged may not be equal in cash value, but cash terms may have to be set aside in order to achieve a deeper reciprocity that is real and equal.

GIVING

OLD TESTAMENT

Genesis 32:13–20; 33:4–5, 8–11

13 And he lodged there that same night; and took of that which came to his hand a present for Esau his brother;

14 Two hundred she goats, and twenty he goats, two hundred ewes, and twenty rams,

15 Thirty milch camels with their colts, forty kine, and ten bulls, twenty she asses, and ten foals.

16 And he delivered them into the hand of his servants, every drove by themselves; and said unto his servants, Pass over before me, and put a space betwixt drove and drove.

17 And he commanded the foremost, saying, When Esau my brother meeteth thee, and asketh thee, saying, Whose art thou? and whither goest thou? and whose are these before thee?

18 Then thou shalt say, They be thy servant Jacob's; it is a present sent unto my lord Esau: and, behold, he is behind us.

19 And so commanded he the second, and the third, and all that followed the droves, saying, On this manner shall ye speak unto Esau, when ye find him.

20 And say ye moreover, Behold, thy servant Jacob is behind us. For he said, I will appease him with the present that goeth before me, and afterward I will see his face; peradventure he will accept of me.

4 And Esau ran to meet him, and embraced him, and fell on his neck, and kissed him: and they wept.

5 And he lifted up his eyes, and saw the women and the children; and said, Who are those with thee? And he said, The children which God hath graciously given thy servant.

8 And he said, What meanest thou by all this drove which I met? And he said, These are to find grace in the sight of my lord.

9 And Esau said, I have enough, my brother; keep that thou hast unto thyself.

10 And Jacob said, Nay, I pray thee, if now I have found grace in thy sight, then receive my present at my hand: for therefore I have seen thy face, as though I had seen the face of God, and thou wast pleased with me.

11 Take, I pray thee, my blessing that is brought to thee; because God hath dealt graciously with me, and because I have enough. And he urged him, and he took it.

Malachi 1:8

8 And if ye offer the blind for sacrifice, is it not evil? and if ye offer the lame and sick, is it not evil? offer it now unto thy governor; will he be pleased with thee, or accept thy person? saith the Lord of hosts.

NEW TESTAMENT

Matthew 2:1, 11

1 Now when Jesus was born in Bethlehem of Judæa in the days of Herod the king, behold, there came wise men from the east to Jerusalem,

11 And when they were come into the house, they saw the young child with Mary his mother, and fell down, and worshipped him: and when they had opened their treasures, they presented unto him gifts; gold, and frankincense, and myrrh.

Matthew 5:42; 10:8

42 Give to him that asketh thee, and from him that would borrow of thee turn not thou away.

8 Freely ye have received, freely give.

Luke 21:1–3

1 And he looked up, and saw the rich men casting their gifts into the treasury.

2 And he saw also a certain poor widow casting in thither two mites.

3 And he said, Of a truth I say unto you, that this poor widow hath cast in more than they all.

Ephesians 2:8

8 For by grace are ye saved through faith; and that not of yourselves: it is the gift of God.

2 Corinthians 8:1–5 (about a relief fund for the poor)

1 Moreover, brethren, we do you to wit of the grace of God bestowed on the churches of Macedonia;

2 How that in a great trial of affliction the abundance of their joy and their deep poverty abounded unto the riches of their liberality.

3 For to their power, I bear record, yea, and beyond their power they were willing of themselves;

4 Praying us with much entreaty that we would receive the gift, and take upon us the fellowship of the ministering to the saints.

5 And this they did, not as we hoped, but first gave their own selves to the Lord, and unto us by the will of God.

James 1:17–18

17 Every good gift and every perfect gift is from above, and cometh down from the Father of lights, with whom is no variableness, neither shadow of turning.

18 Of his own will begat he us with the word of truth, that we should be a kind of firstfruits of his creatures.

GOODNESS

The Old Testament identifies goodness by description rather than by definition. The Book of Proverbs contains poetic descriptions of both the good man and the good woman. There is a touch of Milton's "He for God only, she for God in him," but the picture is a happy one. Its parts fit together in a coherent way. The word "integrity" comes to mind as a synonym for this kind of goodness. Fully integrated with the rest is the relationship of the man and the woman with their God. They are religious, not in some separate sector of their characters, but in their whole being; their entire way of life is adjusted to "He-who-is," to reality itself.

The prophet Micah summed up the nature of goodness with marvelous brevity, but in the Old Testament generally the whole body of God's law is the standard of goodness, since God himself is good and is the source and measure of all goodness. As one of the later rabbis said, "good simply means Torah" (the law).

Jesus endorses this principle in his summary of the law, and he is cool toward those who apply the term "good" flatteringly and without knowledge. In God alone is the certainty of goodness. All goodness is rooted in him, and there is an inevitable correspondence between root and fruit.

Without ever questioning the goodness of divine law, the New Testament tends to transcend all codes and rules of goodness and to speak of it instead as a spontaneous growth rooted in a spirit of love. That is why it can be nourished by contemplation of all that is Christlike.

We use the word "good" in two senses, one moral and the other not. Good behavior is morally virtuous behavior. Good cloth is not morally virtuous cloth, but high-quality cloth. The Bible does the same. God looked at what he had made and saw that it was good (Genesis 1)—that is, qualitatively good. Jesus went about doing good (Acts 10:38)—in other words, being morally good.

The fact that the one word is used in both senses is no accident. Doing right flows from being right in the sense of being sound, well made. To try to get goodness out of us by law, or by moral exhortation, or by punishment, or by social pressure, while paying no attention to what we *are*, is to work against the grain. Goodness goes deep. If you are a good man or a good woman, you have integrity, which means that you are an entire person and that what you are and what you do are all one.

So goodness is not a suit of clothes that you can put on or take off while you yourself remain fundamentally unchanged. Goodness requires a basic orientation toward the good. That is why to *see* good, to contemplate it and love it, can have a more powerful moral effect than any amount of moralizing. It may even produce more goodness spontaneously than a great deal of moral effort produces laboriously. It enthrones goodness in the heart, and from there goodness finds its way out.

Not that moral effort is uncalled for. Once you have a vision of true goodness before you and also a good spirit within you reaching out in love toward that vision, then the striving of the will can be effective. John Wesley's rule stands:

Do all the good you can,
By all the means you can,

In all the ways you can,
In all the places you can,
At all the times you can,
To all the people you can,
As long as ever you can.

GOODNESS

OLD TESTAMENT

Proverbs 2:3, 5, 9, 20

Yea, if thou criest after knowledge,
And liftest up thy voice for understanding;
Then shalt thou understand the fear of the Lord,
And find the knowledge of God.
Then shalt thou understand righteousness, and judgment,
And equity; yea, every good path.
That thou mayest walk in the way of good men,
And keep the paths of the righteous.

Proverbs 31:10–15, 20, 26, 28, 30

Who can find a virtuous woman?
For her price is far above rubies.
The heart of her husband doth safely trust in her,
So that he shall have no need of spoil.
She will do him good and not evil
All the days of her life.
She seeketh wool, and flax,
And worketh willingly with her hands.
She is like the merchants' ships;
She bringeth her food from afar.
She riseth also while it is yet night,
And giveth meat to her household,
And a portion to her maidens.
She stretcheth out her hand to the poor;
Yea, she reacheth forth her hands to the needy.
She openeth her mouth with wisdom;
And in her tongue is the law of kindness.

Her children arise up, and call her blessed;
Her husband also, and he praiseth her.
Favour is deceitful, and beauty is vain:
But a woman that feareth the Lord, she shall be praised.

Psalm 119:65–66, 68

Thou hast dealt well with thy servant,
O Lord, according unto thy word.
Teach me good judgment and knowledge:
For I have believed thy commandments.
Thou art good, and doest good;
Teach me thy statutes.

Micah 6:8

8 He hath shewed thee, O man, what is good; and what doth the Lord require of thee, but to do justly, and to love mercy, and to walk humbly with thy God?

NEW TESTAMENT

Mark 12:28–31

28 And one of the scribes came, and having heard them reasoning together, and perceiving that he had answered them well, asked him, Which is the first commandment of all?

29 And Jesus answered him, The first of all the commandments is, Hear, O Israel; The Lord our God is one Lord:

30 And thou shalt love the Lord thy God with all thy heart, and with all thy soul, and with all thy mind, and with all thy strength: this is the first commandment.

31 And the second is like, namely this, Thou shalt love thy neighbour as thyself. There is none other commandment greater than these.

Mark 10:17–18

17 And when he was gone forth into the way, there came one running, and kneeled to him, and asked him, Good Master, what shall I do that I may inherit eternal life?

18 And Jesus said unto him, Why callest thou me good? there is none good but one, that is, God.

Matthew 7:17–18; 12:33–35

17 Even so every good tree bringeth forth good fruit; but a corrupt tree bringeth forth evil fruit.

18 A good tree cannot bring forth evil fruit, neither can a corrupt tree bring forth good fruit.

33 Either make the tree good, and his fruit good; or else make the tree corrupt, and his fruit corrupt: for the tree is known by his fruit.

34 O generation of vipers, how can ye, being evil, speak good things? for out of the abundance of the heart the mouth speaketh.

35 A good man out of the good treasure of the heart bringeth forth good things: and an evil man out of the evil treasure bringeth forth evil things.

Philippians 4:8

8 Finally, brethren, whatsoever things are true, whatsoever things are honest, whatsoever things are just, whatsoever things are pure, whatsoever things are lovely, whatsoever things are of good report; if there be any virtue, and if there be any praise, think on these things.

GRATITUDE

The Jewish Talmud (a collection of ancient oral laws and traditions) is true to its Old Testament inheritance when it says, "It is forbidden to taste of this world without saying a blessing." And what is to be blessed is the name of God, not the food. Nothing in the world is to be received without thanksgiving. Gratitude takes hold of mere animal gratification and turns it into a means of interpersonal communion between a human being and God.

It goes without saying that a similar spirit of appreciation should exist among human beings, but in the Old Testament that almost literally does go without saying. Its preoccupation is with gratitude to God. To a large extent this is organized through temple rituals and through such things as prescribed grace at meals, but the Psalms make it clear that the range of experiences to be gathered into thanksgiving is far too wide for all of it to be provided for formally. The sensitive Israelite was alive to individual occasions for gratitude as well as to those embodied in the history of the Israelites. Everything from the creation of heaven and earth to the enjoyment of a quiet mind was a taste of the Lord's goodness and was to be acknowledged as such.

The New Testament retains the Old Testament's attitude toward formal thanksgiving but notes that the real gratitude at the heart of a ritual may be less felt by those on the inside of the tradition than by those on the fringe of it—such as the Samaritan leper who was Jewish enough to be sent to a priest to have his cure certified, but non-Jewish enough to be thought of as a foreigner.

At Jesus' last supper the blessings traditionally spoken over bread and wine became the basis of the Christian rite of communion, later to be known as the Eucharist, from the Greek word meaning "gratitude."

In fact, in the New Testament thanksgiving becomes a way of life. Christian obedience is not something given in order to gain blessings; it is something offered out of gratitude for blessings already received and wholly unearned. This is Paul's constant theme. A typical letter from him opens with his thanking God for happy memories of the letter's recipients; Paul's gratitude to them is indistinguishable from his gratitude to God. Then it goes on about grace and the grateful response that should be made to it—in all circumstances, not just when things are going well. Finally it calls on its readers to live and pray their gratitude, to let it shape their relationships with God, with one another, and with all men.

The trouble with ingratitude is not so much the lack of praise for the giver as the lack of appreciation of the gift. To respond with gratitude is to make the whole personality sensitive to the benefit received. Even atheists have been known to wish there were someone to whom to say thank you—on the transcendent scale. Some of them feel the need for a discipline, something akin to prayer, which will keep them sensitive to the fact that we are all receivers of unmerited good. For the believer there is no problem in principle, but the need for discipline remains.

However, where formal thanksgiving is practiced, there is always the danger of formalism. This does not necessarily mean that, for instance, grace is said with no real thought of God. It can mean that grace is said with no real thought of food. Thanksgiving can become too separated from the appreciation of what is being received. The response of gratitude needs to become integrated with the enjoyment of what is given, and both gratitude and enjoyment need to be continuous.

So also with gratitude between people. A child needs to be taught to say thank you not only as a matter of form but also because it enhances both the appreciation of what is received and the child's relationship with the giver. Gratitude makes all life sacramental.

GRATITUDE

OLD TESTAMENT

1 Chronicles 16:4–8

4 And he appointed certain of the Levites to minister before the ark of the Lord, and to record, and to thank and praise the Lord God of Israel:

5 Asaph the chief, and next to him Zechariah, Jeiel, and Shemiramoth, and Jehiel, and Mattithiah, and Eliab, and Benaiah, and Obededom: and Jeiel with psalteries and with harps; but Asaph made a sound with cymbals;

6 Benaiah also and Jahaziel the priests with trumpets continually before the ark of the covenant of God.

7 Then on that day David delivered first this psalm to thank the Lord into the hand of Asaph and his brethren.

8 Give thanks unto the Lord, call upon his name, make known his deeds among the people.

Psalm 92:1–5

It is a good thing to give thanks unto the Lord,
And to sing praises unto thy name, O most High:
To shew forth thy lovingkindness in the morning,
And thy faithfulness every night,
Upon an instrument of ten strings, and upon the psaltery;
Upon the harp with a solemn sound.
For thou, Lord, hast made me glad through thy work:
I will triumph in the works of thy hands.
O Lord, how great are thy works!
And thy thoughts are very deep.

Psalm 136:1–6, 23–26

O give thanks unto the Lord; for he is good:
For his mercy endureth for ever.
O give thanks unto the God of gods:
For his mercy endureth for ever.
O give thanks to the Lord of lords:
For his mercy endureth for ever.
To him who alone doeth great wonders:
For his mercy endureth for ever.
To him that by wisdom made the heavens:
For his mercy endureth for ever.
To him that stretched out the earth above the waters:
For his mercy endureth for ever.
Who remembered us in our low estate:
For his mercy endureth for ever:
And hath redeemed us from our enemies:
For his mercy endureth for ever.
Who giveth food to all flesh:
For his mercy endureth for ever.
O give thanks unto the God of heaven:
For his mercy endureth for ever.

NEW TESTAMENT

Luke 17:11–19

11 And it came to pass, as he went to Jerusalem, that he passed through the midst of Samaria and Galilee.

12 And as he entered into a certain village, there met him ten men that were lepers, which stood afar off:

13 And they lifted up their voices, and said, Jesus, Master, have mercy on us.

14 And when he saw them, he said unto them, Go shew yourselves unto the priests. And it came to pass, that, as they went, they were cleansed.

15 And one of them, when he saw that he was healed, turned back, and with a loud voice glorified God,

16 And fell down on his face at his feet, giving him thanks: and he was a Samaritan.

17 And Jesus answering said, Were there not ten cleansed? but where are the nine?

18 There are not found that returned to give glory to God, save this stranger.

19 And he said unto him, Arise, go thy way: thy faith hath made thee whole.

Matthew 26:20, 26–28

20 Now when the even was come, he sat down with the twelve.

26 And as they were eating, Jesus took bread, and blessed it, and brake it, and gave it to the disciples, and said, Take, eat; this is my body.

27 And he took the cup, and gave thanks, and gave it to them, saying, Drink ye all of it;

28 For this is my blood of the new testament, which is shed for many for the remission of sins.

Philippians 1:3–5

3 I thank my God upon every remembrance of you,

4 Always in every prayer of mine for you all making request with joy,

5 For your fellowship in the gospel from the first day until now.

1 Thessalonians 5:15–18

15 See that none render evil for evil unto any man; but ever follow that which is good, both among yourselves, and to all men.

16 Rejoice evermore.

17 Pray without ceasing.

18 In every thing give thanks: for this is the will of God in Christ Jesus concerning you.

GUILT

The Old Testament recognizes that some men are guilty before the law or before their fellow men, and it assumes that all men are guilty before God. God's attitude toward guilt determines the way in which human beings should deal with it when it arises among them. His attitude is that guilt should be exposed, confessed, and then forgiven.

There is less unanimity on the question of whether we as individuals are responsible only for our own faults or whether we share the guilt of our community and of our ancestors. Many passages express a strong sense of corporate guilt. In a general way a sense of human solidarity in guilt is conveyed in the story of Adam and Eve, but prophets such as Isaiah express a more direct involvement in the faults of a particular society: "I am a man of unclean lips, and I dwell in the midst of a people of unclean lips" (Isaiah 6:5).

Ezekiel, on the other hand, expresses the view that people are judged on their personal record alone. He does so with such force that it would be possible to accuse him of contradicting the explicit terms of one of the Ten Commandments, since this warns that God will visit unborn generations with the sins of their fathers.

The truth is that the Old Testament contains no systematic analysis of the nature of guilt. It is concerned only with prevention and cure—especially cure. If it mentions guilt, it usually does so in the course of appealing for penitence and offering forgiveness.

This applies to both kinds of guilt. Although people are answerable for what they are (which may be the result of other people's behavior) as well as for what they themselves do, God forgives both to the penitent. Old Testament writers knew they had fallen short of what they could be and believed that what they could be fell short of what they should be, but they affirmed that God's mercy is greater than all. Some even believed that a truly innocent man or woman would carry away the guilt of others. Innocence, as well as guilt, brushes off.

The New Testament does not assess the situation any differently, but it brings the remedy nearer. It says that God in Christ is positively pursuing men and women with forgiveness. The innocent guilt-remover has come.

Just as human solidarity in guilt is expressed in the figure of Adam, so potential human solidarity in forgiveness is expressed in the figure of Christ. Neither what we inevitably are nor what we voluntarily have done need keep us from peace with God. Faith in Christ achieves what the sin offerings and guilt offerings of the old dispensation sought to do: it enables us so to identify with innocence that we can be released from guilt.

When modern men and women suffer from feelings of guilt, they bear reluctant testimony to several significant beliefs. They signify their belief in free will: they would not feel they were to blame if nothing could have been different. They also signify their belief that they live in a moral universe: there would be nothing of which to be guilty if no real distinction existed between right and wrong. And they half-signify their belief in some Assessor before whom they are judged: feelings of guilt are commonly associated with expectations of judgment. Half a theology is already implied.

What is lacking is the other half of biblical theology: that which speaks of guilt not in terms of vain regrets or psychological hang-ups but in terms of cure. Men and women who feel that they are permanently and incurably unlovely and unfit to live with are a long way from the Bible. The Bible would say that even if such people really are a plague to themselves, to their neighbors, and to God, yet there is hope for them.

The Bible also requires them to treat other guilty people in the light of this truth.

GUILT

OLD TESTAMENT

Exodus 20:5

5 I the Lord thy God am a jealous God, visiting the iniquity of the fathers upon the children unto the third and fourth generation of them that hate me.

Ezekiel 18:19–21, 23

19 Yet say ye, Why? doth not the son bear the iniquity of the father? When the son hath done that which is lawful and right, and hath kept all my statutes, and hath done them, he shall surely live.

20 The soul that sinneth, it shall die. The son shall not bear the iniquity of the father, neither shall the father bear the iniquity of the son: the righteousness of the righteous shall be upon him, and the wickedness of the wicked shall be upon him.

21 But if the wicked will turn from all his sins that he hath committed, and keep all my statutes, and do that which is lawful and right, he shall surely live, he shall not die.

23 Have I any pleasure at all that the wicked should die? saith the Lord God: and not that he should return from his ways, and live?

Psalm 51:1–7, 10–11

Have mercy upon me, O God, according to thy lovingkindness:
According unto the multitude of thy tender mercies blot out my transgressions.
Wash me throughly from mine iniquity,
And cleanse me from my sin.
For I acknowledge my transgressions:
And my sin is ever before me.
Against thee, thee only, have I sinned,
And done this evil in thy sight:
That thou mightest be justified when thou speakest,
And be clear when thou judgest.
Behold, I was shapen in iniquity;
And in sin did my mother conceive me.
Behold, thou desirest truth in the inward parts:
And in the hidden part thou shalt make me to know wisdom.
Purge me with hyssop, and I shall be clean:
Wash me, and I shall be whiter than snow.
Create in me a clean heart, O God;
And renew a right spirit within me.
Cast me not away from thy presence;
And take not thy holy spirit from me.

Isaiah 53:6 (from the Song of the Lord's Servant)

6 All we like sheep have gone astray; we have turned every one to his own way; and the Lord hath laid on him the iniquity of us all.

NEW TESTAMENT

Luke 15:3–7

3 And he spake this parable unto them, saying,

4 What man of you, having an hundred sheep, if he lose one of them, doth not leave the ninety and nine in the wilderness, and go after that which is lost, until he find it?

5 And when he hath found it, he layeth it on his shoulders, rejoicing.

6 And when he cometh home, he calleth together his friends and neighbours, saying unto them, Rejoice with me; for I have found my sheep which was lost.

7 I say unto you, that likewise joy shall be in heaven over one sinner that repenteth, more than over ninety and nine just persons, which need no repentance.

Acts 2:37–38 (after Peter's pentecostal sermon)

37 Now when they heard this, they were pricked in their heart, and said unto Peter and to the rest of the apostles, Men and brethren, what shall we do?

38 Then Peter said unto them, Repent, and be baptized every one of you in the name of Jesus Christ for the remission of sins, and ye shall receive the gift of the Holy Ghost.

Romans 5:14, 18–19

14 Nevertheless death reigned . . . even over them that had not sinned after the similitude of Adam's transgression, who is the figure of him that was to come.

18 Therefore as by the offence of one judgment came upon all men to condemnation; even so by the righteousness of one the free gift came upon all men unto justification of life.

19 For as by one man's disobedience many were made sinners, so by the obedience of one shall many be made righteous.

Hebrews 9:24; 10:21–22

24 For Christ is not entered into the holy places made with hands, which are the figures of the true; but into heaven itself, now to appear in the presence of God for us:

21 And having an high priest over the house of God;

22 Let us draw near with a true heart in full assurance of faith, having our hearts sprinkled from an evil conscience, and our bodies washed with pure water.

HAPPINESS

In the Bible happiness is regarded as inseparable from living in harmony with the will of God, as is confirmed by the fact that being blessed is indistinguishable from being happy in the Bible's terminology. Many modern translations use the word "happy" where older versions said "blessed" (in the beatitudes, for example). Both words point to the experience of felicity and serenity that is at the heart of happiness in any language.

All the same, ideas about the nature of this blessedness, or happiness, do change and develop as the biblical revelation unfolds. In the earliest sections of the Old Testament the equations are simple: to be obedient to God is to be blessed; to be blessed is to be prosperous in every way; to prosper is to be happy. Happiness is associated with possessions in the widest sense.

This view is then qualified in two ways. First, happiness comes to be associated with wisdom rather than with material rewards as such. Ecclesiastes preaches moderation as the best available path to such limited happiness. Second, there is a challenge to the connection between godliness and blessedness as traditionally understood. The prosperity of the wicked posed a problem. Traditional moralists were inclined to say that such prosperity was bound to be short-lived. Realists such as Job replied that they had not noticed this to be true. Perhaps the moralists should have pursued a new and more inward definition of happiness, one less dependent on fortunate external circumstances.

The New Testament certainly does that. The beatitudes of Jesus challenge all conventional notions of the circumstances in which happiness (blessedness) will be found. This is partly explained by Jesus' teaching that happiness (like forgiveness and all other good things) comes to those who seek to give it rather than to have it. On this view, to strip yourself of the old happiness wrappings (such as wealth), and to do so for the benefit of others, may well let more happiness into your life than the old wrappings ever contained. But a deeper paradox is also at work.

The coming of Jesus marks the advent of a kingdom in which the established order of values and priorities is overturned. To live in the power of that rule is to be happy in all outward circumstances, and the breaking of the old happiness molds may actually foster the discovery of true happiness and of its sources.

The letters that circulated among the first generation of Christians are evidence of a whole community aware of a current running strongly through all experience: the living Spirit of God moves among them with a felicity that transcends all conventional expectations.

The pursuit of happiness may be a right, but catching it cannot be guaranteed. Advertisers sometimes pretend to have a product that can capture it, and the drug cult makes similar claims, but most people know what the Bible affirms—that happiness is an elusive quarry more often encountered when something else is being pursued than when the hunt is for happiness as such.

In the slightly silly grammar of our time, happiness *is*. It exists whether we experience it or not. Stated in religious terms, happiness is the wind of heaven blowing across the fields of time. Only those who dare spread their spiritual wings to it can tell of its power. And they do. From Francis of Assisi in the thirteenth century to many a prisoner of conscience in the twentieth flows a stream of experience making it clear that there is more evidence to back up the paradoxes of the beatitudes than there is to support those who offer to sell us happiness as a commodity.

HAPPINESS

OLD TESTAMENT

Psalm 128:1–4

Blessed is every one that feareth the Lord;
That walketh in his ways.
For thou shalt eat the labour of thine hands:
Happy shalt thou be, and it shall be well with thee.
Thy wife shall be as a fruitful vine by the sides of thine house:
Thy children like olive plants round about thy table.

Proverbs 3:13–14, 17

Happy is the man that findeth wisdom,
And the man that getteth understanding.
For the merchandise of it is better than the merchandise of silver,
And the gain thereof than fine gold.
Her ways are ways of pleasantness,
And all her paths are peace.

Ecclesiastes 5:18–19

18 It is good and comely for one to eat and to drink, and to enjoy the good of all his labour that he taketh under the sun all the days of his life, which God giveth him: for it is his portion.

19 Every man also to whom God hath given riches and wealth, and hath given him power to eat thereof, and to take his portion, and to rejoice in his labour; this is the gift of God.

Jeremiah 12:1

1 Righteous art thou, O Lord, when I plead with thee: yet let me talk with thee of thy judgments: Wherefore doth the way of the wicked prosper? wherefore are all they happy that deal very treacherously?

Job 20:1, 4–5; 21:1, 12–13

Then answered Zophar the Naamathite, and said,

Knowest thou not this of old,
Since man was placed upon earth,
That the triumphing of the wicked is short,
And the joy of the hypocrite but for a moment?

But Job answered and said,

They take the timbrel and harp,
And rejoice at the sound of the organ.
They spend their days in wealth,
And in a moment go down to the grave.

Psalm 68:3

But let the righteous be glad; let them rejoice before God:
Yea, let them exceedingly rejoice.
Sing unto God, sing praises to his name.

NEW TESTAMENT

Matthew 5:3–10 (the beatitudes of Jesus)

3 Blessed are the poor in spirit: for theirs is the kingdom of heaven.

4 Blessed are they that mourn: for they shall be comforted.

5 Blessed are the meek: for they shall inherit the earth.

6 Blessed are they which do hunger and thirst after righteousness: for they shall be filled.

7 Blessed are the merciful: for they shall obtain mercy.

145

8 Blessed are the pure in heart: for they shall see God.

9 Blessed are the peacemakers: for they shall be called the children of God.

10 Blessed are they which are persecuted for righteousness' sake: for theirs is the kingdom of heaven.

Acts 20:35

35 I have shewed you all things, how that so labouring ye ought to support the weak, and to remember the words of the Lord Jesus, how he said, It is more blessed to give than to receive.

John 15:11; 16:33

11 These things have I spoken unto you, that my joy might remain in you, and that your joy might be full.

33 In the world ye shall have tribulation: but be of good cheer; I have overcome the world.

Romans 14:17; 15:13

17 For the kingdom of God is not meat and drink; but righteousness, and peace, and joy in the Holy Ghost.

13 Now the God of hope fill you with all joy and peace in believing, that ye may abound in hope, through the power of the Holy Ghost.

HEALTH

This entry is not about curing sickness (see Illness); it is about health as a positive condition worth studying in itself. In English the words "hale," "heal," "health," "whole," and "holy" are all connected with one another, and in the Bible, too, "health" signifies wholeness. Old Testament references to bodily health are always entwined with references to moral integrity, to religious trust, to a man's relationship with his family, his neighbor, his environment. To be healthy he must be a man as God defines manhood, and that (which includes women too, of course) means being properly adjusted to his place in the scheme of things.

Being healthy also means living within the law and under the rule of wisdom. The Old Testament affirms that the way to live well and long is to live attuned to the will of God as expressed in his law ("Honor thy father and thy mother . . . that it may go well with thee"—Deuteronomy 5:16), but increasingly wisdom becomes the ruling feature of the complete human being ("a wellspring of life to him that hath it . . . sweet to the soul, and healthy to the bones"—Proverbs 16:22, 24).

The simplistic view of Old Testament teaching is that God sends health as a reward for good behavior and sickness as a punishment for sin, but the Book of Job successfully challenges oversimplification. That God's obedient servant would be immune to the ills and accidents of the body was a misinterpretation of promises such as those in Psalm 34 and Psalm 91, a misinterpretation the New

Testament was later to say the devil offered to Jesus (quoting some of these verses in support of the devil's case). Illness and death are not directly attributable to sin, and yet a natural relationship exists between health and holiness. The idea that the body might be made healthy independently of the person as a whole occurred to nobody.

The New Testament endorses the idea of health as wholeness. When Peter describes a man he has healed as having "perfect soundness," the Greek word in the original of Acts is *holokleria* (wholeness), a term that could be used to denote either "something complete in every part" or "a sacrificial animal free of any defect."

For New Testament writers, however, the measure and standard of wholeness was Jesus himself. It is significant that the one short sentence devoted to his boyhood growth speaks of wisdom, of bodily development, of relationship with man, and of relationship with God—the characteristic Old Testament indicators of the complete man. Jesus' concern for the body later made him a healer. His concern for wisdom made him a teacher. His concern for men's relationship with God and with one another made him the central figure of the kingdom he proclaimed and for which he was put to death. His bearing of that affliction was regarded by New Testament writers as completing the full life he taught and embodied (made "perfect through suffering"—Hebrews 2:10).

Health is a relationship between that which is most inward in a man and all that is external to him—or rather it is a network of relationships: between a man and his body, his fellow men, his environment, his culture, and the transcendent reality beyond all these. There is no way by which a fence can be built around any one of those areas—such as the body—in order to allow it to function well regardless of what is happening in other areas of the man's life. If we understood health as fullness of life rather than as mere absence of illness, we would start with a healthy attitude.

The biblical view is that such an attitude is not only correct but is also a way of opening one's life to the positive forces of health that are at work in God's world. Health is not a static thing. There is, in the biblical view, an active power creating and fostering the fullness of life wherever people are open to it.

The Bible even seems to say that there is a healthy way to accept illness and death. They, too, can be made to serve the wholeness of life.

HEALTH

OLD TESTAMENT

Deuteronomy 4:39–40

39 Know therefore this day, and consider it in thine heart, that the Lord he is God in heaven above, and upon the earth beneath: there is none else.

40 Thou shalt keep therefore his statutes, and his commandments, which I command thee this day, that

it may go well with thee, and with thy children after thee, and that thou mayest prolong thy days upon the earth, which the Lord thy God giveth thee, for ever.

Psalm 34:12–14; 91:5–6, 9–13

What man is he that desireth life,
And loveth many days, that he may see good?
Keep thy tongue from evil,
And thy lips from speaking guile.
Depart from evil, and do good;
Seek peace, and pursue it.
Thou shalt not be afraid for the terror by night;
Nor for the arrow that flieth by day;
Nor for the pestilence that walketh in darkness;
Nor for the destruction that wasteth at noonday.
Because thou hast made the Lord, which is my refuge,
Even the most High, thy habitation;
There shall no evil befall thee,
Neither shall any plague come nigh thy dwelling.
For he shall give his angels charge over thee,
To keep thee in all thy ways.
They shall bear thee up in their hands,
Lest thou dash thy foot against a stone.
Thou shalt tread upon the lion and adder:
The young lion and the dragon shalt thou trample under feet.

Proverbs 3:7–8; 4:20–22

Be not wise in thine own eyes:
Fear the Lord, and depart from evil.
It shall be health to thy navel,
And marrow to thy bones.
My son, attend to my words;
Incline thine ear unto my sayings.
Let them not depart from thine eyes;
Keep them in the midst of thine heart.

For they are life unto those that find them,
And health to all their flesh.

NEW TESTAMENT

Luke 2:52

52 And Jesus increased in wisdom and stature, and in favour with God and man.

Luke 11:33–36

33 No man, when he hath lighted a candle, putteth it in a secret place, neither under a bushel, but on a candlestick, that they which come in may see the light.
34 The light of the body is the eye: therefore when thine eye is single, thy whole body also is full of light; but when thine eye is evil, thy body also is full of darkness.
35 Take heed therefore that the light which is in thee be not darkness.
36 If thy whole body therefore be full of light, having no part dark, the whole shall be full of light, as when the bright shining of a candle doth give thee light.

John 10:10

10 I am come that they might have life, and that they might have it more abundantly.

Acts 3:12–16 (after Peter heals a crippled beggar)

12 And when Peter saw it, he answered unto the people, Ye men of Israel, why marvel ye at this? or why look ye so earnestly on us, as though by our own power or holiness we had made this man to walk?

13 The God of Abraham, and of Isaac, and of Jacob, the God of our fathers, hath glorified his Son Jesus; whom ye delivered up, and denied him in the presence of Pilate, when he was determined to let him go.

14 But ye denied the Holy One and the Just, and desired a murderer to be granted unto you;

15 And killed the Prince of life, whom God hath raised from the dead; whereof we are witnesses.

16 And his name through faith in his name hath made this man strong, whom ye see and know: yea, the faith which is by him hath given him this perfect soundness in the presence of you all.

3 John 1–2

1 The elder unto the well-beloved Gaius, whom I love in the truth.

2 Beloved, I wish above all things that thou mayest prosper and be in health, even as thy soul prospereth.

HEAVEN

The writers of the Old Testament believe that God visits the earth but lives in heaven. Human beings do not go to heaven when they die, but may have glimpses or visions of it while they live. Old Testament writers take it for granted (because it was the common assumption of their culture) that we live in a three-story universe with the dead in the basement, the living on the ground floor, and God at the top—over the vault in which the sun, moon, and stars are to be seen. It has been questioned whether they thought the universe was literally and physically constructed in this way. Actually, they were more concerned with the significance of things than with their physical construction, but they certainly looked at the world in the light of these symbols. Inevitably their visions of God involved looking up, but it was the glory of the heavenly vision rather than its altitude that was significant.

To speak of heaven was to say that God is beyond us and above us. He is not to be confused with the world or with anything in it. He is other. And yet the Old Testament also teaches that he is present. Heaven comes, as it were, within the range of human experience, because God lives both "in the high and holy place" and "with him that is of a contrite and humble spirit."

The New Testament also speaks of heaven as a transcendent reality beyond our power to envisage or to express, but now heaven not only touches our lives here on earth but can be our home beyond death as well. This faith had already been adopted by most Jews before the coming of Jesus, but he strengthened it. Generations of affliction had led the Jews to believe that the righteous dead must rise again in order to enjoy what was due to them. Some also believed in paradise as a pleasant waiting place.

Only the Sadducees held out against these beliefs, and Jesus opposed the

Sadducean view on the ground that God had formed a personal relationship with the patriarchs and that a living God can relate only to a living man or woman. Since the patriarchs had been in contact with the eternal during their lives on earth, the eternal must hold them beyond the bounds of mortality.

At the same time Jesus brushed aside any assumption that the life to come is just a resumption of life as we know it. "It's not like that," he said in reply to the Sadducees' conundrum. What it is like he did not say. Conventional pictures appeared in some of his parables, but clearly these provided only the background to a preaching point and were not intended as visions of the heavenly reality. The preaching point made in most of his parables, whatever the setting, was that the kingdom of heaven is an immediate reality to which a response must be made at once. On his lips "the kingdom of heaven" meant the same thing as "the kingdom of God," and it was by accepting the blessings and the demands of this divine rule that men and women could enter into a fullness of life large enough to span the gulf between the living and the dead. The story of the baptism of Jesus expresses vividly the belief that the life of heaven is tangibly present in Jesus himself.

It is not to be wondered at that messages from the dead received through mediums, even if they are accepted as genuine, are disappointingly drab in their picture of heaven. No human mind has the capacity to receive an account of transcendent reality unconditioned by time and space. Perhaps the messages themselves can come only from the suburbs of that experience. What the Bible affirms is that certain present experiences have the quality of heavenly life in them, although the circumstances in which we experience that quality will change indescribably. The experience of union through love, for instance, is one that is said to be of transcendent value. The bereaved lover can be sure that his or her love is going to be fulfilled, though it would be a waste of effort to speculate as to just how.

The biblical heaven is not just a future state and is certainly not best served by our constantly looking beyond death. It is a challenging present reality to be responded to in terms set by everyday relationships. It is the transcendent aspect of every reality, the joy achievable in every experience.

HEAVEN

OLD TESTAMENT

Genesis 28:10–17

10 And Jacob went out from Beer-sheba, and went toward Haran.

11 And he lighted upon a certain place, and tarried there all night, be-cause the sun was set; and he took of the stones of that place, and put them for his pillows, and lay down in that place to sleep.

12 And he dreamed, and behold a ladder set up on the earth, and the top of it reached to heaven: and behold

the angels of God ascending and descending on it.

13 And, behold, the Lord stood above it, and said, I am the Lord God of Abraham thy father, and the God of Isaac: the land whereon thou liest, to thee will I give it, and to thy seed;

14 And thy seed shall be as the dust of the earth, and thou shalt spread abroad to the west, and to the east, and to the north, and to the south: and in thee and in thy seed shall all the families of the earth be blessed.

15 And, behold, I am with thee, and will keep thee in all places whither thou goest, and will bring thee again into this land; for I will not leave thee, until I have done that which I have spoken to thee of.

16 And Jacob awaked out of his sleep, and he said, Surely the Lord is in this place; and I knew it not.

17 And he was afraid, and said, How dreadful is this place! this is none other but the house of God, and this is the gate of heaven.

1 Kings 8:27

27 But will God indeed dwell on the earth? behold, the heaven and heaven of heavens cannot contain thee; how much less this house that I have builded?

Psalm 11:4–5, 7

The Lord is in his holy temple,
The Lord's throne is in heaven:
His eyes behold, his eyelids try, the children of men.
The Lord trieth the righteous:
But the wicked and him that loveth violence his soul hateth.

For the righteous Lord loveth righteousness;
His countenance doth behold the upright.

Isaiah 57:15

15 For thus saith the high and lofty One that inhabiteth eternity, whose name is Holy; I dwell in the high and holy place, with him also that is of a contrite and humble spirit, to revive the spirit of the humble, and to revive the heart of the contrite ones.

NEW TESTAMENT

Matthew 3:16–17; 4:17

16 And Jesus, when he was baptized, went up straightway out of the water: and, lo, the heavens were opened unto him, and he saw the Spirit of God descending like a dove, and lighting upon him:

17 And lo a voice from heaven, saying, This is my beloved Son, in whom I am well pleased.

17 From that time Jesus began to preach, and to say, Repent: for the kingdom of heaven is at hand.

Matthew 22:23–32

23 The same day came to him the Sadducees, which say that there is no resurrection, and asked him,

24 Saying, Master, Moses said, If a man die, having no children, his brother shall marry his wife, and raise up seed unto his brother.

25 Now there were with us seven brethren: and the first, when he had married a wife, deceased, and, having no issue, left his wife unto his brother:

26 Likewise the second also, and the third, unto the seventh.

27 And last of all the woman died also.

28 Therefore in the resurrection whose wife shall she be of the seven? for they all had her.

29 Jesus answered and said unto them, Ye do err, not knowing the scriptures, nor the power of God.

30 For in the resurrection they neither marry, nor are given in marriage, but are as the angels of God in heaven.

31 But as touching the resurrection of the dead, have ye not read that which was spoken unto you by God, saying,

32 I am the God of Abraham, and the God of Isaac, and the God of Jacob? God is not the God of the dead, but of the living.

John 14:1-3

1 Let not your heart be troubled: ye believe in God, believe also in me.

2 In my Father's house are many mansions: if it were not so, I would have told you. I go to prepare a place for you.

3 And if I go and prepare a place for you, I will come again, and receive you unto myself; that where I am, there ye may be also.

HELL

There is not much Old Testament support for the idea of hell as a fiery place of everlasting punishment to which the wicked go after death. Fiery punishments are possible, but they fall on the living—as at Sodom. The dead, good and bad alike, go down to sheol where they live unsubstantial lives from which they ought not to be recalled, though "mediums and spiritists" (Isaiah 8:19, in a modern translation) may know how to recall them. At one time "sheol" was often translated into English as "hell" (e.g., "the pains of hell gat hold upon me," in the old version of Psalm 116:3), but now this mistranslation is usually corrected ("the anguish of the grave came upon me," in the New International Version). Sheol can be regarded as hell insofar as it is a place of separation from God—even the living can feel the misery of sheol when they feel themselves cut off from God—but since the good are there it cannot be regarded as a place of punishment.

Only toward the end of the Old Testament period are there some beginnings to the thought that the faithful departed might return to a real life (see Resurrection). With that idea came the beginnings of a belief in enduring punishment as well as enduring reward.

By New Testament times most people believed in everlasting reward or punishment. The New Testament, however, does not answer metaphysical questions about the nature of hell or about who goes there and whether they will ever get out. The New Testament writers speak of hell only with a moral and religious purpose, and only because every person has to make decisions which are of infinite moral and religious importance. Life with God is on offer, but the offer can be spurned: "beware," says the hell symbol.

That hell is a symbol is clear from the highly pictorial way in which the sayings and parables of Jesus speak of it. To speak of amputation as the answer to moral failings, and therefore as a means of avoiding hell, is clearly not to speak literally.

The good news of the New Testament is that the power of death and hell (or "hades," an appropriate Greek equivalent to the Hebrew "sheol") is broken. Jesus has gone down into that realm and opened it up. Because forgiveness of sins is freely available and Jesus has returned from the dead, neither Hades (the place of death) nor Gehenna (the place of punishment) need be feared.

Where biblical values are concerned, love is still a better motivator than fear. Putting the fear of hell into people does not win a response of the quality and power that putting the love of God into them does. It is characteristic of the Bible to give much attention to the positive motivation and relatively little to the negative.

The dark side of the picture, however, is undoubtedly there. A note of awful severity is struck. If the Bible is to be believed, the full spectrum of possibilities before us includes some dreadful ones.

But the value of this warning is diminished rather than increased if we take it too literally, as can easily happen since ours is a prosaic generation. Most of us are not at home with poetic symbols, especially not with those designed to point to actual realities that can be indicated in no other way. Perhaps the best biblical commentators are the poets—Milton, for instance, who speaks of hell as a state rather than a place: "The mind is its own place, and in itself Can make a Heav'n of Hell, a Hell of Heav'n" (*Paradise Lost*, Book I, l. 254). Or Marlowe, whose Mephistopheles in *Dr. Faustus* carries his hell with him: "Why this is hell, nor am I out of it."

We cannot even lightly dismiss the thought that heaven and hell may be the same thing differently experienced—as, for instance, a long symphony is differently experienced by one who loves music and by one who hates it.

HELL

OLD TESTAMENT

Genesis 13:13; 19:24–25

13 But the men of Sodom were wicked and sinners before the Lord exceedingly.

24 Then the Lord rained upon Sodom and upon Gomorrah brimstone and fire from the Lord out of heaven;

25 And he overthrew those cities, and all the plain, and all the inhabitants of the cities, and that which grew upon the ground.

Psalm 88:3–7, 13–14

For my soul is full of troubles:
And my life draweth nigh unto the grave.
I am counted with them that go down
  into the pit:
I am as a man that hath no strength:
Free among the dead,
Like the slain that lie in the grave,
Whom thou rememberest no more:
And they are cut off from thy hand.
Thou hast laid me in the lowest pit,
In darkness, in the deeps.
Thy wrath lieth hard upon me,
And thou hast afflicted me with all thy
  waves.
But unto thee have I cried, O Lord;
And in the morning shall my prayer pre-
  vent thee.
Lord, why casteth thou off my soul?
Why hidest thou thy face from me?

Isaiah 66:22–24

22 For as the new heavens and the new earth, which I will make, shall remain before me, saith the Lord, so shall your seed and your name remain.

23 And it shall come to pass, that from one new moon to another, and from one sabbath to another, shall all flesh come to worship before me, saith the Lord.

24 And they shall go forth, and look upon the carcases of the men that have transgressed against me: for their worm shall not die, neither shall their fire be quenched; and they shall be an abhorring unto all flesh.

NEW TESTAMENT

Mark 9:42–47

42 And whosoever shall offend one of these little ones that believe in me, it is better for him that a millstone were hanged about his neck, and he were cast into the sea.

43 And if thy hand offend thee, cut it off: it is better for thee to enter into life maimed, then having two hands to go into hell, into the fire that never shall be quenched:

44 Where their worm dieth not, and the fire is not quenched.

45 And if thy foot offend thee, cut it off: it is better for thee to enter halt into life, than having two feet to be cast into hell, into the fire that never shall be quenched:

46 Where their worm dieth not, and the fire is not quenched.

47 And if thine eye offend thee, pluck it out: it is better for thee to enter into the kingdom of God with one eye, than having two eyes to be cast into hell fire.

Luke 16:19–31

19 There was a certain rich man, which was clothed in purple and fine linen, and fared sumptuously every day:

20 And there was a certain beggar named Lazarus, which was laid at his gate, full of sores,

21 And desiring to be fed with the crumbs which fell from the rich man's table: moreover the dogs came and licked his sores.

22 And it came to pass, that the beggar died, and was carried by the angels into Abraham's bosom: the rich man also died, and was buried;

23 And in hell he lifted up his eyes, being in torments, and seeth Abraham afar off, and Lazarus in his bosom.

24 And he cried and said, Father Abraham, have mercy on me, and send Lazarus, that he may dip the tip of his finger in water, and cool my tongue; for I am tormented in this flame.

25 But Abraham said, Son, remember that thou in thy lifetime receivedst thy good things, and likewise Lazarus evil things: but now he is comforted, and thou art tormented.

26 And beside all this, between us and you there is a great gulf fixed: so that they which would pass from hence to you cannot; neither can they pass to us, that would come from thence.

27 Then he said, I pray thee therefore, father, that thou wouldest send him to my father's house:

28 For I have five brethren; that he may testify unto them, lest they also come into this place of torment.

29 Abraham saith unto him, They have Moses and the prophets; let them hear them.

30 And he said, Nay, father Abraham: but if one went unto them from the dead, they will repent.

31 And he said unto him, If they hear not Moses and the prophets, neither will they be persuaded, though one rose from the dead.

Revelation 1:18 (the words of one "like a son of man")

18 I am he that liveth, and was dead; and, behold, I am alive for evermore, Amen; and have the keys of hell and of death.

HOLINESS

To be holy means to be set apart for God. God himself is, of course, the supremely holy being from whom all other holiness is derived. That belief is common to all the strands of thought and periods of time covered by the Old Testament, but at one time God's holiness was thought of as a physically dangerous thing like a live current of electricity. A reading of the story of Uzzah's anxiety about the ark may evoke more sympathy for Uzzah than for God, but the story expressed the sense of fear that human beings felt in the presence of the holy. The ark was a box, central in the worship of Israel through many generations, and a very holy object indeed.

The priesthood and rituals of Israel were developed to shield men and women from this dangerous power and yet make it possible for them to approach God and have dealings with him, though never to see him.

Increasingly the idea of holiness, without ceasing to evoke awe and dread, became moral and personal rather than semiphysical. Holiness flared out against injustice. It was associated with truth and with love. It was worshiped with joy. In Isaiah's vision the prophet's own offenses were purged away by the burning power of holiness. This cleansing prepared him for personal service. All the later prophets speak of holiness in a way that shows it reaching out from the area of ritual to become a controlling factor in every aspect of life. God is "the Holy One of Israel," and human beings are themselves sanctified by their relationship to him.

In the New Testament Jesus is conceived by the Holy Spirit and is himself "the Holy One of God." This truth is recognized less clearly by ordinary men and women than it is by the unholy spirits that were believed to be responsible for most evil and illness. Peter, however, responded to a miracle by saying to Jesus, "Depart from me; for I am a sinful man, O Lord" (Luke 5:8)—a typical response to the holy, fully in line with Old Testament thinking. Later Peter (together with James and John) had an experience of awe and dread in the presence of Jesus. This was on a mountain when the holiness of Jesus expressed itself visibly. This time Peter reacted, as many others have done, by talking nonsense. The experience of the holy transcends the normal usages of language.

The zone of the holy, however, was still expanding. Less and less did it have a geographical location (especially after the destruction of the temple in A.D. 70), more and more a personal location. Holy objects play no very great part in New Testament Christianity; personal holiness does. Contact with Jesus was believed to spread holiness in men and women, and they felt bound to express it in lives characterized by love, joy, and peace.

This does not mean that holiness had become nothing but morality. It was still a sense of the divine, and it still evoked wonder.

Confronted by some trivial change in the familiar pattern of things, the modern humorist is apt to ask, "Is nothing sacred?" It is a good question misapplied. A world in which nothing is sacred, in which nothing evokes awe and wonder and reverence, would be a world that no longer evokes the true depths of human personality. It is a sign of shallowness rather than of maturity never to feel the presence of the holy.

What is more, if there is little of the biblical sense of a holiness that is moral and spiritual, then all kinds of hocus-pocus will flourish on the trade in cheap substitutes. Occult groups will seek after the numinous almost anywhere except where the Bible says it is to be found—and where it will be found to be morally demanding.

HOLINESS

OLD TESTAMEMT

Leviticus 11:44

44 For I am the Lord your God: ye shall therefore sanctify yourselves, and ye shall be holy; for I am holy.

2 Samuel 6:3, 6–7

3 And they set the ark of God upon a new cart, and brought it out of the house of Abinadab that was in Gibeah: and Uzzah and Ahio, the sons of Abinadab, drave the new cart.

6 And when they came to Nachon's threshingfloor, Uzzah put forth his hand to the ark of God, and took hold of it; for the oxen shook it.

7 And the anger of the Lord was kindled against Uzzah; and God smote him there for his error; and there he died by the ark of God.

Exodus 3:2–6

2 And the angel of the Lord appeared unto him in a flame of fire out of the midst of a bush: and he looked, and, behold, the bush burned with fire, and the bush was not consumed.

3 And Moses said, I will now turn aside, and see this great sight, why the bush is not burnt.

4 And when the Lord saw that he turned aside to see, God called unto him out of the midst of the bush, and said, Moses, Moses. And he said, Here am I.

5 And he said, Draw not nigh hither: put off thy shoes from off thy feet, for the place whereon thou standest is holy ground.

6 Moreover he said, I am the God of thy father, the God of Abraham, the God of Isaac, and the God of Jacob. And Moses hid his face; for he was afraid to look upon God.

Isaiah 6:1–7

1 In the year that king Uzziah died I saw also the Lord sitting upon a throne, high and lifted up, and his train filled the temple.

2 Above it stood the seraphims: each one had six wings; with twain he covered his face, and with twain he covered his feet, and with twain he did fly.

3 And one cried unto another, and said, Holy, holy, holy, is the Lord of hosts: the whole earth is full of his glory.

4 And the posts of the door moved at the voice of him that cried, and the house was filled with smoke.

5 Then said I, Woe is me! for I am undone; because I am a man of unclean lips, and I dwell in the midst of a people of unclean lips: for mine eyes have seen the King, the Lord of hosts.

6 Then flew one of the seraphims unto me, having a live coal in his hand, which he had taken with the tongs from off the altar:

7 And he laid it upon my mouth, and said, Lo, this hath touched thy lips; and thine iniquity is taken away, and thy sin purged.

NEW TESTAMENT

Luke 1:35

35 And the angel answered and said unto her, The Holy Ghost shall come upon thee, and the power of the Highest shall overshadow thee: therefore also that holy thing which shall be born of thee shall be called the Son of God.

Mark 1:23–24 (Jesus, teaching at Capernaum)

23 And there was in their synagogue a man with an unclean spirit; and he cried out,

24 Saying, Let us alone; what have we to do with thee, thou Jesus of Nazareth? art thou come to destroy us? I

know thee who thou art, the Holy One of God.

Mark 9:2–7

2 And after six days Jesus taketh with him Peter, and James, and John, and leadeth them up into an high mountain apart by themselves: and he was transfigured before them.

3 And his raiment became shining, exceeding white as snow; so as no fuller on earth can white them.

4 And there appeared unto them Elias with Moses: and they were talking with Jesus.

5 And Peter answered and said to Jesus, Master, it is good for us to be here: and let us make three tabernacles; one for thee, and one for Moses, and one for Elias.

6 For he wist not what to say; for they were sore afraid.

7 And there was a cloud that overshadowed them: and a voice came out of the cloud, saying, This is my beloved Son: hear him.

1 Corinthians 1:2; 3:17

2 To them that are sanctified in Christ Jesus, called to be saints . . .

17 The temple of God is holy, which temple ye are.

HOMOSEXUALITY

The Old Testament verdict is clear. Homosexual activity was a capital offense under the law (Leviticus 20:13)—one of many sexual offenses for which death was the punishment. The Hebrew attitude was that sexuality was for childbearing. To waste semen that could be used fruitfully was an offense in other relationships besides homosexual ones (see Genesis 38:9).

Homosexuality is condemned in the narratives of the Old Testament as well as in its laws, but the stories tend to be about such outrageous behavior that there is plenty to condemn besides homosexuality. There was, for instance, the notorious city of Sodom, where part of the offense was the use of force and the flouting of the sacred laws of hospitality. Also, in the local temples left over from pre-Israelite days, there were male and female prostitutes—both, it is safe to assume, for the use of men. Such places must have lingered on for generations, since steps were being taken to suppress them as late as 621 B.C. Thus homosexuality was mixed up with idolatry and in that company was the more certain of condemnation.

The fear of homosexuality was not so great as to prevent the Old Testament writers from expressing a great respect for deep and passionate relationships between man and man or between woman and woman. There are marvelously tender accounts of the love between David and Jonathan and between Ruth and

Naomi, and there is no thought of forbidden homosexuality in these stories. The person in such a relationship is treated as more important than the person's sex.

In the New Testament, Paul deals very severely with homosexuality in his letter to the Romans—understandably, since he wrote as a bachelor (leaving no room for his position to be misunderstood), as a Jew (believing in the desirability of having sex for the purpose of having children), and to Rome (a city notorious at the time for sexual waywardness). Very significant, however, is the way in which he introduces his attack and the way in which he (as an Old Testament scholar) sees homosexuality in a setting of heathen idolatry.

His argument is that nature reveals enough of God for men and women to be able, if they wish, to distinguish him from the false gods they choose to worship instead. Having turned away from this natural knowledge of God, they have lost their instinct for a natural way of living. It is in this context that homosexuality arises. Sound sexual instincts and sound religious beliefs belong together. This makes all the more important Paul's belief that the power of the Christian gospel will produce not merely moral reform but a radical reconstruction of nature itself.

It is possible to share the Bible's unhappiness about homosexuality without placing blame on individual homosexuals. The biblical position seems to be that homosexuality can arise spontaneously in nature as we know it, but that nature as we know it is in a deep sense unnatural: it is not nature as it should be and could be. The fact that things are as they are cannot be laid at the door of any individual or group of individuals. We all participate in the plight of spoiled humanity, and we share together in the moral responsibility for redeeming it.

This does not satisfy the campaigners for gay liberation. They ask that homosexual love be regarded as a good and holy thing in the same way that heterosexual love is (or should be). They point to the New Testament's stress on love as the highest expression of our humanity, and they claim that any relationship expressing such love has a share of the blessing. To claim this as sanction for physical homosexual activity would be to go a lot further than the biblical writers seem willing to go, but it is true that Jesus spoke of love as a redeeming factor wherever he found it (see Love).

HOMOSEXUALITY

OLD TESTAMENT

Leviticus 18:22

22 Thou shalt not lie with mankind, as with womankind: it is abomination.

Genesis 19:1–13

1 And there came two angels to Sodom at even; and Lot sat in the gate of Sodom: and Lot seeing them rose up to meet them; and he bowed himself with his face toward the ground;

2 And he said, Behold now, my lords, turn in, I pray you, into your servant's house, and tarry all night, and wash your feet, and ye shall rise up early, and go on your ways. And they said, Nay; but we will abide in the street all night.

3 And he pressed upon them greatly; and they turned in unto him, and entered into his house; and he made them a feast, and did bake unleavened bread, and they did eat.

4 But before they lay down, the men of the city, even the men of Sodom, compassed the house round, both old and young, all the people from every quarter:

5 And they called unto Lot, and said unto him, Where are the men which came in to thee this night? bring them out unto us, that we may know them.

6 And Lot went out at the door unto them, and shut the door after him,

7 And said, I pray you, brethren, do not so wickedly.

8 Behold now, I have two daughters which have not known man; let me, I pray you, bring them out unto you, and do ye to them as is good in your eyes: only unto these men do nothing; for therefore came they under the shadow of my roof.

9 And they said, Stand back. And they said again, This one fellow came in to sojourn, and he will needs be a judge: now will we deal worse with thee, than with them. And they pressed sore upon the man, even Lot, and came near to break the door.

10 But the men put forth their hand, and pulled Lot into the house to them, and shut to the door.

11 And they smote the men that were at the door of the house with blindness, both small and great: so that they wearied themselves to find the door.

12 And the men said unto Lot, Hast thou here any besides? son in law, and thy sons, and thy daughters, and whatsoever thou hast in the city, bring them out of this place:

13 For we will destroy this place, because the cry of them is waxen great before the face of the Lord; and the Lord hath sent us to destroy it.

Deuteronomy 23:17–18

17 There shall be no whore of the daughters of Israel, nor a sodomite of the sons of Israel.

18 Thou shalt not bring the hire of a whore, or the price of a dog, into the house of the Lord thy God for any vow: for even both these are abomination unto the Lord thy God.

NEW TESTAMENT

Romans 1:18–27

18 For the wrath of God is revealed from heaven against all ungodliness and unrighteousness of men, who hold the truth in unrighteousness;

19 Because that which may be known of God is manifest in them; for God hath shewed it unto them.

20 For the invisible things of him from the creation of the world are clearly seen, being understood by the

things that are made, even his eternal power and Godhead; so that they are without excuse:

21 Because that, when they knew God, they glorified him not as God, neither were thankful; but became vain in their imaginations, and their foolish heart was darkened.

22 Professing themselves to be wise, they became fools,

23 And changed the glory of the uncorruptible God into an image made like to corruptible man, and to birds, and fourfooted beasts, and creeping things.

24 Wherefore God also gave them up to uncleanness through the lusts of their own hearts, to dishonour their own bodies between themselves:

25 Who changed the truth of God into a lie, and worshipped and served the creature more than the Creator, who is blessed for ever. Amen.

26 For this cause God gave them up unto vile affections: for even their women did change the natural use into that which is against nature:

27 And likewise also the men, leaving the natural use of the woman, burned in their lust one toward another; men with men working that which is unseemly, and receiving in themselves that recompence of their error which was meet.

1 Corinthians 6:9–10

9 Be not deceived: neither fornicators, nor idolaters, nor adulterers, nor effeminate, nor abusers of themselves with mankind,

10 Nor thieves, nor covetous, nor drunkards, nor revilers, nor extortioners, shall inherit the kingdom of God.

2 Corinthians 5:17; 7:1

17 Therefore if any man be in Christ, he is a new creature: old things are passed away; behold, all things are become new.

1 Having therefore these promises, dearly beloved, let us cleanse ourselves from all filthiness of the flesh and spirit, perfecting holiness in the fear of God.

HONESTY

The Old Testament plainly forbids the ordinary, outward dishonesties. At the same time it reports objectively on the amount of cheating that goes on in human affairs. The patriarchs themselves were not above practicing it and were not immune from becoming the victims of it. Jacob contrived to secure the inheritance meant for Esau (see Blessing), but found himself on the painful end of some rather sharp practice by Laban, who covered his cheating, as so many do, with a reference to custom and tradition. Looking back on the small print of the story as reported, it is evident that Laban's words were ambiguous. He could claim not to have broken his explicit agreement, but he could not claim to have acted with the frankness and openness that are essential parts of honesty. He deceived without lying.

It was recognized that in dealings with God no such cover-up was possible, and increasingly it was realized that all dealings—not just those involving the temple—are dealings with God.

By the time the New Testament Gospels were written, Judas was notorious as the betrayer of Christ. This reputation may have reflected backward into accounts of his earlier career, but according to John there was pilferage even within the circle of Jesus' chosen disciples, and Judas was responsible for it. More significant in that story, however, is the fact that even if Judas's words can be taken at their face value and regarded as sincere, the extravagant behavior of Mary was preferred. The sentiments expressed by Judas were at one level admirable, but the open expression of deep and passionate feeling was a higher form of honesty. Endorsing approved codes of conduct is less significant than letting out into the open what is deepest in the heart.

It is appropriate, therefore, that New Testament appeals for honesty should tend to occur as part of a richer and warmer picture of the good life as one motivated throughout by love. Honesty is just one aspect of the full and enduring life that is seen in the visions of the Book of Revelation as belonging to the city of God. It is a civic virtue in that transcendent sense as well as in the more mundane one.

It is not a good idea to present honesty as a merely prudent virtue ("honesty is the best policy"), and it is even worse to present it in negative terms as restrictive and prohibitive. Honesty is, of course, a restraint on certain forms of behavior that may offer short-term advantages, but much more is it a liberating attitude of openness toward the rest of the world.

Perhaps honesty's most active opponent at present is what is known as image building: the calculated attempt to make a good impression regardless of whether or not that impression is a true one! To present an image of oneself that does not correspond to inward fact is to be imprisoned behind a screen of one's own creation. For those who project a false image of themselves there can be no outgoing except through devious and calculated channels designed to keep appearance and reality apart. The self can shrivel in such a prison. And image building is very hard work—boring as well as tiring. Letting the truth show may sometimes be shaming, but it belongs to a much simpler and happier way of life.

Some dictionaries say that the origin of the word "sincere" is obscure, but there is a theory that it goes back to a practice among sculptors of issuing a Latin warrant with their work to guarantee that it was "without wax." This would mean that there were no cracks in the stone cunningly concealed by wax fillings. The Latin for "without wax" just could be the basis of the English word "sincere." Whether or not this is the true explanation, it does provide a good picture of honesty: a solid, three-dimensional thing without flaws.

HONESTY

OLD TESTAMENT

Exodus 20:15

15 Thou shalt not steal.

Genesis 29:16–23, 25–27

16 And Laban had two daughters: the name of the elder was Leah, and the name of the younger was Rachel.

17 Leah was tender eyed; but Rachel was beautiful and well favoured.

18 And Jacob loved Rachel; and said, I will serve thee seven years for Rachel thy younger daughter.

19 And Laban said, It is better that I give her to thee, than that I should give her to another man: abide with me.

20 And Jacob served seven years for Rachel; and they seemed unto him but a few days, for the love he had to her.

21 And Jacob said unto Laban, Give me my wife, for my days are fulfilled, that I may go in unto her.

22 And Laban gathered together all the men of the place, and made a feast.

23 And it came to pass in the evening, that he took Leah his daughter, and brought her to him; and he went in unto her.

25 And it came to pass, that in the morning, behold, it was Leah: and he said to Laban, What is this thou hast done unto me? did not I serve with thee for Rachel? wherefore then hast thou beguiled me?

26 And Laban said, It must not be so done in our country, to give the younger before the firstborn.

27 Fulfil her week, and we will give thee this also for the service which thou shalt serve with me yet seven other years.

2 Kings 22:4–7 (King Josiah's instructions to his secretary)

4 Go up to Hilkiah the high priest, that he may sum the silver which is brought into the house of the Lord, which the keepers of the door have gathered of the people:

5 And let them deliver it into the hand of the doers of the work, that have the oversight of the house of the Lord: and let them give it to the doers of the work which is in the house of the Lord, to repair the breaches of the house,

6 Unto carpenters, and builders, and masons, and to buy timber and hewn stone to repair the house.

7 Howbeit there was no reckoning made with them of the money that was delivered into their hand, because they dealt faithfully.

Psalm 24:3–4

Who shall ascend into the hill of the
   Lord?
Or who shall stand in his holy place?
He that hath clean hands, and a pure
   heart;
Who hath not lifted up his soul unto
   vanity,
Nor sworn deceitfully.

NEW TESTAMENT

John 12:3–8

3 Then took Mary a pound of ointment of spikenard, very costly, and

anointed the feet of Jesus, and wiped his feet with her hair: and the house was filled with the odour of the ointment.

4 Then saith one of his disciples, Judas Iscariot, Simon's son, which should betray him,

5 Why was not this ointment sold for three hundred pence, and given to the poor?

6 This he said, not that he cared for the poor; but because he was a thief, and had the bag, and bare what was put therein.

7 Then said Jesus, Let her alone: against the day of my burying hath she kept this.

8 For the poor always ye have with you; but me ye have not always.

Romans 12:9

9 Let love be without dissimulation. Abhor that which is evil; cleave to that which is good.

2 Corinthians 13:8

8 For we can do nothing against the truth, but for the truth.

Ephesians 5:8–9

8 For ye were sometimes darkness, but now are ye light in the Lord: walk as children of light:

9 (For the fruit of the Spirit is in all goodness and righteousness and truth.)

Revelation 21:25–27 (a vision of the Holy City)

25 And the gates of it shall not be shut at all by day: for there shall be no night there.

26 And they shall bring the glory and honour of the nations into it.

27 And there shall in no wise enter into it any thing that defileth, neither whatsoever worketh abomination, or maketh a lie: but they which are written in the Lamb's book of life.

HOPE

The psalmists and the prophets speak of God as the hope of Israel, but hope is not so much an experience that the Old Testament isolates and examines as it is an essential element in its whole attitude to the future. Hope is built into the structure of the Old Testament's faith and experience. Significantly, when events shake that basic confidence in what lies ahead, the Old Testament remedy is to look at what lies behind.

Some of the most hopefully forward-looking chapters in the Old Testament open with a call to look back. Past, present, and future form a continuous line along the road of a single purpose, and that purpose a gracious one. They do not necessarily form a straight line, nor is the road necessarily a straight one. It may take unexpected turns and pass through some very dark areas, but there is a continuous sense of direction. The road is going somewhere. Goodness experienced at any point along it is a pledge of goodness as its ultimate destination. It is precisely when the situation seems hopeless that Jeremiah addresses God as Hope.

Hope is also the precondition of effective action. The farmer exemplifies it when he sows his seed, especially if he is hungry and weeps to see the seed corn thrown onto the ground when he would much rather eat it. Without hope based on past experience he would sow nothing. Israel is to live in the same way.

New Testament hope was focused on a day of fulfillment beyond the range of world history, but the fact that their hope looked beyond death did not make New Testament Christians indifferent to the present and the future of the world we know. The resurrection of Jesus was, for them, evidence that the end of Israel's long road was in sight, but the Spirit of God reached back to them from the risen Jesus to sustain them in the continuing pilgrimage. The letter to the Hebrews speaks of hope as an anchor that is fastened securely in the invisible world (Hebrews 6:19). What medieval artists pictured as the ship of souls can ride out any storm because it has a bow anchor attached to what lies ahead as well as a stern anchor fastened in past experience.

Indeed, the purpose that constitutes the ground of all human hope is one which transcends even humanity. Nature itself is caught up in the great forward movement. This does not lead to a belief in the inevitability of human improvement (see Progress), but it does mean that even human failure and suffering cannot frustrate the purpose with which we are invited to identify ourselves through faith, hope, and love—Paul's list of the three things which endure.

The Bible does not say that what you fear will not happen. It does say that, even if the worst happens, there is beyond that a good that will be wrung from it and in which you will find the true fulfillment of your hope. Oddly, this does not make men and women resigned to the threatening evil. On the contrary, it gives them more heart to fight against it. Hope is a better spur than desperation.

Our generation, threatened by vast and destructive forces, is often said to be particularly in need of hope. But hope cannot be had just because it would be a useful contribution to mental stability. Nor can it be had on its own. Faith and love are still inseparable from it, and they must be used to dig deeper into events and experience in order to find the underlying purposes with which hope can be aligned. Dickens's Mr. Micawber, with his groundless confidence that "something will turn up," is the most hopeless of men. Hope is not optimism. It is realism—but realism on a scale large enough to encompass the possibility of tragedy.

HOPE

OLD TESTAMENT

Isaiah 51:1–3; 55:12–13

1 Hearken to me, ye that follow after righteousness, ye that seek the Lord: look unto the rock whence ye are hewn, and to the hole of the pit whence ye are digged.

2 Look unto Abraham your father, and unto Sarah that bare you: for I called him alone, and blessed him, and increased him.

3 For the Lord shall comfort Zion: he will comfort all her waste places; and he will make her wilderness like Eden, and her desert like the garden of the Lord; joy and gladness shall be found therein, thanksgiving, and the voice of melody.

12 For ye shall go out with joy, and be led forth with peace: the mountains and the hills shall break forth before you into singing, and all the trees of the field shall clap their hands.

13 Instead of the thorn shall come up the fir tree, and instead of the brier shall come up the myrtle tree.

Psalm 27:2–3

When the wicked, even mine enemies and my foes, came upon me to eat up my flesh,
They stumbled and fell.
Though an host should encamp against me,
My heart shall not fear:
Though war should rise against me,
In this will I be confident.

Jeremiah 14:8

8 O the hope of Israel, the saviour thereof in time of trouble, why shouldest thou be as a stranger in the land, and as a wayfaring man that turneth aside to tarry for a night?

Psalm 126:5–6

They that sow in tears shall reap in joy.
He that goeth forth and weepeth, bearing precious seed,
Shall doubtless come again with rejoicing, bringing his sheaves with him.

NEW TESTAMENT

John 14:18–19, 16–17

18 I will not leave you comfortless: I will come to you.

19 Yet a little while, and the world seeth me no more; but ye see me: because I live, ye shall live also.

16 And I will pray the Father, and he shall give you another Comforter, that he may abide with you for ever;

17 Even the Spirit of truth.

Romans 5:1–5; 8:22–25

1 We have peace with God through our Lord Jesus Christ:

2 By whom also we have access by faith into this grace wherein we stand, and rejoice in hope of the glory of God.

3 And not only so, but we glory in tribulations also: knowing that tribulation worketh patience;

4 And patience, experience; and experience, hope:

5 And hope maketh not ashamed; because the love of God is shed abroad in our hearts by the Holy Ghost which is given unto us.

22 For we know that the whole creation groaneth and travaileth in pain together until now.

23 And not only they, but ourselves also, which have the firstfruits of the Spirit, even we ourselves groan within ourselves, waiting for the adoption, to wit, the redemption of our body.

24 For we are saved by hope: but hope that is seen is not hope: for what a man seeth, why doth he yet hope for?

25 But if we hope for that we see not, then do we with patience wait for it.

1 Peter 1:3, 13

3 Blessed be the God and Father of our Lord Jesus Christ, which according to his abundant mercy hath begotten us again unto a lively hope by the resurrection of Jesus Christ from the dead.

13 Wherefore gird up the loins of your mind, be sober, and hope to the end for the grace that is to be brought unto you at the revelation of Jesus Christ.

HUMILITY

The word "humility" occurs in the Bible in some astonishing contexts. It is by no means confined to the descriptions of little men. Moses, the most towering figure in the Old Testament, is said in the fourth book of the Bible to be the humblest man on earth—one small reason for us not to accept too literally the tradition that Moses was himself the author of the first five books of the Bible!

Of course, the Old Testament does record how power and greatness can rob people of their humility. Eventually it did so in Saul's case. But humility was regarded as a door to greatness rather than as a barrier to it. This attitude rested naturally on the belief that all greatness comes from God, so the humble man who claims no greatness in himself is more open to it than is the proud man.

In the New Testament humility crops up in equally incongruous contexts. In Matthew's Gospel Jesus speaks of his being "humble in heart" in almost the same breath that he speaks of having a unique relationship to God—a God who discloses himself to the humble, just as the Old Testament had insisted. The parable of the guest at a wedding feast is more than a lesson in table manners: it points to a whole way of life in which nothing is claimed, everything is accepted; nothing is of right, all is of grace.

In one of the New Testament's key passages Paul relates such behavior not just to a code of morality or to a static ideal, but to the action of God himself. To live other than humbly would be to blind ourselves to the whole pattern of God's dealings with us through Christ.

Yet no groveling or self-abasement is involved. Humility is simply a matter of opening one's eyes to truth and fact. Paul elsewhere tells everyman "Not to think of himself more highly than he ought, but to think soberly" (Romans 12:3). Abject prostration may be as unsober a posture as stiff-necked pride. Truth is what matters. Humility is not humiliation.

William Temple, onetime archbishop of Canterbury, said, "Humility does not mean thinking less of yourself than of other people, nor does it mean having a low opinion of your own gifts. It means freedom from thinking about yourself one way or the other at all. . . . The humility which consists in being a great deal occupied about yourself, and saying you are of little worth, is not Christian humility. It is one form of self-occupation and a very poor and futile one at that."

There are therefore two reasons why we know that it is a lie when Uriah Heep in Dickens's *David Copperfield* says, "I am well aware that I am the 'umblest person going." Whatever else Heep may be, humble (on the evidence of that speech alone) he cannot be: first, because one cannot boast of humility without abandoning it and, second, because his eyes are on himself. The antidote to pride and every other kind of self-preoccupation is not humiliation but love. Outward-looking, outgoing people can be humble without noticing it, because they are not noticing themselves.

Our society does not foster humility. Some communities are dominated by ideas of hierarchy and class; some revolve around wealth and power; some are meritocracies. All are thereby frustrating their own growth in true human greatness. What is more, they are living on illusions. Their attitudes are false to the facts. Their cure is to see things as they are and to accept what they are given.

HUMILITY

OLD TESTAMENT

Numbers 12:3

3 Now the man Moses was very meek, above all the men which were upon the face of the earth.

1 Samuel 9:17–21; 10:1

17 And when Samuel saw Saul, the Lord said unto him, Behold the man whom I spake to thee of! this same shall reign over my people.

18 Then Saul drew near to Samuel in the gate, and said, Tell me, I pray thee, where the seer's house is.

19 And Samuel answered Saul, and said, I am the seer: go up before me unto the high place: for ye shall eat with me to-day,

20 And on whom is all the desire of Israel? Is it not on thee, and on all thy father's house?

21 And Saul answered and said, Am not I a Benjamite, of the smallest of

the tribes of Israel? and my family the least of all the families of the tribe of Benjamin? wherefore then speakest thou so to me?

1 Then Samuel took a vial of oil, and poured it upon his head, and kissed him, and said, Is it not because the Lord hath anointed thee to be captain over his inheritance?

Proverbs 15:33

The fear of the Lord is the instruction of wisdom;
And before honour is humility.

Jeremiah 9:23–24

23 Let not the wise man glory in his wisdom, neither let the mighty man glory in his might, let not the rich man glory in his riches:

24 But let him that glorieth glory in this, that he understandeth and knoweth me, that I am the Lord.

Psalm 25:9; 149:4

The meek will he guide in judgment:
And the meek will he teach his way.
For the Lord taketh pleasure in his people:
He will beautify the meek with salvation.

NEW TESTAMENT

Matthew 11:25–30

25 At that time Jesus answered and said, I thank thee, O Father, Lord of heaven and earth, because thou hast hid these things from the wise and prudent, and hast revealed them unto babes.

26 Even so, Father: for so it seemed good in thy sight.

27 All things are delivered unto me of my Father: and no man knoweth the Son, but the Father; neither knoweth any man the Father, save the Son, and he to whomsoever the Son will reveal him.

28 Come unto me, all ye that labour and are heavy laden, and I will give you rest.

29 Take my yoke upon you, and learn of me; for I am meek and lowly in heart: and ye shall find rest unto your souls.

30 For my yoke is easy, and my burden is light.

Luke 14:7–11

7 And he put forth a parable to those which were bidden, when he marked how they chose out the chief rooms; saying unto them,

8 When thou art bidden of any man to a wedding, sit not down in the highest room; lest a more honourable man than thou be bidden of him;

9 And he that bade thee and him come and say to thee, Give this man place; and thou begin with shame to take the lowest room.

10 But when thou art bidden, go and sit down in the lowest room; that when he that bade thee cometh, he may say unto thee, Friend, go up higher: then shalt thou have worship in the presence of them that sit at meat with thee.

11 For whosoever exalteth himself shall be abased; and he that humbleth himself shall be exalted.

Philippians 2:5–9

5 Let this mind be in you, which was also in Christ Jesus:

6 Who, being in the form of God, thought it not robbery to be equal with God:

7 But made himself of no reputation, and took upon him the form of a servant, and was made in the likeness of men:

8 And being found in fashion as a man, he humbled himself, and became obedient unto death, even the death of the cross.

9 Wherefore God also hath highly exalted him, and given him a name which is above every name.

IDEAL

The word "ideal" does not occur in the Bible, but the practical function of an ideal is performed in various ways and covered by various words. The Old Testament shows no interest in the ideal as a theoretical concept or as a heavenly reality of which things on earth can be at best only a dim shadow. Philosophy is not its business; abstract speculation about an ideal world is not its concern. What the Old Testament writers do care about intensely is the kind of perfection that can be realized within the conditions actually known to human beings.

One of the words used to point to this practical ideal is the Hebrew word "Torah." It is usually translated as "law," but it really signifies the whole revelation of God's will and purpose. This law is perfect and has the power to make perfect, because it is God's "word" (another term that points to perfection). God's word is the expression of his mind and the vehicle of his spirit, so it has the power to do and not merely to say what is God's will.

A third word relevant to the idea of the ideal is "wisdom." This is looked at elsewhere (see Wisdom), but it, too, speaks of a perfection that reaches out from God to communicate itself to men and women. Whatever the terminology used, the Old Testament ideal is always a practical ideal, neither so remote from the attainments of ordinary mortals as to be irrelevant to them, nor so near to what they normally are as to be no challenge to them. It is a magnet that tends to draw them beyond what they are toward what they might be.

In the New Testament the ideal is brought near by being embodied in the person of Jesus. He is the incarnation of "the Word"—a term used in John's Gospel in much the same way that "wisdom" is used in the Old Testament: the articulated mind of God, communicated to human beings in terms relevant to their actual condition.

Without using the word, all the books of the New Testament represent Jesus as the ideal. He is perfection in human form, and therefore *relevant* perfection, making immediate demands on every aspect of human behavior. It is significant that in speaking of Jesus as the ideal to be formed in Christians as they mature, the New Testament writers repeatedly use the three key ideas they have inherited

170

from the Old Testament: the word, the law, and wisdom. They are thinking of a perfection inherent in the nature of things from the beginning of time, and yet one that has come so close to them that every detail of daily life is checked and challenged by it.

The modern tendency is to make the ideal less relevant and more discouraging. The discouragement arises when the ideal is treated as an immediate expectation rather than a continuing challenge. Those, for instance, who expect an ideal marriage are sure to be let down. There are good marriages but no ideal ones. Those who expect perfection in a marriage partner or in themselves are well on the way to marital disaster. They are inclined to give up as soon as they find a flaw.

On the other hand, an ideal can be too distant. "Oh, yes," say the worldly wise, "in an ideal world it would be different, but as things are we have to cheat a bit"—or lie a bit, or bribe a bit, or rely on force, or whatever it may be. The ideal as a remote and irrelevant perfection is of no earthly use.

The relevant ideal is the one that reaches to where we are and pulls us toward where we are not yet.

IDEAL

OLD TESTAMENT

Deuteronomy 30:11–14

11 For this commandment which I command thee this day, it is not hidden from thee, neither is it far off.

12 It is not in heaven, that thou shouldest say, Who shall go up for us to heaven, and bring it unto us, that we may hear it, and do it?

13 Neither is it beyond the sea, that thou shouldest say, Who shall go over the sea for us, and bring it unto us, that we may hear it, and do it?

14 But the word is very nigh unto thee, in thy mouth, and in thy heart, that thou mayest do it.

Psalm 19:7–9

The law of the Lord is perfect, converting the soul:

The testimony of the Lord is sure, making wise the simple.

The statutes of the Lord are right, rejoicing the heart:

The commandment of the Lord is pure, enlightening the eyes.

The fear of the Lord is clean, enduring for ever:

The judgments of the Lord are true and righteous altogether.

Isaiah 55:8–11

8 For my thoughts are not your thoughts, neither are your ways my ways, saith the Lord.

9 For as the heavens are higher than the earth, so are my ways higher than your ways, and my thoughts than your thoughts.

10 For as the rain cometh down, and the snow from heaven, and returneth not thither, but watereth the

earth, and maketh it bring forth and bud, that it may give seed to the sower, and bread to the eater:

11 So shall my word be that goeth forth out of my mouth: it shall not return unto me void, but it shall accomplish that which I please, and it shall prosper in the thing whereto I sent it.

Proverbs 8:1, 4–6

Doth not wisdom cry?
And understanding put forth her voice?
Unto you, O men, I call;
And my voice is to the sons of man.
O ye simple, understand wisdom:
And, ye fools, be ye of an understanding heart.
Hear; for I will speak of excellent things;
And the opening of my lips shall be right things.

NEW TESTAMENT

John 1:14

14 And the Word was made flesh, and dwelt among us, (and we beheld his glory, the glory as of the only begotten of the Father,) full of grace and truth.

Matthew 5:48

48 Be ye therefore perfect, even as your Father which is in heaven is perfect.

John 14:8–9

8 Philip saith unto him, Lord, shew us the Father, and it sufficeth us.

9 Jesus saith unto him, Have I been so long time with you, and yet hast thou not known me, Philip? he that hath seen me hath seen the Father.

Ephesians 4:13

13 Till we all come in the unity of the faith, and of the knowledge of the Son of God, unto a perfect man, unto the measure of the stature of the fulness of Christ.

Colossians 1:27–28

27 Christ in you, the hope of glory:

28 Whom we preach, warning every man, and teaching every man in all wisdom; that we may present every man perfect in Christ Jesus.

James 1:23–25

23 For if any be a hearer of the word, and not a doer, he is like unto a man beholding his natural face in a glass:

24 For he beholdeth himself, and goeth his way, and straightway forgetteth what manner of man he was.

25 But whoso looketh into the perfect law of liberty, and continueth therein, he being not a forgetful hearer, but a doer of the work, this man shall be blessed in his deed.

ILLNESS

Honour the doctor for his services,
for the Lord created him.
His skill comes from the Most High. . . .

> The Lord created medicines from the earth,
> and a sensible man will not disparage them.
> (Ecclesiastes 38:1–2, 4)

These words (as translated in the New English Bible) come from one of the books that appeared in Israel later than the books of the Hebrew Bible but earlier than those of the New Testament. They represent a considerable change of tone from that used in the Hebrew Old Testament. Doctors play no very great, or greatly respected, part in those books. A disease such as leprosy was diagnosed by the priests, and they were also responsible for certifying its cure. Simpler illnesses and injuries were treated in homely ways by anyone available. Physicians evidently existed (at court, at least), but to consult them instead of seeking a cure through religion was regarded as very foolish.

This is because the Old Testament does not regard illness as something that can be isolated from the rest of human life and treated separately. Illness connects with every aspect of individual and social life, and particularly with sin. This is not to say that people fall ill only because they have themselves done wrong. Job rejected that view, and God supported him. Yet illness was a feature of a flawed world and a disobedient people. It could be removed by God's grace if a person was humble enough to accept the grace—a qualification that very nearly did for Naaman. He had wanted some of the drama then (and now) popularly associated with spiritual healing. He had to be denied it so that his faith would be directed beyond the means of healing to the source of health.

In the New Testament Jesus denies that there is a direct connection beween a man's affliction and his sin—or that of his parents. He does not blame people for being ill. At the same time he does treat healing and forgiveness as acts of the same quality, and by implication regards sin and illness as having much in common. This point is made explicitly in the story of the paralytic, but it is also apparent when Jesus deals with sin or with sickness separately—sometimes more apparent in the original than in translation. For instance, to a woman he has forgiven, he says in our translation, "Thy faith hath saved thee" (Luke 7:50); to one he has healed he says, "Thy faith hath made thee whole" (Mark 5:34). But in the original Greek of the Gospels exactly the same form of words is used in each story. Healing and forgiveness have enough in common to be covered by the same terms.

Yet to remain unhealed did not necessarily signify the absence of faith any more than it denoted the presence of sin. Paul had faith enough, but he was not healed. Instead, he was told that it was better for him to learn a lesson from his "thorn in the flesh," as he called his illness. It was recognized that sickness could be used without being cured, but all New Testament Christians prayed for the sick, and one of the recognized offices among them was that of the healer.

This attitude embraced and did not disparage the work of the physician. Luke, author of the Book of Acts as well as of the Gospel that bears his name, was himself a doctor.

It is the whole person who is sick. This biblical affirmation would now be endorsed by many in the medical profession. A sick man who looks at his sickness in the context of his life may come to see the healing of his illness as the first step in the putting right of his life, or he may see the putting right of his life as the first step in the healing of his illness, or he may see his illness as something he can grow by, even if it is not healed.

Any of the three would be a positive response to illness instead of a negative reaction away from it, and all three are biblical.

ILLNESS

OLD TESTAMENT

Psalm 103:1, 3.

Bless the Lord, O my soul:
And all that is within me, bless his holy
name,
Who forgiveth all thine iniquities;
Who healeth all thy diseases.

2 Kings 5:7–14 (Naaman is sent by the king of Syria with a letter asking that he be healed)

7 And it came to pass, when the king of Israel had read the letter, that he rent his clothes, and said, Am I God, to kill and to make alive, that this man doth send unto me to recover a man of his leprosy? wherefore consider, I pray you, and see how he seeketh a quarrel against me.

8 And it was so, when Elisha the man of God had heard that the king of Israel had rent his clothes, that he sent to the king, saying, Wherefore hast thou rent thy clothes? let him come now to me, and he shall know that there is a prophet in Israel.

9 So Naaman came with his horses and with his chariot, and stood at the door of the house of Elisha.

10 And Elisha sent a messenger unto him, saying, Go and wash in Jordan seven times, and thy flesh shall come again to thee, and thou shalt be clean.

11 But Naaman was wroth, and went away, and said, Behold, I thought, he will surely come out to me, and stand, and call on the name of the Lord his God, and strike his hand over the place, and recover the leper.

12 Are not Abana and Pharpar, rivers of Damascus, better than all the waters of Israel? may I not wash in them, and be clean? So he turned and went away in a rage.

13 And his servants came near, and spake unto him, and said, My father, if the prophet had bid thee do some great thing, wouldest thou not have done it? how much rather then, when he saith to thee, Wash, and be clean?

14 Then went he down, and dipped himself seven times in Jordan, accord-

ing to the saying of the man of God: and his flesh came again like unto the flesh of a little child, and he was clean.

2 Chronicles 16:12

12 And Asa in the thirty and ninth year of his reign was diseased in his feet, until his disease was exceeding great: yet in his disease he sought not to the Lord, but to the physicians.

NEW TESTAMENT

Mark 1:29–34; 2:1, 3–12 (Jesus at Capernaum)

29 And forthwith, when they were come out of the synagogue, they entered into the house of Simon and Andrew, with James and John.

30 But Simon's wife's mother lay sick of a fever, and anon they tell him of her.

31 And he came and took her by the hand, and lifted her up; and immediately the fever left her, and she ministered unto them.

32 And at even, when the sun did set, they brought unto him all that were diseased, and them that were possessed with devils.

33 And all the city was gathered together at the door.

34 And he healed many that were sick of divers diseases, and cast out many devils; and suffered not the devils to speak, because they knew him.

1 And again he entered into Capernaum after some days; and it was noised that he was in the house.

3 And they come unto him, bringing one sick of the palsy, which was borne of four.

4 And when they could not come nigh unto him for the press, they uncovered the roof where he was: and when they had broken it up, they let down the bed wherein the sick of the palsy lay.

5 When Jesus saw their faith, he said unto the sick of the palsy, Son, thy sins be forgiven thee.

6 But there were certain of the scribes sitting there, and reasoning in their hearts,

7 Why doth this man thus speak blasphemies? who can forgive sins but God only?

8 And immediately when Jesus perceived in his spirit that they so reasoned within themselves, he said unto them, Why reason ye these things in your hearts?

9 Whether is it easier to say to the sick of the palsy, Thy sins be forgiven thee; or to say, Arise, and take up thy bed, and walk?

10 But that ye may know that the Son of man hath power on earth to forgive sins, (he saith to the sick of the palsy,)

11 I say unto thee, Arise, and take up thy bed, and go thy way into thine house.

12 And immediately he arose, took up the bed, and went forth before them all.

John 9:1–3

1 And as Jesus passed by, he saw a man which was blind from his birth.

2 And his disciples asked him, saying, Master, who did sin, this man, or his parents, that he was born blind?

3 Jesus answered, Neither hath this man sinned, nor his parents.

2 Corinthians 12:7–9

7 There was given to me a thorn in the flesh, the messenger of Satan to buffet me, lest I should be exalted above measure.

8 For this thing I besought the Lord thrice, that it might depart from me.

9 And he said unto me, My grace is sufficient for thee: for my strength is made perfect in weakness.

INSPIRATION

The inspired prophet of the later parts of the Old Testament, unlike the inspired poet of popular mythology, does not write or speak in a trance as if he were a mere pen in another's hand or the psychic vehicle of another's voice. To be inspired is to be breathed into, but biblical inspiration involves no takeover. The human being, says Genesis, is essentially an organism breathed into by God (see Body). Without inspiration it is impossible to be human.

Certainly inspiration was associated with special people and special gifts. The breath of God could make a man into a prophet, or a mighty warrior, or a lion-killer, or a skilled craftsman, or a man of wisdom. Old Testament passages speak of each of these, and many others, in terms of divine inspiration.

Yet even in the days when an inspired prophet was regarded as an exceptional man who behaved in an exceptional and very noticeable way, Moses could be described as wishing all men to be equally inspired. The prophet Joel expected that wish to be fulfilled. Inspiration was not regarded as the monopoly of a cultural or religious elite. It was for all. And the ultimate effect of inspiration, as the later prophets understood it, was the inbreathing of God's Spirit in such a way that his law would be written on the human heart and instinctively expressed in human lives.

The writers of the New Testament, too, found it impossible to speak of God's Spirit without thinking of its being breathed into men and women, since the original word for "spirit" was the same as that for "breath" (see Spirit). Jesus was heralded as one who would immerse human beings in the Spirit of God and was himself reported as saying, "If ye . . . know how to give good gifts unto your children, how much more shall your heavenly Father give the Holy Spirit to them that ask him" (Luke 11:13). On those disposed to receive it, even though they did not ask, the Spirit was poured out on the Day of Pentecost—an experience of inspiration that is described in Acts under the traditional symbols of wind and fire.

When the New Testament speaks of the Scriptures as being inspired ("God-breathed" would be a very literal translation), it means of course what Christians now refer to as the Old Testament (since The New Testament was still being written). There is still no suggestion that all those laws, prophecies, and other writings were dictated to men so directly that God is their only real author.

The writing of Job is very readily distinguished from that of Ezekiel as is Ecclesiastes from Daniel. The inspired writer speaks his own mind and in his own voice, even when the truth revealed to him is—as in Jeremiah's case, for instance—one that nothing less than divine authority would persuade him to accept.

The same is true of New Testament writers: each has his individual voice. The spirit-filled human personality is not obliterated. Paul, struggling with the problems referred to him by the church at Corinth, claims inspiration—"I think also that I have the Spirit of God" (1 Corinthians 7:40)—but it brings him no certain assurance that he has got the answers right. This is so much the case that he distinguishes between the answers that have a word from the Lord to authenticate them and those that have only his own. Clearly he is aware that his own abilities and limitations are still in play, Spirit-endowed though he was.

But then, Paul believed the whole Christian community to be Spirit-endowed. Some even had the gift "to distinguish between spirits"—that is, to tell true inspirations from false ones.

The biblical democratization of the idea of inspiration is much to be desired. It would rescue us from the elitist claims of cultural snobs and occult practitioners and any who claim private connections with deity. *All* of us have connections with deity, *all* of us are special, *each* of us has his or her inspired gift. Inspiration is everyday, but not commonplace. It is that which gives to each of us a dimension of glory. It is that which makes us what we would otherwise never be; fully ourselves.

INSPIRATION

OLD TESTAMENT

Job 32:8; 33:4

But there is a spirit in man:
And the inspiration of the Almighty giveth them understanding.
The Spirit of God hath made me,
And the breath of the Almighty hath given me life.

Numbers 11:24–29

24 And Moses went out, and told the people the words of the Lord, and gathered the seventy men of the elders of the people, and set them round about the tabernacle.

25 And the Lord came down in a cloud, and spake unto him, and took of the spirit that was upon him, and gave it unto the seventy elders: and it came to pass, that, when the spirit rested upon them, they prophesied, and did not cease.

26 But there remained two of the men in the camp, the name of the one was Eldad, and the name of the

other Medad: and the spirit rested upon them; and they were of them that were written, but went not out unto the tabernacle: and they prophesied in the camp.

27 And there ran a young man, and told Moses, and said, Eldad and Medad do prophesy in the camp.

28 And Joshua the son of Nun, the servant of Moses, one of his young men, answered and said, My lord Moses, forbid them.

29 And Moses said unto him, Enviest thou for my sake? would God that all the Lord's people were prophets, and that the Lord would put his spirit upon them!

Exodus 31:1–5

1 And the Lord spake unto Moses, saying,

2 See, I have called by name Bezaleel the son of Uri, the son of Hur, of the tribe of Judah:

3 And I have filled him with the spirit of God, in wisdom, and in understanding, and in knowledge, and in all manner of workmanship,

4 To devise cunning works, to work in gold, and in silver, and in brass,

5 And in cutting of stones, to set them, and in carving of timber, to work in all manner of workmanship.

Joel 2:28–29

28 I will pour out my spirit upon all flesh; and your sons and your daughters shall prophesy, your old men shall dream dreams, your young men shall see visions:

29 And also upon the servants and upon the handmaids in those days will I pour out my spirit.

Ezekiel 36:26–27

26 A new heart also will I give you, and a new spirit will I put within you: and I will take away the stony heart out of your flesh, and I will give you an heart of flesh.

27 And I will put my spirit within you, and cause you to walk in my statutes, and ye shall keep my judgments, and do them.

NEW TESTAMENT

Luke 3:16

16 John answered, saying unto them all, I indeed baptize you with water; but one mightier than I cometh, the latchet of whose shoes I am not worthy to unloose: he shall baptize you with the Holy Ghost and with fire.

John 20:19, 21–22

19 Then the same day at evening, being the first day of the week, when the doors were shut where the disciples were assembled for fear of the Jews, came Jesus and stood in the midst, and saith unto them, Peace be unto you.

21 Then said Jesus to them again, Peace be unto you: as my Father hath sent me, even so send I you.

22 And when he had said this, he breathed on them, and saith unto them, Receive ye the Holy Ghost.

1 Corinthians 12:4–11

4 Now there are diversities of gifts, but the same Spirit.

5 And there are differences of administrations, but the same Lord.

6 And there are diversities of operations, but it is the same God which worketh all in all.

7 But the manifestation of the Spirit is given to every man to profit withal.

8 For to one is given by the Spirit the word of wisdom; to another the word of knowledge by the same Spirit;

9 To another faith by the same Spirit; to another the gifts of healing by the same Spirit;

10 To another the working of miracles; to another prophecy; to another discerning of spirits; to another divers kinds of tongues; to another the interpretation of tongues:

11 But all these worketh that one and the selfsame Spirit, dividing to every man severally as he will.

2 Timothy 3:16

16 All scripture is given by inspiration of God, and is profitable for doctrine, for reproof, for correction, for instruction in righteousness.

JEALOUSY

The difference between jealousy and envy is glanced at in the entry for envy, but the distinction is sometimes too subtle to worry about. Jealousy in the bad sense is hardly distinguishable from envy. But jealousy does also have a good sense, and then it is hardly distinguishable from zeal—the two English words have the same root (see Zeal). In the Old Testament God is jealous for his people in the sense that they are his and he has no intention of letting them give themselves to idols. This is not an ungenerous attitude since, in fact, the loss would be theirs rather than his.

A husband, too, was allowed to be jealous in relation to his wife. Old Testament law provided for a very grim trial by ordeal to which the wife of a jealous husband could be subjected. It is one of those biblical practices that should not be transferred from biblical times to our own. Given a universally accepted belief in its efficacy, it could have worked, if only for psychological reasons, but it was an attempt to institutionalize the solution to a problem that was (and is) essentially personal. A phenomenon as ugly as marital jealousy, when projected into the public arena, inevitably produces an ugly spectacle.

The New Testament makes it clear (as did the passage from Numbers quoted in the previous entry) that one of the areas in which the wrong kind of envy and jealousy can arise is that of religion. Jesus preached of an openhanded, generous God, but he knew that this concept would deal a blow to religious pride. In his parable of the workers in the vineyard, the employer adopts a generous attitude to his short-time workers and thereby provokes the jealousy of those who have worked longer. Significantly the employer clinches his argument with the rhetorical question, "Is thine eye evil, because I am good?" (Matthew 20:14)—in other words, Are you jealous because I am generous?

The question became something more than rhetorical. When the work of Jesus and his apostles drew popular attention, it provoked the jealousy of the authorities. They were used to being the focus of religious attention and were unwilling to see their position eroded. Pilate, as a detached observer, could see what was happening. He offered to release Jesus in his annual amnesty, "for he knew that for envy they had delivered him" (Matthew 27:18).

Jesus' own apostles, as reported by John, were not immune to the desire to put a fence around their sphere of work and preserve it jealously from encroachment. The great religious figure who managed to put this natural tendency into reverse was John the Baptist—traditionally represented in paintings with a hand pointing away from himself to Christ. His saying about Jesus—"He must increase, but I must decrease"—is the classic anti-jealousy posture. Paul speaks of the absence of jealousy as one of the fruits of the Spirit and the marks of love. Yet he could speak of his being rightly jealous for his converts. He uses the phrase "godly jealousy" to distinguish it from other kinds.

We seem to have a very rough rule of thumb: to be jealous *for* is good; to be jealous *of* is bad.

But rules are not enough. The green-eyed monster jealousy will continue to exercise its spell so long as we think of people and principles and causes as possessions of our own. Love does not sanction license or promiscuity, but it holds its objects in generous and open hands. Such a love provides its own bonds of attachment to what is right. They do not need to be reinforced with institutionalized sanctions or watchful suspicions.

Love not only forbids the bad kind of jealousy; it also promotes the good kind. To be jealous for one's own honor and for one's country's honor is an expression of proper self-love and patriotism. To be jealous for the good name of one's spouse or of one's religious community is an aspect of love for them. To know that one is the object of such jealous love, whether on the human or the transcendent level, is to know that one is valued.

JEALOUSY

OLD TESTAMENT

Exodus 34:14

14 For thou shalt worship no other god: for the Lord, whose name is Jealous, is a jealous God.

Numbers 5:11–23

11 And the Lord spake unto Moses, saying,

12 Speak unto the children of Israel, and say unto them, If any man's wife go aside, and commit a trespass against him,

13 And a man lie with her carnally, and it be hid from the eyes of her husband, and be kept close, and she be defiled, and there be no witness against her, neither she be taken with the manner;

14 And the spirit of jealousy come upon him, and he be jealous of his wife, and she be defiled: or if the spirit of jealousy come upon him, and he be jealous of his wife, and she be not defiled:

15 Then shall the man bring his wife unto the priest, and he shall bring her offering for her, the tenth part of an ephah of barley meal; he shall pour no oil upon it, nor put frankincense thereon; for it is an offering of jealousy, an offering of memorial, bringing iniquity to remembrance.

16 And the priest shall bring her near, and set her before the Lord:

17 And the priest shall take holy water in an earthen vessel; and of the dust that is in the floor of the tabernacle the priest shall take, and put it into the water:

18 And the priest shall set the woman before the Lord, and uncover the woman's head, and put the offering of memorial in her hands, which is the jealousy offering: and the priest shall have in his hand the bitter water that causeth the curse:

19 And the priest shall charge her by an oath, and say unto the woman, If no man have lain with thee, and if thou hast not gone aside to uncleanness with another instead of thy husband, be thou free from this bitter water that causeth the curse:

20 But if thou hast gone aside to another instead of thy husband, and if thou be defiled, and some man have lain with thee beside thine husband:

21 Then the priest shall charge the woman with an oath of cursing, and the priest shall say unto the woman, The Lord make thee a curse and an oath among thy people, when the Lord doth make thy thigh to rot, and thy belly to swell;

22 And this water that causeth the curse shall go into thy bowels, to make thy belly to swell, and thy thigh to rot: And the woman shall say, Amen, amen.

23 And the priest shall write these curses in a book, and he shall blot them out with the bitter water.

NEW TESTAMENT

John 3:26–30 (a story of John the Baptist)

26 And they came unto John, and said unto him, Rabbi, he that was with thee beyond Jordan, to whom thou barest witness, behold, the same baptizeth, and all men come to him.

27 John answered and said, A man can receive nothing, except it be given him from heaven.

28 Ye yourselves bear me witness, that I said, I am not the Christ, but that I am sent before him.

29 He that hath the bride is the bridegroom: but the friend of the bridegroom, which standeth and heareth him, rejoiceth greatly because of the bridegroom's voice: this my joy therefore is fulfilled.

30 He must increase, but I must decrease.

Luke 9:49–50 (a story of John the Apostle)

49 And John answered and said, Master, we saw one casting out devils in thy name; and we forbad him, because he followeth not with us.

50 And Jesus said unto him, Forbid him not: for he that is not against us is for us.

Acts 5:12, 15–18

12 By the hands of the apostles were many signs and wonders wrought among the people . . .

15 Insomuch that they brought forth the sick into the streets, and laid them on beds and couches, that at the least the shadow of Peter passing by might overshadow some of them.

16 There came also a multitude out of the cities round about unto Jerusalem, bringing sick folks, and them which were vexed with unclean spirits: and they were healed every one.

17 Then the high priest rose up, and all they that were with him, (which is the sect of the Sadducees,) and were filled with indignation,

18 And laid their hands on the apostles, and put them in the common prison.

2 Corinthians 11:2

2 For I am jealous over you with godly jealousy: for I have espoused you to one husband, that I may present you as a chaste virgin to Christ.

1 Corinthians 13:4–7

4 Charity suffereth long, and is kind; charity envieth not; charity vaunteth not itself, is not puffed up,

5 Doth not behave itself unseemly, seeketh not her own, is not easily provoked, thinketh no evil;

6 Rejoiceth not in iniquity, but rejoiceth in the truth;

7 Beareth all things, believeth all things, hopeth all things, endureth all things.

JUDGMENT

The story of the judgment of Solomon is told in the Old Testament as an illustration of his wisdom. What makes it so wise, so exemplary, and so appealing a story is partly that Solomon's solution to the problem brings to light a truth that had been concealed, and partly that it tells of the vindication of an insignificant citizen.

Sound judgment in the Old Testament, whether exercised by man or by God, has two salient features: it reveals truths hitherto concealed, and it is tender to the humble and the weak. The prophets promised that the whole world would eventually be subject to such judgment.

The New Testament confirms this promise but adds that in a sense it has already happened. The presence of Jesus in the world has initiated an almost automatic process of judgment. By their response to him, men and women pronounce judgment on themselves. Those who identify with Jesus in faith and love have already passed beyond judgment day. "Verily, verily," says the Jesus of John's Gospel, "he that heareth my word, and believeth on him that sent me, hath everlasting life and shall not come into condemnation; but is passed from death unto life" (John 5:24). This is not because he has already achieved moral perfection, but because of his inward relationship with perfection in the person of Jesus. We are to be judged not by what we have done, but by what we are identified with—not by works, but by faith, as Paul is always saying.

This, however, is a hidden truth that completed judgment must reveal. So the New Testatment speaks of judgment as past, present, and to come. The parable of the sheep and goats uses a conventional picture of ultimate judgment, and it heightens the artificiality of the scene by employing very stylized language with which to describe it. This, however, is only the decor within which the story is set. Its real point is the wholly unexpected content of the judgments pronounced, both favorable and unfavorable.

These suggest that all depends on a man's relationship to the King Judge, but that relationship has been hidden and the king concealed within everyday situations. Judgment is indeed the uncovering of truth, and the truth is that a man's relationship to his neighbor is not only relevant to his relationship with God, it *is* his relationship with God. Morality and mysticism are one.

The end of the world may seem a long way away from today's moral decisions, but the Bible makes them close in principle if not in time. The judgment process is at work now, and we participate in it.

We do this first by seeking the rights and wrongs hidden within things, and by doing so with a special tenderness toward those unable to defend themselves. "As God is my judge" used to be a familiar kind of oath-taking. Well, he is. And quite a lot of judging we should leave to him. But some judgments we have to make ourselves. A posture of moral neutrality is not biblical.

But this daily process of judgment has to be related to the ultimate one, if only because we are ultimately to be judged by the verdicts we have passed. If we have seen evil and smiled on it, that is our condemnation. If we have seen good and identified with it, that is our vindication. The rough justice of the law may have to deal with us in terms of our deeds, but even in that setting it should be clear that mercy can be shown when the bad deed is inwardly renounced and the good inwardly embraced. Ultimate judgment is made in terms of where the heart is.

JUDGMENT

OLD TESTAMENT

1 Kings 3:16–22, 24–27

16 Then came there two women, that were harlots, unto the king, and stood before him.

17 And the one woman said, O my lord, I and this woman dwell in one house; and I was delivered of a child with her in the house.

18 And it came to pass the third day after that I was delivered, that this woman was delivered also: and we were together; there was no stranger with us in the house, save we two in the house.

19 And this woman's child died in the night; because she overlaid it.

20 And she arose at midnight, and took my son from beside me, while thine handmaid slept, and laid it in her bosom, and laid her dead child in my bosom.

21 And when I rose in the morning to give my child suck, behold, it was dead: but when I had considered it in the morning, behold, it was not my son, which I did bear.

22 And the other woman said, Nay; but the living is my son, and the dead is thy son.

24 And the king said, Bring me a sword. And they brought a sword before the king.

25 And the king said, Divide the living child in two, and give half to the one, and half to the other.

26 Then spake the woman whose the living child was unto the king, for her bowels yearned upon her son, and she said, O my lord, give her the living child, and in no wise slay it. But the other said, Let it be neither mine nor thine, but divide it.

27 Then the king answered and said, Give her the living child, and in no wise slay it: she is the mother thereof.

Isaiah 42:1, 3

1 Behold my servant, whom I uphold; mine elect, in whom my soul delighteth; I have put my spirit upon him: he shall bring forth judgment to the Gentiles.

3 A bruised reed shall he not break, and the smoking flax shall he not quench: he shall bring forth judgment unto truth.

NEW TESTAMENT

Matthew 7:1–2; 12:36

1 Judge not, that ye be not judged.

2 For with what judgment ye judge, ye shall be judged: and with what measure ye mete, it shall be measured to you again.

36 But I say unto you, That every idle word that men shall speak, they shall give account thereof in the day of judgment.

Matthew 25:31–45

31 When the Son of man shall come in his glory, and all the holy angels with him, then shall he sit upon the throne of his glory:

32 And before him shall be gathered all nations: and he shall separate

them one from another, as a shepherd divideth his sheep from the goats:

33 And he shall set the sheep on his right hand, but the goats on the left.

34 Then shall the King say unto them on his right hand, Come, ye blessed of my Father, inherit the kingdom prepared for you from the foundation of the world:

35 For I was an hungered, and ye gave me meat: I was thirsty, and ye gave me drink: I was a stranger, and ye took me in:

36 Naked, and ye clothed me: I was sick, and ye visited me: I was in prison, and ye came unto me.

37 Then shall the righteous answer him, saying, Lord, when saw we thee an hungered, and fed thee? or thirsty, and gave thee drink?

38 When saw we thee a stranger, and took thee in? or naked, and clothed thee?

39 Or when saw we thee sick, or in prison, and came unto thee?

40 And the King shall answer and say unto them, Verily I say unto you, Inasmuch as ye have done it unto one

of the least of these my brethren, ye have done it unto me.

41 Then shall he say also unto them on the left hand, Depart from me, ye cursed, into everlasting fire, prepared for the devil and his angels:

42 For I was an hungered, and ye gave me no meat: I was thirsty, and ye gave me no drink:

43 I was a stranger, and ye took me not in: naked, and ye clothed me not: sick, and in prison, and ye visited me not.

44 Then shall they also answer him, saying, Lord, when saw we thee an hungered, or athirst, or a stranger, or naked, or sick, or in prison, and did not minister unto thee?

45 Then shall he answer them, saying, Verily I say unto you, Inasmuch as ye did it not to one of the least of these, ye did it not to me.

John 12:31–32

31 Now is the judgment of this world: now shall the prince of this world be cast out.

32 And I, if I be lifted up from the earth, will draw all men unto me.

JUSTICE

Justice, the Old Testament says, is God's. Human judges administer it, but they do so on God's behalf. The people commit themselves to it, but as part of their duty to God. The priestly tribe of Levi is to pronounce curses on injustice, and these are to be loudly and solemnly endorsed by all the people as a liturgical act of identification with impartial justice.

Of course, ideal justice was not always achieved in practice. So the prophets raised their voices as the spokesmen of both God and the oppressed. They also looked beyond the approximate justice of the courtroom and spoke of a more inward and discerning process such as would make obedience to the requirements of true justice the natural effect of a law written on the heart.

The writers of the New Testament saw Jesus fulfilling this promise. He declined to administer formal justice, warned people of its limitations, and asked them to live by grace and forgiveness rather than by demanding their rights. This, however, was no endorsement of injustice. He speaks of offenses being forgiven when they are acknowledged to be offenses—that is, instances in which the justice of the case has been admitted. Even in his extraordinary parable of the workers in the vineyard (see Competition) no worker gets less than his just due.

Paul also taught that there were better things to do with life than spend it in claiming your rights, especially when this involved taking a fellow Christian ("saint" was the standard word for a believer and implied no claim to moral superiority or special holiness) before a heathen magistrate. But he taught that the magistrate—even the heathen one—was, as an administrator of justice, God's agent (Romans 13:4). As such he was to be treated with respect by Christians.

Paul himself appealed for justice to Caesar, and he never hesitated to claim his rights as a Roman citizen. On one occasion the magistrates of Philippi had Paul and Silas beaten and imprisoned for no other reason than that an angry mob demanded it. In the morning the magistrates ordered the prisoners' release, but Paul was in no mood to ignore the flouting of public justice. "They beat us publicly," he said, "without a trial, even though we are Roman citizens, and threw us into prison. And now do they want to get rid of us quietly? No! Let them come themselves and escort us out" (Acts 16:38–39, New International Version).

And they did. Justice had to be seen as greater than the justices.

"Justice is the public form of love"—that summary has been much used in twentieth-century discussions of the Christian's social duty. The man of love may turn the other cheek when he himself is struck, but when someone else's cheek receives the blow, that same love can express itself as a demand for justice.

Because first-century Christians did not occupy positions of power in the administration of justice, this point of view is implicit rather than explicit in the New Testament. It is, however, very consistent with the position of the Bible as a whole. Both testaments call on people to go far beyond the demands of justice but not to fall short of them. The individual may ignore his or her own rights, but not another person's. And both testaments make clear that this requirement has no social, national, or ethnic limitations. Justice is a law of life for human beings, built into the nature of things by their Creator and therefore of universal application (see Law).

The Bible, however, is not starry-eyed about the degree of justice that can be achieved by courts and forces. The exercise of such rough justice as is enforceable needs to be accompanied by the more inward process of enthroning justice in the hearts of people so that it becomes instinctive.

JUSTICE

OLD TESTAMENT

Deuteronomy 1:16–17

16 And I charged your judges at that time, saying, Hear the causes between your brethren, and judge righteously between every man and his brother, and the stranger that is with him.

17 Ye shall not respect persons in judgment; but ye shall hear the small as well as the great; ye shall not be afraid of the face of man; for the judgment is God's:

Deuteronomy 27:14, 19, 24–26

14 And the Levites shall speak, and say unto all the men of Israel with a loud voice,

19 Cursed be he that perverteth the judgment of the stranger, fatherless, and widow. And all the people shall say, Amen.

24 Cursed be he that smiteth his neighbour secretly. And all the people shall say, Amen.

25 Cursed be he that taketh reward to slay an innocent person. And all the people shall say, Amen.

26 Cursed be he that confirmeth not all the words of this law to do them. And all the people shall say, Amen.

Amos 2:6–7

6 Thus saith the Lord; For three transgressions of Israel, and for four, I will not turn away the punishment thereof; because they sold the righteous for silver, and the poor for a pair of shoes;

7 That pant after the dust of the earth on the head of the poor, and turn aside the way of the meek:

Isaiah 11:3–4 (the promise of a just ruler to come)

3 He shall not judge after the sight of his eyes, neither reprove after the hearing of his ears:

4 But with righteousness shall he judge the poor, and reprove with equity for the meek of the earth.

NEW TESTAMENT

Luke 12:13–14, 57–59; 17:3–5

13 And one of the company said unto him, Master, speak to my brother, that he divide the inheritance with me.

14 And he said unto him, Man, who made me a judge or a divider over you?

57 Yea, and why even of yourselves judge ye not what is right?

58 When thou goest with thine adversary to the magistrate, as thou art in the way, give diligence that thou mayest be delivered from him; lest he hale thee to the judge, and the judge deliver thee to the officer, and the officer cast thee into prison.

59 I tell thee, thou shalt not depart thence, till thou hast paid the very last mite.

3 Take heed to yourselves: If thy brother trespass against thee, rebuke him; and if he repent, forgive him.

4 And if he trespass against thee

seven times in a day, and seven times in a day turn again to thee, saying, I repent; thou shalt forgive him.

5 And the apostles said unto the Lord, Increase our faith.

1 Corinthians 6:1–7

1 Dare any of you, having a matter against another, go to law before the unjust, and not before the saints?

2 Do ye not know that the saints shall judge the world? and if the world shall be judged by you, are ye unworthy to judge the smallest matters?

3 Know ye not that we shall judge angels? how much more things that pertain to this life?

4 If then ye have judgments of things pertaining to this life, set them to judge who are least esteemed in the church.

5 I speak to your shame. Is it so, that there is not a wise man among you? no, not one that shall be able to judge between his brethren?

6 But brother goeth to law with brother, and that before the unbelievers.

7 Now therefore there is utterly a fault among you, because ye go to law one with another. Why do ye not rather take wrong? why do ye not rather suffer yourselves to be defrauded?

Acts 25:11–12 (Paul addressing the court)

11 For if I be an offender, or have committed any thing worthy of death, I refuse not to die: but if there be none of these things whereof these accuse me, no man may deliver me unto them. I appeal unto Cæsar.

12 Then Festus, when he had conferred with the council, answered, Hast thou appealed unto Cæsar? unto Cæsar shalt thou go.

KINDNESS

The Book of Leviticus consists largely of rules and regulations, some of them concerned with rituals that now seem very remote, but many of them with forms of kindness by the practice of which any society could be improved. The repeated refrain in the examples quoted below emphasizes that all relationships are interconnected. The religious laws and the social laws do belong together. One's relationship with, for instance, a neighbor of a different ethnic group cannot be separated from one's relationship with God.

The kindly laws quoted here are the ones particularly relevant to the story of Ruth. The tale begins with Naomi, an Israelite woman who had gone abroad in a time of famine but returns later with a widowed Moabitess daughter-in-law. The theme of the story is kindness—first the kindness Ruth shows to Naomi, then the kindness Boaz shows to Ruth when he finds her among the gleaners in his field. It was, after all, the kindness of Boaz and not the nightingale's song of

Keats's marvelous imagination ". . . that found a path Through the sad heart of Ruth when, sick for home, She stood in tears amid the alien corn."

The story is set in the period of the Judges, but it was told at a much later date to challenge a certain narrowness that sometimes infected Israel's understanding of the relations between men and women, natives and aliens, kinsmen and strangers. Ruth the Moabitess, the story says, became the ancestor of King David and of all the royal line of Bethlehem.

The New Testament is also concerned to extend the boundaries of kindness, and to do so from the same starting point: the inseparability of a human being's relationships with God and with other men and women. The story of the good Samaritan is told as a commentary on this double law. Samaritans were regarded with suspicion by true-born Jews (such as the natives of Jerusalem and Jericho) and with religious contempt by experts on doctrine (such as the priest and the Levite), but kindness was shown to transcend all such distinctions.

There is really no need to ask the Bible whether kindness is a good thing. Few would doubt that it is. The trouble is that kindness is apt to take only familiar forms and to move in familiar grooves around a circle of familiar faces. As Jeanette Stanley said in a religious song of the 1960s:

> People like people who are kind,
> Kind to their mothers, kind to their fathers, kind to their family.
> But do they like people who are kind to an enemy?
> People like people like themselves.

What we need to ask the Bible is how kindness can be given deeper roots and wider branches.

As to the roots of kindness, the biblical picture of life as an interdependent network of relationships, every one of which is also a relationship with God, provides the laws of kindness not only with transcendent authority but also with a natural motivation. Just to see life in those terms is to see, for instance, one's racially different neighbors in a light that makes the exchange of kindnesses instinctive. To be biblical, however, kindness needs to be an action, not just a feeling.

As to the branches, no one can pretend that extending kindness to enemies comes easily, but the New Testament demands it, and the Old Testament opens the road to it when Israel is reminded, "*You* were aliens in Egypt." Know how it feels to be the other. Look at the situation from behind the stranger's eyes. Even an enemy, understood in this way, can be treated with kindness. What is more, the kindness will be appropriate and acceptable to him; it won't be the sort of kindness that humiliates because it will express only the good intentions of the one showing it.

KINDNESS

OLD TESTAMENT

Leviticus 19:33–34; 23:22

33 And if a stranger sojourn with thee in your land, ye shall not vex him.

34 But the stranger that dwelleth with you shall be unto you as one born among you, and thou shalt love him as thyself; for ye were strangers in the land of Egypt: I am the Lord your God.

22 And when ye reap the harvest of your land, thou shalt not make clean riddance of the corners of thy field when thou reapest, neither shalt thou gather any gleaning of thy harvest: thou shalt leave them unto the poor, and to the stranger: I am the Lord your God.

Ruth 1:6–18

6 Then she arose with her daughters in law, that she might return from the country of Moab: for she had heard in the country of Moab how that the Lord had visited his people in giving them bread.

7 Wherefore she went forth out of the place where she was, and her two daughters in law with her; and they went on the way to return unto the land of Judah.

8 And Naomi said unto her two daughters in law, Go, return each to her mother's house: the Lord deal kindly with you, as ye have dealt with the dead, and with me.

9 The Lord grant you that ye may find rest, each of you in the house of her husband. Then she kissed them; and they lifted up their voice, and wept.

10 And they said unto her, Surely we will return with thee unto thy people.

11 And Naomi said, Turn again, my daughters: why will ye go with me? are there yet any more sons in my womb, that they may be your husbands?

12 Turn again, my daughters, go your way; for I am too old to have an husband. If I should say, I have hope, if I should have an husband also to-night, and should also bear sons;

13 Would ye tarry for them till they were grown? would ye stay for them from having husbands? nay, my daughters; for it grieveth me much for your sakes that the hand of the Lord is gone out against me.

14 And they lifted up their voice, and wept again: and Orpah kissed her mother in law; but Ruth clave unto her.

15 And she said, Behold, thy sister in law is gone back unto her people, and unto her gods: return thou after thy sister in law.

16 And Ruth said, Entreat me not to leave thee, or to return from following after thee: for whither thou goest, I will go; and where thou lodgest, I will lodge: thy people shall be my people, and thy God my God:

17 Where thou diest, will I die, and there will I be buried: the Lord do so to me, and more also, if aught but death part thee and me.

18 When she saw that she was stedfastly minded to go with her, then she left speaking unto her.

NEW TESTAMENT

Luke 6:35–36

35 But love ye your enemies, and do good, and lend, hoping for nothing again; and your reward shall be great, and ye shall be the children of the Highest: for he is kind unto the unthankful and to the evil.

36 Be ye therefore merciful, as your Father also is merciful.

Luke 10:27–37 (Jesus has asked an expert to summarize the Law)

27 And he answering said, Thou shalt love the Lord thy God with all thy heart, and with all thy soul, and with all thy strength, and with all thy mind; and thy neighbour as thyself.

28 And he said unto him, Thou hast answered right: this do, and thou shalt live.

29 But he, willing to justify himself, said unto Jesus, And who is my neighbour?

30 And Jesus answering said, A certain man went down from Jerusalem to Jericho, and fell among thieves, which stripped him of his raiment, and wounded him, and departed, leaving him half dead.

31 And by chance there came down a certain priest that way: and when he saw him, he passed by on the other side.

32 And likewise a Levite, when he was at the place, came and looked on him, and passed by on the other side.

33 But a certain Samaritan, as he journeyed, came where he was: and when he saw him, he had compassion on him,

34 And went to him, and bound up his wounds, pouring in oil and wine, and set him on his own beast, and brought him to an inn, and took care of him.

35 And on the morrow when he departed, he took out two pence, and gave them to the host, and said unto him, Take care of him; and whatsoever thou spendest more, when I come again, I will repay thee.

36 Which now of these three, thinkest thou, was neighbour unto him that fell among the thieves?

37 And he said, He that shewed mercy on him. Then said Jesus unto him, Go, and do thou likewise.

LAW

The Old Testament affirms that all just law is of God and is an aspect of a covenant relationship between God and his world. Not just the people of Israel, but all men, all animals, and all nature are bound to him and he to them. This is dramatized in the story of Noah and the rainbow. It is by the laws implicit in that covenant that seasons come and birds migrate and there is order everywhere. The laws of nature are *laws*.

Then a more particular covenant is made with Abraham and his offspring. The first five books of the Bible spell out the detailed legislation by which the covenanted people of Israel are to be ruled. This is state law enforced by judges, but God is its source.

Within both these covenants, however, was the possibility of a more personal relationship between man and God. This new covenant would involve the writing of a moral law into the human heart so that it became an inward necessity rather than an outward constraint. Of this law, too, God was the only possible source.

The New Testament recognizes all three of these types of law but has most to say about the third. The reason for this is that Jesus was believed to have established the new covenant and to have released God's spirit into the hearts of those who entered it. "This cup is the new covenant in my blood," he said over the wine at his last supper.

The old laws, however, were said to have been fulfilled and transcended rather than overthrown. They had at least prepared men and women for the more inward law and they continued to play a supporting role. In any case, Christians were required to exceed the demands of the law, not to fall short of them. For that reason even the laws of the Roman Empire and of its godless local magistrates were to be respected, not just for fear of the consequences of doing otherwise, but for love of the Lord.

To say that a person is law-abiding has come to sound like rather faint praise. We recognize that law-abiding people are the stable core of society, but to modern ears such people sound a little dull—an indication of a rather unenthusiastic contemporary attitude to law generally.

Perhaps this lack of enthusiasm has developed because law has come to be thought of in a quite unbiblical way as just so many regulations put on a statute book by politicians and lawyers. The biblical view of natural law, statute law, and moral law as all flowing from the same source sets every particular law in a larger context. Something of such a context is implied whenever we speak of an unjust law. There could be no such concept unless a Law existed behind the laws, a Law by which the statutes themselves can be judged. The Bible finds this standard inherent in the creation, since its source is in the nature of its Creator.

This suggests that, in the absence of clear evidence to the contrary, we must assume that state laws do carry this august authority. They are to be respected in every way that conscience allows, because by their very existence they bear witness to the order that is built into the nature of things and within which alone human life is possible.

Of course, the conscience that is obedient to moral law may at times have to reject a particular state law. New Testament Christians sometimes did, and some were put to death for it. In principle, however, they were on the side of law, even when it reflected a heathen culture and was imposed by tyrants. It was their experience that the divine Spirit often led them to go far beyond the requirements of state law, rarely to cross it, and never to fall short of it.

"It's not strictly legal, but never mind" is an attitude excluded by the biblical vision of law. But so, too, is its opposite: "So long as it's legal, that's all that matters."

LAW

OLD TESTAMENT

Genesis 9:8–13

8 And God spake unto Noah, and to his sons with him, saying,

9 And I, behold, I establish my covenant with you, and with your seed after you;

10 And with every living creature that is with you, of the fowl, of the cattle, and of every beast of the earth with you; from all that go out of the ark, to every beast of the earth.

11 And I will establish my covenant with you; neither shall all flesh be cut off any more by the waters of a flood; neither shall there any more be a flood to destroy the earth.

12 And God said, This is the token of the covenant which I make between me and you and every living creature that is with you, for perpetual generations:

13 I do set my bow in the cloud, and it shall be for a token of a covenant between me and the earth.

Deuteronomy 29:10–13; 4:1–2

10 Ye stand this day all of you before the Lord your God; your captains of your tribes, your elders, and your officers, with all the men of Israel,

11 Your little ones, your wives, and thy stranger that is in thy camp, from

the hewer of thy wood unto the drawer of thy water:

12 That thou shouldest enter into covenant with the Lord thy God, and into his oath, which the Lord thy God maketh with thee this day:

13 That he may establish thee to-day for a people unto himself, and that he may be unto thee a God, as he hath said unto thee.

1 Now therefore hearken, O Israel, unto the statutes and unto the judgments, which I teach you, for to do them, that ye may live, and go in and possess the land which the Lord God of your fathers giveth you.

2 Ye shall not add unto the word which I command you, neither shall ye diminish aught from it, that ye may keep the commandments of the Lord your God which I command you.

Jeremiah 31:31–33

31 Behold, the days come, saith the Lord, that I will make a new covenant with the house of Israel, and with the house of Judah:

32 Not according to the covenant that I made with their fathers in the day that I took them by the hand to bring them out of the land of Egypt; which my covenant they brake, although I was an husband unto them, saith the Lord:

33 But this shall be the covenant

that I will make with the house of Israel; After those days, saith the Lord, I will put my law in their inward parts, and write it in their hearts; and will be their God, and they shall be my people.

NEW TESTAMENT

Matthew 5:17–19

17 Think not that I am come to destroy the law, or the prophets: I am not come to destroy, but to fulfil.

18 For verily I say unto you, Till heaven and earth pass, one jot or one tittle shall in no wise pass from the law, till all be fulfilled.

19 Whosoever therefore shall break one of these least commandments, and shall teach men so, he shall be called the least in the kingdom of heaven: but whosoever shall do and teach them, the same shall be called great in the kingdom of heaven.

Galatians 3:23–24; 5:18

23 But before faith came, we were kept under the law, shut up unto the faith which should afterwards be revealed.

24 Wherefore the law was our schoolmaster to bring us unto Christ, that we might be justified by faith.

18 But if ye be led of the Spirit, ye are not under the law.

Romans 2:14–15; 3:21

14 For when the Gentiles, which have not the law, do by nature the things contained in the law, these, having not the law, are a law unto themselves:

15 Which shew the work of the law written in their hearts, their conscience also bearing witness, and their thoughts the mean while accusing or else excusing one another;

21 But now the righteousness of God without the law is manifested, being witnessed by the law and the prophets;

1 Peter 2:13, 16

13 Submit yourselves to every ordinance of man for the Lord's sake:

16 As free, and not using your liberty for a cloak of maliciousness, but as the servants of God.

LEISURE

The opening chapters of the Bible describe God as spending six days at work on the creation of the universe and then taking a day off. In this way the Old Testament roots the idea of leisure in the very nature of God. As a response to this, the Sabbath laws made a weekly day of rest obligatory in Israel. The day was holy because it was a sharing in God's own experience of rest. It provided men and women not only with a day of freedom from work but also with a sense of kinship to God.

Labor is not undervalued in the Old Testament (see Work), but there is a feeling that it should be balanced by leisure. A human life should match the natural rhythms of creation. The agricultural year was marked by a number of religious festivals that were undoubted holidays, and the writer of Ecclesiastes celebrated poetically the need for a life of balanced activity and inactivity.

In fact leisure is seen prophetically to stand not only at the beginning of history but also at its end. In the perfected kingdom all men and women will invite their neighbors to share the enjoyment of time off. ("Call" in the Zechariah quotation means to invite to sit down.)

By the time of Jesus, Sabbath laws were sometimes interpreted so rigidly as to become a burden. They freed the workers from toil only to subject them to another set of controls. Jesus was frequently in trouble with Sabbatarians. On one occasion, when he was challenged over the relaxed behavior of his disciples on a Sabbath walk, he first defended them by appealing to the Old Testament itself and then uttered a simple but radical declaration of priorities: patterns of leisure are to be shaped to the needs of men and women, not vice versa.

The Gospels also record a time when Jesus actively sought leisure both for himself and for his disciples. They did not get it, but the story suggests a way of life within which holidays are desirable and right, although they may have to be sacrificed. The New Testament Church continued to value the Sabbath both as fact and as symbol. Paul's letter to the Hebrews speaks of it as an image of heavenly rest. Leisure rather than work is seen as man's final destiny.

Silicon chips, it is said, are going to reduce very significantly the amount of work the human race will need to do in order to live in comfort. Leisure will increase. Too often in the past (and in the present) leisure has been forced on people in the form of unemployment. This means that they have time to enjoy themselves but lack the resources to fill that time with a variety of experiences. The Bible points to a better balance, a more equal sharing of both leisure and resources.

However, even if this balance is achieved, we will still have to equip people mentally and spiritually for handling a great deal of free time. Extended leisure will demand a whole new set of attitudes, because existing attitudes are the product of generations so burdened with work that any leisure time was likely to be seen as an opportunity to enjoy escapist activities. If people are going to work only a few hours of the week, then their leisure will have to be both creative and demanding. Otherwise humans will not remain human. The rhythm of life as Ecclesiastes celebrates it will have to be maintained regardless of which elements in the pattern are wage earning.

The biblical writers naturally did not envisage leisure as it exists today, but the Bible is remarkably free of what has been called the Protestant work ethic. It says that life is essentially a grace freely bestowed. By speaking of rest as an anticipation of heaven, it represents leisure as delight, as the free play of the human spirit. It is an area in which to exercise the gift of freedom.

LEISURE

OLD TESTAMENT

Genesis 2:1–3

1 Thus the heavens and the earth were finished, and all the host of them.

2 And on the seventh day God ended his work which he had made; and he rested on the seventh day from all his work which he had made.

3 And God blessed the seventh day, and sanctified it: because that in it he had rested from all his work which God created and made.

Exodus 20:8–11

8 Remember the sabbath day, to keep it holy.

9 Six days shalt thou labour, and do all thy work:

10 But the seventh day is the sabbath of the Lord thy God: in it thou shalt not do any work, thou, nor thy son, nor thy daughter, thy manservant, nor thy maidservant, nor thy cattle, nor thy stranger that is within thy gates:

11 For in six days the Lord made heaven and earth, the sea, and all that in them is, and rested the seventh day: wherefore the Lord blessed the sabbath day, and hallowed it.

Ecclesiastes 3:1–8, 11

1 To every thing there is a season, and a time to every purpose under the heaven:

2 A time to be born, and a time to die; a time to plant, and a time to pluck up that which is planted;

3 A time to kill, and a time to heal; a time to break down, and a time to build up;

4 A time to weep, and a time to laugh; a time to mourn, and a time to dance;

5 A time to cast away stones, and a time to gather stones together; a time to embrace, and a time to refrain from embracing;

6 A time to get, and a time to lose; a time to keep, and a time to cast away;

7 A time to rend, and a time to sew; a time to keep silence, and a time to speak;

8 A time to love, and a time to hate; a time of war, and a time of peace.

11 He hath made every thing beautiful in his time: also he hath set the world in their heart.

Zechariah 3:10

10 In that day, saith the Lord of hosts, shall ye call every man his neighbour under the vine and under the fig tree.

NEW TESTAMENT

Mark 2:23–28

23 And it came to pass, that he went through the corn fields on the sabbath day; and his disciples began, as they went, to pluck the ears of corn.

24 And the Pharisees said unto him, Behold, why do they on the sabbath day that which is not lawful?

25 And he said unto them, Have

ye never read what David did, when he had need, and was an hungered, he and they that were with him?

26 How he went into the house of God in the days of Abiathar the high priest, and did eat the shewbread, which is not lawful to eat but for the priests, and gave also to them which were with him?

27 And he said unto them, The sabbath was made for man, and not man for the sabbath:

28 Therefore the Son of man is Lord also of the sabbath.

Mark 6:31–33

31 And he said unto them, Come ye yourselves apart into a desert place, and rest a while: for there were many coming and going, and they had no leisure so much as to eat.

32 And they departed into a desert place by ship privately.

33 And the people saw them departing, and many knew him, and ran afoot thither out of all cities, and outwent them, and came together unto him.

Hebrews 4:9–11

9 There remaineth therefore a rest to the people of God.

10 For he that is entered into his rest, he also hath ceased from his own works, as God did from his.

11 Let us labour therefore to enter into that rest, lest any man fall after the same example of unbelief.

Revelation 14:13

13 And I heard a voice from heaven saying unto me, Write, Blessed are the dead which die in the Lord from henceforth: yea, saith the Spirit, that they may rest from their labours; and their works do follow them.

LONELINESS

"It is not good for man to be alone," says the God of Genesis. The book goes on to speak of marriage and also to extol the virtue of hospitality as exemplified by Abraham—hospitality to strangers, since Abraham could not know that his visitors were messengers from God.

The people of the Old Testament lived in large families and close-knit communities, but there is evidence in the Psalms that affliction could still drive a man or woman into spiritual isolation. And such ills could not be healed lightly. Jeremiah had to forgo convivial chatter while burdened with his message. It is better to bear loneliness for a good reason than to cure it in the wrong way.

But the Old Testament is sure that a relationship with God is possible in even the most isolated situation. Daniel exhibits the loneliness of success. He is isolated by his exalted position, surrounded by jealous rivals of another nation and another faith. His only answer is that window open toward Jerusalem.

In the New Testament Jesus proposes a sharing of burdens transcending all time and space, but he goes away alone to pray. He also passes through the ultimate desolation of being abandoned both by men and (as far as his awareness of it went) by God.

His followers believed, however, that his passing through that experience with love unbroken constituted a breakthrough. Never again need humanity be so isolated. As an expression of this, Jesus' followers formed a closely knit but outward-looking social group. Hospitality and openness were reasserted from a new base.

Anyone who has worked in television can testify that loneliness is a major problem of our time. Mother Teresa of Calcutta says that it is *the* major problem of the West. Even to mention the word on a television program is to touch a nerve in a large section of the viewing audience. People may live in crowded cities, seeing a thousand faces a day, and yet feel cut off and isolated. Some seem to feel that only the small screen really speaks to them, and even then it does not necessarily have anything very significant to say.

But what can it say? The need for companionship is at the very root of human existence, says the Bible. Its nerve cannot be cut and should not be anesthetized by television. A hunger for relationship *ought* to be felt, just as a hunger for food should. The biblical promise of spiritual companionship is not designed to dull the pain of isolation and make it acceptable. The biblical view is that the citizens of that crowded city should solve the problem of loneliness by opening themselves and their hopes to one another. They will not do it without suffering rebuffs and woundings (nothing hurts like people), but the Bible does not allow them to opt out.

And yet it makes clear that solitude is not at all the same thing as loneliness. A measure of privacy is as important to the human spirit as the opportunity to communicate. Carlo Carretto, having given up his job as a youth worker and gone to live in a North African desert where he solemnly burned his address book, said that he had not destroyed a single friendship. "On the contrary," he writes, "I have never loved nor prayed so much for my old friends as in the solitude of the desert." And Thomas Merton said, "Go into the desert not to escape other men but in order to find them in God." This, too, is a biblical attitude.

It is evidently possible to be close to people either in solitude or in company. What matters is not to be shut in on yourself but to keep a window open toward others—and sometimes a door for them to come in by.

LONELINESS

OLD TESTAMENT

Genesis 2:18

18 And the Lord God said, It is not good that the man should be alone; I will make him an help meet for him.

Genesis 18:1–5

1 He sat in the tent door in the heat of the day;

2 And he lift up his eyes and looked, and, lo, three men stood by him: and when he saw them, he ran to meet them from the tent door, and bowed himself toward the ground,

3 And said, My Lord, if now I have found favour in thy sight, pass not away, I pray thee, from thy servant:

4 Let a little water, I pray you, be fetched, and wash your feet, and rest yourselves under the tree:

5 And I will fetch a morsel of bread, and comfort ye your hearts; after that ye shall pass on.

Psalm 102:4–7

My heart is smitten, and withered like grass;
So that I forget to eat my bread.
By reason of the voice of my groaning
My bones cleave to my skin.
I am like a pelican of the wilderness:
I am like an owl of the desert.
I watch, and am
As a sparrow alone upon the house top.

Jeremiah 15:17

17 I sat not in the assembly of the mockers, nor rejoiced; I sat alone because of thy hand: for thou hast filled me with indignation.

Daniel 6:3, 6–7, 10

3 Then this Daniel was preferred above the presidents and princes, because an excellent spirit was in him; and the king thought to set him over the whole realm.

6 Then these presidents and princes assembled together to the king, and said thus unto him, King Darius, live for ever.

7 All the presidents of the kingdom, the governors, and the princes, the counsellors, and the captains, have consulted together to establish a royal statute, and to make a firm decree, that whosoever shall ask a petition of any God or man for thirty days, save of thee, O king, he shall be cast into the den of lions.

10 Now when Daniel knew that the writing was signed, he went into his house; and his windows being open in his chamber toward Jerusalem, he kneeled upon his knees three times a day, and prayed, and gave thanks before his God, as he did aforetime.

NEW TESTAMENT

Matthew 11:28–30

28 Come unto me, all ye that labour and are heavy laden, and I will give you rest.

29 Take my yoke upon you, and

learn of me; for I am meek and lowly in heart: and ye shall find rest unto your souls.

30 For my yoke is easy, and my burden is light.

John 16:32

32 Behold, the hour cometh, yea, is now come, that ye shall be scattered, every man to his own, and shall leave me alone: and yet I am not alone, because the Father is with me.

Mark 15:34

34 And at the ninth hour Jesus cried with a loud voice, saying, Eloi, Eloi, lama sabachthani? which is, being interpreted, My God, my God, why hast thou forsaken me?

Matthew 28:16–18, 20

16 Then the eleven disciples went away into Galilee, into a mountain where Jesus had appointed them.

17 And when they saw him, they worshipped him: but some doubted.

18 And Jesus came and spake unto them, saying,

20 Lo, I am with you alway, even unto the end of the world.

Hebrews 10:25; 13:2, 5

25 Not forsaking the assembling of ourselves together, as the manner of some is; but exhorting one another.

2 Be not forgetful to entertain strangers: for thereby some have entertained angels unawares.

5 For he hath said, I will never leave thee, nor forsake thee.

LOVE

The Old Testament demands love from man to God, and from man to man, but it gives priority to God's love for man. All other loves derive from this one, but since God is God and man is man the word often used for God's love can also be translated as "mercy"—as in Psalm 103. At times the divine love seems to focus exclusively on God's people, Israel, but it is increasingly seen to be wider. In spite of that, the language used to describe it becomes increasingly warm and personal.

Romantic love between man and woman is saluted in such Old Testament stories as that of Jacob and Rachel: "Jacob served seven years for Rachel; and they seemed unto him but a few days, for the love he had to her"—Genesis 29:20. That kind of love is celebrated rapturously in the book known as Song of Songs. This long and passionate sequence of poems can be interpreted in all manner of mystical ways, but its root and its force are in the delighted and reciprocal love of man and woman.

Jesus in the New Testament preaches love for enemies as well as for neighbors, and he salutes love wherever he sees it. A contemporary was scandalized when Jesus accepted a demonstration of love from a notorious woman who had misused the man–woman relationship, but love was never to be spurned.

Just as Jesus treated with tenderness the combination of sin plus love, so Paul treated with severity the phenomenon of virtue minus love.

A character in a novel by Iris Murdoch (A *Fairly Honorable Defeat*) says, "Love is the last and secret name of all the virtues." Love does indeed have the modesty to hide itself under many forms of good. Perhaps it is more likely to be genuine when concealed in this way than when it is loudly trumpeted. Love "is not puffed up," says Paul (1 Corinthians 13:4).

Another novelist, Graham Greene, seems to find love concealed in things that are not virtuous in themselves. Many of his stories concern people who violate their own code of good behavior, but do it for love. Are they, the novels seem to ask, condemned or redeemed by so doing? Love takes many forms and wears some strange disguises.

The Bible endorses this. In its original languages there are several words that can be translated as "love," but the distinctions between them are less important than what they have in common. Love always involves a movement outward from the self, a movement of identification with the other. In any case, the New Testament writers choose exactly the same Greek word with which to speak of loving God, loving life, loving your neighbor, loving yourself, loving your enemy, and loving your husband or wife. They also use the word to say that God is love. There are evidently many colors in love's spectrum.

That is why love can take so many forms without changing its essential nature. Love for a suffering human being expresses itself as a bearing or sharing of the other's affliction. Love for an enemy expresses itself as the active pursuit of reconciliation. Love for God expresses itself as awe and obedience. Love between a man and a woman can express itself through sexual union. In all cases union is the theme, and in each case love is the richer and the stronger if it recognizes its kinship with the rest.

The Bible could almost be said to glory in love's hiddenness, diversity, and even ambiguity. The King James Version has chapter headings that are no part of the Bible itself. They were added by the translators. They are summaries of the contents, and sometimes interpretations of what is to come. The second chapter of the Song of Songs has this heading: "The Mutual love of Christ and His Church." To the author of the poem, who lived before Jesus was born, it could not possibly have meant that. The king's scholars were wrong. And yet their confusion is gloriously right.

LOVE

OLD TESTAMENT

Deuteronomy 6:5; Leviticus 19:18

5 And thou shalt love the Lord thy God with all thine heart, and with all thy soul, and with all thy might.

18 Thou shalt love thy neighbour as thyself.

Psalm 103:8, 10–11

The Lord is merciful and gracious,
Slow to anger, and plenteous in mercy.
He hath not dealt with us after our sins;
Nor rewarded us according to our in-
    iquities.
For as the heaven is high above the earth,
So great is his mercy toward them that
    fear him.

Song of Songs 2:2–4, 14, 16

As the lily among thorns,
So is my love among the daughters.

As the apple tree among the trees of the
    wood,
So is my beloved among the sons.
I sat down under his shadow with great
    delight,
And his fruit was sweet to my taste.
He brought me to the banqueting house,
And his banner over me was love.

O my dove, that art in the clefts of the
    rock, in the secret places of the stairs,
Let me see thy countenance, let me hear
    thy voice;
For sweet is thy voice, and thy counte-
    nance is comely.

My beloved is mine, and I am his.

NEW TESTAMENT

Luke 7:36–47

36 And one of the Pharisees desired him that he would eat with him.
And he went into the Pharisee's house,
and sat down to meat.

37 And, behold, a woman in the
city, which was a sinner, when she
knew that Jesus sat at meat in the
Pharisee's house, brought an alabaster
box of ointment,

38 And stood at his feet behind him
weeping, and began to wash his feet
with tears, and did wipe them with the
hairs of her head, and kissed his feet,
and anointed them with the ointment.

39 Now when the Pharisee which
had bidden him saw it, he spake within
himself, saying, This man, if he were
a prophet, would have known who and
what manner of woman this is that
toucheth him: for she is a sinner.

40 And Jesus answering said unto
him, Simon, I have somewhat to say
unto thee. And he saith, Master, say
on.

41 There was a certain creditor
which had two debtors: the one owed
five hundred pence, and the other fifty.

42 And when they had nothing to
pay, he frankly forgave them both. Tell
me therefore, which of them will love
him most?

43 Simon answered and said, I
suppose that he, to whom he forgave
most. And he said unto him, Thou
hast rightly judged.

44 And he turned to the woman,
and said unto Simon, Seest thou this
woman? I entered into thine house,
thou gavest me no water for my feet:
but she hath washed my feet with tears,
and wiped them with the hairs of her
head.

45 Thou gavest me no kiss: but this
woman since the time I came in hath
not ceased to kiss my feet.

46 My head with oil thou didst not
anoint: but this woman hath anointed
my feet with ointment.

47 Wherefore I say unto thee, Her
sins, which are many, are forgiven; for
she loved much: but to whom little is
forgiven, the same loveth little.

1 Corinthians 13:1–3

1 Though I speak with the tongues of men and of angels, and have not charity, I am become as sounding brass, or a tinkling cymbal.

2 And though I have the gift of prophecy, and understand all mysteries, and all knowledge; and though I have all faith, so that I could remove mountains, and have not charity, I am nothing.

3 And though I bestow all my goods to feed the poor, and though I give my body to be burned, and have not charity, it profiteth me nothing.

1 John 4:7–8, 10–11

7 Beloved, let us love one another: for love is of God; and every one that loveth is born of God, and knoweth God.

8 He that loveth not knoweth not God; for God is love.

10 Herein is love, not that we loved God, but that he loved us, and sent his Son to be the propitiation for our sins.

11 Beloved, if God so loved us, we ought also to love one another.

LOYALTY

Elisha was Elijah's servant before he became his successor. His loyalty to the prophet made it possible for him to inherit his master's spirit, with which went both his extraordinary powers and his burdensome responsibilities. The Old Testament story of the day on which the two men parted gives a fascinating picture of whole companies of prophets all along the route of their journey, but the real point is in the repeated opportunities given to Elisha to break the bond between them. On any of these occasions the external bond of master and servant could have been terminated with honor, but the personal bond of relationship held.

Such is loyalty in the Old Testament: a commitment that is tested, but which holds because of its personal and religious depth. The bond between God and Israel was of this kind. Its demand for loyalty was expressed in a formal covenant, but the bond could not be maintained by mere obedience to external laws. Under strain the formal obligations tended to give way. There was need for an inner relationship, a law written in the heart, if loyalty was to be maintained.

In the New Testament the stories of Peter show loyalty under strain. In part they are a story of disloyalty, but the underlying relationship between Jesus and Peter was strong enough for the bond to be remade. Certainly overconfident declarations of loyalty proved fragile. True loyalty is not ensured by verbal promises; still less is it guaranteed by boasts of being more loyal than others. But when all the promises had been broken and all the boasting washed away in tears, love remained. On the basis of that love Jesus repaired the bond with his disciple, not by grappling Peter more closely to himself, but by pointing him to the sheep in whose service Peter's love could be expressed.

Why should the Christian martyr go to the lions when all he need do to escape them is drop a pinch of incense on the altar of a Roman emperor? Why should the modern-day prisoner endure terrible pains and indignities rather than insult his country's flag? Only because of loyalty. And characteristically loyalty is revealed only under stress. To speak of loyalty is usually to speak of someone with a burden to bear and little but a sense of honor to make him or her bear it.

To bear such a burden implies a commitment to some value transcending self-interest. Religion does not have to be dragged in by force: in the concept of loyalty a transcendent dimension already is present. Without it there would be a vacuum at the heart of the idea.

But from a biblical point of view the transcendent dimension should be understood in terms of relationships rather than of purely formal bonds, laws, and promises. This is not to say that external expressions of commitment have no value. Perhaps Peter would not have followed even at a distance if he had not promised to do more. But within and behind each formal bond or covenant (see Commitment) there needs to be a sense of the personal relationship of which each stated obligation is the outward clothing.

These relationships may be between individuals or may involve whole communities, nations, or alliances of nations, but at every level there is need of a deeply felt interpersonal relationship if loyalty to commitment is to hold under stress. When the relationship is there, loyalty is not only stronger but more easily repaired.

Broken loyalty is as painful and as serious as a broken leg, but with time (and a good splint) both can mend.

LOYALTY

OLD TESTAMENT

2 Kings 2:1-12

1 And it came to pass, when the Lord would take up Elijah into heaven by a whirlwind, that Elijah went with Elisha from Gilgal.

2 And Elijah said unto Elisha, Tarry here, I pray thee; for the Lord hath sent me to Bethel. And Elisha said unto him, As the Lord liveth, and as thy soul liveth, I will not leave thee. So they went down to Bethel.

3 And the sons of the prophets that were at Bethel came forth to Elisha, and said unto him, Knowest thou that the Lord will take away thy master from thy head to-day? And he said, Yea, I know it; hold ye your peace.

4 And Elijah said unto him, Elisha,

tarry here, I pray thee; for the Lord hath sent me to Jericho. And he said, As the Lord liveth, and as thy soul liveth, I will not leave thee. So they came to Jericho.

5 And the sons of the prophets that were at Jericho came to Elisha, and said unto him, Knowest thou that the Lord will take away thy master from thy head to-day? And he answered, Yea, I know it; hold ye your peace.

6 And Elijah said unto him, Tarry, I pray thee, here; for the Lord hath sent me to Jordan. And he said, As the Lord liveth, and as thy soul liveth, I will not leave thee. And they two went on.

7 And fifty men of the sons of the prophets went, and stood to view afar off: and they two stood by Jordan.

8 And Elijah took his mantle, and wrapped it together, and smote the waters, and they were divided hither and thither, so that they two went over on dry ground.

9 And it came to pass, when they were gone over, that Elijah said unto Elisha, Ask what I shall do for thee, before I be taken away from thee. And Elisha said, I pray thee, let a double portion of thy spirit be upon me.

10 And he said, Thou hast asked a hard thing: nevertheless, if thou see me when I *am* taken from thee, it shall be so unto thee; but if not, it shall not be so.

11 And it came to pass, as they still went on, and talked, that, behold, there appeared a chariot of fire, and horses of fire, and parted them both asunder; and Elijah went up by a whirlwind into heaven.

12 And Elisha saw it, and he cried, My father, my father, the chariot of Israel, and the horsemen thereof. And he saw him no more.

NEW TESTAMENT

Mark 14:27–31, 53–54, 66–72

27 And Jesus saith unto them, All ye shall be offended because of me this night: for it is written, I will smite the shepherd, and the sheep shall be scattered.

28 But after that I am risen, I will go before you into Galilee.

29 But Peter said unto him, Although all shall be offended, yet will not I.

30 And Jesus saith unto him, Verily I say unto thee, That this day, even in this night, before the cock crow twice, thou shalt deny me thrice.

31 But he spake the more vehemently, If I should die with thee, I will not deny thee in any wise. Likewise also said they all.

53 And they led Jesus away to the high priest: and with him were assembled all the chief priests and the elders and the scribes.

54 And Peter followed him afar off, even into the palace of the high priest: and he sat with the servants, and warmed himself at the fire.

66 And as Peter was beneath in the palace, there cometh one of the maids of the high priest:

67 And when she saw Peter warming himself, she looked upon him, and said, And thou also wast with Jesus of Nazareth.

68 But he denied, saying, I know not, neither understand I what thou sayest. And he went out into the porch; and the cock crew.

69 And a maid saw him again, and began to say to them that stood by, This is one of them.

70 And he denied it again. And a little after, they that stood by said again to Peter, Surely thou art one of them: for thou art a Galilæan, and thy speech agreeth thereto.

71 But he began to curse and to swear, I know not this man of whom ye speak.

72 And the second time the cock crew. And Peter called to mind the word that Jesus said unto him. . . . And when he thought thereon he wept.

John 21:15–17

15 So when they had dined, Jesus saith to Simon Peter, Simon, son of Jonas, lovest thou me more than these? He saith unto him, Yea, Lord; thou knowest that I love thee. He saith unto him, Feed my lambs.

16 He saith to him again the second time, Simon, son of Jonas, lovest thou me? He saith unto him, Yea, Lord; thou knowest that I love thee. He saith unto him, Feed my sheep.

17 He saith unto him the third time, Simon, son of Jonas, lovest thou me? Peter said unto him, Lord, thou knowest all things; thou knowest that I love thee. Jesus saith unto him, Feed my sheep.

MAN

The Old Testament word usually translated as "man" does not denote a male as opposed to a female. It just means "a human being." That is what this entry is about.

Genesis speaks of man (in this sense) as made in the image of God and breathed into by the Spirit of God, but it adds at once that humanity as we know it is not a direct expression of this fact. By Chapter 6 God is said to recognize contrary tendencies as firmly embedded in human nature. Yet the glory remains along with the shame. The Psalms acknowledge both, anticipating Pascal's saying that man is "the glory and scum of the universe."

When the writer of Ecclesiastes describes man as an upright creature universally bent, the Hebrew word he uses for "man" (the one referred to above) is "adam." It is not just the name of an individual in the creation story. It stands for the humanity we all share and of which the first Adam is the representative symbol.

The New Testament Gospel of Luke contains a long list of the ancestors of the family of Jesus, and it ends (having worked backward through time) ". . . the son of Seth, the son of Adam, the son of God." Luke is saying that man's divine origin is not lost. Indeed, in Jesus it is fully recovered. Paul calls him "the last Adam" (1 Corinthians 15:45): a second representative of humanity as a whole.

All parts of the New Testament teach that restored human nature, though found unspoiled only in Jesus, is imparted by him to those who are spiritually united with him. The least within his kingdom is more truly human than the greatest outside it.

The moral demands of the New Testament—demands for love, for honesty, for a unity transcending all human distinctions—are therefore not expressed as mere ethical ideals that men ought to pursue: they are expressed as the natural pattern of life within the new humanity that is coming to birth. But the process is incomplete. Humanity is under construction. Even with their knowledge of Jesus, the New Testament writers such as John and Paul admit that the end of the process is beyond the range of their imagination. "But," says John, "we shall be like him, for we shall see him as he is" (1 John 3:2). The contemplation of true humanity leads to the achievement of true humanity.

Many practical policies would be affected by the adoption of the biblical belief in humanity as man-in-the-making and in every human being as one in whom contrary tendencies are at work. These contrary tendencies are not correctly described as the spiritual versus the material. The material, physical nature of man is perfectly compatible with true humanity. No, the conflict is between two tendencies within the human spirit: the tendency to focus on the self versus the tendency to focus on the other. To deal with human beings without allowing for both these factors is to deal with them unrealistically.

To suppose that man can be perfected by some form of social engineering applied to him from without—whether by way of a political system or of genetic control—is to ignore the deep-seatedness of sin. At least one young mother, seeing children brought up from birth in a kibbutz where all possessions were held in common, was dismayed to hear infant voices shouting "Mine" over every toy. It should not have surprised her. And besides individual selfishness there is also a corporate kind that comes naturally to social groups and communities (see Self and Selfishness). These unhappy facts must always be allowed for.

On the other hand, it is equally a mistake to treat a human being as if there were in him no hunger for the good, nothing to which perfection would appeal. Man is born self-seeking, but the ideal still beckons to him. He needs it made tangible so that he can contemplate it and love it, but when that happens it begins a process not unlike rebirth.

MAN

OLD TESTAMENT

Genesis 6:5–6

5 And God saw that the wickedness of man was great in the earth, and that every imagination of the thoughts of his heart was only evil continually.

6 And it repented the Lord that he had made man on the earth, and it grieved him at his heart.

Psalm 144:3–4

Lord, what is man, that thou takest
knowledge of him!
Or the son of man, that thou makest ac-
count of him!
Man is like to vanity:
His days are as a shadow that passeth away.

Psalm 8:4–8

What is man, that thou are mindful of
him?
And the son of man, that thou visitest
him?
For thou hast made him a little lower
than the angels,
And hast crowned him with glory and
honour.
Thou madest him to have dominion over
the works of thy hands;
Thou hast put all things under his feet:
All sheep and oxen,
Yea, and the beasts of the field;
The fowl of the air, and the fish of the
sea,
And whatsoever passeth through the paths
of the seas.

Psalm 62:9

Surely men of low degree are vanity, and
men of high degree are a lie:
To be laid in the balance,
They are altogether lighter than vanity.

Ecclesiastes 7:20, 29

20 For there is not a just man upon
earth, that doeth good, and sinneth
not.
29 Lo, this only have I found, that
God hath made man upright; but they
have sought out many inventions.

NEW TESTAMENT

John 1:9–13

9 That was the true Light, which
lighteth every man that cometh into
the world.
10 He was in the world, and the
world was made by him, and the world
knew him not.
11 He came unto his own, and his
own received him not.
12 But as many as received him, to
them gave he power to become the
sons of God, even to them that believe
on his name:
13 Which were born, not of blood,
nor of the will of the flesh, nor of the
will of man, but of God.

Luke 7:28

28 For I say unto you, Among those
that are born of women there is not a
greater prophet than John the Baptist:
but he that is least in the kingdom of
God is greater than he.

Acts 17:24–28

24 God that made the world and
all things therein, seeing that he is Lord
of heaven and earth, dwelleth not in
temples made with hands;
25 Neither is worshipped with men's
hands, as though he needed any thing,
seeing he giveth to all life, and breath,
and all things;
26 And hath made of one blood all
nations of men for to dwell on all the
face of the earth, and hath determined
the times before appointed, and the
bounds of their habitation;

27 That they should seek the Lord, if haply they might feel after him, and find him, though he be not far from every one of us:

28 For in him we live, and move, and have our being; as certain also of your own poets have said, For we are also his offspring.

Ephesians 4:17, 22–24

17 This I say therefore, and testify in the Lord, that ye henceforth walk not as other Gentiles walk, in the vanity of their mind . . .

22 That ye put off concerning the former conversation the old man, which is corrupt according to the deceitful lusts;

23 And be renewed in the spirit of your mind;

24 And that ye put on the new man, which after God is created in righteousness and true holiness.

Colossians 3:9–11

9 Lie not one to another, seeing that ye have put off the old man with his deeds;

10 And have put on the new man, which is renewed in knowledge after the image of him that created him:

11 Where there is neither Greek nor Jew, circumcision nor uncircumcision, Barbarian, Scythian, bond nor free: but Christ is all, and in all.

MARRIAGE

Each of the first two chapters of the Old Testament traces the closeness of the marriage relationship right back to the very making of man and woman. The first chapter speaks as if only man and woman together make the full human being: "God created man (adam) in his own image, in the image of God he created him; male and female he created them" (Genesis 1:27). The second chapter, telling the creation story a little differently, explicitly connects it with marriage. Jesus was later to refer to both these texts.

Such passages concentrate on the essence of marriage as a relationship, but the Old Testament is also concerned with marriage as an institution—and for that it legislates. Its laws were framed so as to maximize a man's chances of getting sons, male supremacy being accepted without question. So a husband could have more than one wife, but a wife could have only one husband. A husband could have intercourse with women other than his wife (so long as he did not infringe the rights of another husband), but a wife must have intercourse with none but her husband. The security of the family unit was the primary concern of the legislation, although it also contained some very humane and kindly provisions, such as the excusing of a newly married man from military service.

Legislation, however, defined only minimum standards. Many an Old Testament story tells of a deep relationship between married partners and of a relationship in which the woman's role was far from insignificant. The most revealing of all Old Testament references to marriage are those that see it as a parallel to the relationship between God and his people. This was a common prophetic theme, often accompanied by the denunciation of Israel as an unfaithful wife. God, however, is said by prophets such as Hosea to be like a husband who continues to love his unfaithful wife and continues to seek the mending of the relationship. Hosea's insight seems to have sprung from his own unhappy relationship with his wife, Gomer, but many other marriages must also have been affected by the reflex action of a belief in God as one who maintains a marriage bond even when law and justice declare it broken. He speaks of Israel's God as Ishi (husband) rather than Baali (master).

The New Testament is much less concerned with legislating for marriage as an institution than it is with commending it as a relationship and exploring its significance as an image of the union between God and his people. Jesus spoke of himself as a bridegroom (Mark 2:18–20) and pictured the kingdom of God as a wedding feast. His high view of marriage (see also Divorce) went far beyond the requirements of any law.

His later followers at first played down the importance of marriage. For such critical times it seemed to Paul to be something of a diversion from the task in hand, but even he saw marriage as a parallel to the mystical union of Christ and his church. As always, this reflected back on the understanding of marriage between men and women. It led Paul to speak of reciprocal love in a way that may well have challenged the male-dominated climate of his time, though in other respects he conformed to it.

In the later New Testament books the sense of imminent crisis was less urgent, and the advantages of stable marriage were reaffirmed. The polygamy of the patriarchs was abandoned. Marriage now meant monogamous marriage.

As a source of marital law the Bible is not perfectly satisfactory. It shows marriage in the course of evolution, and the final stages are not expressed in terms of rules. Legislators required to define minimum standards will not find them here, but they will find an understanding of the marriage relationship as being deeply built into the very nature of humanity, and as reflecting the very highest relationship of which human beings are capable. It not only shows marriage to be formed around love but also says what love is—a desire for union at every level.

MARRIAGE

OLD TESTAMENT

Genesis 2:21–24

21 And the Lord God caused a deep sleep to fall upon Adam, and he slept: and he took one of his ribs, and closed up the flesh instead thereof;

22 And the rib, which the Lord God had taken from man, made he a woman, and brought her unto the man.

23 And Adam said, This is now bone of my bones, and flesh of my flesh: she shall be called Woman, because she was taken out of Man.

24 Therefore shall a man leave his father and his mother, and shall cleave unto his wife: and they shall be one flesh.

Deuteronomy 24:5

5 When a man hath taken a new wife, he shall not go out to war, neither shall he be charged with any business: but he shall be free at home one year, and shall cheer up his wife which he hath taken.

Isaiah 54:5–7

5 For thy Maker is thine husband; the Lord of hosts is his name; and thy Redeemer the Holy One of Israel; The God of the whole earth shall he be called.

6 For the Lord hath called thee as a woman forsaken and grieved in spirit, and a wife of youth, when thou wast refused, saith thy God.

7 For a small moment have I forsaken thee; but with great mercies will I gather thee.

Hosea 2:16, 19–20

16 And it shall be at that day, saith the Lord, that thou shalt call me Ishi, and shalt call me no more Baali.

19 And I will betroth thee unto me for ever; yea, I will betroth thee unto me in righteousness, and in judgment, and in lovingkindness, and in mercies.

20 I will even betroth thee unto me in faithfulness: and thou shalt know the Lord.

NEW TESTAMENT

Matthew 19:4–6

4 And he answered and said unto them, Have ye not read, that he which made them at the beginning made them male and female,

5 And said, For this cause shall a man leave father and mother, and shall cleave to his wife: and they twain shall be one flesh?

6 Wherefore they are no more twain, but one flesh. What therefore God hath joined together, let not man put asunder.

1 Corinthians 7:1–4

1 It is good for a man not to touch a woman.

2 Nevertheless, to avoid fornication, let every man have his own wife, and let every woman have her own husband.

3 Let the husband render unto the wife due benevolence: and likewise also the wife unto the husband.

4 The wife hath not power of her own body, but the husband: and likewise also the husband hath not power of his own body, but the wife.

Ephesians 5:22–29

22 Wives, submit yourselves unto your own husbands, as unto the Lord.

23 For the husband is the head of the wife, even as Christ is the head of the church: and he is the saviour of the body.

24 Therefore as the church is subject unto Christ, so let the wives be to their own husbands in every thing.

25 Husbands, love your wives, even as Christ also loved the church, and gave himself for it;

26 That he might sanctify and cleanse it with the washing of water by the word,

27 That he might present it to himself a glorious church, not having spot, or wrinkle, or any such thing; but that it should be holy and without blemish.

28 So ought men to love their wives as their own bodies. He that loveth his wife loveth himself.

29 For no man ever yet hated his own flesh; but nourisheth and cherisheth it, even as the Lord the church:

1 Timothy 5:14

14 I will therefore that the younger women marry, bear children, guide the house, give none occasion to the adversary to speak reproachfully.

MATERIALISM

Materialism does not mean living by material things. It means living *for* them. Living *by* them is inevitable, since human life is an embodied form of existence. So the Old Testament is unashamedly concerned about the material world, but the people of whom it approves are the servants of a purpose that transcends the material. Israel's struggle for existence in the wilderness and its building of prosperity in Canaan were material struggles, but their purpose was the fashioning of a free people, freely responding to God in the way required by his law—a way of brotherliness toward one another and of reverence before him.

Unfortunately, "success" (defined in materialistic terms) could easily blind people to its own real significance, and so turn to failure. Not only the prophets who denounced luxury but also the Book of Wisdom writers who often appreciated it were concerned to define success in nonmaterialistic terms, not so that material things could be dismissed from consideration, but so that they could be valued and used at their true worth. When valued for what they are, say such books as Ecclesiastes and Proverbs, material things are just a medium in which to develop personal relationships with others and with God.

The Old Testament is quoted in the New when Jesus speaks of man's not living by bread alone. Neither in Deuteronomy nor in the Gospels does this mean that bread is unimportant. What is folly, however, is the attitude of the man in the parable who "stores up things for himself" and who makes his life depend on his possessions instead of making his possessions the instruments of his personal and interpersonal life.

Jesus' Sermon on the Mount is both a celebration of the goodness of the material world and an appeal to look beyond it. Only the man or woman who gives priority to the values of the kingdom of God can truly value and rightly handle material things. Such a man, apparently, was Paul, since he could claim to have learned how to find contentment in either abundance or want.

If and when people become insensitive to the values that transcend the material, then the life of the world turns in on itself: goals have to be defined in material terms; lives have to be measured against materialistic standards. This is materialism. In the long term it is a way of death to the human spirit, and even in the short term it spoils, paradoxically, the appreciation of all things material. Materialists are really possessed by their possessions. Material things can be truly valued only by those who have some measure of what Hans Kung has called "inward freedom from possessions."

Once material things are seen as a means and not an end, they will be not only better appreciated but also better distributed and more secure. If human brotherhood had always been valued above material possessions so that material things were used as the instruments of brotherhood, then we might be free of some of the deep divisions between classes, nations, and races that now threaten our material prosperity. As it is, we must start where we are, but the preaching of worldwide brotherhood will produce little human solidarity till the words are clothed in tangible, material forms.

It is as true of societies as it is of individuals that they need to give their heart to a nonmaterial form of wealth if they are to see material things in their true and glorious light. The unworldly Thomas Traherne, the seventeenth-century mystic, taught us how to "enjoy the world aright." That he meant the material world was clear when, in his great "Thanksgiving for the Body," he gave thanks for

> Springs, Rivers, Fountains, Oceans,
> Gold, Silver and precious Stones.
> Corn, Wine, and Oyl,
> The Sun, Moon and Stars,
> Cities, Nations, Kingdoms.
> And the Bodies of Men, the greatest Treasures of all,
> For each other.

MATERIALISM

OLD TESTAMENT

Deuteronomy 8:10–16

10 When thou hast eaten and art full, then thou shalt bless the Lord thy God for the good land which he hath given thee.

11 Beware that thou forget not the Lord thy God, in not keeping his commandments, and his judgments, and his statutes, which I command thee this day:

12 Lest when thou hast eaten and art full, and hast built goodly houses, and dwelt therein;

13 And when thy herds and thy flocks multiply, and thy silver and thy gold is multiplied, and all that thou hast is multiplied;

14 Then thine heart be lifted up, and thou forget the Lord thy God, which brought thee forth out of the land of Egypt, from the house of bondage;

15 Who led thee through that great and terrible wilderness, wherein were fiery serpents, and scorpions, and drought, where there was no water; who brought thee forth water out of the rock of flint;

16 Who fed thee in the wilderness with manna, which thy fathers knew not, that he might humble thee, and that he might prove thee, to do thee good at thy latter end.

Amos 6:1, 4–7

1 Woe to them that are at ease in Zion, and trust in the mountain of Samaria,

4 That lie upon beds of ivory, and stretch themselves upon their couches, and eat the lambs out of the flock, and the calves out of the midst of the stall;

5 That chant to the sound of the viol, and invent to themselves instruments of music, like David;

6 That drink wine in bowls, and anoint themselves with the chief ointments: but they are not grieved for the affliction of Joseph.

7 Therefore now shall they go captive with the first that go captive, and the banquet of them that stretched themselves shall be removed.

Proverbs 15:16–17

Better is little with the fear of the Lord
Than great treasure and trouble therewith.
Better is a dinner of herbs where love is,
Than a stalled ox and hatred therewith.

Ecclesiastes 4:6

6 Better is an handful with quietness, than both the hands full with travail and vexation of spirit.

NEW TESTAMENT

Matthew 4:1–4

1 Then was Jesus led up of the Spirit into the wilderness to be tempted of the devil.

2 And when he had fasted forty days and forty nights, he was afterward an hungered.

3 And when the tempter came to him, he said, If thou be the Son of God, command that these stones be made bread.

4 But he answered and said, It is written, Man shall not live by bread alone, but by every word that proceedeth out of the mouth of God.

Luke 12:15–21

15 And he said unto them, Take heed, and beware of covetousness: for a man's life consisteth not in the abundance of things which he possesseth.

16 And he spake a parable unto them, saying, The ground of a certain rich man brought forth plentifully:

17 And he thought within himself, saying, What shall I do, because I have no room where to bestow my fruits?

18 And he said, This will I do: I will pull down my barns, and build greater; and there will I bestow all my fruits and my goods.

19 And I will say to my soul, Soul, thou hast much goods laid up for many years; take thine ease, eat, drink, and be merry.

20 But God said unto him, Thou fool, this night thy soul shall be re-quired of thee: then whose shall those things be, which thou hast provided?

21 So is he that layeth up treasure for himself, and is not rich toward God.

Matthew 6:31–33

31 Therefore take no thought, saying, What shall we eat? or, What shall we drink? or, Wherewithal shall we be clothed?

32 (For after all these things do the Gentiles seek:) for your heavenly Father knoweth that ye have need of all these things.

33 But seek ye first the kingdom of God, and his righteousness; and all these things shall be added unto you

Philippians 4:11–13

11 I have learned, in whatsoever state I am, therewith to be content.

12 I know both how to be abased, and I know how to abound: every where and in all things I am instructed both to be full and to be hungry, both to abound and to suffer need.

13 I can do all things through Christ which strengtheneth me.

MERCY

Mercy is not just being good to people: it is being good to people who do not deserve such treatment—often in the face of their positive demerits. The Old Testament position is that, since all men and women stand in need of this treatment from God, it is only fitting that they should show mercy to one another, as David did when he had Saul "at his mercy."

Weak people are always afraid that mercy is the same thing as laxity and that standards of morality and justice will collapse if bad men and women are spared the penalty to be exacted, but those who ask for mercy do by that very act affirm and uphold the standards of justice. Had they not offended against those standards, no occasion for mercy would have arisen. The real answer to badness is goodness—not the mere obliteration of the bad, but the loving acknowledgment of the good as it is seen in God. And from that goodness, prophets and psalmists affirm, mercy is inseparable.

The New Testament is all about God's mercy actively ensuring that men and women shall not suffer the consequences of their wrongdoing. This is described as the central purpose of Christ's presence. Yet its effect is not so much a lowering of standards as a raising of them, and that includes an increased demand for mercy between one human being and another.

There is no question of meriting mercy. It is sheer grace, an expression of the loving will of God and nothing else. But one has a natural obligation to respond to mercy by becoming merciful. Not to live by mercy is a sign of not really having accepted it in the first place. But as always in the New Testament, the good life is seen as following and flowing out of the act and gift of grace rather than as preceding it. It is a result of being forgiven rather than a precondition for it (see Forgiveness).

There is a story about a woman who came to the Emperor Napoleon to plead for the life of her son, who had been condemned to death under military law. "Your son," said the emperor, "has done nothing to deserve mercy."

"If he had," said the woman, "it would not be mercy."

There is no answer to that. The more we hedge mercy about with conditions and qualifications, the less merciful it is. It may be something else of great importance (such as retributive justice), but it is not mercy. Mercy is essentially unmerited. It need not even ask for mitigating circumstances.

That is what makes its existence so precarious in societies dominated by standards of merit. Earned rewards and deserved punishments are felt to have their place in the nature of things. Unearned rewards and undeserved pardons seem to challenge this settled order. So they do. And yet ultimately life is a gift rather than an achievement. The best things in it are not merely free but unmerited. In common experience, grace goes deeper and is more certain than justice.

If that fact were let into consciousness more often and allowed to influence behavior more widely, the effects would be considerable. Yet standards of justice would not be overthrown. Mercy, after all, can be shown and accepted only where an offense is acknowledged to exist and where consequently standards of justice are affirmed. The granting and receiving of pardon may in fact make the standard clearer and more commanding than punishment would. Mercy, though unconditional, does impose its own obligations.

"Mercy rejoiceth against judgment," says the New Testament James (2:13). But not against justice. Justice and mercy are ultimately one. They spring from the same divine root.

MERCY

OLD TESTAMENT

Psalm 25:6–7

Remember, O Lord, thy tender mercies
and thy lovingkindnesses;
For they have been ever of old.
Remember not the sins of my youth, nor
my transgressions:

Zechariah 7:9

9 Thus speaketh the Lord of hosts, saying, Execute true judgment, and shew mercy and compassions every man to his brother.

1 Samuel 24:2–4, 8–11, 16–17

2 Then Saul took three thousand chosen men out of all Israel, and went to seek David and his men upon the rocks of the wild goats.

3 And he came to the sheepcotes by the way, where was a cave; and Saul went in to cover his feet: and David and his men remained in the sides of the cave.

4 And the men of David said unto him, Behold the day of which the Lord said unto thee, Behold, I will deliver thine enemy into thine hand, that thou mayest do to him as it shall seem good unto thee. Then David arose, and cut off the skirt of Saul's robe privily.

8 David also arose afterward, and went out of the cave, and cried after Saul, saying, My lord the king. And when Saul looked behind him, David stooped with his face to the earth, and bowed himself.

9 And David said to Saul, Wherefore hearest thou men's words, saying, Behold, David seeketh thy hurt?

10 Behold, this day thine eyes have seen how that the Lord had delivered thee to-day into mine hand in the cave: and some bade me kill thee: but mine eye spared thee; and I said, I will not put forth mine hand against my lord; for he is the Lord's anointed.

11 Moreover, my father, see, yea, see the skirt of thy robe in my hand: for in that I cut off the skirt of thy robe, and killed thee not, know thou and see that there is neither evil nor transgression in mine hand, and I have not sinned against thee; yet thou huntest my soul to take it.

16 And it came to pass, when David had made an end of speaking these words unto Saul, that Saul said, Is this thy voice, my son David? And Saul lifted up his voice, and wept.

17 And he said to David, Thou art more righteous than I: for thou hast rewarded me good, whereas I have rewarded thee evil.

Habakkuk 3:2

2 O Lord, in wrath remember mercy.

NEW TESTAMENT

John 3:16–17

16 For God so loved the world, that he gave his only begotten Son, that whosoever believeth in him should not perish, but have everlasting life.

17 For God sent not his Son into the world to condemn the world; but that the world through him might be saved.

Matthew 5:7

7 Blessed are the merciful: for they shall obtain mercy.

Matthew 18:23–33

23 Therefore is the kingdom of heaven likened unto a certain king, which would take account of his servants.

24 And when he had begun to reckon, one was brought unto him, which owed him ten thousand talents.

25 But forasmuch as he had not to pay, his lord commanded him to be sold, and his wife, and children, and all that he had, and payment to be made.

26 The servant therefore fell down, and worshipped him, saying, Lord, have patience with me, and I will pay thee all.

27 Then the lord of that servant was moved with compassion, and loosed him, and forgave him the debt.

28 But the same servant went out, and found one of his fellow-servants, which owed him an hundred pence: and he laid hands on him, and took him by the throat, saying, Pay me that thou owest.

29 And his fellow-servant fell down at his feet, and besought him, saying, Have patience with me, and I will pay thee all.

30 And he would not: but went and cast him into prison, till he should pay the debt.

31 So when his fellow-servants saw what was done, they were very sorry, and came and told unto their lord all that was done.

32 Then his lord, after that he had called him, said unto him, O thou wicked servant, I forgave thee all that debt, because thou desiredst me:

33 Shouldest not thou also have had compassion on thy fellow-servant, even as I had pity on thee?

Romans 9:14–16; 11:32

14 What shall we say then? Is there unrighteousness with God? God forbid.

15 For he saith to Moses, I will have mercy on whom I will have mercy, and I will have compassion on whom I will have compassion.

16 So then it is not of him that willeth, nor of him that runneth, but of God that sheweth mercy.

32 For God hath concluded them all in unbelief, that he might have mercy upon all.

MIRACLES

To the men of the Old Testament everything happened by the direct decision of God, so one event was just as possible as another. Though exceptional, it was as easy for God to make the sun stand still as it was for him to keep it moving.

Significantly, the miracles to which the writers come back again and again are not the most extraordinary ones, but those that they see as most clearly expressing God's loving purpose—supremely, the deliverance from Egypt.

In the New Testament the three words commonly used for miracles meant "powers," "wonders," and "signs." The second of these never appeared without the third, which suggests that the exceptional is to be studied for its significance rather than its oddity.

Jesus evidently regarded a mere display of miraculous power as a temptation of the devil, though such displays were much sought after by his generation—and by later ones. However, even if we deny that miracles are a ground for belief, we must read the exceptional events going on around Jesus as evidence of the kingdom's presence.

The supreme New Testament miracle is the resurrection of Jesus from the dead, but the New Testament treats even this as natural given the circumstances: "it was not possible that he should be holden of it."

"I don't believe in miracles," people say. In a sense the Bible does not ask them to—not to believe *in* miracles, not to make miracles the ground and object of faith. God alone is that. The biblical writers believe that miracles happen (which is different from believing *in* them), but they insist that faith can do without them. From outside the relationship of faith in God, miracles look very significant. From inside it, such wonders are so natural that there seems no great point in putting a line around certain events and calling them miraculous—as if God were not active in the others.

Yet the word "miracle" is needed. A world without wonders would be an impoverished world, and a God who confined himself to the obvious and the familiar would be the center of an impoverished religion. Definitions are needed.

It is quite easy to define the miraculous in such a way that a miracle can never happen. For instance, if a miracle is "something contrary to the laws of nature," and if the laws of nature are just an account of what actually happens in the world, then a miracle cannot actually happen. Each time one appears to happen, the laws of nature have to be redefined to allow for it, and once that is done the event is no longer (by definition) miraculous.

A recent book, *Miracles* by Goeffrey Ashe, offers a better definition of a miracle as "a divinely ordained exception." This at least rules out two misunderstandings.

First, it says that Walt Whitman is using the wrong word when he says (expressing an entirely proper sentiment), "To me every hour of the light and dark is a miracle, Every cubic inch of space is a miracle." If everything is a miracle, nothing is.

Goeffrey Ashe's definition also rules out the idea that every extraordinary event can be called miraculous. A miracle is not just an exceptional event, but a divinely ordained one. It is not an event of purely human significance, whether spoon bending by the power of the mind or wart charming by the power of

219

magic. It is above all an expression of the mind and purpose of God, a message for the mind to read rather than boggle at.

The age of miracles need never pass so long as the world's potential is imperfectly realized. It is reasonable to believe that the creation is designed to respond to faith in ways as yet undiscovered. Its laws may not be set aside, but they can be opened up.

MIRACLES

OLD TESTAMENT

Joshua 10:12–13

12 Then spake Joshua to the Lord in the day when the Lord delivered up the Amorites before the children of Israel, and he said in the sight of Israel, Sun, stand thou still upon Gibeon; and thou, Moon, in the valley of Ajalon.

13 And the sun stood still, and the moon stayed, until the people had avenged themselves upon their enemies. Is not this written in the book of Jasher? So the sun stood still in the midst of heaven, and hasted not to go down about a whole day.

1 Kings 17:8–15

8 And the word of the Lord came unto him, saying,

9 Arise, get thee to Zarephath, which belongeth to Zidon, and dwell there: behold, I have commanded a widow woman there to sustain thee.

10 So he arose and went to Zarephath. And when he came to the gate of the city, behold, the widow woman was there gathering of sticks: and he called to her, and said, Fetch me, I pray thee, a little water in a vessel, that I may drink.

11 And as she was going to fetch it, he called to her, and said, Bring me, I pray thee, a morsel of bread in thine hand.

12 And she said, As the Lord thy God liveth, I have not a cake, but an handful of meal in a barrel, and a little oil in a cruse: and, behold, I am gathering two sticks, that I may go in and dress it for me and my son, that we may eat it, and die.

13 And Elijah said unto her, Fear not; go and do as thou hast said: but make me thereof a little cake first, and bring it unto me, and after make for thee and for thy son.

14 For thus saith the Lord God of Israel, The barrel of meal shall not waste, neither shall the cruse of oil fail, until the day that the Lord sendeth rain upon the earth.

15 And she went and did according to the saying of Elijah: and she, and he, and her house, did eat many days.

Psalm 78:12–13

Marvellous things did he in the sight of
   their fathers,
In the land of Egypt, in the field of Zoan.
He divided the sea, and caused them to
   pass through;
And he made the waters to stand as an
   heap.

NEW TESTAMENT

Matthew 4:5–7

5 Then the devil taketh him up into the holy city, and setteth him on a pinnacle of the temple.

6 And saith unto him, If thou be the Son of God, cast thyself down: for it is written, He shall give his angels charge concerning thee: and in their hands they shall bear thee up, lest at any time thou dash thy foot against a stone.

7 Jesus said unto him, It is written again, Thou shalt not tempt the Lord thy God.

Matthew 11:2–6

2 Now when John had heard in the prison the works of Christ, he sent two of his disciples,

3 And said unto him, Art thou he that should come, or do we look for another?

4 Jesus answered and said unto them, Go and shew John again those things which ye do hear and see:

5 The blind receive their sight, and the lame walk, the lepers are cleansed, and the deaf hear, the dead are raised

up, and the poor have the gospel preached to them.

6 And blessed is he, whosoever shall not be offended in me.

Mark 8:12

12 And he sighed deeply in his spirit, and saith, Why doth this generation seek after a sign? verily I say unto you, There shall no sign be given unto this generation.

Acts 2:22–24, 43

22 Ye men of Israel, hear these words; Jesus of Nazareth, a man approved of God among you by miracles and wonders and signs, which God did by him in the midst of you, as ye yourselves also know:

23 Him, being delivered by the determinate counsel and foreknowledge of God, ye have taken, and by wicked hands have crucified and slain:

24 Whom God hath raised up, having loosed the pains of death: because it was not possible that he should be holden of it.

43 And fear came upon every soul: and many wonders and signs were done by the apostles.

MISTAKES

The Old Testament does distinguish between wrong actions done deliberately and wrong actions done unintentionally (nearer to what we would call mistakes), but it regards both as sins. The reason for this is rooted in the Old Testament's strong belief that the difference between right and wrong is written into the nature of things. A wrong action is not exempt from evil consequences just because it was done in ignorance or with an innocent motive. This may seem harsh, but the idea was to face up to the facts so that the situation could be remedied.

Once the mistake has been made, the Old Testament says clearly that there is no alternative but to turn back. The Hebrew word for "repent" primarily signifies not a feeling of moral contrition but the action of changing course. Even God is said to change his course. When the Israelites in the wilderness made the mistake of thinking that Moses was never going to come down from Mount Sinai, they turned to idolatry. God decided to destroy them, but Moses persuaded him to change his mind.

In the Old Testament, idolatry is the most fundamental of all mistakes. It is fantasy, and from this all forms of error flow. Doing right follows from thinking right, and thinking right follows from seeing things as they are at the most fundamental level. Prophets who foster illusions as to the nature of ultimate reality are liable to lead everybody into mistakes of every kind and at every level. Fantasy is the father of error.

In the New Testament Gospels, Jesus regards his critics as mistaken and sees their mistakes as grounded in fundamental error as to the nature of God. He also regarded other levels of unreality as leading to other mistakes. He mocked the mistakes men make because they lack a sense of proportion and because they see other people's mistakes much more clearly than they see their own. At the same time Jesus warned that making a fundamental misjudgment can be as disastrous as building a house without a foundation.

The Gospels are astonishingly frank about the mistakes made by the apostles of Jesus. Two of them, for example, sought positions of authority under him, which was to mistake the nature of his rule. One of them promised to follow him to the death, which was to mistake his own resolution. One of them even betrayed Jesus (conceivably with the mistaken idea that it would help force him to take a stand before the authorities) and then made the final mistake of committing suicide. Jesus preached perfection, but dealt very gently with many people who fell far short of it—so long as they had the sense to face the fact of their own imperfection.

The Bible seems to regard mistakes as both more serious and less final than do most modern thinkers. This seriousness is a result of the Bible's essential realism. Doing the wrong thing is harmful. A mistake cannot be disregarded just because the person who made it "meant no harm" or "didn't know."

On the other hand, a wrong can be put right. In view of the fact that we all make mistakes, one might assume that most of us would have learned to handle them. This does not appear to be so. Some people go obstinately on with a mistake rather than admit they have made one, and others quit altogether rather than try to correct their mistakes. We need to consider the biblical view that if there is that in the nature of things which makes every mistake harmful, there is also that in the nature of things which makes the hurt healable—if attended to.

We may want to insist that there are such things as "innocent mistakes" and that to treat them all as sins is to be too dramatic about them, but there is also wisdom in seeing that human beings are all of a piece and that a connection exists between fundamental beliefs and trivial actions, between one's attitude toward ultimate reality and one's handling of everyday issues.

MISTAKES

OLD TESTAMENT

Exodus 32:1–4, 7, 10–14

1 And when the people saw that Moses delayed to come down out of the mount, the people gathered themselves together unto Aaron, and said unto him, Up, make us gods, which shall go before us; for as for this Moses, the man that brought us up out of the land of Egypt, we wot not what is become of him.

2 And Aaron said unto them, Break off the golden earrings, which are in the ears of your wives, of your sons, and of your daughters, and bring them unto me.

3 And all the people brake off the golden earrings which were in their ears, and brought them unto Aaron.

4 And he received them at their hand, and fashioned it with a graving tool, after he had made it a molten calf: and they said, These be thy gods, O Israel, which brought thee up out of the land of Egypt.

7 And the Lord said unto Moses, Go, get thee down; for thy people, which thou broughtest out of the land of Egypt, have corrupted themselves:

10 Now therefore let me alone, that my wrath may wax hot against them, and that I may consume them: and I will make of thee a great nation.

11 And Moses besought the Lord his God, and said, Lord,

12 Turn from thy fierce wrath, and repent of this evil against thy people.

13 Remember Abraham, Isaac, and Israel, thy servants.

14 And the Lord repented of the evil which he thought to do unto his people.

Leviticus 5:17–18

17 And if a soul sin, and commit any of these things which are forbidden to be done by the commandments of the Lord; though he wist it not, yet is he guilty, and shall bear his iniquity.

18 And he shall bring a ram without blemish out of the flock, with thy estimation, for a trespass offering, unto the priest: and the priest shall make an atonement for him concerning his ignorance wherein he erred and wist it not, and it shall be forgiven him.

Isaiah 9:16

16 For the leaders of this people cause them to err; and they that are led of them are destroyed.

Jeremiah 23:32

32 Behold, I am against them that prophesy false dreams, saith the Lord, and do tell them, and cause my people to err by their lies.

NEW TESTAMENT

Mark 12:24, 27

24 And Jesus answering said unto them, Do ye not therefore err, because ye know not the scriptures, neither the power of God?

27 He is not the God of the dead, but the God of the living: ye therefore do greatly err.

Luke 6:39, 41–42, 47–49

39 Can the blind lead the blind? shall they not both fall into the ditch?

41 And why beholdest thou the mote that is in thy brother's eye, but perceivest not the beam that is in thine own eye?

42 Either how canst thou say to thy brother, Brother, let me pull out the mote that is in thine eye, when thou thyself beholdest not the beam that is in thine own eye?

47 Whosoever cometh to me, and heareth my sayings, and doeth them, I will shew you to whom he is like:

48 He is like a man which built an house, and digged deep, and laid the foundation on a rock: and when the flood arose, the stream beat vehemently upon that house, and could not shake it: for it was founded upon a rock.

49 But he that heareth, and doeth not, is like a man that without a foundation built an house upon the earth; against which the stream did beat vehemently, and immediately it fell; and the ruin of that house was great.

Matthew 27:3–5

3 Then Judas, which had betrayed him, when he saw that he was condemned, repented himself, and brought again the thirty pieces of silver to the chief priests and elders,

4 Saying, I have sinned in that I have betrayed the innocent blood. And they said, What is that to us? see thou to that.

5 And he cast down the pieces of silver in the temple, and departed, and went and hanged himself.

Galatians 6:1–3

1 Brethren, if a man be overtaken in a fault, ye which are spiritual, restore such an one in the spirit of meekness; considering thyself, lest thou also be tempted.

2 Bear ye one another's burdens, and so fulfil the law of Christ.

3 For if a man think himself to be something, when he is nothing, he deceiveth himself.

MONEY

The Old Testament story of Jeremiah's field at Anathoth provides not only an interesting picture of ancient coinage in use but also a very significant picture of a man putting his money where his faith is. Jeremiah was in prison in Jerusalem. He had warned that the policy being followed by the government of the day would bring the Babylonians down on them. This had happened, and Jeremiah had been imprisoned on the ground that he was evidently sympathetic toward the enemy. It does not always pay to have been proved right.

For the moment, however, the Babylonians had lifted the siege of Jerusalem. Business could be resumed, though the village of Anathoth, where Jeremiah had relatives, must still have been in Babylonian hands. As next of kin Jeremiah had a legal right to buy some land there. Few purchasers would have given much for a title so unlikely to be enforceable, but for Jeremiah it was an opportunity to use his money as a sign of his confidence in the future of God's people. His buying the land was a very public and very convincing expression of his belief that, beyond the present chastisement, God would restore Israel to the enjoyment of its lands.

To the Old Testament writers, money is as valuable as what it will do. And no more. It is not of value in itself (see Values). The prophets insisted that there are blessings to be had which transcend the power of money either to buy or to measure.

Several of the New Testament parables of Jesus involve money, but they are not *about* money. That is, they are not designed to teach its proper use. They are about different ways of responding to the kingdom of God. Money in these stories is a metaphor for life itself.

All the same, the parallel can to some extent be read both ways. In the parable of the talents, the details about the use of money provide no model, any more than the details about the behavior of the grasping businessman provide a true picture of God, but it is true that the real question is not "What have you received?" but "What have you done with it?" And this does apply to money as well as to membership in the people of God, which was the subject under consideration when the story was told. Money is again seen to be a means and not an end.

The importance of the issue has nothing to do with the amount at stake. The widow's mite is more than enough to open or close a way through money to abundant life.

The special problem of riches is looked at in the entry for Wealth. Here, however, we are concerned with money itself, whether much or little is involved. And money, as the classical economists confirmed, is just a means of exchange. As such it is very useful. As anything else—as an end rather than a means, for instance, or as a measure of human value—it is a menace. But you can hardly blame money for that.

When people make this mistake it is because they have fallen into the ancient trap of focusing on what is near in such a way that what is beyond it becomes a confusing blur. The mistake about money is an instructive example of an error that can as easily, but perhaps not as obviously, be made with relationships, with time, with natural resources, and with spiritual gifts. In all cases a sort of depth of vision (in a metaphorical sense) is needed in order to see the more distant possibilities to be approached through what lies immediately to hand.

In his *Prayers of Life* Michael Quoist meditates on a bank note—no improper subject for religious meditation. As he says, "We can hardly respect money enough for the blood and toil it represents. Money is frightening. It can serve or destroy man."*

MONEY

OLD TESTAMENT

Jeremiah 32:6–15

6 And Jeremiah said, The word of the Lord came unto me, saying,

7 Behold, Hanameel the son of Shallum thine uncle shall come unto thee, saying, Buy thee my field that is in Anathoth: for the right of redemption is thine to buy it.

8 So Hanameel mine uncle's son came to me in the court of the prison according to the word of the Lord, and said unto me, Buy my field, I pray thee, that is in Anathoth, which is in the country of Benjamin: for the right of inheritance is thine, and the redemption is thine; buy it for thyself. Then I knew that this was the word of the Lord.

9 And I bought the field of Hanameel my uncle's son, that was in An-

athoth, and weighed him the money, even seventeen shekels of silver.

10 And I subscribed the evidence, and sealed it, and took witnesses, and weighed him the money in the balances.

11 So I took the evidence of the purchase, both that which was sealed according to the law and custom, and that which was open:

12 And I gave the evidence of the purchase unto Baruch, the son of Neriah, the son of Maaseiah, in the sight of Hanameel mine uncle's son, and in the presence of the witnesses that subscribed the book of the purchase, before all the Jews that sat in the court of the prison.

13 And I charged Baruch before them, saying,

14 Thus saith the Lord of hosts, the God of Israel; Take these evidences,

*Michael Quoist, *Prayers of Life* (Dublin: Gill/Logos, 1963).

this evidence of the purchase, both which is sealed, and this evidence which is open; and put them in an earthen vessel, that they may continue many days.

15 For thus saith the Lord of hosts, the God of Israel; Houses and fields and vineyards shall be possessed again in this land.

Isaiah 55:1–2

1 Ho, every one that thirsteth, come ye to the waters, and he that hath no money; come ye, buy, and eat; yea, come, buy wine and milk without money and without price.

2 Wherefore do ye spend money for that which is not bread? and your labour for that which satisfieth not? hearken diligently unto me, and eat ye that which is good, and let your soul delight itself in fatness.

NEW TESTAMENT

Matthew 25:14–28

14 For the kingdom of heaven is as a man travelling into a far country, who called his own servants, and delivered unto them his goods.

15 And unto one he gave five talents, to another two, and to another one; to every man according to his several ability; and straightway took his journey.

16 Then he that had received the five talents went and traded with the same, and made them other five talents.

17 And likewise he that had received two, he also gained other two.

18 But he that had received one went and digged in the earth, and hid his lord's money.

19 After a long time the lord of those servants cometh, and reckoneth with them.

20 And so he that had received five talents came and brought other five talents, saying, Lord, thou deliveredst unto me five talents: behold, I have gained beside them five talents more.

21 His lord said unto him, Well done, thou good and faithful servant: thou hast been faithful over a few things, I will make thee ruler over many things: enter thou into the joy of thy lord.

22 He also that had received two talents came and said, Lord, thou deliveredst unto me two talents: behold, I have gained two other talents beside them.

23 His lord said unto him, Well done, good and faithful servant; thou hast been faithful over a few things, I will make thee ruler over many things: enter thou into the joy of thy lord.

24 Then he which had received the one talent came and said, Lord, I knew thee that thou art an hard man, reaping where thou hast not sown, and gathering where thou hast not strawed:

25 And I was afraid, and went and hid thy talent in the earth: lo, there thou hast that is thine.

26 His lord answered and said unto him, Thou wicked and slothful servant, thou knewest that I reap where I sowed not, and gather where I have not strawed:

27 Thou oughtest therefore to have

put my money to the exchangers, and then at my coming I should have received mine own with usury.

28 Take therefore the talent from him, and give it unto him which hath ten talents.

Mark 12:41–43

41 And Jesus sat over against the treasury, and beheld how the people cast money into the treasury: and many that were rich cast in much.

42 And there came a certain poor widow, and she threw in two mites, which make a farthing.

43 And he called unto him his disciples, and saith unto them, Verily I say unto you, That this poor widow hath cast more in, than all they which have cast into the treasury.

MORALITY

The Bible never separates true religion from right conduct. Not only are both God's concern, but even the word "both" is questionable. Worshiping God and serving your neighbor constitute at bottom a single activity. Life is one, and all of it is from God. So morality and theology are indistinguishable from each other.

In the Old Testament all behavior is connected with the idea of the covenant. Men and women are united to God (and therefore to one another) by a solemn treaty. Good behavior is that which confirms this bond. Bad behavior is that which disrupts it. The terms of the covenant are spelled out at length in many Old Testament books, but they are summarized in the Ten Commandments—provided here (with some abbreviation) in their Deuteronomic version. These are mostly negatives, but the life indicated within the boundaries of the prohibitions forms a balanced pattern of harmonious relationships with God, with time, with family, with neighbors, and with things.

The Psalms constantly express a love of the law, and by the law they mean the whole content of God's revealed will for men and women, including the moral virtues. What the psalmists love is not a set of hampering prohibitions, but a positive and beautiful way of life.

Of course, moral codes *can* be interpreted as hampering prohibitions, and merely keeping within them *can* be regarded as a sufficient moral achievement. There is evidence in the New Testament of some people doing these things. So Jesus insists that goodness is in God alone and flows out into the actions of human beings from within themselves. Behavior controlled in this way cannot stop at the keeping of commandments.

Jesus reaffirms the law, but interprets it as above all a summons to live for others, to be sensitive to the plight of one's neighbor—including one's Samaritan neighbor (not always regarded by Jews as qualifying for the title), and one's female neighbor (not always regarded as amounting to very much at all), and one's immoral neighbor. In John, Chapter 4, Jesus meets someone who has each disqualification: an immoral Samaritan woman. He not only shows kindness to her but also asks a kindness of her. Morality is not just do-gooding. It is the embracing of all goodness everywhere.

To live morally is, according to the Bible, to live in harmony with the way in which man and his world have been put together. To break with that pattern is not to claim a larger liberty. It is more like claiming to be a bird when you are in fact a mammal—a claim that can be dangerous if you live on the edge of a cliff.

It is of course possible to separate morality from religion. It is even possible to look at the pattern of outward behavior to which the Bible points and to regard that as biblical morality. It is, however, a process something like picking flowers and examining them without their roots. As in the case of the flowers, one thing to be noticed about the morally good life as the Bible depicts it is that it is regarded as very beautiful. The ancient connection between beauty, truth, and goodness seems to be indissoluble. The good life may not be prudent or respectable (it led Jesus to crucifixion), and it is certainly no insurance against suffering (it led Job through agony), but it has a way of flowering that men and women find altogether lovely.

So perhaps morality is best fostered not by proliferating the commandments and prohibitions that mark the boundaries of immorality, but by contemplating positive goodness wherever it is incarnate. When goodness kindles imagination and love, it offers us a chance to develop those inner conditions from which moral behavior grows as naturally as fruit grows on trees.

MORALITY

OLD TESTAMENT

Deuteronomy 5:7–9, 11–14, 16–21

7 Thou shalt have none other gods before me.

8 Thou shalt not make thee any graven image, or any likeness of any thing that is in heaven above, or that is in the earth beneath, or that is in the waters beneath the earth:

9 Thou shalt not bow down thyself unto them, nor serve them:

11 Thou shalt not take the name of the Lord thy God in vain:

12 Keep the sabbath day to sanctify it, as the Lord thy God hath commanded thee.

13 Six days thou shalt labour, and do all thy work:

14 But the seventh day is the sabbath of the Lord thy God: in it thou shalt not do any work,

16 Honour thy father and thy mother.

229

17 Thou shalt not kill.

18 Neither shalt thou commit adultery.

19 Neither shalt thou steal.

20 Neither shalt thou bear false witness against thy neighbour.

21 Neither shalt thou desire thy neighbour's wife, neither shalt thou covet thy neighbour's house, his field, or his manservant, or his maidservant, his ox, or his ass, or any thing that is thy neighbour's.

Psalm 119:97, 101–04

O how love I thy law!
It is my meditation all the day.
I have refrained my feet from every evil
   way,
That I might keep thy word.
I have not departed from thy judgments:
For thou hast taught me.
How sweet are thy words unto my taste!
Yea, sweeter than honey to my mouth!
Through thy precepts I get understanding:
Therefore I hate every false way.

Micah 6:8

8 He hath shewed thee, O man, what is good; and what doth the Lord require of thee, but to do justly, and to love mercy, and to walk humbly with thy God?

NEW TESTAMENT

Luke 18:18–22

18 And a certain ruler asked him, saying, Good Master, what shall I do to inherit eternal life?

19 And Jesus said unto him, Why callest thou me good? none is good, save one, that is, God.

20 Thou knowest the commandments, Do not commit adultery, Do not kill, Do not steal, Do not bear false witness, Honour thy father and thy mother.

21 And he said, All these have I kept from my youth up.

22 Now when Jesus heard these things, he said unto him, Yet lackest thou one thing: sell all that thou hast, and distribute unto the poor, and thou shalt have treasure in heaven: and come, follow me.

Matthew 22:35–40

35 Then one of them, which was a lawyer, ask him a question, tempting him, and saying,

36 Master, which is the great commandment in the law?

37 Jesus said unto him, Thou shalt love the Lord thy God with all thy heart, and with all thy soul, and with all thy mind.

38 This is the first and great commandment.

39 And the second is like unto it, Thou shalt love thy neighbour as thyself.

40 On these two commandments hang all the law and the prophets.

Luke 6:43–45

43 For a good tree bringeth not forth corrupt fruit; neither doth a corrupt tree bring forth good fruit.

44 For every tree is known by his own fruit. For of thorns men do not gather figs, nor of a bramble bush gather they grapes.

45 A good man out of the good

treasure of his heart bringeth forth that which is good; and an evil man out of the evil treasure of his heart bringeth forth that which is evil: for of the abundance of the heart his mouth speaketh.

Galatians 5:14; 6:10

14 For all the law is fulfilled in one word, even in this; Thou shalt love thy neighbour as thyself.

10 As we have therefore opportunity, let us do good unto all men, especially unto them who are of the household of faith.

3 John 11

11 Beloved, follow not that which is evil, but that which is good. He that doeth good is of God: but he that doeth evil hath not seen God.

MOURNING

David was the ideal king, but the Old Testament reports his faults and inconsistencies with great frankness. When it came to mourning his dead he was unpredictable. On the death of Bathsheba's child he grieved less than was expected. His commonsense reply to those who were puzzled by his behavior may have struck them as almost too sensible and unemotional, but having expressed his love while the child was alive he was perhaps entitled to grieve less when the child was dead. Certainly he was not to be blamed if he declined to exhibit a grief he did not feel.

On the other hand, when David's son Absalom was killed in battle fighting against his father, the king's grief at the death of his rebellious son outweighed every other consideration. David had to be reminded that he owed a debt of gratitude to the living as well as a debt of grief to the dead.

So the Old Testament does recognize limits beyond which mourning should not go, but the absolute propriety of uninhibited grieving over the death of a loved one is fully recognized.

The New Testament, unlike most of the Old, affirms that death is not the end, but this does not make New Testament writers indifferent to the sorrows of the bereaved. The care of widows in particular was a special concern of the young Christian church, and Jesus himself was reported to have wept openly at the grave of his friend Lazarus. Not even the fact that Lazarus was to be raised from the dead was felt to make these tears inappropriate. The family mourned, and Jesus mourned with them.

His own appearances after his resurrection were also to those who mourned his death. His return to life was not used to confound his enemies or to move the indifferent. It was known only to those who already cared and grieved. This

231

suggests that the love that expresses itself in mourning can be a way of opening up to life rather than a way of shutting off life, as has sometimes been supposed.

Psychiatrists and social workers now speak of "the right to mourn." It might be said that this right had never been denied, but that would not be altogether true. The bereaved often report that after a rush of sympathy at the beginning, they seem to be shunned during the weeks and months of grieving, almost as if they had an infectious disease. People are embarrassed by another's sorrow, and if they do make contact they see to it that conversation will be about anything but the one who died—which, we are told, is the one subject about which the bereaved do want to talk.

There must be many exceptions to these rules, but just as there has been almost a conspiracy of silence about death, so also has there been a weakening of our capacity to grieve openly and naturally and to accept the grieving of others. The Bible approves no such inhibitions.

But mourning must not stand in the way of living. As the Bible sees it, it should be an enrichment of living and should leave the mourners more open to the needs of those who survive as well as drawing love out in directions that transcend the boundaries of this life.

The rites and rituals of mourning vary from place to place and from time to time. Being to such an extent culturally conditioned, none of them can be regarded as obligatory from a biblical or from any other point of view. But in most societies they do provide an acceptable language in which to say what needs to be said: an expression of both sorrow and love—a sorrow and love that are not lost in the grave but that reach beyond it and around it.

MOURNING

OLD TESTAMENT

2 Samuel 12:15–23

15 And the Lord struck the child that Uriah's wife bare unto David, and it was very sick.

16 David therefore besought God for the child; and David fasted, and went in, and lay all night upon the earth.

17 And the elders of his house arose, and went to him, to raise him up from the earth: but he would not, neither did he eat bread with them.

18 And it came to pass on the seventh day, that the child died. And the servants of David feared to tell him that the child was dead: for they said, Behold, while the child was yet alive, we spake unto him, and he would not hearken unto our voice: how will he then vex himself, if we tell him that the child is dead?

19 But when David saw that his servants whispered, David perceived that the child was dead: therefore David said unto his servants, Is the child dead? And they said, He is dead.

20 Then David arose from the earth, and washed, and anointed himself, and changed his apparel, and came into the house of the Lord, and worshipped: then he came to his own house; and when he required, they set bread before him, and he did eat.

21 Then said his servants unto him, What thing is this that thou hast done? thou didst fast and weep for the child, while it was alive; but when the child was dead, thou didst rise and eat bread.

22 And he said, While the child was yet alive, I fasted and wept: for I said, Who can tell whether God will be gracious to me, that the child may live?

23 But now he is dead, wherefore should I fast? can I bring him back again? I shall go to him, but he shall not return to me.

2 Samuel 19:1–7

1 And it was told Joab, Behold, the king weepeth and mourneth for Absalom.

2 And the victory that day was turned into mourning unto all the people: for the people heard say that day how the king was grieved for his son.

3 And the people gat them by stealth that day into the city, as people being ashamed steal away when they flee in battle.

4 But the king covered his face, and the king cried with a loud voice, O my son Absalom, Absalom, my son, my son!

5 And Joab came into the house to the king, and said, Thou hast shamed this day the faces of all thy servants, which this day have saved thy life, and the lives of thy sons and of thy daughters, and the lives of thy wives, and the lives of thy concubines;

6 In that thou lovest thine enemies, and hatest thy friends. For thou hast declared this day, that thou regardest neither princes nor servants: for this day I perceive, that if Absalom had lived, and all we had died this day, then it had pleased thee well.

7 Now therefore arise, go forth, and speak comfortably unto thy servants.

NEW TESTAMENT

Matthew 5:4

4 Blessed are they that mourn: for they shall be comforted.

John 11:32–35

32 Then when Mary was come where Jesus was, and saw him, she fell down at his feet, saying unto him, Lord, if thou hadst been here, my brother had not died.

33 When Jesus therefore saw her weeping, and the Jews also weeping which came with her, he groaned in the spirit, and was troubled,

34 And said, Where have ye laid him? They said unto him, Lord, come and see.

35 Jesus wept.

John 20:11–16

11 But Mary stood without at the sepulchre weeping: and as she wept, she stooped down, and looked into the sepulchre,

12 And seeth two angels in white

sitting, the one at the head, and the other at the feet, where the body of Jesus had lain.

13 And they say unto her, Woman, why weepest thou? She saith unto them, Because they have taken away my Lord, and I know not where they have laid him.

14 And when she had thus said, she turned herself back, and saw Jesus standing, and knew not that it was Jesus.

15 Jesus saith unto her, Woman, why weepest thou? whom seekest thou? She, supposing him to be the gardener, saith unto him, Sir, if thou have borne him hence, tell me where thou hast laid him, and I will take him away.

16 Jesus saith unto her, Mary. She turned herself, and saith unto him, Rabboni; which is to say, Master.

Romans 12:15

15 Rejoice with them that do rejoice, and weep with them that weep.

MURDER

The Old Testament makes a number of distinct points. First, man is made in the image of God, so killing a man (or a woman) is a serious matter. Although parts of the Old Testament come from a period when war was just a seasonal event, and although the Old Testament itself required capital punishment for a number of offenses, it regards murder as a deeply sacrilegious crime. An unsolved murder had to be solemnly purged by an entire community.

Second, the offense is not to be concealed or excused, though from the first, murder has been both committed and (unsuccessfully) concealed and excused. It has its beginning in the envy and anger arising between the two sons of Adam: Cain and Abel (see Aggression and Crime).

Third, murder is not to be disguised by using devious means to carry it out. David, having seduced Bathsheba, got her husband killed in battle. He remained individually answerable to God for that death.

The New Testament retains and enhances the Old Testament's sense of the sacredness of life, but it cannot be taken as necessarily either endorsing or abrogating the Old Testament's approval of capital punishment for murder. New Testament Christians were in no position to decide that issue. They were victims rather than judges. John the Baptist, Jesus, and Stephen all suffered violent deaths, which were murders dressed up as something else.

So the New Testament emphasis is naturally on the attitudes that lead to murder rather than on the punishments that should follow it. Jesus spoke of anger as a road to murder—one which led so surely in that direction that it could be regarded as the moral equivalent. Other motivations were revealed in the story of the death of John the Baptist.

The killing of Jesus was done with due respect for legal formalities, but the sentence was passed by a man who knew that it was a wrong one. Pilate washed his hands in vain. It is not that easy for any man to free himself of responsibility for the life of another.

Perhaps that is the point to be taken. Legally, murder does have to be isolated. Police and judiciary must treat it as a particular offense of the utmost gravity. But morally and spiritually murder is part of a pattern to which all contribute through anger, envy, and resentment. The cutting off of a human life is the extension into criminality of the cutting off of human beings as practiced in many legal ways. In order to oppose murder it is necessary not only to detest it and punish it but also to throw into reverse the whole pattern of events that leads toward it.

And the Bible's view is that such a reversal is possible. The prohibition of murder is one side of a coin. Call it the negative side. The other side of the same coin, the positive side, is the sanctity of human life. To diminish in any way the value attaching to the life of a human being is to begin traveling along a road at the far end of which is murder.

Providing criminals with sociological excuses for their crimes has doubtless been overdone, but there is room for a far more positive appreciation of human personality to show itself in the life of human communities. This appreciation can be expressed in education, in the communications media, in legislation, and in the courts. If there is a biblical case against capital punishment even for murder, then it has its roots in the biblical reverence for life. The Bible itself does not make that case, but we have yet to work out all the implications of the Bible's fundamental belief in man as the image of God.

MURDER

OLD TESTAMENT

Genesis 9:6

6 Whoso sheddeth man's blood, by man shall his blood be shed: for in the image of God made he man.

Exodus 20:13

13 Thou shalt not kill.

Deuteronomy 21:1–4, 6–8

1 If one be found slain in the land which the Lord thy God giveth thee to possess it, lying in the field, and it be not known who hath slain him:

2 Then thy elders and thy judges shall come forth, and they shall measure unto the cities which are round about him that is slain:

3 And it shall be, that the city which is next unto the slain man, even the elders of that city shall take an heifer, which hath not been wrought with, and which hath not drawn in the yoke;

4 And the elders of that city shall bring down the heifer unto a rough valley, which is neither eared nor sown,

and shall strike off the heifer's neck there in the valley:

6 And all the elders of that city, that are next unto the slain man, shall wash their hands over the heifer that is beheaded in the valley:

7 And they shall answer and say, Our hands have not shed this blood, neither have our eyes seen it.

8 Be merciful, O Lord, unto thy people Israel, whom thou hast redeemed, and lay not innocent blood unto thy people of Israel's charge. And the blood shall be forgiven them.

2 Samuel 11:1, 14–15; 12:7, 9–10

1 And it came to pass, after the year was expired, at the time when kings go forth to battle, that David sent Joab, and his servants with him, and all Israel; and they destroyed the children of Ammon, and besieged Rabbah.

14 And it came to pass in the morning, that David wrote a letter to Joab, and sent it by the hand of Uriah.

15 And he wrote in the letter, saying, Set ye Uriah in the forefront of the hottest battle, and retire ye from him, that he may be smitten, and die.

7 And Nathan said to David . . . Thus saith the Lord God of Israel . . .

9 Wherefore hast thou despised the commandment of the Lord, to do evil in his sight? thou hast killed Uriah the Hittite with the sword, and hast taken his wife to be thy wife, and hast slain him with the sword of the children of Ammon.

10 Now therefore the sword shall never depart from thine house; because thou hast despised me.

NEW TESTAMENT

Matthew 5:21–22

21 Ye have heard that it was said by them of old time, Thou shalt not kill; and whosoever shall kill shall be in danger of the judgment:

22 But I say unto you, That whosoever is angry with his brother without a cause shall be in danger of the judgment.

Mark 6:19–28 (Herod's wife plots against John the Baptist)

19 Therefore Herodias had a quarrel against him, and would have killed him; but she could not:

20 For Herod feared John, knowing that he was a just man and an holy, and observed him; and when he heard him, he did many things, and heard him gladly.

21 And when a convenient day was come, that Herod on his birthday made a supper to his lords, high captains, and chief estates of Galilee;

22 And when the daughter of the said Herodias came in, and danced, and pleased Herod and them that sat with him, the king said unto the damsel, Ask of me whatsoever thou wilt, and I will give it thee.

23 And he sware unto her, Whatsoever thou shalt ask of me, I will give it thee, unto the half of my kingdom.

24 And she went forth, and said unto her mother, What shall I ask? And she said, The head of John the Baptist.

25 And she came in straightway with

haste unto the king, and asked, saying, I will that thou give me by and by in a charger the head of John the Baptist.

26 And the king was exceeding sorry; yet for his oath's sake, and for their sakes which sat with him, he would not reject her.

27 And immediately the king sent an executioner, and commanded his head to be brought: and he went and beheaded him in the prison,

28 And brought his head in a charger, and gave it to the damsel: and the damsel gave it to her mother.

Matthew 27:24, 26

24 When Pilate saw that he could prevail nothing, but that rather a tumult was made, he took water, and washed his hands before the multitude, saying, I am innocent of the blood of this just person: see ye to it.

26 Then released he Barabbas unto them: and when he had scourged Jesus, he delivered him to be crucified.

NATURE

Old Testament writers did not have the detailed knowledge of natural law available today, but they lived too close to nature itself to be unaware of the forces at work. They understood the orderly chain of cause and effect. They could read the signs. They knew how to make the most of the soil and the seasons, how to breed good flocks and good herds.

Yet none of this hid God from them. He was not distanced from them by the workings of the natural order. He was immediately present in it and directly responsible for it. The natural laws and forces governing its operation did not take over from him; they were his. As Job was shown, the internal workings of the system were as much a cause for wonder as were its results.

Humanity's role in the natural order was a distinctive one. Adam was required to exercise a measure of control over the natural world. His naming the animals was a symbol of his mastery over them through understanding. But men and women, in the Old Testament picture, did not stand apart from nature. They were part of it, subject to its laws as any other creature was.

The prologue to John's Gospel also affirms that nature is rational because it is grounded in the word (or reason: *logos*) of God. Man's place is special, but yet to be fully achieved.

Jesus himself reads the world of nature in a way that is different from, though not inconsistent with, John's interpretation and that of the Old Testament. He sees it as wealth outpoured in such abundance that we need never doubt the giver's willingness and ability to meet our needs. What we must do is reach to the heights of our own nature (by seeking God's kingdom) so that the rest of nature can fall into place under and around us ("all these things shall be added unto you").

The parables of Jesus are the work of one who has looked with an affectionate and discerning eye on the work of the good shepherd, the careful husbandman, and the perhaps slightly too random sower. The kingdom he preached in the parables, miraculous as it was, had strong affinities with the natural processes of growth. It was a transcendent extension of the natural order rather than the abolition of it.

What the kingdom did radically contradict was humanity's anxious, possessive attitude toward natural things, an attitude that springs from no longer feeling at one with them. Conservation was not an issue of the time, but its spiritual roots are biblical.

Alexander Pope's sardonic epitaph intended for Sir Isaac Newton was a joke with some truth in it:

Nature and Nature's laws lay hid in night:
God said, *Let Newton be!* and all was light.

Certainly nature's laws, after Newton, became better known and more methodically observed. Newton, for instance, provided a physical explanation of the rainbow, where previously only theological and mythical explanations were to be had. Some thought that by doing so he robbed the rainbow of its august religious significance. Keats was one of these. He objected to the learning that could "unweave the rainbow." He complained that whereas "There was an awful rainbow once in heaven," now it is given "In the dull catalogue of common things."

The Bible knows no such catalogue. It finds common things as wonderful as unusual ones. It regards the regular working of the natural law as awesome in itself. It suggests that we should not let our knowledge take away our sense of glory in things. On the contrary, we should regard the knowledge itself as a vision of glory.

Where the scientific understanding of nature has perhaps obscured the biblical picture is by giving the mistaken impression—and it is a mistake scientifically as well as biblically—that we should see ourselves as standing over nature, surveying it, assessing it, using it from some position apart from it. We are not in such a position. We are embedded in nature, part of it, one with it. Only from within nature can we see it as a vision of glory.

NATURE

OLD TESTAMENT

*Job 38:4–7, 16–20, 22, 28–29, 41;
39:1, 5–6, 19, 26–27*

Where wast thou when I laid the foundations of the earth?
Declare, if thou hast understanding.
Who hath laid the measures thereof, if thou knowest?
Or who hath stretched the line upon it?
Whereupon are the foundations thereof fastened?
Or who laid the corner stone thereof;
When the morning stars sang together,
And all the sons of God shouted for joy?

Hast thou entered into the springs of the sea?
Or hast thou walked in the search of the depth?
Have the gates of death been opened unto thee?
Or hast thou seen the doors of the shadow of death?
Hast thou perceived the breadth of the earth?
Declare if thou knowest it all.

Where is the way where light dwelleth?
And as for darkness, where is the place thereof,
That thou shouldest take it to the bound thereof,
And that thou shouldest know the paths to the house thereof?

Hast thou entered into the treasures of the snow?
Or hast thou seen the treasures of the hail,
Hath the rain a father?
Or who hath begotten the drops of dew?
Out of whose womb came the ice?
And the hoary frost of heaven, who hath gendered it?

Who provideth for the raven his food?
When his young ones cry unto God,
They wander for lack of meat.
Knowest thou the time when the wild goats of the rock bring forth?
Or canst thou mark when the hinds do calve?
Who hath sent out the wild ass free?
Or who hath loosed the bands of the wild ass?
Whose house I have made the wilderness,
And the barren land his dwellings.

Hast thou given the horse strength?
Hast thou clothed his neck with thunder?
Doth the hawk fly by thy wisdom,
And stretch her wings toward the south?
Doth the eagle mount up at thy command,
And make her nest on high?

NEW TESTAMENT

John 1:1–5

1 In the beginning was the Word, and the Word was with God, and the Word was God.

2 The same was in the beginning with God.

3 All things were made by him; and without him was not any thing made that was made.

4 In him was life; and the life was the light of men.

5 And the light shineth in darkness; and the darkness comprehended it not.

Luke 12:22–31

22 And he said unto his disciples, Therefore I say unto you, Take no

thought for your life, what ye shall eat; neither for the body, what ye shall put on.

23 The life is more than meat, and the body is more than raiment.

24 Consider the ravens: for they neither sow nor reap; which neither have storehouse nor barn; and God feedeth them: how much more are ye better than the fowls?

25 And which of you with taking thought can add to his stature one cubit?

26 If ye then be not able to do that thing which is least, why take ye thought for the rest?

27 Consider the lilies how they grow: they toil not, they spin not; and yet I say unto you, that Solomon in all his glory was not arrayed like one of these.

28 If then God so clothe the grass, which is to-day in the field, and to-morrow is cast into the oven; how much more will he clothe you, O ye of little faith?

29 And seek not ye what ye shall eat, or what ye shall drink, neither be ye of doubtful mind.

30 For all these things do the nations of the world seek after: and your Father knoweth that ye have need of these things.

31 But rather seek ye the kingdom of God; and all these things shall be added unto you.

Mark 4:30–32

30 And he said, Whereunto shall we liken the kingdom of God? or with what comparison shall we compare it?

31 It is like a grain of mustard seed, which, when it is sown in the earth, is less than all the seeds that be in the earth:

32 But when it is sown, it groweth up, and becometh greater than all herbs, and shooteth out great branches; so that the fowls of the air may lodge under the shadow of it.

NEIGHBOR

The Old Testament Book of Proverbs gives a practical account of neighborliness. Other books spell out in detail the behavior required of the good neighbor. But there is also a mystical strand in the Old Testament's description of the bond between neighbors. The commandment in Leviticus, later to be much quoted in the New Testament, expresses a sense of unity—almost of identity—between neighbors. This arose from the Hebrew understanding of life and of community: each individual is unique, but the boundaries of his life overlap the boundaries of other lives; he does not exist apart from his relationships. The community, the company of neighbors, is an organic growth.

The prophets Isaiah, Jeremiah, Ezekiel, and Hosea all expressed this by speaking of Israel as a vine or a vineyard. The idea is in the Psalms, too. The vine metaphor speaks of God as the source of the community's life, but as a source from which the members could cut themselves off by not being good neighbors to one another—by practicing oppression and injustice, for instance.

The New Testament continues to blend the practical with the mystical. Jesus' golden rule is a practical code of conduct, but in the Gospel of John, Jesus also takes up the metaphor of the vineyard. Before this time a likeness of a vine had actually been stamped on coins (by the Maccabees) as a national emblem. Jesus could not speak of the vine without evoking thoughts of community, and to speak of himself as the vine was to speak of himself as the inclusive representative of the whole people, renewing the deep-rooted unity of branch with branch, neighbor with neighbor.

Paul used another image of organic unity, that of the body. The community he spoke of was the Christian church, not a geographical neighborhood; but just as Christ was seen as the revelation of the true human being, so his body was seen as the revelation of the true human community. And this community was one in which the old ethnic and social distinctions were absorbed in the new neighborliness.

In any event, Jesus had already made it clear that when ethnic and social distinctions remained, the claims of neighborliness overrode them. He delivered his parable of the Good Samaritan (see Kindness) in answer to the question, "Who is my neighbor?" The implied answer is "He who behaves like one." The fact that the good neighbor in the story was a Samaritan (regarded by the Jews as ethnically impure and religiously heretical) was very much to the point. And the Samaritan in the story was the hero, not the victim. This is not a story of a good Jew helping a wounded man in spite of his being an alien. It is the alien who does the helping: neighborliness is reciprocal; it is to be accepted as well as offered.

A modern urban community may conceal the significance of neighborliness, but it does not remove it. In fact, city dwellers, far removed from the sources of food and drink, are more interdependent than anyone else. The neighbor relationship is still an organic one. We may choose our friends, but we and our neighbors are one by physical necessity—and by something deeper than that.

There is still room for the biblical view of neighborliness as a mystical matter as well as a practical one. On the practical side, neighborliness needs to express itself both corporately and individually. Human needs are so large and so complex that they need to be served by the whole community organizing its kindness professionally, yet they are also so individual and personal that they need to be met by one-to-one relationships. Both corporate and individual neighborliness needs to be sustained by the visionary way of seeing ourselves and other people, not as alien and separated individuals, but as parts of a transcendent unity.

The Jewish philosopher Martin Buber has taught us to think of real life as meeting, as I–Thou relationships rather than as I–It relationships. That understanding of the connection between neighbors is rooted in the Bible's sublime picture of what it means to be human. As Buber says, "in each Thou we address the eternal Thou."

NEIGHBOR

OLD TESTAMENT

Leviticus 19:18

18 Thou shalt love thy neighbour as thyself.

Isaiah 5:1-2, 7

1 My well-beloved hath a vineyard in a very fruitful hill:

2 And he fenced it, and gathered out the stones thereof, and planted it with the choicest vine, and built a tower in the midst of it, and also made a winepress therein: and he looked that it should bring forth grapes, and it brought forth wild grapes.

7 For the vineyard of the Lord of hosts is the house of Israel, and the men of Judah his pleasant plant: and he looked for judgment, but behold oppression; for righteousness, but behold a cry.

Zechariah 8:16-17

16 These are the things that ye shall do; Speak ye every man the truth to his neighbour; execute the judgment of truth and peace in your gates:

17 And let none of you imagine evil in your hearts against his neighbour; and love no false oath: for all these are things that I hate, saith the Lord.

Proverbs 3:28-29; 14:21; 26:18-20

Say not unto thy neighbour, Go, and come again,
And to morrow I will give;
When thou hast it by thee.
Devise not evil against thy neighbour,
Seeing he dwelleth securely by thee.
He that despiseth his neighbour sinneth:
But he that hath mercy on the poor, happy is he.
As a mad man who casteth firebrands,
Arrows, and death,
So is the man that deceiveth his neighbour,
And saith, Am not I in sport?
Where no wood is, there the fire goeth out:
So where there is no talebearer, the strife ceaseth.

NEW TESTAMENT

Matthew 7:12

12 Therefore all things whatsoever ye would that men should do to you, do ye even so to them: for this is the law and the prophets.

John 15:1-2, 4-5

1 I am the true vine, and my Father is the husbandman.

2 Every branch in me that beareth not fruit he taketh away: and every

branch that beareth fruit, he purgeth it, that it may bring forth more fruit.

4 Abide in me, and I in you. As the branch cannot bear fruit of itself, except it abide in the vine; no more can ye, except ye abide in me.

5 I am the vine, ye are the branches.

Romans 13:10

10 Love worketh no ill to his neighbour: therefore love is the fulfilling of the law.

1 Corinthians 12:12–14, 21, 26

12 For as the body is one, and hath many members, and all the members of that one body, being many, are one body: so also is Christ.

13 For by one Spirit are we all baptized into one body, whether we be Jews or Gentiles, whether we be bond or free; and have been all made to drink into one Spirit.

14 For the body is not one member, but many.

21 And the eye cannot say unto the hand, I have no need of thee: nor again the head to the feet, I have no need of you.

26 And whether one member suffer, all the members suffer with it; or one member be honoured, all the members rejoice with it.

1 John 2:9–10; 4:20–21

9 He that saith he is in the light, and hateth his brother, is in darkness even until now.

10 He that loveth his brother abideth in the light, and there is none occasion of stumbling in him.

20 If a man say, I love God, and hateth his brother, he is a liar: for he that loveth not his brother whom he hath seen, how can he love God whom he hath not seen?

21 And this commandment have we from him, That he who loveth God love his brother also.

OBEDIENCE

In the Old Testament obedience is never an impersonal or merely mechanical activity; it is always part of a personal relationship. To obey is to respect the natural authority of one over another (for instance, of God over man), not in order to deprive the second of his proper dignity or of his personal responsibility, but to establish him within an order by which he will be nurtured, honored, and made complete. That, at any rate, is the principle. Without the principle, some of the stories would be hard to take.

The difficult stories are those in which God is said to ask something that seems inconsistent with his goodness. In the end, however, even those stories yield points that remain valid within the completed concept of obedience. God is said to want Agag hewn in pieces; yet out of this comes the classical statement of the priority of obedience over sacrifice. He asks Abraham to be ready to sacrifice his son; yet out of this comes the discovery that the *will* to obey is all that God needs.

Each piece of the jigsaw puzzle needs to be fitted in with the rest, so that the jagged edges are absorbed in the total picture of a relationship—a relationship to the authority of God that is so happy and so stabilizing that the Psalms are forever singing of it with delight.

The New Testament also distinguishes real from nominal obedience. What counts is not the formal pledging of obedience, however respectful the form of words, but the aligning of the will to implement that pledge.

According to the New Testament, perfect obedience is offered only by Jesus himself. During the agony in the Garden of Gethsemane he submitted himself to the Father's will, and he remained constant to that will through all that was to follow. Others can only identify themselves with the obedience of Jesus. This they do by fixing their faith and love on him, and the effect is that they thereby express at least the *will* to offer the same obedience. The will is enough. In that posture they can claim the privilege of a child of God.

Obedience is not at present a greatly admired virtue—except in children and domestic animals. Too many atrocities have been performed by men who afterward defended themselves by saying that they were only obeying orders. Obeying orders is, in any event, often taken to be a rather mechanical and impersonal activity. Computers can be programmed to respond obediently to a given impulse. Human beings should take more of the responsibility on themselves.

Against the mechanical view can be set the Bible's picture of obedience as a responsible activity involving the free and personal acknowledgment of authority. Obedience is its true self when it is part of a relationship in which love and trust are its motives. To submit merely because one fears the consequences of disobedience is not so much to obey as to conform. Biblical obedience goes deeper.

An understanding of the importance of love and trust here is important not only for those from whom obedience is required but also for those who require obedience from others. Parents demanding obedience of their children and backing up their demand with the because-I'll-clout-you-if-you-don't type of argument may be concealing rather than revealing their real claim to authority, and may therefore be damaging rather than strengthening their children's capacity to obey—in the true spirit of obedience. Parents who are themselves seen to be under the authority of their own principles are the ones who are in the best position to give valid orders.

Significantly, obedience can be weakened by two direct opposites: overindulgence and neglect. The spoiled child and the deprived child, different as their experiences may be, both grow up outside a framework of acknowledged authority expressed in a personal relationship. Neither child has much experience of the loving and trusting authority from which true obedience grows.

OBEDIENCE

OLD TESTAMENT

Genesis 22:1–2, 9–13

1 And it came to pass after these things, that God did tempt Abraham, and said unto him, Abraham: and he said, Behold, here I am.

2 And he said, Take now thy son, thine only son Isaac, whom thou lovest, and get thee into the land of Moriah; and offer him there for a burnt offering upon one of the mountains which I will tell thee of.

9 And they came to the place which God had told him of; and Abraham built an altar there, and laid the wood in order, and bound Isaac his son, and laid him on the altar upon the wood.

10 And Abraham stretched forth his hand, and took the knife to slay his son.

11 And the angel of the Lord called unto him out of heaven, and said, Abraham, Abraham: and he said, Here am I.

12 And he said, Lay not thine hand upon the lad, neither do thou any thing unto him: for now I know that thou fearest God, seeing thou hast not withheld thy son, thine only son from me.

13 And Abraham lifted up his eyes, and looked, and behold behind him a ram caught in a thicket by his horns: and Abraham went and took the ram, and offered him up for a burnt offering in the stead of his son.

Exodus 19:3, 5; 24:7

3 And Moses went up unto God, and the Lord called unto him out of the mountain, saying, Thus shalt thou say to the house of Jacob, and tell the children of Israel:

5 Now therefore, if ye will obey my voice indeed, and keep my covenant, then ye shall be a peculiar treasure unto me above all people:

7 And he took the book of the covenant, and read in the audience of the people: and they said, All that the Lord hath said will we do, and be obedient.

1 Samuel 15:18–22 (Samuel reproves Saul)

18 And the Lord sent thee on a journey, and said, Go and utterly destroy the sinners the Amalekites, and fight against them until they be consumed.

19 Wherefore then didst thou not obey the voice of the Lord, but didst fly upon the spoil, and didst evil in the sight of the Lord?

20 And Saul said unto Samuel, Yea, I have obeyed the voice of the Lord, and have gone the way which the Lord sent me, and have brought Agag the king of Amalek, and have utterly destroyed the Amalekites.

21 But the people took of the spoil, sheep and oxen, the chief of the things which should have been utterly destroyed, to sacrifice unto the Lord thy God in Gilgal.

22 And Samuel said, Hath the Lord as great delight in burnt offerings and sacrifices, as in obeying the voice of the Lord? Behold, to obey is better than sacrifice, and to hearken than the fat of rams.

NEW TESTAMENT

Matthew 21:28–31; 7:21

28 But what think ye? A certain man had two sons; and he came to the first, and said, Son, go work to-day in my vineyard.

29 He answered and said, I will not: but afterward he repented, and went.

30 And he came to the second, and said likewise. And he answered and said, I go, sir: and went not.

31 Whether of them twain did the will of his father? They say unto him, The first.

21 Not every one that saith unto me, Lord, Lord, shall enter into the kingdom of heaven; but he that doeth the will of my Father which is in heaven.

Luke 22:39–42

39 And he came out, and went, as he was wont, to the mount of Olives; and his disciples also followed him.

40 And when he was at the place, he said unto them, Pray that ye enter not into temptation.

41 And he was withdrawn from them about a stone's cast, and kneeled down, and prayed,

42 Saying, Father, if thou be willing, remove this cup from me: nevertheless not my will, but thine, be done.

Hebrews 5:7–9

7 Who in the days of his flesh, when he had offered up prayers and supplications with strong crying and tears unto him that was able to save him from death, and was heard in that he feared;

8 Though he were a Son, yet learned he obedience by the things which he suffered;

9 And being made perfect, he became the author of eternal salvation unto all them that obey him.

Romans 5:19

19 By the obedience of one shall many be made righteous.

ORDER

The Old Testament begins with chaos, and it sees chaos as continuing just below the surface. The making and keeping of order is the work of God's Spirit, but man is called to contribute to it. A framework of natural law and rhythmic order is built into all creation, but all the same the early chapters of Genesis describe God as telling man to subdue the world—that is, to continue the ordering process under his direction.

Social and political order in the Old Testament is treated similarly. It is ordained: men are to live in a hierarchy of judges and kings, priests and high priests, citizens and elders, sons and fathers—all and always with God as the supreme head. Yet there is no finality about any one pattern: kings are raised up and set aside, kingdoms are divided and united. Order is an absolute good demanded by God as the context for human life, but no particular order is guaranteed permanence. Particular orders and systems of order are the flexible—even disposable—instruments of divine order.

Rehoboam, Solomon's son, found this to be true. By resisting change he lost control of ten out of the twelve tribes of Israel. And the God of Israel, the God of order, did nothing to prevent it. In fact he brought it about. The Old Testament's position seemed to be that disorder was to be resisted only when it was a move toward chaos. Sometimes disorder was not that at all but the precursor of a changed pattern of order newly emerging.

In the New Testament, Christianity similarly appears as a new order challenging an existing one. Certainly the new church was *for* order and *against* chaos. Jesus appointed twelve apostles—the same number as the tribes of Israel, for he was reconstructing the people of God. His followers formed a church with recognized orders and offices.

Yet the Christians were seen as a disorderly force. Two of them arrived in a Greek city firmly ruled by Rome and were greeted as "those who have turned the world upside down." Not uncharacteristically the defenders of law and order in its established form expressed their determination to adhere to orderly ways by creating a near riot with the help of what seems to have been an early example of a rent-a-mob.

It has been said (was it by G. K. Chesterton?) that once the world has been turned upside down it will be found to be the right way up. Every form of order has to resist chaos and yet be open to its own replacement by a better form of order. Tennyson's King Arthur going to his death expressed it memorably:

> And slowly answer'd Arthur from the barge:
> The old order changeth, yielding place to new,
> And God fulfils himself in many ways,
> Lest one good custom should corrupt the world.

However, as the Bible sees it, chaos lies only just beneath the surface of human life. Order must be firmly maintained in order for life to be viable—firmly, but not inflexibly. The breaking down of an established and conventional order often seems to those who have lived securely within it to mark the return of chaos. They should ask what is the alternative to the existing system: is it threatened by chaos or by a new order? If the latter, is it going to be better or worse than the old?

One measure by which to judge this is the degree of personal security and freedom to be enjoyed within the system. True order, as the Bible describes it, always provides a framework for the development of personal freedom and interpersonal cooperation. It is not compatible with a rigid system of control.

The flexibility of any particular system of order is especially important where growth and development have to be allowed for. Many colonial powers learned this too slowly, but it applies in families as well. Is adolescent rebellion an eruption of chaos or a necessary change from one form of rule to another?

ORDER

OLD TESTAMENT

Genesis 1:1–2

1 In the beginning God created the heaven and the earth.

2 And the earth was without form, and void; and darkness was upon the face of the deep. And the spirit of God moved upon the face of the waters.

Job 10:20–22

Are not my days few? cease then,
And let me alone, that I may take comfort a little,
Before I go whence I shall not return,
Even to the land of darkness and the shadow of death;
A land of darkness, as darkness itself;
And of the shadow of death, without any order,
And where the light is as darkness.

1 Kings 12:1–8, 14–16

1 And Rehoboam went to Shechem: for all Israel were come to Shechem to make him king.

2 And it came to pass, when Jeroboam the son of Nebat, who was yet in Egypt, heard of it, (for he was fled from the presence of king Solomon, and Jeroboam dwelt in Egypt;)

3 That they sent and called him. And Jeroboam and all the congrega-tion of Israel came, and spake unto Rehoboam, saying,

4 Thy father made our yoke grievous: now therefore make thou the grievous service of thy father, and his heavy yoke which he put upon us, lighter, and we will serve thee.

5 And he said unto them, Depart yet for three days, then come again to me. And the people departed.

6 And king Rehoboam consulted with the old men, that stood before Solomon his father while he yet lived, and said, How do ye advise that I may answer this people?

7 And they spake unto him, saying, If thou wilt be a servant unto this people this day, and wilt serve them, and answer them, and speak good words to them, then they will be thy servants for ever.

8 But he forsook the counsel of the old men, which they had given him, and consulted with the young men that were grown up with him, and which stood before him:

14 And spake to them after the counsel of the young men, saying, My father made your yoke heavy, and I will add to your yoke: my father also chastised you with whips, but I will chastise you with scorpions.

15 Wherefore the king hearkened not unto the people; for the cause was from the Lord, that he might perform his saying, which the Lord spake by Ahijah the Shilonite unto Jeroboam the son of Nebat.

16 So when all Israel saw that the king hearkened not unto them, the people answered the king, saying, What portion have we in David? neither have we inheritance in the son of Jesse: to your tents, O Israel: now see to thine own house, David. So Israel departed unto their tents.

NEW TESTAMENT

Mark 3:13–15

13 And he goeth up into a mountain, and calleth unto him whom he would: and they came unto him.

14 And he ordained twelve, that they should be with him, and that he might send them forth to preach,

15 And to have power to heal sicknesses, and to cast out devils.

Ephesians 4:11–13;
1 Corinthians 14:40

11 And he gave some, apostles; and some, prophets; and some, evangelists; and some, pastors and teachers;

12 For the perfecting of the saints, for the work of the ministry, for the edifying of the body of Christ:

13 Till we all come in the unity of the faith, and of the knowledge of the Son of God.

40 Let all things be done decently and in order.

Acts 17:1–7

1 They came to Thessalonica, where there was a synagogue of the Jews:

2 And Paul, as his manner was, went in unto them, and three sabbath days reasoned with them out of the scriptures,

3 Opening and alleging, that Christ must needs have suffered, and risen again from the dead: and that this Jesus, whom I preach unto you, is Christ.

4 And some of them believed, and consorted with Paul and Silas; and of the devout Greeks a great multitude, and of the chief women not a few.

5 But the Jews which believed not, moved with envy, took unto them certain lewd fellows of the baser sort, and gathered a company, and set all the city on an uproar, and assaulted the house of Jason, and sought to bring them out to the people.

6 And when they found them not, they drew Jason and certain brethren unto the rulers of the city, crying, These that have turned the world upside down are come hither also;

7 Whom Jason hath received: and these all do contrary to the decrees of Cæsar, saying that there is another king, one Jesus.

PATIENCE

The Old Testament says firmly that patience is a characteristic of God. He endures generations of human perversity without writing off the enterprise.

Those who are slow to anger are therefore commended, but since their endurance rests on the patience of an ever-active God, there is always in it an element of hope. It is a patient waiting, an expectation of eventual vindication.

The patience of Job is proverbial, but in fact the greater part of the Book of Job is concerned with his lack of patience, or at least with his discontent with his friends' false explanations of his sufferings. Job's submissiveness, reported in the early chapters of the book, should be read with due allowance for the great protest that is to come.

The New Testament also salutes both patient waiting and patient enduring. A picture of patient waiting is drawn in the character of Simeon—and again it is a waiting full of hope and expectation, finally of fulfillment. As an example of patient enduring, the New Testament points repeatedly at Jesus on the cross, but this is still not a picture of mere resignation. It is the road to eventual victory. Patience is a matter of being harnessed to an ongoing purpose that has the power eventually to prevail. One may have to endure much while awaiting its fulfillment, but to react with anger or resentment would be to break faith with that purpose. Patience is connected to all three of the theological virtues: faith, hope, and love.

It is in this sense that patience is recommended to the followers of Jesus. They are not asked to fold their hands and leave everything to fate. They are given a high purpose and asked to exercise the active virtue of patience in its pursuit:

> Patience is a virtue,
> Get it if you can.
> Seldom found in woman,
> Never found in man.

This cynical old rhyme may have been an early blow against male chauvinism, but would probably now be rejected as sexual stereotyping. The sexes must be allowed an equal claim to a lack of virtue! For the rhyme does take it for granted that patience is a good thing.

True patience certainly is, but there are substitutes not too easily distinguished from it. In some situations, for example, resignation (easily mistaken for patience) is a fault. In other situations discontent (easily mistaken for impatience) is a virtue. Charles Kingsley spoke of "that divine discontent which is the parent of upward aspiration." He said of it that it is "the very germ of all virtue."

So the biblical examples could well be used as a sort of test for distinguishing true patience from false. And the crux seems to be that true patience involves the steady pursuit of a purpose, whereas false patience means just putting up with things and offering them no purposeful resistance.

Patience, then, since it always has a goal, is the very opposite of sitting still. And yet a certain inward stillness is very much a part of it. What used to be called "waiting on God" was not quiescence, nor was it waiting *for* God. It was a way of being still with the sort of stillness a great-winged bird can display when gliding on a rising current of air. Those who demand quick results and instant satisfactions alienate themselves from any purpose larger than a passing one. Those who move in time with the largest purpose are inwardly still and outwardly unshakable. They are the ones who will display patience as a virtue.

PATIENCE

OLD TESTAMENT

Exodus 34:6–7

6 And the Lord passed by before him, and proclaimed, The Lord, The Lord God, merciful and gracious, longsuffering, and abundant in goodness and truth,

7 Keeping mercy for thousands, forgiving iniquity and transgression and sin.

Proverbs 14:29–30

He that is slow to wrath is of great understanding:
But he that is hasty of spirit exalteth folly.
A sound heart is the life of the flesh:
But envy the rottenness of the bones.

Psalm 37:5–7

Commit thy way unto the Lord;
Trust also in him; and he shall bring it to pass.
And he shall bring forth thy righteousness as the light,
And thy judgment as the noonday.
Rest in the Lord, and wait patiently for him.

Job 1:13–21

13 And there was a day when his sons and his daughters were eating and drinking wine in their eldest brother's house:

14 And there came a messenger unto Job, and said, The oxen were ploughing, and the asses feeding beside them:

15 And the Sabeans fell upon them, and took them away; yea, they have slain the servants with the edge of the sword; and I only am escaped alone to tell thee.

16 While he was yet speaking, there came also another, and said, The fire of God is fallen from heaven, and hath burned up the sheep, and the servants, and consumed them; and I only am escaped alone to tell thee.

17 While he was yet speaking, there came also another, and said, The Chaldeans made out three bands, and fell upon the camels, and have carried them away, yea, and slain the servants with the edge of the sword; and I only am escaped alone to tell thee.

18 While he was yet speaking, there came also another, and said, Thy sons and thy daughters were eating and drinking wine in their eldest brother's house:

19 And, behold, there came a great wind from the wilderness, and smote the four corners of the house, and it fell upon the young men, and they are dead; and I only am escaped alone to tell thee.

20 Then Job arose, and rent his mantle, and shaved his head, and fell down upon the ground, and worshipped,

21 And said, Naked came I out of my mother's womb, and naked shall I return thither: the Lord gave, and the Lord hath taken away; blessed be the name of the Lord.

NEW TESTAMENT

Luke 2:25–30

25 And, behold, there was a man in Jerusalem, whose name was Simeon; and the same man was just and devout, waiting for the consolation of Israel: and the Holy Ghost was upon him.

26 And it was revealed unto him by the Holy Ghost, that he should not see death, before he had seen the Lord's Christ.

27 And he came by the Spirit into the temple: and when the parents brought in the child Jesus, to do for him after the custom of the law,

28 Then took he him up in his arms, and blessed God, and said,

29 Lord, now lettest thou thy servant depart in peace, according to thy word:

30 For mine eyes have seen thy salvation.

Hebrews 12:1–3

1 Let us run with patience the race that is set before us,

2 Looking unto Jesus the author and finisher of our faith; who for the joy that was set before him endured the cross, despising the shame, and is set down at the right hand of the throne of God.

3 For consider him that endured such contradiction of sinners against himself, lest ye be wearied and faint in your minds.

Galatians 5:5

5 For we through the Spirit wait for the hope of righteousness by faith.

James 5:7–8

7 Be patient therefore, brethren, unto the coming of the Lord. Behold, the husbandman waiteth for the precious fruit of the earth, and hath long patience for it, until he receive the early and latter rain.

8 Be ye also patient; stablish your hearts.

PEACE

"Shalom," the Old Testament word for peace, can also be translated "totality"; the adjective "shalem" is normally translated "whole." Peace means everything that belongs to the harmony of all things: prosperity, personal relationships, good weather, national freedom . . . everything. The Old Testament sees Israel's peace as rooted in its covenant with God, but from there it branches into all of life. Ezekiel is only one of several prophets who speak of even the taming of wild nature as part of the peace process.

But there is a false peace often proclaimed by false prophets. It is the illusory security of those who practice injustice behind the protection of superior force. Prophets such as Jeremiah and Ezekiel had a double task: first to convince people that peace was threatened by such behavior, and then (when this had been proved right) to convince them that peace was possible on God's terms. What was not possible was to live out of harmony with God's will and yet experience harmony in relation to men and nature.

The New Testament claimed that this expectation of peace was fulfilled in Jesus, though the old world continued and the heavenly kingdom was for the time being hidden within it. The idea of Jesus as the new king was open to misinterpretation in the circumstances of the time. Instead of being seen as the head of a transcendent kingdom of peace, he could easily be taken to be the leader of a secular movement of national liberation through war. His teaching was carefully framed to minimize this misunderstanding and in one notable gesture—not fully understood till later—he dramatized its repudiation.

This was his triumphal entry into Jerusalem, which could so easily have been a triumphal*ist* entry into the capital city. The whole significance of the event was transformed by his choosing to ride not on a horse, the conventional symbol of war, but on a donkey. In this way he fulfilled a prophecy by Zechariah that contained not only the words quoted in John's Gospel but also these, which immediately followed:

> I will cut off the chariot from Ephraim,
> and the horse from Jerusalem,
> and the battle bow shall be cut off;
> and he shall speak peace unto the heathen.
> (Zechariah 9:10)

While continuing the Old Testament belief in the wide extent of God's peace, the New Testament increased the sense of its depth. The Psalms had spoken movingly of inner peace, but the New Testament had more to say about it—and about its ability to stand up to external disquiet. Jesus was seen as the possessor and bequeather of peace even when he stood on the brink of crucifixion.

Peace, it is often said, is not just the absence of war between nations. Nor is it just the presence of good relations between nations. It is personal as well as national, inward as well as outward, ecological as well as human.

To say that "peace is indivisible" is to say that it can be enjoyed in one of its aspects only (in the long term at least) if it is present in all its aspects. It involves living in harmony with the laws of our being, and that involves our attitude toward ourselves, toward each other, and toward our whole environment.

Clearly this is a positive rather than a passive role. Jesus said, "Blessed are the peacemakers [the *doers* of peace], for they shall be called the children of God." Activities such as peacemaking can meet with plenty of opposition. Peace has to be deep enough and wide enough to contain such conflicts and to resolve them in the total harmony.

PEACE

OLD TESTAMENT

Isaiah 52:7

7 How beautiful upon the mountains are the feet of him that bringeth good tidings, that publisheth peace; that bringeth good tidings of good, that publisheth salvation; that saith unto Zion, Thy God reigneth!

Ezekiel 34:25

25 And I will make with them a covenant of peace, and will cause the evil beasts to cease out of the land: and they shall dwell safely in the wilderness, and sleep in the woods.

Isaiah 48:18, 22

18 O that thou hadst hearkened to my commandments! then had thy peace been as a river, and thy righteousness as the waves of the sea:

22 There is no peace, saith the Lord, unto the wicked.

Micah 4:2–4

2 The law shall go forth of Zion, and the word of the Lord from Jerusalem.

3 And he shall judge among many people, and rebuke strong nations afar off; and they shall beat their swords into ploughshares, and their spears into pruning-hooks: nation shall not lift up a sword against nation, neither shall they learn war any more.

4 But they shall sit every man under his vine and under his fig tree; and none shall make them afraid: for the mouth of the Lord of hosts hath spoken it.

Isaiah 9:6–7

6 For unto us a child is born, unto us a son is given: and the government shall be upon his shoulder: and his name shall be called Wonderful, Counsellor, The mighty God, The everlasting Father, The Prince of Peace.

7 Of the increase of his government and peace there shall be no end.

NEW TESTAMENT

Luke 2:13–14 (after an angel has announced the birth of Jesus)

13 And suddenly there was with the angel a multitude of the heavenly host praising God, and saying,

14 Glory to God in the highest and on earth peace, good will toward men.

John 12:12–16

12 On the next day much people that were come to the feast, when they heard that Jesus was coming to Jerusalem,

13 Took branches of palm trees, and went forth to meet him, and cried, Hosanna: Blessed is the King of Israel that cometh in the name of the Lord.

14 And Jesus, when he had found a young ass, sat thereon; as it is written,

15 Fear not, daughter of Sion: behold, thy King cometh, sitting on an ass's colt.

16 These things understood not his disciples at the first: but when Jesus was glorified, then remembered they that these things were written of him, and that they had done these things unto him.

John 14:27

27 Peace I leave with you, my peace I give unto you: not as the world giveth, give I unto you. Let not your heart be troubled, neither let it be afraid.

Philippians 4:7

7 And the peace of God, which passeth all understanding, shall keep your hearts and minds through Christ Jesus.

POLITICS

The Old Testament is an intensely political volume. Its thesis is that divine law must govern human life, and, since human life is lived in communities, political activity is inevitably part of it. So the law books lay down the rules of political life, and the prophetic books denounce the politicians who break those rules.

Israel, however, was not a democracy. It was a theocracy, and the ultimate sovereignty of God was mediated by his chosen leaders, such as Moses, and by his anointed kings, such as David. Authority could be delegated, as it was by Moses (see Society), but only to those who were themselves ruled by the Spirit of God. It was rule from above with checks from beyond and from below. If kings ceased to serve the divine purpose, they were displaced. If leaders abused their position, prophets rose up from among the people to denounce them in the name of the Lord.

What is more, the divine concern with politics was not limited to the politics of Israel. An Israelite (such as Mordecai, whose story is told at length in the Book of Esther) might hold political power in a nation other than Israel, and God would support him in his work. A non-Israelite might hold political power over Israel, and God could use him, as he did Cyrus the Persian.

But the prophets did not limit themselves to the politics of the day. Though they commented freely on current issues, they also kept alive a vision of a better order to come. This order would transcend all political systems and would include the regeneration of nature itself, but it was from the contemplation of such perfection that the prophets turned back to the politics of their own day and passed judgment.

Jesus preached the advent of this long-awaited kingdom. His kingdom was not an earthly political unit, but as the manifestation of an ideal community it was a challenge to all political systems (see Society). It was simultaneously hidden (like leavening in dough) and revealed (like a city on a hill).

The opponents of Jesus naturally tried to prove that his teaching was political and seditious. In his reply to their question about paying taxes to Caesar—a question framed with all the political skills of flattery and duplicity—he could not have meant that he regarded a whole area of life as being outside God's concern. That would have been contrary to the whole tenor of his teaching and of the Bible as a whole. He must have meant that within the all-embracing rule of God there was room for political authority also to be exercised.

The New Testament speaks throughout of two ages overlapping in such a way that the Christian lives in the kingdoms of this world and in the kingdom of heaven, both at the same time. And the wider world of earthly kingdoms was not a world without God. Their rulers were also God's servants, even if they did not know it. In their letters, both Paul and Peter addressed themselves to the political realities of their time. There was no point in telling Christians to seek political power for themselves, given the circumstances of the time, but both Peter and Paul were clear that such power operated under the rule of God. It had to be respected when rightly used, and resisted when it required disobedience to divine law.

The Bible sees man as a political animal, but as one who is held between two forces. On one side is the force of immediate political reality: politics as the art of the possible, the technique of doing what is expedient within the limitations imposed by the circumstances of a particular time. On the other side is the force of the divine order and the transcendent community—not a mere dream or ideal, but a present experience to those who are prepared to participate in that order of things as well as in the passing one.

Political wisdom is to live in both systems without schizophrenia. Mere expediency on the one hand and mere idealism on the other are to be avoided. Always the expedient is to be chosen in the light of the transcendent; always the ideal is to be served in terms of the realistic.

POLITICS

OLD TESTAMENT

Psalm 127:1

Except the Lord build the house,
They labour in vain that build it:
Except the Lord keep the city,
The watchman waketh but in vain.

Micah 3:9-11

9 Hear this, I pray you, ye heads of the house of Jacob, and princes of the house of Israel, that abhor judgment, and pervert all equity.

10 They build up Zion with blood, and Jerusalem with iniquity.

11 The heads thereof judge for reward, and the priests thereof teach for hire, and the prophets thereof divine for money.

Isaiah 45:1-2, 5

1 Thus saith the Lord to his anointed, to Cyrus, whose right hand I have holden, to subdue nations before him; and I will loose the loins of kings, to open before him the two leaved gates; and the gates shall not be shut;

2 I will go before thee, and make the crooked places straight: I will break in pieces the gates of brass, and cut in sunder the bars of iron:

5 I am the Lord, and there is none else, there is no God beside me: I girded thee, though thou hast not known me.

Jeremiah 30:18, 20-21

18 Thus saith the Lord; Behold, I will bring again the captivity of Jacob's tents, and have mercy on his dwellingplaces; and the city shall be builded upon her own heap, and the palace shall remain after the manner thereof.

20 Their children also shall be as aforetime, and their congregation shall be established before me, and I will punish all that oppress them.

21 And their nobles shall be of themselves, and their governor shall proceed from the midst of them.

NEW TESTAMENT

Matthew 5:14; 13:33

14 Ye are the light of the world. A city that is set on an hill cannot be hid.

33 Another parable spake he unto them; The kingdom of heaven is like unto leaven, which a woman took, and hid in three measures of meal, till the whole was leavened.

Luke 20:20-25

20 And they watched him, and sent forth spies, which should feign them-

selves just men, that they might take hold of his words, that so they might deliver him unto the power and authority of the governor.

21 And they asked him, saying, Master, we know that thou sayest and teachest rightly, neither acceptest thou the person of any, but teachest the way of God truly:

22 Is it lawful for us to give tribute unto Cæsar, or no?

23 But he perceived their craftiness, and said unto them, Why tempt ye me?

24 Shew me a penny. Whose image and superscription hath it? They answered and said, Cæsar's.

25 And he said unto them, Render therefore unto Cæsar the things which be Cæsar's, and unto God the things which be God's.

John 18:36

36 Jesus answered, My kingdom is not of this world: if my kingdom were of this world, then would my servants fight, that I should not be delivered to the Jews: but now is my kingdom not from hence.

Romans 13:5–6

5 Wherefore ye must needs be subject [to rulers], not only for wrath, but also for conscience sake.

6 For, for this cause pay ye tribute also: for they are God's ministers, attending continually upon this very thing.

1 Peter 2:13–14

13 Submit yourselves to every ordinance of man for the Lord's sake: whether it be to the king, as supreme;

14 Or unto governors, as unto them that are sent by him for the punishment of evildoers, and for the praise of them that do well.

POVERTY

Those who are poor (whether deservedly or not) are made by the Old Testament a legal charge on those who are not poor. The law was often ignored, and the prophets were quick to announce doom as a consequence, but relief for the poor was an absolute obligation on the community, not just a gesture left to those with charitable feelings. And relief was to be provided in such a way as not to diminish the poor man's status as a brother.

But the Old Testament also uses the word "poor" to denote people who were not necessarily hard up. In the simple, hard-working, pious people the health of Israel was believed to reside, and from these "poor" (to use what was almost the technical term for them) salvation was to come.

The New Testament takes up this expectation in Mary's song, the Magnificat, itself a direct echo of Hannah's song in 1 Samuel. The poor—meaning those who live in simplicity rather than those who live in wretchedness—are still at the center of Israel's hope.

But between the Testaments there had developed an interest in voluntary poverty of an extreme kind, and this also is reflected in the New Testament. John the Baptist, for example, appears on the scene practicing the most austere life-style imaginable. Later, Jesus tells a rich young man to give his entire fortune to the poor, and he sends out his disciples moneyless and defenseless, bereft of all material security.

But these instructions represented a way of removing the barriers created by possessions rather than the pursuit of poverty as an end in itself. Jesus' own life-style was often contrasted with that of John because it was not particularly austere. When an extravagantly expensive gesture was performed in his honor, Jesus accepted it. Of course, when he said, "Ye have the poor always with you," he was neither dismissing their needs nor wearily acknowledging a boring perennial problem. His statement was (besides being a quotation from the Old Testament) a salute to the fact that possessions can be used to express love in many ways—including the relief of poverty, but not only the relief of poverty. To do "a beautiful thing," to make a fragrant gesture in honor of one about to die, is to act with the kind of grace that will also respond to the needs of the poor, and will respond in a way that is gracious, not humiliating (see Sympathy).

The Bible does not deal with the "problem" of poverty so much as with the poor as people. Its attitude is personal and concrete rather than sociological and abstract. The world itself cannot but confront us with the fact of poverty. The Bible not only confirms what ought to be obvious—that the needs of the poor (including poor communities) must be the responsibility of the wealthy (including wealthy nations)—but also stirs the imagination to see in the poor something much more than a burdensome problem. The poor are precious. They are a revelation of life's essence. They are to be loved.

Involuntary poverty is a world sickness to be cured, but voluntary poverty (or at any rate simplicity) can be a way to health. It removes the barriers between one human being and others. It strips the artificial coverings from the reality of life. It makes for a plainness of life-style in which other forms of wealth and power can be discovered.

One February morning in 1209, in a little Italian chapel that had recently been rebuilt, the priest celebrating Mass read as the Gospel one of the accounts telling how Jesus sent out his apostles without money, without food, and with minimal clothing. One member of the congregation was innocent enough to take the message quite literally as applying to himself. He embraced poverty. Powerless as that rendered him (by all conventional standards), Saint Francis then cheerfully diverted the course of history and enriched the world. Poverty is a complex and potent thing.

POVERTY

OLD TESTAMENT

Deuteronomy 15:7–8, 10–11

7 If there be among you a poor man of one of thy brethren within any of thy gates in thy land which the Lord thy God giveth thee, thou shalt not harden thine heart, nor shut thine hand from thy poor brother:

8 But thou shalt open thine hand wide unto him, and shalt surely lend him sufficient for his need, in that which he wanteth.

10 Thou shalt surely give him, and thine heart shall not be grieved when thou givest unto him: because that for this thing the Lord thy God shall bless thee in all thy works, and in all that thou puttest thine hand unto.

11 For the poor shall never cease out of the land: therefore I command thee, saying, Thou shalt open thine hand wide unto thy brother, to thy poor, and to thy needy, in thy land.

Amos 5:11

11 Forasmuch therefore as your treading is upon the poor, and ye take from him burdens of wheat: ye have built houses of hewn stone, but ye shall not dwell in them; ye have planted pleasant vineyards, but ye shall not drink wine of them.

Proverbs 19:17; 21:13

He that hath pity upon the poor lendeth
 unto the Lord;
And that which he hath given will he pay
 him again.

Whoso stoppeth his ears at the cry of the
 poor,
He also shall cry himself, but shall not
 be heard.

1 Samuel 2:7–8

7 The Lord maketh poor, and maketh rich: he bringeth low, and lifteth up.

8 He raiseth up the poor out of the dust, and lifteth up the beggar from the dunghill, to set them among princes, and to make them inherit the throne of glory.

NEW TESTAMENT

Luke 1:52–53

52 He hath put down the mighty from their seats, and exalted them of low degree.

53 He hath filled the hungry with good things; and the rich he hath sent empty away.

Mark 1:4, 6

4 John did baptize in the wilderness, and preach the baptism of repentance for the remission of sins.

6 And John was clothed with camel's hair, and with a girdle of a skin about his loins; and he did eat locusts and wild honey.

Luke 6:20

20 And he lifted up his eyes on his disciples, and said, Blessed be ye poor: for yours is the kingdom of God.

Mark 6:7–9

7 And he called unto him the twelve, and began to send them forth by two and two; and gave them power over unclean spirits;

8 And commanded them that they should take nothing for their journey, save a staff only; no scrip, no bread, no money in their purse:

9 But be shod with sandals; and not put on two coats.

Matthew 26:6–13

6 Now when Jesus was in Bethany, in the house of Simon the leper,

7 There came unto him a woman having an alabaster box of very precious ointment, and poured it on his head, as he sat at meat.

8 But when his disciples saw it, they had indignation, saying, To what purpose is this waste?

9 For this ointment might have been sold for much, and given to the poor.

10 When Jesus understood it, he said unto them, Why trouble ye the woman? for she hath wrought a good work upon me.

11 For ye have the poor always with you; but me ye have not always.

12 For in that she hath poured this ointment on my body, she did it for my burial.

13 Verily I say unto you, Wheresoever this gospel shall be preached in the whole world, there shall also this, that this woman hath done, be told for a memorial of her.

James 2:2–5

2 For if there come unto your assembly a man with a gold ring, in goodly apparel, and there come in also a poor man in vile raiment;

3 And ye have respect to him that weareth the gay clothing, and say unto him, Sit thou here in a good place; and say to the poor, Stand thou there, or sit here under my footstool:

4 Are ye not then partial in yourselves, and are become judges of evil thoughts?

5 Hearken, my beloved brethren, Hath not God chosen the poor of this world rich in faith, and heirs of the kingdom which he hath promised to them that love him?

POWER

There is evidence in the Old Testament of a time when Israel's God was thought of as simply the most powerful among many gods. Naturally all power was then thought of in competitive terms. Elijah was able to slaughter the prophets of Baal because he had demonstrated on Mount Carmel that his God could do greater feats than theirs. The dramatic story in 1 Kings 18 (too long to quote here) tells how he and his rivals each prepared the materials for a burnt offering, but neither was allowed to set fire to it. The kindling had to be done supernaturally. Baal's worshipers made the first attempt, spurred on in their prayers by the mocking Elijah. When they failed, Elijah made his own task more difficult by having water poured on his pile of wood. Then he called on the Lord, and fire came down from heaven to consume his sacrifice.

Elijah's taunts against the Baal worshipers were well directed, but his own argument was a crude one of which he was himself soon to feel the inadequacy.

When Israel came to see that the Lord was not just the *most* powerful but the *all*-powerful God—the only God—this new understanding involved a reappraisal of power generally. Power came to look less competitive, less arbitrary, more purposeful. It was found to be always related to the divine law and plan. It was no longer thought of as significant in itself, regardless of what it was used for. Significant power was power such as that which liberated the Israelites from Egyptian domination. A mere wonder such as Aaron's performance with his staff left the situation unaltered.

To the prophets, power was increasingly moral power, not because they had no interest in sheer clout but because they believed that real power just seeped away unless it was aligned with the moral purpose that God had written into the creation. So Micah speaks of power and might, not as the ability to get one's own way or to become top nation, but as the ability to show Israel where it had got its values wrong.

The New Testament closely linked power with authority; the word for "authority" can actually be translated as "power" in some contexts. Jesus had manifest power because he had intrinsic authority, and that from God. Power is again a matter of being in line with the divine purpose.

New Testament writers, however, were well aware of other forces at work in the world. There was the power of evil, conceived of in the most concrete and personal terms. And there was the power of all those human authorities who knew nothing of divine law and who could—and did—exert their power against the Christian cause. To the New Testament writers, however, neither of these— neither misplaced spiritual power operating from beyond the world nor undisciplined human power operating within it—was of final importance. Christians believed that the resurrection of Jesus showed that all other forces had outreached themselves and were doomed to fade away.

The Bible suggests a good question to raise when power is under discussion: "Power to do what?" Significant power is always related to purpose. To pursue power as if it were an end in itself can lead an individual to madness and a nation to overkill.

According to the Bible, power does not lie around in packages waiting to be picked up and used as we may choose. In the short term it may look like that, but in the long term the power at loose in the world works according to certain laws and is subject to natural checks and balances. The discussion of purpose should precede the discussion of power. Whether the power seeker is an individual or a superpower, the recommended way is to decide first what purposes to pursue and then, if these seem intrinsically valid, seek the power to do just those things—never power for its own sake, never the power to do just anything.

POWER

OLD TESTAMENT

Exodus 7:8–13

8 And the Lord spake unto Moses and unto Aaron, saying,

9 When Pharaoh shall speak unto you, saying, Shew a miracle for you: then thou shalt say unto Aaron, Take thy rod, and cast it before Pharaoh, and it shall become a serpent.

10 And Moses and Aaron went in unto Pharaoh, and they did so as the Lord had commanded: and Aaron cast down his rod before Pharaoh, and before his servants, and it became a serpent.

11 Then Pharaoh also called the wise men and the sorcerers: now the magicians of Egypt, they also did in like manner with their enchantments.

12 For they cast down every man his rod, and they became serpents: but Aaron's rod swallowed up their rods.

13 And he hardened Pharaoh's heart, and he hearkened not unto them; as the Lord had said.

Exodus 14:21–25; 15:1, 6

21 And Moses stretched out his hand over the sea; and the Lord caused the sea to go back by a strong east wind all that night, and made the sea dry land, and the waters were divided.

22 And the children of Israel went into the midst of the sea upon the dry ground: and the waters were a wall unto them on their right hand, and on their left.

23 And the Egyptians pursued, and went in after them to the midst of the sea, even all Pharaoh's horses, his chariots, and his horsemen.

24 And it came to pass, that in the morning watch the Lord looked unto the host of the Egyptians through the pillar of fire and of the cloud, and troubled the host of the Egyptians,

25 And took off their chariot wheels, that they drave them heavily: so that the Egyptians said, Let us flee from the face of Israel; for the Lord fighteth for them against the Egyptians.

1 Then sang Moses and the children of Israel this song unto the Lord, and spake, saying, I will sing unto the Lord, for he hath triumphed gloriously: the horse and his rider hath he thrown into the sea.

6 Thy right hand, O Lord, is become glorious in power: thy right hand, O Lord, hath dashed in pieces the enemy.

Micah 3:8

8 But truly I am full of power by the spirit of the Lord, and of judgment, and of might, to declare unto Jacob his transgression, and to Israel his sin.

NEW TESTAMENT

Luke 4:31–36

31 And [Jesus] came down to Capernaum, a city of Galilee, and taught them on the sabbath days.

32 And they were astonished at his doctrine: for his word was with power.

33 And in the synagogue there was a man, which had a spirit of an unclean devil, and cried out with a loud voice,

34 Saying, Let us alone; what have we to do with thee, thou Jesus of Nazareth? art thou come to destroy us? I know thee who thou art; the Holy One of God.

35 And Jesus rebuked him, saying, Hold thy peace, and come out of him. And when the devil had thrown him in the midst, he came out of him, and hurt him not.

36 And they were all amazed, and spake among themselves, saying, What a word is this! for with authority and power he commandeth the unclean spirits, and they come out.

Acts 1:3, 7–9

3 He shewed himself alive after his passion by many infallible proofs, being seen of them forty days, and speaking of the things pertaining to the kingdom of God.

7 And he said unto them, It is not for you to know the times or the seasons, which the Father hath put in his own power.

8 But ye shall receive power, after that the Holy Ghost is come upon you: and ye shall be witnesses unto me both in Jerusalem, and in all Judæa, and in Samaria, and unto the uttermost part of the earth.

9 And when he had spoken these things, while they beheld, he was taken up; and a cloud received him out of their sight.

Ephesians 1:18–23 (the apostle prays to "the Father of Glory")

18 That ye may know what is the hope of his calling, and what the riches of the glory of his inheritance in the saints,

19 And what is the exceeding greatness of his power to us-ward who believe, according to the working of his mighty power,

20 Which he wrought in Christ, when he raised him from the dead, and set him at his own right hand in the heavenly places,

21 Far above all principality, and power, and might, and dominion, and every name that is named, not only in this world, but also in that which is to come:

22 And hath put all things under his feet, and gave him to be the head over all things to the church,

23 Which is his body, the fulness of him that filleth all in all.

PRAISE

The Bible insists that worship must always be directed to God (see Worship). To let it stop short at something created instead of passing through to the Creator is the dreaded sin of idolatry against which the Old Testament speaks so fiercely. Praise, however, though it is central to the worship of God and always shaped by the appreciation of his nature, can legitimately spill over into the praise of men, so long as they are doing at their own level and in their own way what God does in his infinite way. Not only can praise be given to God or man, it can even be given *by* God *to* men, as when Moses reported God's commendation of the people's ideas.

The Old Testament does not hesitate to "praise famous men" (a phrase from Ecclesiastes, a Jewish book of the period between the Old and New Testaments) when their deeds mirror the nature and work of God—that is, when they defeat their enemies (David), display wisdom (Solomon), create order and beauty (Hezekiah), show steadfast love (Ruth), or do what is right (various kings).

In the New Testament, Jesus gives praise where it is due, and refuses it where it is sought. He was particularly hard on those who made their religion a means of getting praise for themselves rather than an inward and hidden giving of praise to God. This applied both to religion as prayer and to religion as almsgiving.

On one occasion Jesus even ruled on a family quarrel where praise and blame were involved. Martha blamed Mary for neglecting the chores. Jesus praised her for choosing what was more important. He also accepted praise aimed in his own direction, regarding it as in the nature of things. With characteristic hyperbole he spoke of the very stones insisting on the open acknowledgment of God's representative.

The reason why fulsome and undiscriminating praise is so objectionable is that merited praise is so important. It is the cheer by which we greet achievement. If we did not let it out, we would be the poorer. What is more, the unsaluted achievement, though not intrinsically diminished, is lacking in power to encourage others. It needs to be acknowledged in order to provide a standard for others.

A child who never receives a "well done" will hardly know the good of which he or she is capable. Discriminating praise can be of positive value—which means also that the cessation of praise when the same child makes a mess of things can serve as a warning to him or her. Discriminating praise, however, makes it clear that the thing done well is done for its own sake. It is not done in order to win praise.

To give praise where it is due—and therefore to know where it is due—is an important function. And it is a very democratic one. The praise that comes through official channels or is whipped up by political bosses and media flaks is of little significance compared with the spontaneous admiration of people at large. The true power of praise is in the hands of the man or woman in the crowd, the parent of the ordinary child.

Praise does, however, demand a capacity to recognize the good when we see it. It needs standards. The biblical answer to this need is not so much to lay down a code as to keep the spirit sensitive to true worth through the praise of transcendent goodness.

PRAISE

OLD TESTAMENT

Deuteronomy 5:28

28 And the Lord heard the voice of your words, when ye spake unto me; and the Lord said unto me, I have heard the voice of the words of this people, which they have spoken unto thee: they have well said all that they have spoken.

2 Chronicles 31:20–21

20 And thus did Hezekiah throughout all Judah, and wrought that which was good and right and truth before the Lord his God.

21 And in every work that he began in the service of the house of God, and in the law, and in the commandments, to seek his God, he did it with all his heart, and prospered.

Proverbs 27:2; 28:4

Let another man praise thee, and not thine own mouth;
A stranger, and not thine own lips.
They that forsake the law praise the wicked:
But such as keep the law contend with them.

Isaiah 42:5, 8

5 Thus saith God the Lord, he that created the heavens, and stretched them out; he that spread forth the earth, and that which cometh out of it; he that giveth breath unto the people upon it, and spirit to them that walk therein:

8 I am the Lord: that is my name: and my glory will I not give to another, neither my praise to graven images.

Psalm 150

Praise ye the Lord.
Praise God in his sanctuary:
Praise him in the firmament of his power.
Praise him for his mighty acts:
Praise him according to his excellent greatness.
Praise him with the sound of the trumpet:
Praise him with the psaltery and harp.
Praise him with the timbrel and dance:
Praise him with stringed instruments and organs.
Praise him upon the loud cymbals:
Praise him upon the high sounding cymbals.
Let every thing that hath breath praise the Lord.
Praise ye the Lord.

NEW TESTAMENT

Matthew 6:2–4

2 Therefore when thou doest thine alms, do not sound a trumpet before thee, as the hypocrites do in the synagogues and in the streets, that they may have glory of men. Verily I say unto you, They have their reward.

3 But when thou doest alms, let not thy left hand know what thy right hand doeth:

4 That thine alms may be in secret: and thy Father which seeth in secret himself shall reward thee openly.

Luke 10:38–42

38 Now it came to pass, as they went, that he entered into a certain village: and a certain woman named Martha received him into her house.

39 And she had a sister called Mary, which also sat at Jesus' feet, and heard his word.

40 But Martha was cumbered about much serving, and came to him, and said, Lord, dost thou not care that my sister hath left me to serve alone? bid her therefore that she help me.

41 And Jesus answered and said unto her, Martha, Martha, thou art careful and troubled about many things:

42 But one thing is needful: and Mary hath chosen that good part, which shall not be taken away from her.

Luke 19:37–40

37 And when he was come nigh, even now at the descent of the mount of Olives, the whole multitude of the disciples began to rejoice and praise God with a loud voice for all the mighty works that they had seen;

38 Saying, Blessed be the King that cometh in the name of the Lord: peace in heaven, and glory in the highest.

39 And some of the Pharisees from among the multitude said unto him, Master, rebuke thy disciples.

40 And he answered and said unto them, I tell you that, if these should hold their peace, the stones would immediately cry out.

1 Corinthians 4:4–5

4 He that judgeth me is the Lord.

5 Therefore judge nothing before the time, until the Lord come, who both will bring to light the hidden things of darkness, and will make manifest the counsels of the hearts: and then shall every man have praise of God.

PRAYER

The entire Book of Psalms demonstrates the nature of Old Testament prayer, and it has been used in the devotions of pious Jews, Christians, and others through every century since it was compiled. Many other Old Testament passages vibrate with the same notes: reverence, love, thankfulness, confession, pleading. But Old Testament prayer is not always so submissive or so timeless.

Abraham bargaining with God for the people of Sodom is one picture of a man at prayer. The assumptions are that all situations are flexible and that God himself is persuadable. Prayer is a dialogue. Those who press their case may, through God, alter the course of events going on around them.

So Hezekiah, having received a challenging letter from his powerful enemy the king of Assyria, takes the letter with him to the temple in Jerusalem and physically spreads it out before God in order to pray over it—rather as some in our own time have made a point of praying over their newspapers.

In the New Testament, Jesus not only teaches prayer but also prays. He stands on the human side of the dialogue. But then the New Testament says that God is always involved in the asking as well as the answering.

At its very simplest level, prayer is a way of concentrating the mind and of assembling all the inner resources of the human personality. As the Bible understands it, these resources are then turned outward. Prayer is the action of a creature who is a free personality but who is not alone in the world. His spirit moves outward to meet with the response of a Spirit that is not himself, though it is also in himself.

The real difficulty of prayer today is not making a case for it or finding time for it: it is finding room for it in our mental picture of the way the world works. That picture may be almost unconscious. It may be one that we picked up years ago, almost by accident, and that has remained unexamined ever since. It may even be inconsistent with information and opinions subsequently acquired. But if, deep down, we are governed by a picture of reality as a crudely mechanical and inflexible system, prayer will be squeezed out.

Admittedly it would be impossible for us to go back to the biblical world picture in all its simplicity. It is possible to believe in prayer as confidently as the people of the Bible did, but not to have the same mental picture of how prayer works. We have a different view of the universe, of the laws that operate in it, of the way its parts fit together and influence one another. To the biblical writers, each separate event *was* a separate event. And each separate event was individually arranged by God. To ask him to do this rather than that was not to ask for any interruption in the orderly processes of nature as then understood.

We cannot go back to that position, but we can go a long way beyond the rigid, mechanical view of natural law that saw each event as the inevitable and unalterable result of other physical causes. The laws of cause and effect now look much subtler and more flexible; they seem responsive to influences that are personal rather than physical. It is becoming possible to see a place for prayer within the laws that order the universe, rather than as a challenge to them.

It is tempting to talk about a control system with feedback, but this could make the picture too impersonal again. Prayer, as the Bible sees it, is above all a

268

personal relationship with God. The governing picture is that of a world designed to foster and reward the exercise of all that belongs to personality: free will, love, concentration, benevolence. In such a world prayer is a built-in, ever present, and entirely natural possibility.

PRAYER

OLD TESTAMENT

Genesis 18:22–32

22 And the men turned their faces from thence, and went toward Sodom: but Abraham stood yet before the Lord.

23 And Abraham drew near, and said, Wilt thou also destroy the righteous with the wicked?

24 Peradventure there be fifty righteous within the city: wilt thou also destroy and not spare the place for the fifty righteous that are therein?

25 That be far from thee to do after this manner, to slay the righteous with the wicked: and that the righteous should be as the wicked, that be far from thee: Shall not the Judge of all the earth do right?

26 And the Lord said, if I find in Sodom fifty righteous within the city, then I will spare all the place for their sakes.

27 And Abraham answered and said, Behold now, I have taken upon me to speak unto the Lord, which am but dust and ashes:

28 Peradventure there shall lack five of the fifty righteous: wilt thou destroy all the city for lack of five? And he said, If I find there forty and five, I will not destroy it.

29 And he spake unto him yet again, and said, Peradventure there shall be forty found there. And he said, I will not do it for forty's sake.

30 And he said unto him, Oh let not the Lord be angry, and I will speak: Peradventure there shall thirty be found there. And he said, I will not do it, if I find thirty there.

31 And he said, Behold now, I have taken upon me to speak unto the Lord: Peradventure there shall be twenty found there. And he said, I will not destroy it for twenty's sake.

32 And he said, Oh let not the Lord be angry, and I will speak yet but this once: Peradventure ten shall be found there. And he said, I will not destroy it for ten's sake.

2 Kings 19:14–16

14 And Hezekiah received the letter of the hand of the messengers, and read it: and Hezekiah went up into the house of the Lord, and spread it before the Lord.

15 And Hezekiah prayed before the Lord, and said, O Lord God of Israel, which dwellest between the cherubims, thou art the God, even thou alone, of all the kingdoms of the earth; thou hast made heaven and earth.

16 Lord, bow down thine ear, and hear: open, Lord, thine eyes, and see: and hear the words of Sennacherib, which hath sent him to reproach the living God.

NEW TESTAMENT

Matthew 6:5–13; 7:9–11;
Luke 11:9–10

5 And when thou prayest, thou shalt not be as the hypocrites are: for they love to pray standing in the synagogues and in the corners of the streets, that they may be seen of men. Verily I say unto you, They have their reward.

6 But thou, when thou prayest, enter into thy closet, and when thou hast shut thy door, pray to thy Father which is in secret; and thy Father which seeth in secret shall reward thee openly.

7 But when ye pray, use not vain repetitions, as the heathen do: for they think that they shall be heard for their much speaking.

8 Be not ye therefore like unto them: for your Father knoweth what things ye have need of, before ye ask him.

9 After this manner therefore pray ye: Our Father which art in heaven, Hallowed be thy name.

10 Thy kingdom come. Thy will be done in earth, as it is in heaven.

11 Give us this day our daily bread.

12 And forgive us our debts, as we forgive our debtors.

13 And lead us not into temptation, but deliver us from evil: For thine is the kingdom, and the power, and the glory, for ever. Amen.

9 Or what man is there of you, whom if his son ask bread, will he give him a stone?

10 Or if he ask a fish, will he give him a serpent?

11 If ye then, being evil, know how to give good gifts unto your children, how much more shall your Father which is in heaven give good things to them that ask him?

9 And I say unto you, Ask, and it shall be given you; seek, and ye shall find; knock, and it shall be opened unto you.

10 For every one that asketh receiveth; and he that seeketh findeth; and to him that knocketh it shall be opened.

Romans 8:26–27

26 The Spirit also helpeth our infirmities: for we know not what we should pray for as we ought: but the Spirit itself maketh intercession for us with groanings which cannot be uttered.

27 And he that searcheth the hearts knoweth what is the mind of the Spirit, because he maketh intercession for the saints according to the will of God.

PRIDE

"Pride goes before a fall" is a summary of an Old Testament proverb (Proverbs 16:18), but from the point of view of the Old Testament as a whole, this is something of an understatement. Pride *is* the fall. It is the essence of all sin. Adam and Eve lose paradise because of their desire to "be as gods, knowing good

270

and evil" (Genesis 3:5). In all their descendants this proud desire to displace God, although it may express itself as no more than a determination to break one of his commandments, is the essential cause of downfall.

Relevant readings can be found in almost any book of the Old Testament, but the Book of Daniel is a mine of stories designed to show the inevitable doom of those who are governed by pride. Belshazzar's feast is the story of a non-Israelite, a king of Babylon, who presumes to use for his own glorification the vessels from God's ransacked temple in Jerusalem. Immediately the writing appears on the wall. Daniel is summoned to interpret it, and what happens then is reported in the passage quoted here.

In the New Testament the coming of Jesus is celebrated in a song that explicitly endorses the Old Testament's theme that the proud will be abased and the humble exalted. Jesus had to keep pressing this lesson. He did so by making statements of principle, by telling parables and offering practical advice (against seeking the prominent place at table, for instance), and by forbidding titles to his followers (a commandment they have often ignored).

Paul's message is also directed against pride and therefore toward humility, but never toward humiliation. He does not even ask people to think badly of themselves—only to think accurately. Rather than suppress that exuberant spirit which, when it loses touch with reality, can express itself as pride, he just changes its orientation, boasting of his Lord's shameful death rather than his own attainments. There is no answer to his logic in 1 Corinthians 4:7—"What hast thou, that thou didst not receive? Now if thou didst receive it, why dost thou glory as if thou hadst not received it?" If it's a gift, why treat it as an achievement?

The Bible does not object to pride because it makes us feel good. Religion has no particular interest in making us feel bad. Biblical religion attacks pride only because it is a sign that we have got things wrong. We have mistaken our place in the world, and since that place is in fact a very significant one, getting it wrong has universally disastrous consequences—including the loss of that significant place.

Paradoxically our pride is precisely what makes us insignificant. Pride is a mistaken view of ourselves. To correct it we do not have to minimize our virtues and gifts, we just have to recognize that they *are* gifts. Being thankful is as good a feeling as being proud, and it has the advantage of being soundly based on fact.

This approach is particularly useful in relation to the corporate forms of pride: national pride, community pride, team pride. Taking pride in something or someone can be perfectly proper so long as three conditions are fulfilled. First, the object of pride must be truly admirable by objective standards. Second, the quality we admire must really be present in and not just projected onto the beloved group in a spirit of chauvinism. Third, this quality must be seen as a gift to be acknowledged with gratitude rather than as an accomplishment for lack of which others can be regarded as our inferiors.

PRIDE

OLD TESTAMENT

Daniel 5:13, 16–28

13 Then was Daniel brought in before the king. And the king spake and said unto Daniel, Art thou that Daniel, which art of the children of the captivity of Judah, whom the king my father brought out of Jewry?

16 I have heard of thee, that thou canst make interpretations, and dissolve doubts: now if thou canst read the writing, and make known to me the interpretation thereof, thou shalt be clothed with scarlet, and have a chain of gold about thy neck, and shalt be the third ruler in the kingdom.

17 Then Daniel answered and said before the king, Let thy gifts be to thyself, and give thy rewards to another; yet I will read the writing unto the king, and make known to him the interpretation.

18 O thou king, the most high God gave· Nebuchadnezzar thy father a kingdom, and majesty, and glory, and honour:

19 And for the majesty that he gave him, all people, nations, and languages, trembled and feared before him: whom he would he slew; and whom he would he kept alive; and whom he would he set up; and whom he would he put down.

20 But when his heart was lifted up, and his mind hardened in pride, he was deposed from his kingly throne, and they took his glory from him:

21 And he was driven from the sons of men; and his heart was made like the beasts, and his dwelling was with the wild asses: they fed him with grass like oxen, and his body was wet with the dew of heaven; till he knew that the most high God ruled in the kingdom of men, and that he appointeth over it whomsoever he will.

22 And thou his son, O Belshazzar, hast not humbled thine heart, though thou knewest all this;

23 But hast lifted up thyself against the Lord of heaven; and they have brought the vessels of his house before thee, and thou, and thy lords, thy wives, and thy concubines, have drunk wine in them; and thou hast praised the gods of silver, and gold, of brass, iron, wood, and stone, which see not, nor hear, nor know: and the God in whose hand thy breath is, and whose are all thy ways, hast thou not glorified:

24 Then was the part of the hand sent from him; and this writing was written.

25 And this is the writing that was written, MENE, MENE, TEKEL, UPHARSIN.

26 This is the interpretation of the thing: MENE; God hath numbered thy kingdom, and finished it.

27 TEKEL; Thou art weighed in the balances, and art found wanting.

28 PERES; Thy kingdom is divided, and given to the Medes and Persians.

NEW TESTAMENT

Luke 1:46–55 (the Magnificat of Mary)

46 And Mary said, My soul doth magnify the Lord,

47 And my spirit hath rejoiced in God my Saviour.

48 For he hath regarded the low estate of his handmaiden: for, behold, from henceforth all generations shall call me blessed.

49 For he that is mighty hath done to me great things; and holy is his name.

50 And his mercy is on them that fear him from generation to generation.

51 He hath shewed strength with his arm; he hath scattered the proud in the imagination of their hearts.

52 He hath put down the mighty from their seats, and exalted them of low degree.

53 He hath filled the hungry with good things: and the rich he hath sent empty away.

54 He hath holpen his servant Israel, in remembrance of his mercy;

55 As he spake to our fathers, to Abraham, and to his seed for ever.

Matthew 23:8–12

8 But be not ye called Rabbi: for one is your Master, even Christ; for all ye are brethren.

9 And call no man your father upon the earth: for one is your Father, which is in heaven.

10 Neither be ye called masters: for one is your Master, even Christ.

11 But he that is greatest among you shall be your servant.

12 And whosoever shall exalt himself shall be abased; and he that shall humble himself shall be exalted.

Romans 12:3

3 For I say, through the grace given unto me, to every man that is among you, not to think of himself more highly than he ought to think; but to think soberly, according as God hath dealt to every man the measure of faith.

Galatians 6:14

14 But God forbid that I should glory, save in the cross of our Lord Jesus Christ, by whom the world is crucified unto me, and I unto the world.

PROGRESS

The Old Testament starts with regress rather than progress. It opens with a picture of perfection and then tells of man's falling away from it—and of God's using a flaming sword to bar his return.

But the history of Israel, for all the disasters that overtook the nation, is a history dominated by a sense of purposive movement toward a goal. The whole Bible resounds with the conviction that to move from servitude to freedom (especially inner freedom) is to move forward, and to move from anarchy to the rule of just law (especially when it is written on the heart) is to move forward. Perhaps that paradisal vision in the early chapters should be regarded as a picture of God's ultimate intention for humanity and should be seen as a goal rather than as a point of departure. Creative purposes, after all, are normally fulfilled at the end rather than at the beginning.

Not that the divine goal is a human utopia to be approached step by step through the centuries of history. It is a transcendent order that cuts into history from outside it. Yet when a prophet such as Isaiah spoke of the coming kingdom he revealed what could and what could not be counted as progress in ordinary daily affairs. Secure domestic life, a drop in infant mortality, the gathering of harvest by the farmer who has worked for it, the pacifying of the natural order, the enjoyment of international peace: all these are characteristics of the goal and are therefore criteria of progress.

Naturally there were those—the author of Ecclesiastes among them—who saw no signs whatsoever of progress—or even of change.

The New Testament abounds with images of change. Its writers believed that the transcendent order of things had come within range of human experience in the person of Jesus. From one point of view this was progress, because it happened as the climax of a historical process. From another point of view it was not, because it was eternity invading time and eclipsing all mere stage-by-stage movement.

In the enormous eleventh chapter of Hebrews, of which only fragments are quoted here, the writer looks back over the centuries and sees them as a great march forward to the point at which he stands. Yet he does not see the earlier pioneers as having been left behind. The fulfillment somehow embraces them all.

The difficulty about progress is that we sometimes think we are seeing it when all we are seeing is change. The world-weary writer of Ecclesiastes could not see even that, but the world-weary Malcolm Muggeridge sees worse—progress backward:

I consider that the way of life in urbanized, rich countries, as it exists today, and as it is likely to go on developing, is probably the most degraded and unillumined ever to come to pass on the earth. *

Certainly change is not always change for the better, and the march of time is not necessarily the march of progress. But then, change is not necessarily change for the worse either. What the Bible offers is neither a denunciation of human efforts at improvement nor an assurance that things will just naturally get better. It does, however, offer some criteria for judging which way is forward and which backward, plus some assurance that real gains will be supported by the power at the heart of things.

Every situation can be handled well or badly. To handle it well is to create a new situation that can be handled even better. So real progress is possible, both

*Malcolm Muggeridge, *Jesus Rediscovered* (Garden City, N.Y.: Doubleday, 1979).

individually and corporately. But the community does not consist of generations of people each standing on the shoulders of its predecessor and so reaching greater heights, nor does individual life consist necessarily of mounting success. True progress relates not so much to the past as to the transcendent. Chronological order is unimportant. At every moment a way forward is open.

PROGRESS

OLD TESTAMENT

Genesis 3:23–24

23 Therefore the Lord God sent him forth from the garden of Eden, to till the ground from whence he was taken.

24 So he drove out the man; and he placed at the east of the garden of Eden Cherubims, and a flaming sword which turned every way, to keep the way of the tree of life.

Isaiah 65:13, 19–25

13 Therefore thus saith the Lord God,

19 I will rejoice in Jerusalem, and joy in my people: and the voice of weeping shall be no more heard in her, nor the voice of crying.

20 There shall be no more thence an infant of days, nor an old man that hath not filled his days: for the child shall die an hundred years old; but the sinner being an hundred years old shall be accursed.

21 And they shall build houses, and inhabit them; and they shall plant vineyards, and eat the fruit of them.

22 They shall not build, and another inhabit; they shall not plant, and another eat: for as the days of a tree are the days of my people, and mine elect shall long enjoy the work of their hands.

23 They shall not labour in vain, nor bring forth for trouble; for they are the seed of the blessed of the Lord, and their offspring with them.

24 And it shall come to pass, that before they call, I will answer; and while they are yet speaking, I will hear.

25 The wolf and the lamb shall feed together, and the lion shall eat straw like the bullock: and dust shall be the serpent's meat. They shall not hurt nor destroy in all my holy mountain, saith the Lord.

Ecclesiastes 1:9–10

9 The thing that hath been, it is that which shall be; and that which is done is that which shall be done: and there is no new thing under the sun.

10 Is there any thing whereof it may be said, See, this is new? it hath been already of old time, which was before us.

NEW TESTAMENT

Matthew 13:16–17

16 But blessed are your eyes, for they see: and your ears, for they hear.

17 For verily I say unto you, That

many prophets and righteous men have desired to see those things which ye see, and have not seen them; and to hear those things which ye hear and have not heard them.

Hebrews 11:13–16; 32–40 (after mentioning Abel, Enoch, Noah, Abraham, and Sarah)

13 These all died in faith, not having received the promises, but having seen them afar off, and were persuaded of them, and embraced them, and confessed that they were strangers and pilgrims on the earth.

14 For they that say such things declare plainly that they seek a country.

15 And truly, if they had been mindful of that country from whence they came out, they might have had opportunity to have returned.

16 But now they desire a better country, that is, an heavenly: wherefore God is not ashamed to be called their God: for he hath prepared for them a city.

32 And what shall I more say? for the time would fail me to tell of Gedeon, and of Barak, and of Samson, and of Jephthæ; of David also, and Samuel, and of the prophets:

33 Who through faith subdued kingdoms, wrought righteousness, obtained promises, stopped the mouths of lions,

34 Quenched the violence of fire, escaped the edge of the sword, out of weakness were made strong, waxed valiant in fight, turned to flight the armies of the aliens.

35 Women received their dead raised to life again: and others were tortured, not accepting deliverance; that they might obtain a better resurrection:

36 And others had trial of cruel mockings and scourgings, yea, moreover of bonds and imprisonment:

37 They were stoned, they were sawn asunder, were tempted, were slain with the sword: they wandered about in sheepskins and goatskins; being destitute, afflicted, tormented;

38 (Of whom the world was not worthy:) they wandered in deserts, and in mountains, and in dens and caves of the earth.

39 And these all, having obtained a good report through faith, received not the promise:

40 God having provided some better things for us, that they without us should not be made perfect.

PROPHECY

Everyone in Old Testament times agreed that when the Lord spoke through one of his prophets he was to be obeyed. The snag was that false prophets existed and were not easily distinguished from true ones. Deuteronomy proposed testing on a sort of verification principle. The difficulty with this test was partly that it depended too much on just one aspect of prophecy (that of prediction), and partly that it yielded its verdict too late to be of much practical use.

In the meantime the prestige of prophecy was exploited shamelessly. The strong king Ahab of Israel kept a troop of four hundred prophets who could be relied on to prophesy in line with the king's wishes. The weak king Jehoshaphat of Judah, a reluctant ally, sought a different verdict elsewhere. A messenger was sent to fetch Micaiah (well known to Ahab as a prophet who said the wrong thing). The messenger tried to persuade even Micaiah to agree with the four hundred, but he refused to make prophecy subordinate to policy.

The true prophet always spoke under the compulsion of truth as he had seen it in his encounters with God. Often, as with Jeremiah, the message was as unwelcome to the prophet himself as it was to his hearers.

New Testament writers were happy to see Jesus as the fulfillment of Old Testament prophecy. Indeed, Jesus on one occasion seems to have taken considerable pains deliberately to fulfill a prophecy. This was his way of making clear just what kind of king he was and what kind of kingdom he preached—a very necessary clarification at a time when many Jews were looking for a military leader.

But prophecy was not thought to have ended with the fulfillment by Jesus of Old Testament hopes. It continued in the New Testament church and was valued by Paul far above the gift of ecstatic "speaking in tongues." This new kind of prophecy evidently had little to do with prediction (prediction never was the whole of prophecy, anyway) and much to do with the preaching of the fundamentals on which life could be built with security.

Today the place to look for prophecy in a newspaper is not the astrological column but the editorial. No doubt the incidence of false prophets is almost as high there as it was among Ahab's well-drilled prophetic squad, but the editorial task of analyzing events in order to find the fundamental principles involved is the essentially prophetic one. A certain amount of forecasting does result, but a true prophet could be wrong in his predictions for tomorrow and right in his interpretation of today. That is what counts.

The biblical view is that a prophecy which is politic and convenient and popular needs to be looked at with some suspicion. The view that is unexpected and challenging needs to be taken more seriously—especially if it springs from some bringing together of current events and ultimate reality.

And yet the truth of a prophetic voice is in no way established by the speaker's fervor, or by his going into a trance, or by any display of the paranormal. Nor is it established by the fact that he or she lives a long way off in the East or lived a long way back in the past. The only test is whether the prophet reveals the way things are and the way they are going. The fact that there are foundations on which life will stand—and others on which it will not—is what makes prophecy possible. The man or woman who can speak prophetically is the one whose vision embraces both ultimate purposes and immediate practicalities. This prophet's words may well be taken to be true now, and proved to be true in future.

PROPHECY

OLD TESTAMENT

Deuteronomy 18:21–22

21 And if thou say in thine heart, How shall we know the word which the Lord hath not spoken?

22 When a prophet speaketh in the name of the Lord, if the thing follow not, nor come to pass, that is the thing which the Lord hath not spoken, but the prophet hath spoken it presumptuously: thou shalt not be afraid of him.

1 Kings 22:4–8, 13–14

4 And he said unto Jehoshaphat, Wilt thou go with me to battle to Ramoth–gilead? And Jehoshaphat said to the king of Israel, I am as thou art, my people as thy people, my horses as thy horses.

5 And Jehoshaphat said unto the king of Israel, Inquire, I pray thee, at the word of the Lord to-day.

6 Then the king of Israel gathered the prophets together, about four hundred men, and said unto them, Shall I go against Ramoth–gilead to battle, or shall I forbear? And they said, Go up; for the Lord shall deliver it into the hand of the king.

7 And Jehoshaphat said, Is there not here a prophet of the Lord besides, that we might inquire of him?

8 And the king of Israel said unto Jehoshaphat, There is yet one man, Micaiah the son of Imlah, by whom we may inquire of the Lord; but I hate him; for he doth not prophesy good concerning me, but evil.

13 And the messenger that was gone to call Micaiah spake unto him, saying, Behold now, the words of the prophets declare good unto the king with one mouth: let thy word, I pray thee, be like the word of one of them, and speak that which is good.

14 And Micaiah said, As the Lord liveth, what the Lord saith unto me, that will I speak.

Jeremiah 23:16–18

16 Thus saith the Lord of hosts, Hearken not unto the words of the prophets that prophesy unto you: they make you vain: they speak a vision of their own heart, and not out of the mouth of the Lord.

17 They say still unto them that despise me, The Lord hath said, Ye shall have peace; and they say unto every one that walketh after the imagination of his own heart, No evil shall come upon you.

18 For who hath stood in the counsel of the Lord, and hath perceived and heard his word? who hath marked his word, and heard it?

Amos 3:8

8 The lion hath roared, who will not fear? the Lord God hath spoken, who can but prophesy?

NEW TESTAMENT

Matthew 21:1–5

1 And when they drew nigh unto Jerusalem, and were come to Beth-

phage, unto the mount of Olives, then sent Jesus two disciples,

2 Saying unto them, Go into the village over against you, and straightway ye shall find an ass tied, and a colt with her: loose them, and bring them unto me.

3 And if any man say aught unto you, ye shall say, The Lord hath need of them, and straightway he will send them.

4 All this was done, that it might be fulfilled which was spoken by the prophet, saying,

5 Tell ye the daughter of Sion, Behold, thy King cometh unto thee, meek, and sitting upon an ass, and a colt the foal of an ass.

Acts 3:18, 22, 24–25

18 But those things, which God before had shewed by the mouth of all his prophets, that Christ should suffer, he hath so fulfilled.

22 For Moses truly said unto the fathers, A prophet shall the Lord your God raise up unto you of your brethren, like unto me; him shall ye hear in all things whatsoever he shall say unto you.

24 Yea, and all the prophets from Samuel and those that follow after, as many as have spoken, have likewise foretold of these days.

25 Ye are the children of the prophets, and of the covenant which God made with our fathers.

1 Corinthians 14:1–5

1 Follow after charity, and desire spiritual gifts, but rather that ye may prophesy.

2 For he that speaketh in an unknown tongue speaketh not unto men, but unto God: for no man understandeth him; howbeit in the spirit he speaketh mysteries.

3 But he that prophesieth speaketh unto men to edification, and exhortation, and comfort.

4 He that speaketh in an unknown tongue edifieth himself; but he that prophesieth edifieth the church.

5 I would that ye all spake with tongues, but rather that ye prophesied.

PROVIDENCE

The Old Testament speaks of God as not only providing for the wants of all, but as deciding the course of every event. Even bad things are his responsibility (see Disaster). He is sovereign over all.

Yet just how he chooses to rule is a matter of some dispute. Joseph says to his brothers who had sold him into slavery, "Ye thought evil against me; but God meant it unto good" (Genesis 50:20). This suggests ruling by overruling: a purpose that prevails while other purposes work independently within it.

At least three views of providence are very clearly represented in the poetic-dialogue sections of the Book of Job. The first view is that of Job's friends, who

279

say that God controls events so as to reward the good with prosperity and punish the bad with suffering. Job, expressing the second view, denies that this is so, but implies that it ought to be. The voice of God in the closing chapters speaks only of the wonders of nature—and implies the third view: that providence is framed to a larger design than that of a meritocracy under which each would get his or her moral deserts.

The New Testament says that this supreme design is the making of sons: men and women in a personal relationship to God as Father. There is no suggestion that the course of nature and of history is therefore outside God's control. On the contrary, the fall of every sparrow is provided for within this purpose. But what matters is not so much that the Creator should control the course of every event as that his creative purpose should be forwarded through it—even in spite of it. The sun rises and the rain falls upon the just and the unjust, but for all that, the pattern of events is flexible enough to respond to asking, seeking, knocking. The world is providentially governed to favor the development of personal freedom and personal relationships.

Paul says that nothing which happens can "separate us from the love of God which is in Christ Jesus" (again see Disaster) and that the pains and sufferings of the creation are the birth pangs by which sonship to God is brought into the world. But even Paul's account of the grand design is followed by a reverently agnostic doxology in which he quotes twice from the Old Testament.

Not so many decades ago "Providence" was the standard reverential substitute for the word "God." "Trust to Providence," people said. They meant "trust God," but they especially meant "trust God to arrange everything for the best." The word went with the idea of God as the Super-Planner, ordaining and controlling every event. But this emphasis seems to have arisen as a backlash to scientific materialism and determinism. Some said, "Nothing is under the control of a personal God, and the mechanical operation of cause and effect is unalterable." In answer, the religious felt they had to say, "Everything is under the control of a personal God, and he intervenes all the time to make things happen the way he wants." An earlier and less rigid view was expressed by Shakespeare in *Hamlet* (act V, scene ii): "There's a divinity which shapes our ends, Rough-hew them how we will."

This view of providence as a purpose that prevails where it does not choose to control is more in harmony with both the view of God developed in the Bible and the view of the world developing in science. There is room for randomness, for accident, and for evil—but not for the frustration of creation's ultimate purpose. Providence does not mean that every event is arranged; it means that every contingency is provided for. Many hateful things happen. Sometimes human beings are responsible, sometimes not. But nothing has happened or can happen of which it would be true to say (on this view of all-pervasive providence) that no good can be wrested from it and that no good purpose can prevail over it.

Providence means that the universe is neither a random conjunction of accidents nor an inexorable system of inflexible laws. It serves a purpose, and that purpose has personality as its source and as its goal.

PROVIDENCE

OLD TESTAMENT

Psalm 145:9, 14–16

The Lord is good to all:
And his tender mercies are over all his
  works.
The Lord upholdeth all that fall,
And raiseth up all those that be bowed
  down.
The eyes of all wait upon thee;
And thou givest them their meat in due
  season.
Thou openest thine hand,
And satisfiest the desire of every living
  thing.

Psalm 66:5–7

Come and see the works of God:
He is terrible in his doing toward the
  children of men.
He turned the sea into dry land:
They went through the flood on foot:
There did we rejoice in him.
He ruleth by his power for ever;
His eyes behold the nations.

Job 16:1, 9, 16–17; 34:1; 35:12; 38:1–7

Then Job answered and said,

He teareth me in his wrath, who hateth
  me:
He gnasheth upon me with his teeth;
Mine enemy sharpeneth his eyes upon
  me.
My face is foul with weeping,
And on my eyelids is the shadow of death;

Not for any injustice in mine hands:
Also my prayer is pure.

Furthermore Elihu answered and said,

Job hath spoken without knowledge,
And his words were without wisdom.
Yea, surely God will not do wickedly,
Neither will the Almighty pervert judg-
  ment.

Then the Lord answered Job out of the whirlwind, and said,

Who is this that darkeneth counsel
By words without knowledge?
Gird up now thy loins like a man;
For I will demand of thee, and answer
  thou me.
Where wast thou when I laid the foun-
  dations of the earth?
Declare, if thou hast understanding.
Who hath laid the measures thereof, if
  thou knowest?
Or who hath stretched the line upon it?
Whereupon are the foundations thereof
  fastened?
Or who laid the corner stone thereof;
When the morning stars sang together,
And all the sons of God shouted for joy?

NEW TESTAMENT

Matthew 10:29–31; 7:7–8

29 Are not two sparrows sold for a farthing? and one of them shall not fall on the ground without your Father.

30 But the very hairs of your head are all numbered.

31 Fear ye not therefore, ye are of more value than many sparrows.

7 Ask, and it shall be given you; seek, and ye shall find; knock, and it shall be opened unto you:

8 For every one that asketh receiveth; and he that seeketh findeth; and to him that knocketh it shall be opened.

Romans 8:19, 22, 28–29; 11:33–36

19 For the earnest expectation of the creature waiteth for the manifestation of the sons of God.

22 For we know that the whole creation groaneth and travaileth in pain together until now.

28 And we know that all things work together for good to them that love God, to them who are the called according to his purpose.

29 For whom he did foreknow, he also did predestinate to be conformed to the image of his Son, that he might be the firstborn among many brethren.

33 O the depth of the riches both of the wisdom and knowledge of God! how unsearchable are his judgments, and his ways past finding out!

34 For who hath known the mind of the Lord? or who hath been his counsellor?

35 Or who hath first given to him, and it shall be recompensed unto him again?

36 For of him, and through him, and to him, are all things: to whom be glory for ever. Amen.

PUNISHMENT

The Old Testament recognizes two kinds of punishment administered by God. One is the retributive punishment that expresses God's abhorrence of evil. It is universal and virtually spontaneous. The meeting of holiness and iniquity is rather like the meeting of a naked flame with an explosive gas. According to the cautionary tales of the Old Testament, this punishment can strike a man dead or turn a woman to salt. God alone is justified in administering this kind of punishment. It is not a model for human beings to follow.

The other kind of punishment is disciplinary. God applies this only to his own people, and they are to copy it in their treatment of one another. For both God and man, disciplinary punishment is an active expression of love, not a withdrawal of love.

The New Testament affirms that disciplinary punishment is to be continued. It is administered by God, it is to be administered by the church, and it is even administered (with many lapses) by civil authorities who know nothing of God. Since both Jesus and Paul suffered unjust punishments at the hands of Roman officials, Paul's belief that secular punishments could normally be seen as instruments of God's rule was the more remarkable.

As to the more fundamental breach between holy God and sinful humanity, the New Testament writers believed that it had been healed. Christians need no longer fear retributive justice from God. The civil authorities' unjust punishment of Jesus, which he bore with such love, had opened a way past it. By identifying with Christ's death on the cross, the Christian could renounce egoism and embrace holiness, at least in principle. On this basis, punishment could be remitted and reconciliation achieved, since God deals with us not on the basis of what we have done or are, but in terms of what we have set our hearts on (see Righteousness).

Moreover, God's own action made this reconciliation possible. The New Testament sees Jesus as fulfilling the role of God's suffering servant in Isaiah 53, wherein it was said that "the chastisement of our peace was upon him"—in other words, he bore the punishment through which we could secure pardon.

In our time it is quite possible to picture a man who without hypocrisy preaches forgiveness on a Sunday morning, administers disciplinary punishment to his children on Sunday afternoon, and on Monday from a magistrate's bench sentences a criminal to the punishment provided by the state.

In his role as a preacher he will set no limit to mercy. He may even speak of Jesus as taking our punishment upon himself vicariously—a principle the law will not allow him to apply on Monday.

At home his discipline will have to be—and be seen to be—an expression of love. It will also have to be an expression of known law and not a venting of his own annoyance. He will administer punishment as one who is himself under discipline (see Discipline).

On the bench he will impose punishments that are in part disciplinary but that may also contain an element of secularized retribution insofar as society feels it must express its abhorrence of crime quite apart from the question of whether the punishment helps the criminal.

But he is one man, not three. Each of his roles must influence the others. Even in court his sentencing policy will be directed toward achieving the criminal's endorsement of the law as good rather than his submission to it for fear of punishment. When the goodness of what is right has been accepted, mercy can put aside punishment—but only because what punishment aims at has already been achieved.

PUNISHMENT

OLD TESTAMENT

Genesis 19:15–17, 24, 26

15 And when the morning arose, then the angels hastened Lot, saying, Arise, take thy wife, and thy two daughters, which are here; lest thou be consumed in the iniquity of the city.

16 And while he lingered, the men

laid hold upon his hand, and upon the hand of his wife, and upon the hand of his two daughters; the Lord being merciful unto him: and they brought him forth, and set him without the city.

17 And it came to pass, when they had brought them forth abroad, that he said, Escape for thy life; look not behind thee, neither stay thou in all the plain; escape to the mountain, lest thou be consumed.

24 Then the Lord rained upon Sodom and upon Gomorrah brimstone and fire from the Lord out of heaven;

26 But his wife looked back from behind him, and she became a pillar of salt.

Isaiah 13:9, 11

9 Behold, the day of the Lord cometh, cruel both with wrath and fierce anger, to lay the land desolate: and he shall destroy the sinners thereof out of it.

11 And I will punish the world for their evil, and the wicked for their iniquity; and I will cause the arrogancy of the proud to cease, and will lay low the haughtiness of the terrible.

Deuteronomy 8:5; 7:6

5 Thou shalt also consider in thine heart, that, as a man chasteneth his son, so the Lord thy God chasteneth thee.

6 For thou art an holy people unto the Lord thy God.

Proverbs 17:10; 23:13–14

A reproof entereth more into a wise man
Than an hundred stripes into a fool.
Withhold not correction from the child:
For if thou beatest him with the rod, he
  shall not die.
Thou shalt beat him with the rod,
And shalt deliver his soul from hell.

2 Samuel 7:8, 14–15

8 Now therefore so shalt thou say unto my servant David, Thus saith the Lord of hosts.

14 I will be his father, and he shall be my son. If he commit iniquity, I will chasten him with the rod of men, and with the stripes of the children of men:

15 But my mercy shall not depart away from him.

NEW TESTAMENT

John 18:29–31; 19:16

29 Pilate then went out unto them, and said, What accusation bring ye against this man?

30 They answered and said unto him, If he were not a malefactor, we would not have delivered him up unto thee.

31 Then said Pilate unto them, Take ye him, and judge him according to your law. The Jews therefore said unto him, It is not lawful for us to put any man to death.

16 Then delivered he him therefore unto them to be crucified.

Romans 6:8; 8:1

8 Now if we be dead with Christ, we believe that we shall also live with him:

1 There is therefore now no condemnation to them which are in Christ Jesus.

Hebrews 12:10–11

10 For they [our fathers] verily for a few days chastened us after their own pleasure; but he for our profit, that we might be partakers of his holiness.

11 Now no chastening for the present seemeth to be joyous, but grievous: nevertheless afterward it yieldeth the peaceable fruit of righteousness unto them which are exercised thereby.

Romans 13:3–5

3 For rulers are not a terror to good works, but to the evil. Wilt thou then not be afraid of the power? do that which is good, and thou shalt have praise of the same.

4 For he is the minister of God to thee for good. But if thou do that which is evil, be afraid; for he beareth not the sword in vain: for he is the minister of God, a revenger to execute wrath upon him that doeth evil.

5 Wherefore ye must needs be subject, not only for wrath, but also for conscience' sake.

James 2:12–13

12 So speak ye, and so do, as they that shall be judged by the law of liberty.

13 For he shall have judgment without mercy, that hath shewed no mercy; and mercy rejoiceth against judgment.

PURPOSE

At the time when Israel was suffering military defeat and exile, much Old Testament thinking was directed to the subject of purpose. It was felt that God has purposes, and human beings have purposes, and the trouble arises when these two do not coincide. In the long run, God's purposes will prevail, but in the short term, he does not prevent men and women from carrying out their own designs. On the contrary, God's tactic is to let men and women have their way. The distress that follows from pursuing these essentially alien goals will teach them to align their own purposes with the divine ones.

They will not then become puppets. Indeed, only then will they become truly free. But the purposes they will set themselves and will freely pursue will be in harmony with their own nature as defined by the purposes of God.

The New Testament provides the same picture of two wills or purposes at work in the world, the human and the divine. It adds that the divine purpose is made fully known and effective through Jesus. Those who pray, "thy kingdom come," are submitting themselves to it.

But this is again a liberating rather than an enslaving process. It may be, as it was with Jesus himself, that fidelity to the larger purpose will mean the yielding up of lesser ones—even of life itself. But this, Jesus says, is the way of fulfillment, while mere self-seeking defeats its own purpose. Within the great design there is room for a host of lesser purposes, each of them reflecting something of the larger plan. As Jesus moves toward death in the fulfillment of his own majestic purpose, he can be called aside to endorse and promote the lesser purposes of others, such as the two blind men on the road from Jericho to Jerusalem.

Purposeless people are people adrift—and unhappily adrift at that. Human nature works best when all its faculties are homing in on some goal. But if men and women picture the entire creation as purposeless, it is no wonder that their own lives become similarly disoriented.

Some very down-to-earth and everyday effects result from the biblical vision of eternal purpose. The Bible sees the world as neither a random display of accidents nor a rigid system of mechanical laws. Both randomness and law may be present, but the creation is designed to serve a purpose, and that purpose is the evolution of beings capable of having purposes of their own. Inevitably such free personalities may adopt wrong purposes—which means purposes hostile to their true nature as determined by the larger design that has called their freedom into being. In spite of this, the overall purpose goes forward. In fact men and women learn their true nature partly by pursuing goals that are alien to it, so the larger purpose goes forward in any event.

Such a picture makes getting up in the morning worthwhile even when the day ahead promises little gratification for the immediate appetites and ambitions that tend to take over when a sense of larger purpose is lacking. And, significantly, these lesser goals are the ones that are *not* freely chosen but are dictated by the selfish gene. The woman who submits to no outside will is actually less free than the one who does; the man who can contemplate laying down his life as a means of furthering a purpose larger than life is the truly free man.

Within the purpose that has been set for each of us, we will choose to adopt many lesser purposes. Some of them will be quite playful and trivial ones, but we can look for them to reflect in their miniature way the supreme intention to bring into being a network of loving relationships between free persons. Only if we can see things in this light will we set out to improve our golf handicap, to grow a better marrow, or to move up in the next round of promotions at work.

PURPOSE

OLD TESTAMENT

Isaiah 14:24–27

24 The Lord of hosts hath sworn, saying, Surely as I have thought, so shall it come to pass; and as I have purposed, so shall it stand:

25 That I will break the Assyrian in my land, and upon my mountains tread him under foot: then shall his yoke depart from off them, and his burden depart from off their shoulders.

26 This is the purpose that is purposed upon the whole earth: and this is the hand that is stretched out upon all the nations.

27 For the Lord of hosts hath purposed, and who shall disannul it? and his hand is stretched out, and who shall turn it back?

Psalm 81:11–12

But my people would not hearken to my voice;
And Israel would none of me.
So I gave them up unto their own hearts' lust:
And they walked in their own counsels.

Jeremiah 29:4, 10–14

4 Thus saith the Lord of hosts, the God of Israel, unto all that are carried away captives, whom I have caused to be carried away from Jerusalem unto Babylon;

10 That after seventy years be accomplished at Babylon I will visit you, and perform my good word toward you, in causing you to return to this place.

11 For I know the thoughts that I think toward you, saith the Lord, thoughts of peace, and not of evil, to give you an expected end.

12 Then shall ye call upon me, and ye shall go and pray unto me, and I will hearken unto you.

13 And ye shall seek me, and find me, when ye shall search for me with all your heart.

14 And I will be found of you, saith the Lord: and I will turn away your captivity, and I will gather you from all the nations, and from all the places whither I have driven you, saith the Lord; and I will bring you again into the place whence I caused you to be carried away captive.

NEW TESTAMENT

Luke 11:2

2 And he said unto them, When ye pray, say, Our Father which art in heaven, Hallowed be thy name. Thy kingdom come. . . .

John 6:38–40; 7:16–17; 8:32

38 For I came down from heaven, not to do mine own will, but the will of him that sent me.

39 And this is the Father's will which hath sent me, that of all which he hath given me I should lose nothing, but should raise it up again at the last day.

40 And this is the will of him that sent me, that every one which seeth

the Son, and believeth on him, may have everlasting life: and I will raise him up at the last day.

16 My doctrine is not mine, but his that sent me.

17 If any man will do his will, he shall know of the doctrine, whether it be of God, or whether I speak of myself.

32 And ye shall know the truth, and the truth shall make you free.

Matthew 16:24–25

24 Then said Jesus unto his disciples, If any man will come after me, let him deny himself, and take up his cross, and follow me.

25 For whosoever will save his life shall lose it: and whosoever will lose his life for my sake shall find it.

Matthew 20:29–34

29 And as they departed from Jericho, a great multitude followed him.

30 And, behold, two blind men sitting by the way side, when they heard that Jesus passed by, cried out, saying, Have mercy on us, O Lord, thou son of David.

31 And the multitude rebuked them, because they should hold their peace: but they cried the more, saying, Have mercy on us, O Lord, thou son of David.

32 And Jesus stood still, and called them, and said, What will ye that I shall do unto you?

33 They said unto him, Lord, that our eyes may be opened.

34 So Jesus had compassion on them, and touched their eyes: and immediately their eyes received sight, and they followed him.

Ephesians 1:9–12; 3:11

9 [God] having made known unto us the mystery of his will, according to his good pleasure which he hath purposed in himself:

10 That in the dispensation of the fulness of time he might gather together in one all things in Christ, both which are in heaven, and which are on earth; even in him:

11 In whom also we have obtained an inheritance, being predestinated according to the purpose of him who worketh all things after the counsel of his own will:

12 That we should be to the praise of his glory, who first trusted in Christ.

11 According to the eternal purpose which he purposed in Christ Jesus our Lord.

RECONCILIATION

The first Old Testament passage quoted here is a story of reconciliation after a long history of division. Laban had long been practicing low cunning on Jacob. Jacob had long been replying with what might be called a slightly higher cunning. Now Jacob had slipped away to return to his native land with his wives

("My daughters," said Laban) and his flocks ("Offspring of my animals," said Laban). Laban's pursuit has brought them together on neutral ground.

On that ground they are able to achieve a sufficient measure of reconciliation and to express it in the sharing of a meal and the building of a pillar that will stand as a reminder of the covenant between them. Probably all members of both clans would contribute a stone to the building of the cairn. The names of the tower meant "witness heap" (first in Aramaic and then in Hebrew) and also "watchtower," because it spoke of the God who watched over and was involved in the reconciliation of the two parties.

Where two are to be reconciled, a third is commonly required as mediator. In the reconciliation of Saul and David (which did not last) the role of mediator was played by Jonathan. In more enduring unions, God was the reconciler. Ezekiel's acted-out prophecy with two sticks would be thought of as actually initiating the divine action of bringing together and binding into one the long-divided kingdoms of Israel and Judah.

Jesus taught that reconciliation between human beings had priority even over the worship of God, but the whole New Testament projects onto the largest possible screen the classic three-sided pattern of reconciliation, and it sees Jesus as the reconciling agent between God and a whole world at odds with him. Jesus is said to provide in his own person the common ground on which estranged parties can meet: neighbor with neighbor, Jew with Gentile, man with God. The role of arbiter is a costly one. To love those who are divided is to be torn apart, but it is their identification with a reconciler's suffering that brings together those who have been divided. The cross stands as the symbol of all reconciliation as well as being for Jesus the literal cost of it.

Take any two factions at odds with each other. The choice is a wide one: the two partners in a broken marriage; the two groups of nations known (none too accurately) as the East and the West; the pro and the anti lobby on any issue; the two neighbors at loggerheads over some dispute concerning their properties; the two tribes facing each other within a community and brandishing their religious totems in hope of securing God's blessing on their bombs and bullets. All these are in need of the healing activity known as reconciliation.

The list is not only long but lengthening. At one time people on opposite sides of the world were not so much divided as merely separated. There was no connection between them. Now they are involved with each other enough to be actively divided. Without reconciliation they cannot even be themselves because they are locked into a crippling relationship of disharmony. Few lessons more desperately need to be learned than the technique of reconciliation.

According to the Bible reconciliation can begin when each party finds, outside the area of dispute, some piece of common ground on which to meet the other party. Most often this is provided by a third party who can relate to each of them. A dramatic symbol can play its part, too: perhaps Jews and Palestinians might someday build a cairn to mark a boundary and a covenant between them. More trivial divisions might yield to lighter treatment. In a suburban contretemps, for example, a third resident might interest both the embattled neighbors in a neighborhood sports club. This club, which stands outside the area of dispute, could provide the ground on which to build reconciliation.

Will this third neighbor be accused of interfering? Possibly. But the classic pattern of biblical reconciliation makes clear that the mediator's role is costly as well as necessary.

RECONCILIATION

OLD TESTAMENT

Genesis 31:25–26, 43–50

25 Then Laban overtook Jacob. Now Jacob had pitched his tent in the mount: and Laban with his brethren pitched in the mount of Gilead.

26 And Laban said to Jacob, What hast thou done, that thou hast stolen away unawares to me, and carried away my daughters, as captives taken with the sword?

43 These daughters are my daughters, and these children are my children, and these cattle are my cattle, and all that thou seest is mine: and what can I do this day unto these my daughters, and unto their children which they have born?

44 Now therefore come thou, let us make a covenant, I and thou; and let it be for a witness between me and thee.

45 And Jacob took a stone, and set it up for a pillar.

46 And Jacob said unto his brethren, Gather stones; and they took stones, and made an heap: and they did eat there upon the heap.

47 And Laban called it Jegar-sahadu-tha: but Jacob called it Galeed.

48 And Laban said, This heap is a witness between me and thee this day. Therefore was the name of it called Galeed;

49 And Mizpah; for he said, The Lord watch between me and thee, when we are absent one from another.

50 If thou shalt afflict my daughters, or if thou shalt take other wives beside my daughters, no man is with us; see, God is witness betwixt me and thee.

1 Samuel 19:1–2, 4–7

1 And Saul spake to Jonathan his son, and to all his servants, that they should kill David.

2 But Jonathan Saul's son delighted much in David:

4 And Jonathan spake good of David unto Saul his father, and said unto him, Let not the king sin against his servant, against David; because he hath not sinned against thee, and because his works have been to thee-ward very good:

5 For he did put his life in his hand, and slew the Philistine, and the Lord wrought a great salvation for all Israel: thou sawest it, and didst rejoice:

wherefore then wilt thou sin against innocent blood, to slay David without a cause?

6 And Saul hearkened unto the voice of Jonathan: and Saul sware, As the Lord liveth, he shall not be slain.

7 And Jonathan called David, and Jonathan shewed him all those things. And Jonathan brought David to Saul, and he was in his presence, as in times past.

Ezekiel 37:15–19

15 The word of the Lord came again unto me, saying,

16 Moreover, thou son of man, take thee one stick, and write upon it, For Judah, and for the children of Israel his companions: then take another stick, and write upon it, For Joseph, the stick of Ephraim, and for all the house of Israel his companions:

17 And join them one to another into one stick; and they shall become one in thine hand.

18 And when the children of thy people shall speak unto thee, saying, Wilt thou not shew us what thou meanest by these?

19 Say unto them, Thus saith the Lord God; Behold, I will take the stick of Joseph, which is in the hand of Ephraim, and the tribes of Israel his fellows, and will put them with him, even with the stick of Judah, and make them one stick, and they shall be one in mine hand.

NEW TESTAMENT

Matthew 5:23–24

23 Therefore if thou bring thy gift to the altar, and there rememberest that thy brother hath aught against thee;

24 Leave there thy gift before the altar, and go thy way; first be reconciled to thy brother, and then come and offer thy gift.

Ephesians 2:15–16, 18

15 Having abolished in his flesh the enmity, even the law of commandments contained in ordinances; for to make in himself of twain one new man, so making peace;

16 And that he might reconcile both unto God in one body by the cross, having slain the enmity thereby:

18 For through him we both have access by one Spirit unto the Father.

2 Corinthians 5:18–19

18 And all things are of God, who hath reconciled us to himself by Jesus Christ, and hath given to us the ministry of reconciliation;

19 To wit, that God was in Christ, reconciling the world unto himself, not imputing their trespasses unto them; and hath committed unto us the word of reconciliation.

1 Timothy 2:5

5 For there is one God, and one mediator between God and men, the man Christ Jesus.

1 Peter 3:8–9

8 Finally, be ye all of one mind, having compassion one of another, love as brethren, be pitiful, be courteous:

9 Not rendering evil for evil, or railing for railing: but contrariwise blessing.

291

REPENTANCE

In some modern translations of the Old Testament, human beings are said to "repent" whereas God is said to "relent." This is the correct modern usage of the words, but in the original Hebrew the same word was sometimes used for both man's change of heart and God's. In order to repent it was not always necessary to have sinned. How could sin be a prerequisite if God himself repented? The Hebrew word for "repent" denoted a change of course made in the light of altered circumstances.

Of course in humanity's case contrition was often called for. It could be individual or (as in the story of Ezra) corporate. But repentance was not so much a feeling of guilt as a practical change of attitude and action.

As such, repentance was part of the Old Testament's view of a highly flexible order of things. "What is done is done" was not the current philosophy. On the contrary, what is done can be undone, redone, done differently, or canceled out as if it had never been done at all. Even the seemingly irresistible course of history could be diverted by a change of heart. Man could repent, God would relent, and a fresh start would be made.

The New Testament contains not only renewed calls to repentance—from John, from Jesus, from Peter, from Paul, from just about every preacher in the book—but more strikingly a renewed assurance that such a change of direction (or change of mind, to give the New Testament Greek word for repentance its literal meaning) could totally transform the human condition. Forgiveness, purification, a fresh start in a new world were all possible consequences.

Jesus was often in trouble for keeping bad company, but he said this was just the company that needed his message. His mission was to those who could be made to see the need for a change of course.

"Repentance" sounds like a word that belongs to the dark side of religion, a word that could well be discarded by a generation which has learned to think of guilt as just a psychological affliction to be cured by self-knowledge. In fact, "repentance" is one of the most optimistic words in the Bible. Its context is invariably a hopeful one. It says not only that you are free to change your mind and your ways but also that your environment will respond to your doing so.

Certainly feelings of contrition and the acknowledgment of faults can be part of the process of repentance. There is a sense of guilt that is spiritually correct, as well as a guilt complex that is psychologically wrong. Man is a responsible being and is only belittled by the view that nothing is his own fault and his personal responsibility. What enables him to remain both responsible and hopeful is the assurance that to acknowledge his fault is to open the door to a radical process of change.

It also helps if he can lay hold of the Biblical emphasis in both Hebrew and Greek on repentance as not so much a feeling as an act. The true opposite of repentance is obstinacy. The right symbol for the impenitent man is the mule. He is the man who goes doggedly on along the line he has adopted even when it is clearly the wrong one. He has no belief in the feasibility of change. Perhaps he is bemused by the very unbiblical picture of the world as an inflexible system of cause and effect, or by the equally unbiblical picture of it as a moralistic trial in which every fault is indelibly recorded.

The more flexible and biblical attitude to life is a far more cheerful one. If things have gone wrong, the real answer is not a sedative—still less an overdose. The biblical recommendation to those who have fallen flat on their faces is to pick themselves up, dust themselves off (an almost biblical image of contrition), and start again in a different direction. Perhaps it is good that we are using here the old King James Version of the Old Testament in which the subject of the verb "to repent" is usually "God."

REPENTANCE

OLD TESTAMENT

Jeremiah 18:7–10

7 At what instant I shall speak concerning a nation, and concerning a kingdom, to pluck up, and to pull down, and to destroy it;

8 If that nation, against whom I have pronounced, turn from their evil, I will repent of the evil that I thought to do unto them.

9 And at what instant I shall speak concerning a nation, and concerning a kingdom, to build and to plant it;

10 If it do evil in my sight, that it obey not my voice, then I will repent of the good, wherewith I said I would benefit them.

Joel 2:13–14

13 And rend your heart, and not your garments, and turn unto the Lord your God: for he is gracious and merciful, slow to anger, and of great kindness, and repenteth him of the evil.

14 Who knoweth if he will return and repent, and leave a blessing behind him; even a meat offering and a drink offering unto the Lord your God?

Ezra 9:3–6

3 And when I heard this thing, I rent my garment and my mantle, and plucked off the hair of my head and of my beard, and sat down astonied.

4 Then were assembled unto me every one that trembled at the words of the God of Israel, because of the transgression of those that had been carried away; and I sat astonied until the evening sacrifice.

5 And at the evening sacrifice I arose up from my heaviness; and having rent my garment and my mantle, I fell upon my knees, and spread out my hands unto the Lord my God,

6 And said, O my God, I am ashamed and blush to lift up my face to thee, my God: for our iniquities are increased over our head, and our trespass is grown up unto the heavens.

Job 42:5–6

I have heard of thee by the hearing of the
   ear:
But now mine eye seeth thee.
Wherefore I abhor myself, and repent
In dust and ashes.

NEW TESTAMENT

Matthew 3:1–2, 7–8, 11

1 In those days came John the Baptist, preaching in the wilderness of
Judæa,

2 And saying, Repent ye: for the
kingdom of heaven is at hand.

7 But when he saw many of the
Pharisees and Sadducees come to his
baptism, he said unto them, O generation of vipers, who hath warned you
to flee from the wrath to come?

8 Bring forth therefore fruits meet
for repentance:

11 I indeed baptize you with water
unto repentance: but he that cometh
after me is mightier than I, whose shoes
I am not worthy to bear: he shall baptize you with the Holy Ghost, and with
fire.

Mark 2:16–17

16 And when the scribes and Pharisees saw him eat with publicans and
sinners, they said unto his disciples,
How is it that he eateth and drinketh
with publicans and sinners?

17 When Jesus heard it, he saith
unto them, They that are whole have
no need of the physician, but they that
are sick: I came not to call the righteous, but sinners to repentance.

Luke 15:8–10

8 Either what woman having ten
pieces of silver, if she lose one piece,
doth not light a candle, and sweep the
house, and seek diligently till she find
it?

9 And when she hath found it, she
calleth her friends and her neighbours
together, saying, Rejoice with me; for
I have found the piece which I had
lost.

10 Likewise, I say unto you, there
is joy in the presence of the angels of
God over one sinner that repenteth.

Acts 17:30

30 And the times of this ignorance
God winked at; but now commandeth
all men everywhere to repent.

1 John 1:8–9

8 If we say that we have no sin, we
deceive ourselves, and the truth is not
in us.

9 If we confess our sins, he is faithful and just to forgive us our sins, and
to cleanse us from all unrighteousness.

RESURRECTION

The Old Testament does not believe that a human life can be altogether
extinguished, but that is a very different thing from believing in resurrection.

Sheol, the abode of the dead, was generally thought to be a meaningless place from which there was no return to real life.

A few choice beings such as Enoch and Elijah were believed to have been spared going to sheol at all, and such a man might even restore life to one who had died. These, however, were only examples of death delayed or evaded. Real resurrection from the dead appears in only a few Old Testament texts such as the one from the Book of Daniel quoted here.

Yet the Old Testament lays the foundations for a belief in resurrection by its repeated affirmation that life is essentially renewable. Ezekiel, for instance, uses resurrection language to speak of the whole nation's being restored to life and vigor (see the prophecy of the dry bones under Hope). Or again, to sin and be forgiven is to experience a kind of resurrection: God is he "Who forgiveth all thine iniquities; who healeth all thy diseases; who redeemeth thy life from destruction; who crowneth thee with loving kindness and tender mercies" (Psalm 103:3–4). Faith in a God who will not allow his purposes to be frustrated was forcing men and women toward a belief in resurrection: "God will redeem my soul from the power of the grave: for he shall receive me" (Psalm 49:15).

By New Testament times only the diehard Sadducees still disbelieved in resurrection, and Jesus argued against them that God's personal relationship with the patriarchs of old made it impossible to think of them as eternally separated from God: "He is not a God of the dead, but of the living: for all live unto him" (Luke 20:38).

Like Elijah, Jesus was reported to have recalled the dead to life—most dramatically in the story of Lazarus, the brother of Martha and Mary. Jesus' own resurrection, however, was regarded as something altogether different. His death was not delayed or evaded: it was met and defeated, never to return.

The significance of Jesus' resurrection is explored throughout the New Testament. It was a vindication of all that Jesus had said and done. It was a token of what for others was still to come, for he rose as "the first fruits of them that slept" (1 Corinthians 15:20). Speculative questions about the form of that experience were dismissed by Paul with a peremptory "Fool!" (1 Corinthians 15:36).

Resurrection, however, is not treated in the New Testament as something that can be experienced only beyond death. It is seen as a quality of life that can be appropriated at once and will immediately influence every facet of behavior. "If ye be risen with Christ," says Paul in Colossians 3, and immediately goes on to describe in detail the characteristics of resurrection life as it is lived here and now.

Is it true that life can be caught up into a force that makes it indestructible? More is at stake than a belief in life after death, though that would be plenty. The biblical view of resurrection is an affirmation about the nature of all human life and of the world itself. It says that we are part of a system in which renewal is always a possibility. The laws of entropy do not have the last word. It is not true that everything is perpetually running down so that it must all end in decay and death. Life is a renewable resource.

The man or woman who believes in resurrection in this broad, biblical sense will neither cling to existing forms and institutions nor readily write them off: he or she will be prepared for them to rise again and to assume a new embodiment for the purpose. This belief has sociological as well as personal consequences. All that and heaven too!

RESURRECTION

OLD TESTAMENT

1 Kings 17:17–23

17 And it came to pass after these things, that the son of the woman, the mistress of the house, fell sick; and his sickness was so sore, that there was no breath left in him.

18 And she said unto Elijah, What have I to do with thee, O thou man of God? art thou come unto me to call my sin to remembrance, and to slay my son?

19 And he said unto her, Give me thy son. And he took him out of her bosom, and carried him up into a loft, where he abode, and laid him upon his own bed.

20 And he cried unto the Lord, and said, O Lord my God, hast thou also brought evil upon the widow with whom I sojourn, by slaying her son?

21 And he stretched himself upon the child three times, and cried unto the Lord, and said, O Lord my God, I pray thee, let this child's soul come into him again.

22 And the Lord heard the voice of Elijah; and the soul of the child came into him again, and he revived.

23 And Elijah took the child, and brought him down out of the chamber into the house, and delivered him unto his mother: and Elijah said, See, thy son liveth.

Psalm 6:5; 88:10–12

For in death there is no remembrance of
   thee:
In the grave who shall give thee thanks?
Wilt thou shew wonders to the dead?
Shall the dead arise and praise thee?
Shall thy lovingkindness be declared in
   the grave?
Or thy faithfulness in destruction?
Shall thy wonders be known in the dark?
And thy righteousness in the land of
   forgetfulness?

Daniel 12:2

2 And many of them that sleep in the dust of the earth shall awake, some to everlasting life, and some to shame and everlasting contempt.

NEW TESTAMENT

Luke 7:11–15

11 And it came to pass the day after, that he went into a city called Nain;

and many of his disciples went with him, and much people.

12 Now when he came nigh to the gate of the city, behold, there was a dead man carried out, the only son of his mother, and she was a widow: and much people of the city was with her.

13 And when the Lord saw her, he had compassion on her, and said unto her, Weep not.

14 And he came and touched the bier: and they that bare him stood still. And he said, Young man, I say unto thee, Arise.

15 And he that was dead sat up, and began to speak. And he delivered him to his mother.

John 11:23–26

23 Jesus saith unto her, Thy brother shall rise again.

24 Martha saith unto him, I know that he shall rise again in the resurrection at the last day.

25 Jesus said unto her, I am the resurrection, and the life: he that believeth in me, though he were dead, yet shall he live:

26 And whosoever liveth and believeth in me shall never die.

Mark 16:1–6

1 And when the sabbath was past, Mary Magdalene, and Mary the mother of James, and Salome, had bought sweet spices, that they might come and anoint [the body of Jesus].

2 And very early in the morning the first day of the week, they came unto the sepulchre at the rising of the sun.

3 And they said among themselves, Who shall roll us away the stone from the door of the sepulchre?

4 And when they looked, they saw that the stone was rolled away: for it was very great.

5 And entering into the sepulchre, they saw a young man sitting on the right side, clothed in a long white garment; and they were affrighted.

6 And he saith unto them, Be not affrighted: Ye seek Jesus of Nazareth, which was crucified: he is risen; he is not here: behold the place where they laid him.

1 Corinthians 15:3–8, 12–14

3 For I delivered unto you first of all that which I also received, how that Christ died for our sins according to the scriptures;

4 And that he was buried, and that he rose again the third day according to the scriptures:

5 And that he was seen of Cephas, then of the twelve:

6 After that, he was seen of above five hundred brethren at once; of whom the greater part remain unto this present, but some are fallen asleep.

7 After that, he was seen of James; then of all the apostles.

8 And last of all he was seen of me also, as of one born out of due time.

12 Now if Christ be preached that he rose from the dead, how say some among you that there is no resurrection of the dead?

13 But if there be no resurrection of the dead, then is Christ not risen:

14 And if Christ be not risen, then is our preaching vain, and your faith is also vain.

REVERENCE

In the Old Testament reverence is above all reverence for God. His very name was too holy to be spoken. Even when passages from the Bible came to be read in synagogue worship, a word meaning Lord had to be substituted for the sacred name Jahweh (said by some to be derived from the Hebrew for "I am"). In most English translations old and new this substitution is still made with LORD in small capitals to distinguish it from "Lord" in ordinary upper and lower type when the original has "Adonai."

This reverence for God spilled over into respect for all that was attached to him: the law, the Sabbath, the priesthood, the temple. And not only that: parents had to be treated with respect because God set them in authority over their children, and the world had to be revered because God made it. All of these received a measure of reverence only because of their association with God. All the veneration they received was intended to pass through them to God himself. For it to stop short would be idolatry.

Reverence for God undoubtedly contained an element of fear—chiefly that deep-rooted dread of the numinous, the feeling of awe before that which is altogether other than we are. But there was more to reverence than that. It was joy, too. And it always demanded a life of simple goodness rather than an attitude of abject prostration before the holy.

Jesus, however, encountered in New Testament times people who had systematized and classified the sacred so that reverence was in danger of becoming, for them, a mechanical obedience to regulations. This seems to have been behind his attack on those who considered some oaths binding and others not, according to the degree of holiness attributed to the thing sworn by. Nothing is ultimately holy except God, and anything that connects us with him derives from that contact enough holiness to demand reverence.

In the parable of the tenants, those who refused to give the son their respect serve as a metaphor for all who break the connection between the ultimate object of reverence and that which conveys it to us. As Paul said in a slightly different context (Romans 11:16), "if the root be holy, so are the branches."

Totally to withhold reverence (or its secular equivalent, respect) in the interests of democratic equality has enjoyed something of a vogue. As a principle, a case could even be made for this refusal to show reverence, but the principle is rarely applied consistently. There seems to be in humanity an instinct for reverence. People need to look up to something. Dethroning one object of awe appears only to leave a vacuum that human nature abhors. All too soon a new (and not often a better) god takes the vacant throne. To withhold reverence from its traditional objects and give it instead to film stars, or to pop singers, or to wealth, or to muscle is hardly progress.

What is needed is not a prescribed classification of things to be reverenced or respected, but a capacity to respond to anything and everything that reflects ultimate goodness, beauty, and truth—however imperfectly. To revere the right things for the right reasons, and to see through them and beyond them to the source of that rightness, is humanly healthy.

When Albert Schweitzer spoke of "reverence for life" he extended the idea in a direction to which the Bible was already pointing. If there is sacredness at the center of things, then everything is sacred. If there is nothing to be reverenced at the heart of reality, then nothing is sacred. The consequences of a belief that nothing deserves reverence would not be felt only in the realm of religion. All life would be affected—and belittled.

REVERENCE

OLD TESTAMENT

Exodus 3:13–15

13 And Moses said unto God, Behold, when I come unto the children of Israel, and shall say unto them, The God of your fathers hath sent me unto you; and they shall say to me, What is his name? what shall I say unto them?

14 And God said unto Moses, I AM THAT I AM: and he said, Thus shalt thou say unto the children of Israel, I AM hath sent me unto you.

15 And God said moreoever unto Moses, Thus shalt thou say unto the children of Israel, The Lord God of your fathers, the God of Abraham, the God of Isaac, and the God of Jacob, hath sent me unto you: this is my name for ever, and this is my memorial unto all generations.

Deuteronomy 28:58–59

58 If thou wilt not observe to do all the words of this law that are written in this book, that thou mayest fear this glorious and fearful name, THE LORD THY GOD;

59 Then the Lord will make thy plagues wonderful, and the plagues of thy seed, even great plagues, and of long continuance, and sore sicknesses.

Leviticus 26:1–2

1 Ye shall make you no idols nor graven image, neither rear you up a standing image, neither shall ye set up any image of stone in your land, to bow down unto it: for I am the Lord your God.

2 Ye shall keep my sabbaths, and reverence my sanctuary: I am the Lord.

Psalm 5:3–4, 7

My voice shalt thou hear in the morning, O Lord;
In the morning will I direct my prayer unto thee, and will look up.
For thou art not a God that hath pleasure in wickedness:
Neither shall evil dwell with thee.
But as for me, I will come into thy house in the multitude of thy mercy:

And in thy fear will I worship toward thy holy temple.

Isaiah 59:19

19 So shall they fear the name of the Lord from the west, and his glory from the rising of the sun.

NEW TESTAMENT

Matthew 23:16–22

16 Woe unto you, ye blind guides, which say, Whosoever shall swear by the temple, it is nothing; but whosoever shall swear by the gold of the temple, he is a debtor!

17 Ye fools and blind: for whether is greater, the gold, or the temple that sanctifieth the gold?

18 And, Whosoever shall swear by the altar, it is nothing; but whosoever sweareth by the gift that is upon it, he is guilty.

19 Ye fools and blind: for whether is greater, the gift, or the altar that sanctifieth the gift?

20 Whoso therefore shall swear by the altar, sweareth by it, and by all things thereon.

21 And whoso shall swear by the temple, sweareth by it, and by him that dwelleth therein.

22 And he that shall swear by heaven, sweareth by the throne of God, and by him that sitteth thereon.

Luke 20:9–16

9 Then began he to speak to the people this parable; A certain man planted a vineyard, and let it forth to husbandmen, and went into a far country for a long time.

10 And at the season he sent a servant to the husbandmen, that they should give him of the fruit of the vineyard: but the husbandmen beat him, and sent him away empty.

11 And again he sent another servant: and they beat him also, and entreated him shamefully, and sent him away empty.

12 And again he sent a third: and they wounded him also, and cast him out.

13 Then said the lord of the vineyard, What shall I do? I will send my beloved son: it may be they will reverence him when they see him.

14 But when the husbandmen saw him, they reasoned among themselves, saying, This is the heir: come, let us kill him, that the inheritance may be ours.

15 So they cast him out of the vineyard, and killed him. What therefore shall the lord of the vineyard do unto them?

16 He shall come and destroy these husbandmen, and shall give the vineyard to others. And when they heard it they said, God forbid.

Hebrews 12:28–29

28 Wherefore we receiving a kingdom which cannot be moved, let us have grace, whereby we may serve God acceptably with reverence and godly fear:

29 For our God is a consuming fire.

RIGHT

The Old Testament does not think much of the man who is "right in his own eyes." It has much more objective standards. King after king had his life assessed in the same way: either he did or did not do "what was right in the eyes of the Lord." God's law was the supreme definition of rightness, and this rightness was built into the very structure of the universe. Two things followed.

One was that the right could not be ignored with impunity. A natural connection existed between right behavior and well-being—not that right behavior was a guarantee of individual peace and prosperity; the story of Job disproved that. But written into the nature of things there was believed to be a right way to live and a right way to use the world. Human life could be lived properly on no other terms. The man who tried it was a "fool"—that is, he was wrong in both his thinking and his behavior. Intellectual rightness and moral rightness amounted to the same thing.

The other consequence resulting from the objective reality of the right was that everybody had "rights." The king who disregarded the just claims of the people could not argue that "What I say is right just because I am the one who is saying it." The people could (and the prophets did) appeal over the king's head to the divine law. Their rights were grounded in standards of right and wrong that could not be altered to suit the convenience of those in power.

The New Testament insists equally strongly on the objective reality of the right, only stressing that what matters is an inward correspondence to the heart of the law rather than an outward conformity to its details. And rightness was still seen to be a matter both of doing right and of thinking right. Goodness (that which is morally right) and truth (that which is intellectually right) were inseparable. The lawyer who engaged Jesus in dialogue was right in the sense that his reply was correct (literally "upright") and also right in the sense that the rule he put forward was just. On these lines life works: "Do this and you will live."

The New Testament, however, had to face the fact that Jesus himself did this and died—ignominiously. To be right is no guarantee of success by any ordinary definition of the term. The might that goes with right is the ultimate power, but it is not a force that can be harnessed to take us where we wish to go. Those who put themselves under the rule of the right and good must do so without reservations or conditions. The New Testament, like the Old, is sure that the right will prevail, and the Christians of the New Testament were prepared to defy authority on that basis—but where, when, and how right would prevail remained a mystery that the Christians did not think they were meant to resolve.

The English word "right" covers a multitude of meanings: my opinion is right; he did right; human rights—not to mention right as opposed to left. The ambiguity is no accident. All these meanings grow from the same stock. To get the sum right and to do right are both ways of falling in line with the facts. They are forms of obedience to the way things are. One is intellectual, and the other is moral, but both imply that there is a reality outside us with which we do well to harmonize intellectually and morally.

And that reality, that order which provides the norms of truth and goodness, is where our rights are rooted. If they were given by statute, they could be taken away by statute. We can say that this would be a wrong thing to do only because there is an objective standard of rightness against which all conduct can be measured. To think the truth (i.e., to be right), to act justly (to be righteous), and to have a just claim (to have rights) are all ways of relating correctly to an underlying order of things that is given—and that will prevail.

RIGHT

OLD TESTAMENT

Proverbs 14:12

There is a way which seemeth right unto a man,
But the end thereof are the ways of death.

Isaiah 45:19

19 I the Lord speak righteousness, I declare things that are right.

Psalm 1:1–3

Blessed is the man that walketh not in the counsel of the ungodly,
Nor standeth in the way of sinners,
Nor sitteth in the seat of the scornful.
But his delight is in the law of the Lord;
And in his law doth he meditate day and night.
And he shall be like a tree planted by the rivers of water,
That bringeth forth his fruit in his season.

2 Kings 22:2

2 And he [Josiah] did that which was right in the sight of the Lord, and walked in all the way of David his father, and turned not aside to the right hand or to the left.

Isaiah 10:1–2

1 Woe unto them that decree unrighteous decrees, and that write grievousness which they have prescribed;
2 To turn aside the needy from judgment, and to take away the right from the poor of my people, that widows may be their prey, and that they may rob the fatherless!

Job 16:11–12, 16–17; 23:11–12

God hath delivered me to the ungodly,
And turned me over into the hands of the wicked.
I was at ease, but he hath broken me asunder:
He hath also taken me by my neck, and shaken me to pieces,
My face is foul with weeping,
And on my eyelids is the shadow of death;
Not for any injustice in mine hands:
Also my prayer is pure.
My foot hath held his steps,
His way have I kept, and not declined.

Neither have I gone back from the commandment of his lips;
I have esteemed the words of his mouth more than my necessary food.

NEW TESTAMENT

Luke 10:25–28

25 And, behold, a certain lawyer stood up, and tempted him, saying, Master, what shall I do to inherit eternal life?

26 He said unto him, What is written in the law? how readest thou?

27 And he answering said, Thou shalt love the Lord thy God with all thy heart, and with all thy soul, and with all thy strength, and with all thy mind; and thy neighbour as thyself.

28 And he said unto him, Thou hast answered right: this do, and thou shalt live.

Matthew 23:23–24

23 Woe unto you, scribes and Pharisees, hypocrites! for ye pay tithe of mint and anise and cummin, and have omitted the weightier matters of the law, judgment, mercy, and faith: these ought ye to have done, and not to leave the other undone.

24 Ye blind guides, which strain at a gnat, and swallow a camel.

John 8:15–16

15 Ye judge after the flesh; I judge no man.

16 And yet if I judge, my judgment is true: for I am not alone, but I and the Father that sent me.

Acts 4:18–20

18 And they called them [Peter and John], and commanded them not to speak at all nor teach in the name of Jesus.

19 But Peter and John answered and said unto them, Whether it be right in the sight of God to hearken unto you more than unto God, judge ye.

20 For we cannot but speak the things which we have seen and heard.

1 John 2:3–6

3 And hereby we do know that we know him, if we keep his commandments.

4 He that saith, I know him, and keepeth not his commandments, is a liar, and the truth is not in him.

5 But whoso keepeth his word, in him verily is the love of God perfected: hereby know we that we are in him.

6 He that saith he abideth in him ought himself also so to walk, even as he walked.

RIGHTEOUSNESS

To be righteous means in the Old Testament to correspond to a norm, and the Old Testament norm is God. The righteous live by the law that flows from the nature of God. Their way of life is not necessarily a moral achievement on the part of the righteous. They certainly need not feel smug about it. But they are in fact living in a way that works. A plant growing in the right soil would have the same experience.

Some people in Old Testament times thought of peace and prosperity not as the natural (and therefore widely dispersed) fruits of righteousness, but as prizes individually awarded for good conduct. Job and the writer of Ecclesiastes challenged that view. A righteous man could suffer; an unrighteous one might prosper. Nevertheless, the norm remained. Righteousness was to be pursued because it was right, not because it paid.

One day, it was hoped, righteousness would be perfectly embodied, but before that could happen a new order would have to come about—a new kind of Israel under a new kind of king.

New Testament writers claimed to have seen this "Righteous One"—the "Holy One and the Just," as Peter said in his sermon (Acts 3:14). But they now understood that such righteousness is well beyond human achievement. The best that men and women can do is hunger for it. According to Jesus that would be enough. To receive the rewards of righteousness you do not have to *be* good; you simply have to identify with goodness. To see it, recognize it, welcome it: that is enough to put you in line for receiving righteousness as a gift. To some who "trusted in themselves that they were righteous" Jesus told a seemingly scandalous story about a man who was justified (that is, pronounced righteous) simply on the ground of his penitence and love—and in preference to a man who was the very epitome of self-proclaimed goodness.

Paul was giving no new twist to Christianity when he taught that the true righteousness by which we live in harmony with God is never our own: it is a gift bestowed by grace and received by faith. Certainly good actions will follow, but they are the natural result of being at peace with God, not a condition for receiving that peace. To have faith in Christ is to be oriented toward the true norm, and that is to be justified. In the Greek of the New Testament the word "justified," whether in the parable of Jesus or in a letter from Paul, is at root the word "righteous."

The first bit of good news for modern men and women is that there *are* norms. We do not have to make up our own standards of good and bad, right and wrong. Some modern apostles of freedom rather gave the impression that we did. Young people in particular found that a great burden. Mostly they borrowed someone else's standards; that was easier than devising their own. But since all standards were thought to be relative and changeable, people found it difficult to live by them with confidence.

Well, according to the Bible, standards are not all relative and changeable. Their embodiment in codes and laws and moralities may be rough and tentative, but an underlying reality of righteousness exists, and it is fixed and certain. That is quite a relief.

And it is good news, too, that our value and acceptability are not limited to our small measure of success in living up to that perfection. Moralists may be alarmed by the idea that a loved ideal is a more important indicator of righteousness than any actually achieved level of conventional goodness, but moralism is not very biblical. Your true righteousness is where your heart is. It is the object of faith and love rather than the measure of ethical success already arrived at. Biblical righteousness has nothing to do with self-righteousness.

RIGHTEOUSNESS

OLD TESTAMENT

Psalm 119:137–138, 160

Righteous art thou, O Lord,
And upright are thy judgments.
Thy testimonies that thou hast commanded are righteous
And very faithful.
Thy word is true from the beginning:
And every one of thy righteous judgments endureth for ever.

Psalm 92:12–13

The righteous shall flourish like the palm tree:
He shall grow like a cedar in Lebanon.
Those that be planted in the house of the Lord
Shall flourish in the courts of our God.

Job 29:14; 30:25–26

I put on righteousness, and it clothed me:
My judgment was as a robe and a diadem.
Did not I weep for him that was in trouble?
Was not my soul grieved for the poor?
When I looked for good, then evil came unto me:
And when I waited for light, there came darkness.

Ecclesiastes 7:15

15 All things have I seen in the days of my vanity: there is a just man that perisheth in his righteousness, and there is a wicked man that prolongeth his life in his wickedness.

Isaiah 11:1, 3–5

1 And there shall come forth a rod out of the stem of Jesse, and a Branch shall grow out of his roots.

3 He shall not judge after the sight of his eyes, neither reprove after the hearing of his ears:

4 But with righteousness shall he judge the poor, and reprove with equity for the meek of the earth:

5 And righteousness shall be the girdle of his loins, and faithfulness the girdle of his reins.

NEW TESTAMENT

Matthew 5:6, 20

6 Blessed are they which do hunger and thirst after righteousness: for they shall be filled.

20 For I say unto you, That except your righteousness shall exceed the

righteousness of the scribes and Pharisees, ye shall in no case enter into the kingdom of heaven.

Matthew 10:40–41

40 He that receiveth you receiveth me, and he that receiveth me receiveth him that sent me.

41 He that receiveth a prophet in the name of a prophet shall receive a prophet's reward; and he that receiveth a righteous man in the name of a righteous man shall receive a righteous man's reward.

Luke 18:9–14

9 And he spake this parable unto certain which trusted in themselves that they were righteous, and despised others:

10 Two men went up into the temple to pray; the one a Pharisee, and the other a publican.

11 The Pharisee stood and prayed thus with himself, God, I thank thee, that I am not as other men are, extortioners, unjust, adulterers, or even as this publican.

12 I fast twice in the week, I give tithes of all that I possess.

13 And the publican, standing afar off, would not lift up so much as his eyes unto heaven, but smote upon his breast, saying, God be merciful to me a sinner.

14 I tell you, this man went down to his house justified rather than the other: for every one that exalteth himself shall be abased; and he that humbleth himself shall be exalted.

Romans 3:21–24; 6:13

21 But now the righteousness of God without the law is manifested, being witnessed by the law and the prophets;

22 Even the righteousness of God which is by faith of Jesus Christ unto all and upon all them that believe: for there is no difference:

23 For all have sinned, and come short of the glory of God;

24 Being justified freely by his grace through the redemption that is in Christ Jesus.

13 Yield yourselves unto God, as those that are alive from the dead, and your members as instruments of righteousness unto God.

SACRIFICE

"I desire mercy, and not sacrifice" (Hosea 6:6) was a characteristic cry delivered by the Old Testament prophets in God's behalf. But mercy and sacrifice should never have become alternatives to each other. A whole variety of sacrificial acts could be required of a faithful Israelite: some involved killing an animal, some did not; some expressed thankfulness, some penitence, some communion—but none of them was said to put the offerer right with God regardless of his personal attitude. Justice and mercy were required as well, not instead.

That is not to say that the prophets were complaining unnecessarily. They knew that, all too likely, people would come to think of sacrifice as a way of buying God off, a system for making it all right to do wrong, but that was never Old Testament teaching. Even the "sin offering" related only to accidental breaches of a ritual requirement. It had nothing to do with deliberate wrongdoing.

The prophetic denunciations doubtless hit many a target, but they passed by the man who reverently laid his hands on the head of the finest lamb in his flock and then released its life so that he and his family and his God might have fellowship in that unspoiled life as it passed back to its maker.

The sacrifice offered by Joseph and Mary after the birth of Jesus was appropriate to a family that could not afford to offer a year-old lamb. Sacrifice was still a very real form of devotion in Israel, though it ended with the destruction of the temple in A.D. 70.

By then the followers of Jesus had developed a different attitude. They taught that much of what sacrifice symbolized could be expressed directly from the human heart. For the rest, the perfect expression of absolute dedication was not a slaughtered animal but the story of Jesus himself. Inevitably they used the language and imagery of sacrifice in speaking of the life of Jesus. His self-offering to death said more than could ever be said by the ritual killing of a spotless lamb. He was himself all that the lamb prefigured under the old system, and he was more, since even deliberate wrongdoing could now be confessed and forgiven through identification with his essentially moral act of loving oblation. What the earlier sacrifices offered was now seen as only a picture and a foretaste of the new.

Given the New Testament belief in Jesus as the incarnation of God, Christ's sacrifice meant that God had made himself not only his own high priest but his own sacrificial victim too—a thought that C. S. Lewis in his pre-Christian days found very moving so long as it was embodied in pagan myth and not in Christian history.

By tying the notion of divine self-sacrifice to a real historical character, Christianity has provided a solid basis for the persistent belief that self-giving is the highest form of life. Sacrificial imagery with its constant use of the blood as a symbol may seem grotesque in modern culture, but a world in which nobody made sacrifices would be a world populated by a diminished humanity. The sacrifices people make for their children, or for each other, or for their friends or their community, are often regarded as the finest things about them. Rightly, the Bible would say.

Of course, it has to be *self*-giving. The wartime general who bravely "sacrifices" the lives of thousands of ordinary soldiers is as far from the point as it is possible to get. And yet it is still true that self-offering will often need the stimulus of an act of sacrifice by somebody else. The inner self needs an external sacrifice, or a symbol of sacrifice, with which it can identify. Human beings find that life more readily follows than precedes such gestures. The token—whether it is the bunch of flowers offered by a lover or the sacrifice of the Mass offered by a Roman Catholic priest—expresses what life can only slowly learn to perform: the total oblation of the very self.

SACRIFICE

OLD TESTAMENT

Leviticus 3:1–2

1 And if his oblation be a sacrifice of peace offering, if he offer it of the herd; whether it be a male or female, he shall offer it without blemish before the Lord.

2 And he shall lay his hand upon the head of his offering, and kill it at the door of the tabernacle of the congregation: and Aaron's sons the priests shall sprinkle the blood upon the altar round about.

1 Chronicles 21:22–24

22 Then David said to Ornan, Grant me the place of this threshing-floor, that I may build an altar therein unto the Lord: thou shalt grant it me for the full price: that the plague may be stayed from the people.

23 And Ornan said unto David, Take it to thee, and let my lord the king do that which is good in his eyes: lo, I give thee the oxen also for burnt offerings, and the threshing instruments for wood, and the wheat for the meat offering; I give it all.

24 And king David said to Ornan, Nay; but I will verily buy it for the full price: for I will not take that which is thine for the Lord, nor offer burnt offerings without cost.

Amos 5:16, 21–24

16 Therefore the Lord, the God of hosts, the Lord, saith thus;

21 I hate, I despise your feast days, and I will not smell in your solemn assemblies.

22 Though ye offer me burnt offerings and your meat offerings, I will not accept them: neither will I regard the peace offerings of your fat beasts.

23 Take thou away from me the noise of thy songs; for I will not hear the melody of thy viols.

24 But let judgment run down as waters, and righteousness as a mighty stream.

Psalm 4:5

Offer the sacrifices of righteousness,
And put your trust in the Lord.

NEW TESTAMENT

Luke 2:22–24

22 And when the days of her [Mary's] purification according to the law of Moses were accomplished, they brought him to Jerusalem, to present him to the Lord;

23 (As it is written in the law of the Lord, Every male that openeth the womb shall be called holy to the Lord;)

24 And to offer a sacrifice according to that which is said in the law of

the Lord, A pair of turtledoves, or two young pigeons.

John 1:29

29 The next day John seeth Jesus coming unto him, and saith, Behold the Lamb of God, which taketh away the sin of the world.

1 Corinthians 5:7

7 Christ our passover is sacrificed for us:

Hebrews 7:23–27; 9:12–14

23 And they truly were many priests, because they were not suffered to continue by reason of death:

24 But this man, because he continueth ever, hath an unchangeable priesthood.

25 Wherefore he is able also to save them to the uttermost that come unto God by him, seeing he ever liveth to make intercession for them.

26 For such an high priest became us, who is holy, harmless, undefiled, separate from sinners, and made higher than the heavens;

27 Who needeth not daily, as those high priests, to offer up sacrifice, first for his own sins, and then for the people's: for this he did once, when he offered up himself.

12 Neither by the blood of goats and calves, but by his own blood he entered in once into the holy place, having obtained eternal redemption for us.

13 For if the blood of bulls and of goats, and the ashes of an heifer sprinkling the unclean, sanctifieth to the purifying of the flesh:

14 How much more shall the blood of Christ, who through the eternal Spirit offered himself without spot to God, purge your conscience from dead works to serve the living God?

1 Peter 2:5

5 Ye also, as lively stones, are built up a spiritual house, an holy priesthood, to offer up spiritual sacrifices, acceptable to God by Jesus Christ.

SADNESS

Tears are quite a feature of the Old Testament. The whole Bible affirms the goodness of life and is undoubtedly grateful for it, but the good life for which it is so thankful was never thought to be one of unbroken cheerfulness. Sorrow was always one element in the rich experience of living. One Old Testament book (admittedly a short one) is actually called the Book of Lamentations.

The titles of the books in the Bible are no part of the original text, and the Lamentations of Jeremiah (the full title of this one) may not be correct. But the book expresses in poetry the sadness of Jerusalem at a time of defeat. Its sadness is the reverse side of the good experience of civic pride and love. Moreover, this sadness is intensified by the very quality of that good experience. It is the sadness of a people who believe that they are in some way special in God's sight. This belief, too, makes their sorrow exceptional. The greatness of their joy defined the depths of their sadness. Mediocrity knows no such depths—or heights.

Nor, incidentally, did the sad experience so blunt the poet's enjoyment of his craft as to prevent his making the first four poems in his book alphabetic acrostics: the verses all begin with the successive letters of the Hebrew alphabet. The author was not just having fun with the city's misery. He did not enjoy it. But his sorrow contributed to the refining of his art. He needed all his skill to measure out so exactly and so beautifully the depths of the city's sorrow.

The Psalm quoted here expresses just as beautifully the sadness of Jerusalemites who had been exiled to Babylon. It is significant that the word "joy" should occur in this lament. The experiences of joy and of sorrow cannot be parted.

Both the psalmist and the author of Lamentations go on to pray for vengeance on those responsible for their affliction. Jeremiah himself was much more free of that desire. In the mixture of experiences to which sadness belongs, bitterness and hatred are not such necessary or intrinsic ingredients as joy and love.

Jerusalem was still the occasion for tears in New Testament times. The New Testament sees sorrow as a natural part of the perfect life in an imperfect world. A fruitful part of it, too.

Of course, sorrow can be overdone. Paul asked his converts in Corinth not to allow excessive sorrow to overwhelm one of their number whom they had disciplined, and he himself was glad to have been spared "sorrow upon sorrow" (Philippians 2:27).

To cherish sorrow as an end in itself would be quite unbiblical. Indeed, the desired end is the wiping away of all tears:

> Joy and Woe are woven fine
> A clothing for the Soul divine;
> Under every grief and pine
> Runs a joy with silken twine.

So wrote William Blake in *Songs of Innocence*. He was not saying merely that every cloud has a compensatory silver lining. He was saying that joy and woe are the warp and woof of the same experience. He was also pointing out that only in this experience of joy and sorrow can the divine spirit in man live on this earth. In this he was true to the witness of the Bible.

Blake belonged to a generation that wept more freely than most of us do today. We may choose to remain more inhibited at the dark end of the emotional spectrum, but we still need to understand the proper place of sadness in human experience. It is too closely related to love and to joy to be banished from the full life. It must not be allowed to weigh so heavily as to upset the balance of life (see Depression), but the pursuit of happiness is made stronger rather than weaker by the experience of sorrow. The generation that declared the pursuit of happiness to be a human right was the generation of Blake—and of Wordsworth, who found among his deepest and richest experiences that of hearing "the still, sad music of humanity."

SADNESS

OLD TESTAMENT

Lamentations 1:8–12

Jerusalem hath grievously sinned; therefore she is removed:

All that honoured her despise her, because they have seen her nakedness:

Yea, she sigheth, and turneth backward.

Her filthiness is in her skirts; she remembereth not her last end;

Therefore she came down wonderfully: she had no comforter.

O Lord, behold my affliction: for the enemy hath magnified himself.

The adversary hath spread out his hand upon all her pleasant things:

For she hath seen that the heathen entered into her sanctuary,

Whom thou didst command that they should not enter into thy congregation.

All her people sigh, they seek bread;

They have given their pleasant things for meat to relieve the soul:

See, O Lord, and consider; for I am become vile.

Is it nothing to you, all ye that pass by?

Behold, and see if there be any sorrow like unto my sorrow, which is done unto me,

Wherewith the Lord hath afflicted me in the day of his fierce anger.

Psalm 137:1–6

By the rivers of Babylon,
There we sat down, yea, we wept,
When we remembered Zion.

We hanged our harps
Upon the willows in the midst thereof.

For there they that carried us away captive required of us a song;

And they that wasted us required of us mirth, saying,

Sing us one of the songs of Zion.

How shall we sing the Lord's song
In a strange land?

If I forget thee, O Jerusalem,
Let my right hand forget her cunning.

If I do not remember thee,
Let my tongue cleave to the roof of my mouth;

If I prefer not Jerusalem
Above my chief joy.

NEW TESTAMENT

Luke 19:41–42

41 And when he was come near, he beheld the city, and wept over it,

42 Saying, If thou hadst known, even thou, at least in this thy day, the things which belong unto thy peace! but now they are hid from thine eyes.

Luke 23:28–29

28 But Jesus turning unto them said, Daughters of Jerusalem, weep not for me, but weep for yourselves, and for your children.

29 For, behold, the days are coming, in the which they shall say, Blessed

are the barren, and the wombs that never bare, and the paps which never gave suck.

2 Corinthians 2:4–7; 7:8–10

4 For out of much affliction and anguish of heart I wrote unto you with many tears; not that ye should be grieved, but that ye might know the love which I have more abundantly unto you.

5 But if any have caused grief, he hath not grieved me, but in part: that I may not overcharge you all.

6 Sufficient to such a man is this punishment, which was inflicted of many.

7 So that contrariwise ye ought rather to forgive him, and comfort him, lest perhaps such a one should be swallowed up with overmuch sorrow.

8 For though I made you sorry with a letter, I do not repent, though I did repent: for I perceive that the same epistle hath made you sorry, though it were but for a season.

9 Now I rejoice, not that ye were made sorry, but that ye sorrowed to repentance: for ye were made sorry after a godly manner, that ye might receive damage by us in nothing.

10 For godly sorrow worketh repentance to salvation not to be repented of.

Revelation 7:17

17 God shall wipe away all tears from their eyes.

SALVATION

To "save," to "be saved," "salvation": it is interesting that these terms originally meant what the nonreligious would like them to mean now. "Salvation" was not a preacher's word so much as a soldier's and politician's. F. J. Taylor says, "In the Old Testament salvation is expressed by a word which has the root meaning of 'to be wide' or 'spacious,' 'to develop without hindrance,' and thus ultimately 'to have victory in battle.' "*

The real savior was always God, but his instrument could be a soldier such as Gideon. As the Old Testament moves on, the idea of salvation becomes increasingly complex: it is needed individually and daily; its instrument can be a humble man, or even a despised and rejected one; it is accomplished by wisdom rather than by might. Clearly the whole concept of salvation has become wider and deeper, covering deliverance from inner constraints as well as outer ones.

*F. J. Taylor, in A *Theological Word Book of the Bible*, ed. A. Richardson (London: SCM Press, 1950).

The New Testament naturally sees Jesus as the suffering savior of whom the Book of Isaiah had spoken, but Jesus himself made the idea of salvation if anything more complex than ever. He said that people were lost and that he had come to save them, yet he said that the way of salvation involved a readiness to lose one's life rather than a determination to save it. Few understood. As he hung on the cross, Jesus heard the word "save" used by bystanders, by soldiers, and by one of his fellow sufferers, but none of them meant what he had tried to teach as the meaning of the word.

The real meaning became clearer after Jesus had died and so disposed of some of the false meanings. "Salvation" came to be a comprehensive term covering a comprehensive experience. On the one hand was a whole way of life characterized by various forms of bondage—bondage to evil and bondage to death among them. On the other hand was a way of life characterized by Christ's own freedom from evil and mastery of death. To be saved was to be transferred from the one life to the other.

Paul insisted that this transfer was brought about not by human merit, but by God's grace working through faith. The roots of that idea were imbedded in the teaching of Jesus, and his followers spoke of it as a matter of experience. Yet it never made them in the least passive: God did the saving, but that did not mean that nothing was required of the saved. Asked whether salvation is the work of God or of man, Paul seems to say that it is entirely God's doing—so work hard at it: "Work out your own salvation with fear and trembling. For it is God which worketh in you" (Philippians 2:12–13). If that seems illogical, it could be that we just lack the language with which to say how the eternal relates to the temporal, the human to the divine.

Such a view of salvation at least delivers us from the specious attraction of the "savior" with a too simple solution—one that usually involves our voting for him, fighting for him, buying his product, or offering him unquestioned obedience. Salvation, in the broad biblical sense, does not come out of a gun, a ballot box, or a supermarket, although war, voting, and marketing—like all other aspects of life—are profoundly influenced by it.

The comprehensive view of salvation as freedom "to develop without hindrance" covers both inward and outward conditions. The belief that it is a gift to be accepted rather than a purchase to be made with one's own moral or material resources strips it of all pride, vanity, and boasting. The discovery that to accept the gift is to come under a whole new set of moral imperatives and to draw on a whole new set of moral and spiritual resources makes it an active rather than a passive experience.

In other words, salvation is an antidote to pessimism and despondency. The human condition may be grim, but it includes a transcendent dimension out of which can come the power to transform that condition entirely.

313

SALVATION

OLD TESTAMENT

Judges 6:14–16

14 And the Lord looked upon him [Gideon], and said, Go in this thy might, and thou shalt save Israel from the hand of the Midianites: have not I sent thee?

15 And he said unto him, Oh my Lord, wherewith shall I save Israel? behold, my family is poor in Manasseh, and I am the least in my father's house.

16 And the Lord said unto him, Surely I will be with thee, and thou shalt smite the Midianites as one man.

Psalm 68:19–20

Blessed be the Lord, who daily loadeth
us with benefits,
Even the God of our salvation.
He that is our God is the God of salvation;
And unto God the Lord belong the issues from death.

Ecclesiastes 9:13–16

13 This wisdom have I seen also under the sun, and it seemed great unto me:

14 There was a little city, and few men within it; and there came a great king against it, and besieged it, and built great bulwarks against it:

15 Now there was found in it a poor wise man, and he by his wisdom delivered the city; yet no man remembered that same poor man.

16 Then said I, Wisdom is better than strength: nevertheless the poor man's wisdom is despised, and his words are not heard.

Isaiah 52:10, 13–15; 53:11–12

10 The Lord hath made bare his holy arm in the eyes of all the nations; and all the ends of the earth shall see the salvation of our God.

13 Behold my servant shall deal prudently, he shall be exalted and extolled, and be very high.

14 As many were astonied at thee; his visage was so marred more than any man, and his form more than the sons of men:

15 So shall he sprinkle many nations; the kings shall shut their mouths at him:

11 By his knowledge shall my righteous servant justify many; for he shall bear their iniquities.

12 Therefore will I divide him a portion with the great, and he shall divide the spoil with the strong; because he hath poured out his soul unto death: and he was numbered with the transgressors; and he bore the sin of many and made intercession for the transgressors.

NEW TESTAMENT

Luke 19:10

10 For the Son of man is come to seek and to save that which was lost.

Luke 9:23–24

23 And he said to them all, If any man will come after me, let him deny

himself, and take up his cross daily, and follow me.

24 For whosoever will save his life shall lose it: but whosoever will lose his life for my sake, the same shall save it.

Luke 23:35–39

35 And the people stood beholding. And the rulers also with them derided him, saying, He saved others; let him save himself, if he be Christ, the chosen of God.

36 And the soldiers also mocked him, coming to him, and offering him vinegar,

37 And saying, If thou be the king of the Jews, save thyself.

38 And a superscription also was written over him in letters of Greek, and Latin, and Hebrew, THIS IS THE KING OF THE JEWS.

39 And one of the malefactors which were hanged railed on him, saying, If thou be Christ, save thyself and us.

Titus 3:3–7

3 For we ourselves also were sometimes foolish, disobedient, deceived, serving divers lusts and pleasures, living in malice and envy, hateful, and hating one another.

4 But after that the kindness and love of God our Saviour toward man appeared,

5 Not by works of righteousness which we have done, but according to his mercy he saved us, by the washing of regeneration, and renewing of the Holy Ghost;

6 Which he shed on us abundantly through Jesus Christ our Saviour;

7 That being justified by his grace, we should be made heirs according to the hope of eternal life.

Ephesians 2:8–9

8 For by grace are ye saved through faith; and that not of yourselves: it is the gift of God:

9 Not of works, lest any man should boast.

SELF

Selfishness is the subject of a separate entry. But what is a self anyway, whether turned inward as selfishness or outward as love? According to the Old Testament it is an image of God. In God there is by nature all that belongs to selfhood: awareness, freedom, power of decision, choice. In man these things are present as God's gift. They are sustained in being by man's relationship with God.

A word that comes to mind—now somewhat dated (except in connection with some kinds of music)—is "soul." The biblical words that used to be translated as "soul" are now often translated as "self"—or, more simply, "those souls" becomes "them," and "my soul" becomes "me." This is right. The word denotes simply the living being. The Hebrew word "Nephesh," which can be translated as "soul," can be used of animals as well as human beings. In both Testaments the word "self," "soul," and "life" can often be regarded as interchangeable.

Yet in some passages the emphasis seems so concentrated on the inner core of conscious selfhood that the distinctive term "soul" still seems to be required. Take, for example, the passage from Deuteronomy quoted here—one that has played a great part in Jewish worship. Loving God with all your soul means loving him with the full force of your selfhood.

Since the Old Testament is not given to introspection, selfhood is not much analyzed or defined, but it is abundantly illustrated in some of the intensely personal Psalms. It is the consciousness of a human being struggling to grow in understanding of three things: his own significance; the significance of the world around him; the significance of his relationship with that God from whom he is inseparable but over against whom he stands as a free individual. The psalmist attains self-knowledge not so much by looking inward as by looking outward and upward. He knows himself through God's knowledge of him.

In all the first three New Testament Gospels Jesus warns that human beings should take care not to exchange their selfhood (or their souls) even for the whole world. His parable of the rich fool illustrates how easily and unthinkingly one can make such an exchange (see Materialism). More mysteriously he speaks in the fourth Gospel of the opposite process: that of nourishing one's life with the spiritual food which Jesus himself is—an image that is not hard to interpret, even though the language used may seem grotesque to a modern ear. Just as all selfhood is nourished by relationship with another self, so transcendent selfhood (or eternal life) is nourished by relationship with the selfhood of God.

Another biblical word that points to the self is "name." To have a name is to possess personal identity. In the symbolism of the Book of Revelation, the writing of a name into the book of life was a promise of eternal identity.

Faust was not the only man to be tempted to trade his soul, his selfhood, for something less, but few face a choice as dramatic as his. This kind of temptation happens gradually as men and women forget what they really are as persons and allow themselves to conform to some alternative mold made ready for them as producers, or consumers, or sex objects, or even as just members of "the masses."

The bargain is a bad one because selfhood is of transcendent significance, but its preservation demands constant awareness of transcendent values. The living self is that which is alive to the meaning of things. Food, for instance, is not just body fuel to a living self. It is taken in full awareness of its taste, of all that has gone into its making, and even of its poetic significance as an image or symbol— perhaps its sacramental significance as a point of meeting with God. Every experience is savored so as to taste its quality as an encounter between the self and its environment.

SELF

OLD TESTAMENT

Genesis 1:27

27 So God created man in his own image, in the image of God created he him; male and female created he them.

Deuteronomy 6:4–5; 8:2–3

4 Hear, O Israel: The Lord our God is one Lord:

5 And thou shalt love the Lord thy God with all thine heart, and with all thy soul, and with all thy might.

2 And thou shalt remember all the way which the Lord thy God led thee these forty years in the wilderness, to humble thee, and to prove thee, and to know what was in thine heart, whether thou wouldst keep his commandments, or no.

3 And he humbled thee, and suffered thee to hunger, and fed thee with manna, which thou knewest not, neither did thy fathers know; that he might make thee know that man doth not live by bread only, but by every word that proceedeth out of the mouth of the Lord doth man live.

Psalm 139:1–10, 23–24

O Lord, thou hast searched me, and known me.
Thou knowest my downsitting and mine uprising.
Thou understandest my thought afar off.
Thou compassest my path and my lying down,
And art acquainted with all my ways.
For there is not a word in my tongue,
But, lo, O Lord, thou knowest it altogether.
Thou hast beset me behind and before,
And laid thine hand upon me.
Such knowledge is too wonderful for me;
It is high, I cannot attain unto it.
Whither shall I go from thy spirit?
Or whither shall I flee from thy presence?
If I ascend up into heaven, thou art there:
If I make my bed in hell, behold, thou art there.
If I take the wings of the morning,
And dwell in the uttermost parts of the sea;
Even there shall thy hand lead me,
And thy right hand shall hold me.
Search me, O God, and know my heart:
Try me, and know my thoughts:
And see if there be any wicked way in me,
And lead me in the way everlasting.

NEW TESTAMENT

Matthew 16:26

26 For what is a man profited, if he shall gain the whole world, and lose his own soul? or what shall a man give in exchange for his soul?

John 6:47–57

47 Verily, verily, I say unto you, He that believeth on me hath everlasting life.

48 I am that bread of life.

49 Your fathers did eat manna in the wilderness, and are dead.

50 This is the bread which cometh down from heaven, that a man may eat thereof, and not die.

51 I am the living bread which came down from heaven: if any man eat of this bread, he shall live for ever: and the bread that I will give is my flesh, which I will give for the life of the world.

52 The Jews therefore strove among themselves, saying, How can this man give us his flesh to eat?

53 Then Jesus said unto them, Verily, verily, I say unto you, Except ye eat the flesh of the Son of man, and drink his blood, ye have no life in you.

54 Whoso eateth my flesh, and drinketh my blood, hath eternal life; and I will raise him up at the last day.

55 For my flesh is meat indeed, and my blood is drink indeed.

56 He that eateth my flesh, and drinketh my blood, dwelleth in me, and I in him.

57 As the living Father hath sent me, and I live by the Father: so he that eateth me, even he shall live by me.

1 Corinthians 15:45, 47, 49

45 And so it is written, the first man Adam was made a living soul; the last Adam was made a quickening spirit.

47 The first man is of the earth, earthy: the second man is the Lord from heaven.

49 And as we have borne the image of the earthy, we shall also bear the image of the heavenly.

Revelation 3:5 (the Living One speaks in a vision)

5 He that overcometh, the same shall be clothed in white raiment; and I will not blot out his name out of the book of life, but I will confess his name before my Father, and before his angels.

SELFISHNESS

The Old Testament certainly prefers generosity to selfishness. "If there be among you a poor man," said the law, "thou shalt not harden thine heart, nor shut thine hand" (Deuteronomy 15:7). At the same time the Old Testament was very realistic about the proper place of self-interest in human affairs: "Love thy neighbor as thyself," said Leviticus 19:18.

The difference between selfishness and a proper self-interest is nicely illustrated in the story of Esther—a mere fragment of which is quoted here. It is the all too familiar story of a Jewish pogrom, but with an unusual twist: for once the Jews were able to turn the tables on their persecutors.

As they told the story, Esther was queen of Persia in the time of Xerxes I, perhaps the most powerful ruler in the world at that time (c.485–c.465 B.C.). Esther did not attain that position easily. She had been taken into the king's harem after a year of beauty treatments—six months with oil of myrrh and six with perfumes and cosmetics. She then pleased the king so much that he made her queen. During all this time she neglected (advisedly) to tell her husband that she was Jewish. But she kept in touch with her people through her guardian, Mordecai, who became practically a resident at the palace gate.

Then the appeal of naked self-interest is demonstrated. Haman, the villain of the story, persuaded the king that the Jews in Persia were a nonconforming minority and that "it is not for the king's profit" to tolerate them. Rulers are commonly susceptible to an appeal to their self-interest, and when Haman offered to put ten thousand talents of silver into the royal treasury to meet the cost of a final solution, the king authorized him to go ahead.

The passages quoted here begin at this point in the story, and they show Esther naturally inclined, at first, toward the selfish policy of keeping quiet. Then, however, she submits herself to Mordecai's bolder policy when it is presented to her as an appeal to both patriotism and long-term self-interest. In line with the Old Testament understanding of human nature, selfishness is overcome not so much by sheer unselfishness as by seeing that both the self and the other share a common interest.

Jesus in the New Testament quotes the Old Testament law about loving your neighbor as yourself, and this (as is often pointed out) does imply loving yourself. He did demand practical unselfishness of a very rare kind, yet even he allowed an element of self-interest into his appeal. He told his disciples to deny themselves but not to destroy themselves. Self-denial could take as extreme a form as acceptance of crucifixion for others and yet be a way to life. Self-destruction could take as easy a form as self-indulgence and yet be a way to the death of self. The saving of that essential self was a legitimate goal. And Jesus' argument was that men and women will be dealt with as they themselves deal with others, so that even enlightened self-interest would point to a policy of giving rather than grasping, of generosity rather than selfishness.

Paul uses a similar argument to back up his appeal for unselfishness in the very practical matter of a collection he is making for the impoverished Christians of Jerusalem—the mother church, but a remote one as far as his correspondents were concerned.

Selfishness is not only a sin; it is a mistake. It is a road that does not in fact lead to self-fulfillment because it starts from a wrong understanding of what the self is. Selfishness assumes that the self is an isolated thing, separable from all other selves. So it confronts each issue with the question "What's in it for me?" That approach builds a wall around the self and within that wall the self dies.

The true self is not an isolated thing, but a social thing. It lives and grows and becomes rich within a network of relationships, and these are maintained in health by the outgoing of the self in generosity and self-giving rather than by the defense of the self through grasping and selfishness.

SELFISHNESS

OLD TESTAMENT

Esther 4:5–5:3; 7:3 (Mordecai has appeared at the King's gate in sackcloth and ashes)

5 Then called Esther for Hatach, one of the king's chamberlains, whom he had appointed to attend upon her, and gave him a commandment to Mordecai, to know what it was, and why it was.

6 So Hatach went forth to Mordecai unto the street of the city, which was before the king's gate.

7 And Mordecai told him of all that had happened unto him, and of the sum of the money that Haman had promised to pay to the king's treasuries for the Jews, to destroy them.

8 Also he gave him the copy of the writing of the decree that was given at Shushan to destroy them, to shew it unto Esther, and to declare it unto her, and to charge her that she should go in unto the king, to make supplication unto him, and to make request before him for her people.

9 And Hatach came and told Esther the words of Mordecai.

10 Again Esther spake unto Hatach, and gave him commandment unto Mordecai;

11 All the king's servants, and the people of the king's provinces, do know, that whosoever, whether man or woman, shall come unto the king into the inner court, who is not called, there is one law of his to put him to death, except such to whom the king shall hold out the golden sceptre, that he may live: but I have not been called to come in unto the king these thirty days.

12 And they told to Mordecai Esther's words.

13 Then Mordecai commanded to answer Esther, Think not with thyself that thou shalt escape in the king's house, more than all the Jews.

14 For if thou altogether holdest thy peace at this time, then shall there enlargement and deliverance arise to the Jews from another place; but thou and thy father's house shall be destroyed: and who knoweth whether thou art come to this kingdom for such a time as this?

15 Then Esther bade them return Mordecai this answer,

16 Go, gather together all the Jews that are present in Shushan, and fast ye for me, and neither eat nor drink three days, night or day: I also and my maidens will fast likewise; and so will I go in unto the king, which is not according to the law: and if I perish, I perish.

17 So Mordecai went his way, and did according to all that Esther had commanded him.

1 Now it came to pass on the third day, that Esther put on her royal apparel, and stood in the inner court of the king's house, over against the king's house: and the king sat upon his royal throne in the royal house, over against the gate of the house.

2 And it was so, when the king saw Esther the queen standing in the court, that she obtained favour in his sight:

and the king held out to Esther the golden sceptre that was in his hand. So Esther drew near, and touched the top of the sceptre.

3 Then said the king unto her, What wilt thou, queen Esther? and what is thy request? it shall be even given thee to the half of the kingdom.

3 Then Esther the queen answered and said, If I have found favour in thy sight, O king, and if it please the king, let my life be given me at my petition, and my people at my request.

NEW TESTAMENT

Luke 6:30–34, 38; 9:23–25

30 Give to every man that asketh of thee; and of him that taketh away thy goods ask them not again.

31 And as ye would that men should do to you, do ye also to them likewise.

32 For if ye love them which love you, what thank have ye? for sinners also love those that love them.

33 And if ye do good to them which do good to you, what thank have ye? for sinners also do even the same.

34 And if ye lend to them of whom ye hope to receive, what thank have ye? for sinners also lend to sinners, to receive as much again.

38 Give, and it shall be given unto you; good measure, pressed down, and shaken together, and running over, shall men give into your bosom. For with the same measure that ye mete withal it shall be measured to you again.

23 And he said to them all, if any man will come after me, let him deny himself, and take up his cross daily, and follow me.

24 For whosoever will save his life shall lose it: but whosoever will lose his life for my sake, the same shall save it.

25 For what is a man advantaged, if he gain the whole world, and lose himself, or be cast away?

2 Corinthians 9:6–7, 11

6 But this I say, He which soweth sparingly shall reap also sparingly; and he which soweth bountifully shall reap also bountifully.

7 Every man according as he purposeth in his heart, so let him give; not grudgingly, or of necessity: for God loveth a cheerful giver.

11 Being enriched in every thing to all bountifulness, which causeth through us thanksgiving to God.

SERVICE

In Old Testament Hebrew the same word (or words from the same root) could be used to denote either the service of the priest in the temple or of the laborer in the field, either a service of worship such as the Passover or the inward devotion of the heart such as David asked Solomon to give to God. At the beginning of the Book of Exodus, the Hebrews are forced to render service to the Egyptians—meaning that they must work for them. By Chapter 12 the Hebrews are preparing to escape and are being told that when they are settled in freedom they must celebrate their deliverance by rendering service to God—meaning that they must worship him. Words with the same Hebrew root are used to denote both the work and the worship. The two actions are akin.

The real difference between the service rendered to the Egyptians and the service rendered to God was not that one was manual and the other ritual: God, after all, required both forms equally. The real difference was that the first was enforced and unjust, the second voluntary and due. True service is part of a relationship that binds the one serving and the one served in mutual fellowship. The labor imposed by a task master is false service.

So Joshua is described as inviting a voluntary commitment to the Lord's service. This commitment will involve much more than ritual. It will cover work in the fields, life in the home, justice in the courts, the relief of poverty . . . everything. But everything as part of a relationship binding God and Israel together. In no sense are the service of God and the service of humanity rivals. The two are synonymous.

How costly as well as how rewarding all this could be was discovered later. Some of what was involved was expressed in the Suffering Servant poems of the Book of Isaiah.

Jesus spoke of the servant role as his own and as the right one for his followers (see Ambition). He also said that it was impossible to serve two masters (see Wealth) or to perform an excess of service (see Duty). Yet according to John's Gospel he still needed at the end of his life to demonstrate the truth that humble service is fitting in one who comes from God and is returning to God.

In the remainder of the New Testament the service of God and the service of humanity become if possible even more deeply inseparable. The language of practical service merges completely into that of liturgical services and sacrificial worship. In some contexts, such as Philippians 2:30, the very word "liturgy" (in its original Greek form) is used when referring to material assistance.

The early Christian church not only saw all work as the service of God in Christ, but neither wanted nor expected ever to be free of it. In the exalted vision of the heavenly city in the Book of Revelation, service still has its place.

The modern tendency to separate voluntary service from necessary work is not biblical. The Bible sees daily labor, voluntary service, and religious worship as aspects of the same integrated activity referred to as service. Such service involves the contemplative side of life as well as the active. It is done with such a will that the voluntary overrides the compulsory even when one is performing an inescapable duty.

The concept of service not only covers the whole of life and makes a unity of it but also delivers those who accept it from any idea of service as a duty from which they are allowed time off. To ask how much of my time is to be given to my neighbor and how much reserved to myself, or how much of my money is to be given to God and how much is for me, is to divide one part of life from another and many parts of life from God. The biblical notion of service regards every activity as being related to the transcendent, so that Mary and Martha, for example, are both serving the same end.

SERVICE

OLD TESTAMENT

Joshua 24:14–22

14 Now therefore fear the Lord, and serve him in sincerity and in truth: and put away the gods which your fathers served on the other side of the flood, and in Egypt; and serve ye the Lord.

15 And if it seem evil unto you to serve the Lord, choose you this day whom ye will serve; whether the gods which your fathers served that were on the other side of the flood, or the gods of the Amorites, in whose land ye dwell: but as for me and my house, we will serve the Lord.

16 And the people answered and said, God forbid that we should forsake the Lord, to serve other gods;

17 For the Lord our God, he it is that brought us up and our fathers out of the land of Egypt, from the house of bondage, and which did those great signs in our sight, and preserved us in all the way wherein we went, and among all the people through whom we passed:

18 And the Lord drave out from before us all the people, even the Amorites which dwelt in the land:

therefore will we also serve the Lord; for he is our God.

19 And Joshua said unto the people, Ye cannot serve the Lord: for he is an holy God; he is a jealous God; he will not forgive your transgressions nor your sins.

20 If ye forsake the Lord, and serve strange gods, then he will turn and do you hurt, and consume you, after that he hath done you good.

21 And the people said unto Joshua, Nay; but we will serve the Lord.

22 And Joshua said unto the people, Ye are witnesses against yourselves that ye have chosen you the Lord, to serve him. And they said, We are witnesses.

1 Chronicles 28:6–7, 9

6 And he said unto me [David], Solomon thy son, he shall build my house and my courts: for I have chosen him to be my son, and I will be his father.

7 Moreover I will establish his kingdom for ever, if he be constant to do my commandments and my judgments, as at this day.

9 And thou, Solomon my son, know thou the God of thy father, and

serve him with a perfect heart and with a willing mind: for the Lord searcheth all hearts, and understandeth all the imaginations of the thoughts.

Isaiah 42:1–4

1 Behold my servant, whom I uphold; mine elect, in whom my soul delighteth; I have put my spirit upon him: he shall bring forth judgment to the Gentiles.

2 He shall not cry, nor lift up, nor cause his voice to be heard in the street.

3 A bruised reed shall he not break, and the smoking flax shall he not quench: he shall bring forth judgment unto truth.

4 He shall not fail nor be discouraged, till he have set judgment in the earth: and the isles shall wait for his law.

NEW TESTAMENT

John 13:3–5, 12–17

3 Jesus knowing that the Father had given all things into his hands, and that he was come from God, and went to God;

4 He riseth from supper, and laid aside his garments; and took a towel, and girded himself.

5 After that he poureth water into a basin, and began to wash the disciples' feet, and to wipe them with the towel wherewith he was girded.

12 So after he had washed their feet, and had taken his garments, and was set down again, he said unto them, Know ye what I have done to you?

13 Ye call me Master and Lord: and ye say well; for so I am.

14 If I then, your Lord and Master, have washed your feet; ye also ought to wash one another's feet.

15 For I have given you an example, that ye should do as I have done to you.

16 Verily, verily, I say unto you, The servant is not greater than his lord; neither he that is sent greater than he that sent him.

17 If ye know these things, happy are ye if ye do them.

Ephesians 5:1–2

1 Be ye therefore followers of God, as dear children;

2 And walk in love, as Christ also hath loved us, and hath given himself for us an offering and a sacrifice to God for a sweet-smelling savour.

Colossians 3:23–24 (to servants)

23 And whatsoever ye do, do it heartily, as to the Lord, and not unto men;

24 Knowing that of the Lord ye shall receive the reward of the inheritance: for ye serve the Lord Christ.

Revelation 22:3

3 The throne of God and of the Lamb shall be in it; and his servants shall serve him.

SEX

The Old Testament treats human sexuality with a mixture of reverence, distrust, and familiarity. Perhaps the last of these dominates. It is taken for granted that sexuality is solidly built into human nature and expresses itself in the actions and attitudes of every man and woman: "God created man in his own image, in the image of God he created him; male and female created he them" (Genesis 1:27). The history books in the Old Testament are full of what might now be called "explicit sex," and this is because the religion of Israel saw no reason why it should be concealed.

At the same time a man's sexual organs were regarded as too sacred to be seen by his children (perhaps because of their association with the mystery of the engendering of life), and a woman's bleeding rendered her ritually unclean (perhaps because blood was thought of as containing life itself). This mixture of frankness and awe was focused in the rite that made an Israelite male physically distinguishable from the men of neighboring nations: the rite of circumcision. The sign and seal of Israel's covenant with God was located in the sex organs of its men, and the image of that covenant was in the marriage of man and woman.

Ezekiel's allegory of unfaithful Jerusalem used sexual imagery to tell the whole history of the city, so deeply was sex rooted in man and therefore in his understanding of God.

Belief in the virgin birth of Jesus is not prominent in the New Testament—Mark, John, and Paul make absolutely no reference to it—but it is often taken to be evidence of the New Testament's generally low estimate of sexuality. In fact, however, in the two Christmas stories in which the virgin birth is mentioned—those of Matthew and Luke—the intention seems to be to exalt the initiative of God rather than to demean the sexuality of man.

Jesus himself was very demanding in his sex ethics (lust, he said, is the moral equivalent of adultery) but notoriously gentle with those who failed to live up to accepted codes (see Love).

Paul thought it good to be celibate in the circumstances of his time, but he regarded the marriage bond as a true image of the relationship between Christ and his people (see Marriage) and the physical union of the sexes as so significant that it could join a prostitute to the body of Christ. This is surely the very opposite of a low view of sex. The New Testament never treats sex as merely an animal activity. Sex involves all of a man's or a woman's humanity and spirituality.

So frankness on matters of sex is not incompatible with a sense of its mystery. The modern (and biblical) attitude of openness toward all that is involved in being male or female has sometimes led to the modern (and nonbiblical) tendency to remove the personal and spiritual factors from the relationships between men and women. But to treat a relationship as just an instrument of the sexual function is to debase both humanity and sexuality. A generation that knew all about sex and nothing about love would be an impoverished one. Sex education has to take account of this.

The true riches of sexuality are enjoyed by those for whom the physical is a mirror of the spiritual—and more than a mirror, a partner. The giving and receiving to which biology compels us can be the key to a whole way of life characterized by the search for union through the way of exchange. If we are ever to reach such mystical goals as the losing of ourselves in one another or in the infinite, it will be because our sexuality set us on that road; and if we are ever to find ourselves again, our identity enlarged by that experience, it will be thanks to that in our bodies which enables us to go out of ourselves in love and be given ourselves back again in being loved.

SEX

OLD TESTAMENT

Genesis 9:20–23

20 And Noah began to be an husbandman, and he planted a vineyard:

21 And he drank of the wine, and was drunken; and he was uncovered within his tent.

22 And Ham, the father of Canaan, saw the nakedness of his father, and told his two brethren without.

23 And Shem and Japheth took a garment, and laid it upon both their shoulders, and went backward, and covered the nakedness of their father; and their faces were backward, and they saw not their father's nakedness.

Leviticus 12:1–5

1 And the Lord spake unto Moses, saying,

2 Speak unto the children of Israel, saying, If a woman have conceived seed, and born a man child: then she shall be unclean seven days; according to the days of the separation for her infirmity shall she be unclean.

3 And in the eighth day the flesh of his foreskin shall be circumcised.

4 And she shall then continue in the blood of her purifying three and thirty days; she shall touch no hallowed thing, nor come into the sanctuary, until the days of her purifying be fulfilled.

5 But if she bear a maid child, then she shall be unclean two weeks, as in her separation: and she shall continue in the blood of her purifying threescore and six days.

Ezekiel 16:1–8

1 Again the word of the Lord came unto me, saying,

2 Son of man, cause Jerusalem to know her abominations,

3 And say, Thus saith the Lord God unto Jerusalem: Thy birth and thy nativity is of the land of Canaan; thy father was an Amorite, and thy mother an Hittite.

4 And as for thy nativity, in the day thou wast born thy navel was not cut, neither wast thou washed in water to supple thee; thou wast not salted at all, nor swaddled at all.

5 None eye pitied thee, to do any of these unto thee, to have compassion upon thee; but thou wast cast out in the open field, to the loathing of thy person, in the day that thou wast born.

6 And when I passed by thee, and saw thee polluted in thine own blood, I said unto thee when thou wast in thy blood, Live; yea, I said unto thee when thou wast in thy blood, Live.

7 I have caused thee to multiply as the bud of the field, and thou hast increased and waxen great, and thou art come to excellent ornaments: thy breasts are fashioned, and thine hair is grown, whereas thou wast naked and bare.

8 Now when I passed by thee, and looked upon thee, behold, thy time was the time of love; and I spread my skirt over thee, and covered thy nakedness: yea, I sware unto thee, and entered into a covenant with thee, saith the Lord God, and thou becamest mine.

NEW TESTAMENT

Matthew 1:18–20

18 Now the birth of Jesus Christ was on this wise: When as his mother Mary was espoused to Joseph, before they came together, she was found with child of the Holy Ghost.

19 Then Joseph her husband, being a just man, and not willing to make her a public example, was minded to put her away privily.

20 But while he thought on these things, behold, the angel of the Lord appeared unto him in a dream, saying, Joseph, thou son of David, fear not to take unto thee Mary thy wife: for that which is conceived in her is of the Holy Ghost.

Mark 10:6–8

6 From the beginning of the creation God made them male and female.

7 For this cause shall a man leave his father and mother, and cleave to his wife;

8 And they twain shall be one flesh: so then they are no more twain, but one flesh.

1 Corinthians 6:15–18; 7:1–2, 7–9

15 Know ye not that your bodies are the members of Christ? shall I then take the members of Christ, and make them the members of an harlot? God forbid.

16 What? know ye not that he which is joined to an harlot is one body? for two, saith he, shall be one flesh.

17 But he that is joined unto the Lord is one spirit.

18 Flee fornication. Every sin that a man doeth is without the body; but he that committeth fornication sinneth against his own body.

1 It is good for a man not to touch a woman.

2 Nevertheless, to avoid fornication, let every man have his own wife, and let every woman have her own husband.

7 For I would that all men were even as I myself. But every man hath his proper gift of God, one after this manner, and another after that.

8 I say therefore to the unmarried and widows, It is good for them if they abide even as I.

9 But if they cannot contain, let them marry: for it is better to marry than to burn.

SIN

In the Old Testament "sin" is a deviation from right order, whether deliberate or accidental, whether conscious or unconscious. The whole moral and natural scheme of things is underwritten by God, so there can be no wrongdoing that is not sinning against him. "Against thee, thee only, have I sinned," says the author of Psalm 51:4. Even foreigners such as the people of Gaza and Tyre and Edom, although they were deemed to have no knowledge of the true God, were said by Amos to be sinning against him in their acts of inhumanity. Equally, for an Israelite to break faith with a foreigner was to sin against God.

But the Old Testament also specified how sin can be dealt with. Sin as an inner sickness leading to unwitting offenses against ritual laws could be atoned for by sacrifice, and sin as deliberate wrongdoing could be forgiven if confessed. When the wrongdoing involved others in the loss of their rights, then restitution had to be made as part of the process of confession and forgiveness.

In the New Testament, Jesus treats sin as so akin to sickness that forgiving and healing become two parts of the single process of putting men and women back on their feet. Jesus said that his special mission was to those who were aware of their inner sickness, but he did not accept that any were actually free from it. Indeed, those who were outwardly righteous were in most danger of keeping their inner corruption hidden, and therefore unhealed. Hence his vivid denunciation of hypocrites as whitewashed tombs, "which indeed appear beautiful outward, but are within full of dead men's bones, and of all uncleanness" (Matthew 23:27).

As always, the New Testament's primary concern is with the inner territory of the spirit rather than with the letter of the outward law, and it is in that inner area that the sources of sin are to be replaced by the Spirit of God. This replacement occurs, the New Testament says, once faith has performed the mysterious transaction by which Christ's innocence is exchanged for the believer's guilt; this is not a miscarriage of justice, but a loving union of identities.

Of course, Christians could not claim to have ceased sinning from then on. They had to admit that sin still existed but that it was now an anomaly where once it had been natural.

"There is honor," it is said, "even among thieves." Certainly it would be difficult to find a man or a woman who has absolutely no code of right and wrong, no sense of ever having fallen below standard. A person might admit only to "having made mistakes," but—regardless of the term used—he or she will admit to having done the wrong thing at times.

A difficulty arises, however, when one has a moral code without having the religious concept of sin. When wrongdoing is not understood as sin, there is little that can be done about it. Mistakes seem more indelible than sins. Admittedly an individual may say "sorry" to another individual and may receive that individual's forgiveness, but the apology solves only part of the problem—and is not always possible anyway. The man or woman who has done wrong has thrown life out of alignment with the nature of things, has damaged the structure on which human life depends. Putting matters right involves going further back, and further in, than just the one-to-one relationship. The environment in which we live and move and have our being needs also to be part of the process of repair, and for that to happen we need to be aware of a transcendent order responsive to human penitence and active in the cause of healing.

An increased understanding of human behavior as sin would make life not more morbid, but more hopeful. It would transform morality from an inflexible system of law into something personal—and therefore mendable.

SIN

OLD TESTAMENT

Amos 1:6, 9, 11

6 Thus saith the Lord; For three transgressions of Gaza, and for four, I will not turn away the punishment thereof; because they carried away captive the whole captivity, to deliver them up to Edom:

9 Thus saith the Lord; For three transgressions of Tyrus, and for four, I will not turn away the punishment thereof; because they delivered up the whole captivity to Edom, and remembered not the brotherly covenant:

11 Thus saith the Lord; For three transgressions of Edom, and for four, I will not turn away the punishment thereof; because he did pursue his brother with the sword, and did cast off all pity, and his anger did tear perpetually, and he kept his wrath for ever.

Deuteronomy 24:14–15

14 Thou shalt not oppress an hired servant that is poor and needy, whether he be of thy brethren, or of thy strangers that are in thy land within thy gates:

15 At his day thou shalt give him his hire, neither shall the sun go down upon it; for he is poor, and setteth his heart upon it: lest he cry against thee unto the Lord, and it be sin unto thee.

Numbers 5:5–7

5 And the Lord spake unto Moses, saying,

6 Speak unto the children of Israel, When a man or woman shall commit

any sin that men commit, to do a trespass against the Lord, and that person be guilty;

7 Then they shall confess their sin which they have done: and he shall recompense his trespass with the principal thereof, and add unto it the fifth part thereof, and give it unto him against whom he hath trespassed.

Isaiah 1:18

18 Come now, and let us reason together, saith the Lord: though your sins be as scarlet, they shall be as white as snow; though they be red like crimson, they shall be as wool.

NEW TESTAMENT

Matthew 9:10–13

10 And it came to pass, as Jesus sat at meat in the house, behold, many publicans and sinners came and sat down with him and his disciples.

11 And when the Pharisees saw it, they said unto his disciples, Why eateth your Master with publicans and sinners?

12 But when Jesus heard that, he said unto them, They that be whole need not a physician, but they that are sick.

13 But go ye and learn what that meaneth, I will have mercy, and not sacrifice: for I am not come to call the righteous, but sinners to repentance.

Luke 5:17–25

17 And it came to pass on a certain day, as he was teaching, that there were Pharisees and doctors of the law sitting by, which were come out of every town of Galilee, and Judæa, and Jerusalem: and the power of the Lord was present to heal them.

18 And, behold, men brought in a bed a man which was taken with a palsy: and they sought means to bring him in, and to lay him before him.

19 And when they could not find by what way they might bring him in because of the multitude, they went upon the housetop, and let him down through the tiling with his couch into the midst before Jesus.

20 And when he saw their faith, he said unto him, Man, thy sins are forgiven thee.

21 And the scribes and the Pharisees began to reason, saying, Who is this which speaketh blasphemies? Who can forgive sins, but God alone?

22 But when Jesus perceived their thoughts, he answering said unto them, What reason ye in your hearts?

23 Whether is easier, to say, Thy sins be forgiven thee; or to say, Rise up and walk?

24 But that ye may know that the Son of man hath power upon earth to forgive sins, (he said unto the sick of the palsy,) I say unto thee, Arise, and take up thy couch, and go into thine house.

25 And immediately he rose up before them, and took up that whereon he lay, and departed to his own house, glorifying God.

2 Corinthians 5:21; 7:1

21 For he hath made him to be sin

for us, who knew no sin; that we might be made the righteousness of God in him.

1 Having therefore these promises, dearly beloved, let us cleanse ourselves from all filthiness of the flesh and spirit, perfecting holiness in the fear of God.

SOCIETY

The Old Testament always sees the individual in a social context. He *is* an individual, and so is responsible for his own life, but he exists only within a network of relationships. He may go off to the desert to be alone with God, but (like Elijah at Horeb) he is sent back into the community to obey God in a social and political setting (see Worship).

The shape of Old Testament society changed from time to time. It differed during the nomadic period, for instance, from what it was after the Israelites settled in Canaan. At all times social responsibility had to be shared, and increasingly it had to be widely shared. Always the object was to build a cohesive community responsive to the will of God.

That object shaped all the laws and institutions of Israelite society, although it was never fully attained. The recurring phrase, "You shall be my people, and I will be your God," was always spoken in the future tense. The fulfillment of the promise was said to be coming in a new order under a divinely gifted king, but it is very significant that under the rule of that king the individual was expected to grow in stature and significance. Far from everything's being left to the anointed ruler, the new society was expected to be one in which the individual would know the law for himself, would have God's spirit within him, and would support his neighbor.

The New Testament sees Jesus as that king, and it sees the kingdom he preached as the promised new order of society. But the New Testament is concerned with two social orders existing simultaneously.

One of these is the fellowship of Christians: a coherent community increasingly equipped with its own leadership and its own rules. This is the successor to the old Israel as the people of God—an idea symbolized by Jesus' choosing twelve apostles to match the number of the tribes of Israel. At its inception this society practiced a kind of voluntary communism. That may have been imprudent, and certainly Paul later had to organize collections for the impoverished Christians of Jerusalem, but it was a move that expressed a delighted sense of unity and interdependence.

But beyond this "holy nation" stood the human community at large. It featured emperors, laws, magistrates, armies, and prisons. New Testament Christians had very little political influence in that society, but they took it very seriously—not just because it was likely to persecute them, but because it had its own proper place within the purposes of God. Membership in the redeemed society involved an attitude of loyalty and responsibility toward the larger society, not an attitude of indifference to it.

Social progress nearly always seems to depend on minorities who pioneer an alternative life-style within the framework of an existing order. There is usually tension between the majority and the minority. Sometimes the minority is virtually forced out and has to form a New England or a Pennsylvania elsewhere, but even the rejecting society ultimately accepts some of what had been pioneered within it.

Tension often exists within the minority society, too—especially when its members find themselves asked by the larger society to do things that have been excluded from its way of life. Christians, for instance, have often been uncertain whether the pacifism that is obligatory for them as a Christian community should require them to refuse to perform military service in the larger, nonpacifist communities of which they are also members. There is no easy answer to such questions. Probably they should be answered differently at different times as social forms develop. But the tensions engendered by a double loyalty can be creative tensions, since from a biblical point of view they are just different aspects of the service of one God.

SOCIETY

OLD TESTAMENT

Exodus 18:13–24

13 And it came to pass on the morrow, that Moses sat to judge the people: and the people stood by Moses from the morning unto the evening.

14 And when Moses' father in law saw all that he did to the people, he said, What is this thing that thou doest to the people? why sittest thou thyself alone, and all the people stand by thee from morning unto even?

15 And Moses said unto his father in law, Because the people come unto me to inquire of God:

16 When they have a matter, they come unto me; and I judge between one and another, and I do make them know the statutes of God, and his laws.

17 And Moses' father in law said unto him, The thing that thou doest is not good.

18 Thou wilt surely wear away, both thou, and this people that is with thee: for this thing is too heavy for thee; thou art not able to perform it thyself alone.

19 Hearken now unto my voice, I will give thee counsel, and God shall be with thee: Be thou for the people to God-ward, that thou mayest bring the causes unto God:

20 And thou shalt teach them or-

dinances and laws, and shalt shew them the way wherein they must walk, and the work that they must do.

21 Moreover thou shalt provide out of all the people able men, such as fear God, men of truth, hating covetousness; and place such over them, to be rulers of thousands, and rulers of hundreds, rulers of fifties, and rulers of tens:

22 And let them judge the people at all seasons: and it shall be, that every great matter they shall bring unto thee, but every small matter they shall judge: so shall it be easier for thyself, and they shall bear the burden with thee.

23 If thou shalt do this thing, and God command thee so, then thou shalt be able to endure, and all this people shall also go to their place in peace.

24 So Moses hearkened to the voice of his father in law, and did all that he had said.

Isaiah 32:1–2, 5

1 Behold, a king shall reign in righteousness, and princes shall rule in judgment.

2 And a man shall be as an hiding place from the wind, and a covert from the tempest; as rivers of water in a dry place, as the shadow of a great rock in a weary land.

5 The vile person shall be no more called liberal, nor the churl said to be bountiful.

NEW TESTAMENT

Matthew 20:25–28

25 But Jesus called them unto him, and said, Ye know that the princes of the Gentiles exercise dominion over them, and they that are great exercise authority upon them.

26 But it shall not be so among you: but whosoever will be great among you, let him be your minister;

27 And whosoever will be chief among you, let him be your servant:

28 Even as the Son of man came not to be ministered unto, but to minister, and to give his life a ransom for many.

Acts 2:41–47

41 Then they that gladly received his word were baptized: and the same day there were added unto them about three thousand souls.

42 And they continued stedfastly in the apostles' doctrine and fellowship, and in breaking of bread, and in prayers.

43 And fear came upon every soul: and many wonders and signs were done by the apostles.

44 And all that believed were together, and had all things common;

45 And sold their possessions and goods, and parted them to all men, as every man had need.

46 And they, continuing daily with one accord in the temple, and breaking bread from house to house, did eat their meat with gladness and singleness of heart,

47 Praising God, and having favour with all the people. And the Lord added to the church daily such as should be saved.

Romans 12:4–5

4 For as we have many members in

one body, and all members have not the same office:

5 So we, being many, are one body in Christ, and every one members one of another.

1 Peter 2:9–10, 12, 15, 17

9 But ye are a chosen generation, a royal priesthood, an holy nation, a peculiar people; that ye should shew forth the praises of him who hath called you out of darkness into his marvellous light:

10 Which in time past were not a people, but are now the people of God: which had not obtained mercy, but now have obtained mercy.

12 Having your conversation honest among the Gentiles: that, whereas they speak against you as evildoers, they may by your good works, which they shall behold, glorify God in the day of visitation.

15 For so is the will of God, that with well-doing ye may put to silence the ignorance of foolish men.

17 Honour all men.

SPIRIT

Both the Old Testament Hebrew and the New Testament Greek used a single word to denote wind, breath, and spirit. Such a fact is always of more than linguistic importance. It means that the people using those languages actually thought of spirit (whether man's or God's) in the same way that they thought of the wind in the trees or the breath in the lungs. The same kind of invisible yet tangible force gave movement to the branches and life to men and animals. This force was both natural and supernatural, except that no such distinction could be drawn.

The Spirit of God in the Old Testament is divine power coming out from God himself and entering into the history of the world. The spirit of humanity is God's gift of human life—and the change from a capital S to a small one is not, and could not have been, an Old Testament differentiation. Everything from the subduing of primal chaos (see Order) to the skill of the jeweler (see Calling) was the work of the divine Spirit. But more was to come. Israel, resurrected and remade, would consciously experience the Spirit in the life of every individual (see Inspiration).

In the New Testament account of the life of Jesus, the Spirit of God is responsible for his conception and becomes visible at his baptism. Jesus' death and resurrection were followed by a great experience of the power of the Spirit on the Day of Pentecost. From then on, all that Jesus had been to his disciples when he confronted them outwardly he continued to be to them inwardly through the indwelling of the Spirit of God. His disciples claimed that in this experience the hopes of the Old Testament prophets were fulfilled.

Given this belief in the Spirit's power, it is possibly surprising that according to the New Testament the Spirit can be resisted or even quenched. But it is characteristic of the biblical view of spiritual power that it does not override or obliterate personal freedom and responsibility. On the contrary, it enhances them. In the New Testament the chief mark of the Spirit's presence is love.

The trinitarian idea of God as Father, Son, and Holy Spirit was developed in its fullness after the time of the New Testament, but the whole Bible massively affirms that the Spirit is God's.

The English language (in common with most other European languages) enables us to make distinctions that the Hebrew and Greek of the Bible do not make. Such distinctions are worth making. Indeed, the Bible itself, while relating all created things to the Spirit of God, does acknowledge a special relationship between the Spirit of God and man; a still more special one with Israel; a unique one with Jesus; a peculiarly rich and intimate one with the followers of Jesus. In speaking of these things we may well be glad we have words that do not also mean "wind" or "breath." It would be a mistake, however, to make the distinctions absolute and to forget their common biblical roots.

It is helpful to remain aware of the connection between natural and supernatural; between humanity and God and beast; between the sacred and the profane, the holy and the secular. The Bible sees a clear opposition between the holy and the evil, but almost none between the holy and the secular. The Spirit is encountered in all things and in all things is either reverenced or resisted. To be concerned about the church and unconcerned about the environment would be as outrageous as the New Testament says it is to love God and hate your brother.

The biblical account of Spirit is a vision of the connectedness of things. But it is also a vision of each individual's capacity for an inward, personal, and intensely private relationship to the transcendent. The awesome significance of being human could hardly be more strongly stated than by saying that we not only carry a divine flame within us but actually have the power to snuff it out.

SPIRIT

OLD TESTAMENT

Psalm 104:24, 30

O Lord, how manifold are thy works!
In wisdom hast thou made them all:
The earth is full of thy riches.
Thou sendest forth thy spirit, they are created:
And thou renewest the face of the earth.

Psalm 31:5

Into thine hand I commit my spirit:
Thou hast redeemed me, O Lord God of truth.

Ezekiel 37:1–12, 14

1 The hand of the Lord was upon me, and carried me out in the spirit of

335

the Lord, and set me down in the midst of the valley which was full of bones,

2 And caused me to pass by them round about: and, behold, there were very many in the open valley; and, lo, they were very dry.

3 And he said unto me, Son of man, can these bones live? And I answered, O Lord God, thou knowest.

4 Again he said unto me, Prophesy upon these bones, and say unto them, O ye dry bones, hear the word of the Lord.

5 Thus saith the Lord God unto these bones; Behold, I will cause breath to enter into you, and ye shall live:

6 And I will lay sinews upon you, and will bring up flesh upon you, and cover you with skin, and put breath in you, and ye shall live; and ye shall know that I am the Lord.

7 So I prophesied as I was commanded: and as I prophesied, there was a noise, and behold a shaking, and the bones came together, bone to his bone.

8 And when I beheld, lo, the sinews and the flesh came up upon them, and the skin covered them above: but there was no breath in them.

9 Then said he unto me, Prophesy unto the wind, prophesy, son of man, and say to the wind, Thus saith the Lord God; Come from the four winds, O breath, and breathe upon these slain, that they may live.

10 So I prophesied as he commanded me, and the breath came into them, and they lived, and stood up upon their feet, an exceeding great army.

11 Then he said unto me, Son of man, these bones are the whole house of Israel: behold, they say, Our bones are dried, and our hope is lost: we are cut off for our parts.

12 Therefore prophesy and say unto them, Thus saith the Lord God; Behold, O my people, I will open your graves, and cause you to come up out of your graves, and bring you into the land of Israel.

14 And shall put my spirit in you, and ye shall live.

NEW TESTAMENT

Luke 1:35

35 And the angel answered and said unto her [Mary], The Holy Ghost shall come upon thee, and the power of the Highest shall overshadow thee: therefore also that holy thing which shall be born of thee shall be called the Son of God.

Mark 1:7–11

7 And [John the Baptist] preached, saying, There cometh one mightier than I after me, the latchet of whose shoes I am not worthy to stoop down and unloose.

8 I indeed have baptized you with water: but he shall baptize you with the Holy Ghost.

9 And it came to pass in those days, that Jesus came from Nazareth of Galilee, and was baptized of John in Jordan.

10 And straightway coming up out of the water, he saw the heavens opened, and the Spirit like a dove descending upon him:

11 And there came a voice from heaven, saying, Thou art my beloved Son, in whom I am well pleased.

John 15:26

26 But when the Comforter is come, whom I will send unto you from the Father, even the Spirit of truth, which proceedeth from the Father, he shall testify of me.

Acts 2:14–18 (to the crowd at Pentecost)

14 But Peter, standing up with the eleven, lifted up his voice, and said unto them, Ye men of Judæa, and all ye that dwell at Jerusalem, be this known unto you, and hearken to my words:

15 For these are not drunken, as ye suppose, seeing it is but the third hour of the day.

16 But this is that which was spoken by the prophet Joel;

17 And it shall come to pass in the last days, saith God, I will pour out of my Spirit upon all flesh: and your sons and your daughters shall prophesy, and your young men shall see visions, and your old men shall dream dreams:

18 And on my servants and on my handmaidens I will pour out in those days of my Spirit; and they shall prophesy.

Romans 5:5; 1 Thessalonians 5:19

5 The love of God is shed abroad in our hearts by the Holy Ghost which is given unto us.

19 Quench not the Spirit.

STRESS

The word "stress" is said to cover, among other things, "physical, mental, or emotional tension; a situation or factor causing this." The term is not biblical but the experience is. And the Old Testament is inclined to regard the absence of stress as a graver symptom than its presence. The Old Testament's view of life is that it was never meant to be easy.

Jeremiah, for instance, knew the tension that arose from physical suffering, from inner conflict, and from being at odds with his community. His faith in God, far from keeping him clear of such stresses, was the very thing that got him into them. His being the Lord's prophet at all was the result of an inner compulsion from which he would gladly have been free. Emotional tension has rarely been more vividly expressed than in the words of Jeremiah: "Then I said, I will not make mention of him, nor speak any more in his name. But his word was in mine heart as a burning fire shut up in my bones, and I was weary with forbearing, and I could not stay" (20:9).

To have an unpatriotic and unwelcome message of doom to deliver made the strain worse. Later, having been proved right, Jeremiah might have expected to be accepted. Instead, he was required still to swim against the tide by preaching messages of hope and encouragement when everyone else was proclaiming doom. The rope that once pulled him from a well (and how splendid it is to have so circumstantially convincing a story from two and a half millennia ago) was a metaphor for his whole life: the rope was his salvation, but it threatened to cut into his flesh; the strain was intolerable, but the alternative was death.

Yet the prophetic message was never one of stoic endurance, nor did the prophets speak of suffering as necessarily purifying or ennobling. Their promise was only that the power of God was there. In fire and flood God's presence could be experienced.

The New Testament is equally clear that a stress-free life is no part of the Christian promise. What is offered is a way of bearing stress—a way that makes the experience creative without its ceasing to be painful. Physical suffering, family tension, and social insecurity were all part of what the disciples were told to expect, but they were also told that in those experiences they would discover the power of God's Spirit. The yoke is a natural image of stress and strain, and yet, Jesus offers his yoke to the heavy laden, saying, "My yoke is easy, and my burden is light" (Matthew 11:30).

The Gospels show Jesus himself in the Garden of Gethsemane under extreme tension. Having submitted himself to the will of God, he is strengthened, but even after this strengthening he is described as praying in such anguish that his sweat was like drops of blood.

The Bible does suggest a way to cope with stress (see also Anxiety, Depression), but not a means to avoid it. Stress is to be neither evaded nor cultivated.

There are those who cultivate it, however. There is a type of man who is not so much a troubleshooter as a troubleseeker. There is a type of woman who considers a straightforward relationship boring and who insists on spicing it with emotional complications of some sort. And there are innumerable variations on these themes.

There are also those who try to evade stress. They refuse to hear bad news. They shrink the range of life and experience the better to cocoon themselves. They will not face up to old age or death. Sooner or later, however, the cocoon is broken open and they must face reality like everyone else.

The biblical word for both the cultivators and the evaders of stress is "fools." Wisdom is to take the inevitable strains without resentment, trusting that there is that in man and in his environment that can use tension as a means of growth.

STRESS

OLD TESTAMENT

Amos 6:1

1 Woe to them that are at ease in Zion, and trust in the mountain of Samaria.

Jeremiah 38:1–13

1 Jeremiah had spoken unto all the people, saying,

2 Thus saith the Lord, He that remaineth in this city shall die by the sword, by the famine, and by the pestilence: but he that goeth forth to the Chaldeans shall live; for he shall have his life for a prey, and shall live.

3 Thus saith the Lord, This city shall surely be given into the hand of the king of Babylon's army, which shall take it.

4 Therefore the princes said unto the king, We beseech thee, let this man be put to death: for thus he weakeneth the hands of the men of war that remain in this city, and the hands of all the people, in speaking such words unto them: for this man seeketh not the welfare of this people, but the hurt.

5 Then Zedekiah the king said, Behold, he is in your hand: for the king is not he that can do any thing against you.

6 Then took they Jeremiah, and cast him into the dungeon of Malchiah the son of Hammelech, that was in the court of the prison: and they let down Jeremiah with cords. And in the dungeon there was no water, but mire: so Jeremiah sunk in the mire.

7 Now when Ebed-melech the Ethiopian, one of the eunuchs which was in the king's house, heard that they had put Jeremiah in the dungeon; the king then sitting in the gate of Benjamin;

8 Ebed-melech went forth out of the king's house, and spake to the king, saying,

9 My lord the king, these men have done evil in all that they have done to Jeremiah the prophet, whom they have cast into the dungeon; and he is like to die for hunger in the place where he is: for there is no more bread in the city.

10 Then the king commanded Ebed-melech the Ethiopian, saying, Take from hence thirty men with thee, and take up Jeremiah the prophet out of the dungeon, before he die.

11 So Ebed-melech took the men with him, and went into the house of the king under the treasury, and took thence old cast clouts and old rotten rags, and let them down by cords into the dungeon to Jeremiah.

12 And Ebed-melech the Ethiopian said unto Jeremiah, Put now these old cast clouts and rotten rags under thine armholes under the cords. And Jeremiah did so.

13 So they drew up Jeremiah with cords, and took him up out of the dungeon: and Jeremiah remained in the court of the prison.

Isaiah 43:2–3

2 When thou passest through the waters, I will be with thee; and through

the rivers, they shall not overflow thee: when thou walkest through the fire, thou shalt not be burned; neither shall the flame kindle upon thee.

3 For I am the Lord thy God, the Holy One of Israel, thy Saviour.

NEW TESTAMENT

Mark 13:9-13

9 But take heed to yourselves: for they shall deliver you up to councils; and in the synagogues ye shall be beaten: and ye shall be brought before rulers and kings for my sake, for a testimony against them.

10 And the gospel must first be published among all nations.

11 But when they shall lead you, and deliver you up, take no thought beforehand what ye shall speak, neither do ye premeditate: but whatsoever shall be given you in that hour, that speak ye: for it is not ye that speak, but the Holy Ghost.

12 Now the brother shall betray the brother to death, and the father the son; and children shall rise up against their parents, and shall cause them to be put to death.

13 And ye shall be hated of all men for my name's sake: but he that shall endure unto the end, the same shall be saved.

Luke 22:39-44

39 And he came out, and went, as he was wont, to the mount of Olives; and his disciples also followed him.

40 And when he was at the place, he said unto them, Pray that ye enter not into temptation.

41 And he was withdrawn from them about a stone's cast, and kneeled down, and prayed,

42 Saying, Father, if thou be willing, remove this cup from me: nevertheless not my will, but thine, be done.

43 And there appeared an angel unto him from heaven, strengthening him.

44 And being in an agony he prayed more earnestly: and his sweat was as it were great drops of blood falling down to the ground.

1 Peter 4:12-13

12 Beloved, think it not strange concerning the fiery trial which is to try you, as though some strange thing happened unto you:

13 But rejoice, inasmuch as ye are partakers of Christ's sufferings; that, when his glory shall be revealed, ye may be glad also with exceeding joy.

SUFFERING

The problem of suffering is an intensely modern one, but it has probably never been stated more forcibly than in the Old Testament Book of Job. And perhaps the chief lesson of the book is that to state the problem openly and in the presence of God is the way to deal with it—not to answer the problem, but to set it in a context where pain seems as natural as joy and where both are inseparable from coming alive to the divine glory. The one thing suffering does not do is the very thing Job begins by feeling it has done: make life pointless.

Another thing suffering does not do is what Job's friends insisted that it did: come as a punishment for wrongdoing. Job himself, while denying that this was the case, did feel that it ought to be. In the end he is persuaded to withdraw that belief, and his friends are told plainly that they are wrong. Suffering is not punishment.

Yet none of Job's questions is answered. After thirty-six chapters of sublimely dramatic speeches in verse form (precipitated into a culture that had no tradition of verse drama; emanating from the sheer force of the issue discussed), God speaks. His chapters are magnificent (see Nature), but he nowhere speaks of the problem of suffering and never explains himself or his policy. These chapters do not offer even a glance at the possibility of a compensatory life after death. Instead, Job is shown the wonder of the world we have in the form in which we have it. Obviously our world is not a meritocracy that rewards moral virtue or punishes the lack of it. Suffering is a mystery within a world of mysteries. The very reason for existing at all remains unexplained. But existence is glorious. Job withdraws his complaint because he has learned to live in the world as it is, and to worship its God as he is.

In a prose postscript (that could well be part of an earlier story into which the inspired poet has inserted the verse dialogue) Job's fortunes are restored, but before that happens he has already been reconciled to the way the world is.

Several New Testament writers seized on the Suffering Servant poems in the Book of Isaiah as a way of interpreting the suffering of Jesus. The popular view at the time still was (and still is) that of Job's friends. Goodness, it was thought, must surely procure immunity from suffering. So Jesus was expected to prove his messiahship by descending from the cross. Instead, he suffered and died on it. His followers believed that by doing this in unbroken fellowship with them and with God he brought the two parties together.

The New Testament does not suggest (as some have) that God was determined to punish somebody for humanity's wickedness and that he did not mind hitting the wrong target so long as somebody got hurt. Rather it sees the human condition as one in which suffering is inevitable and one which could be brought to perfection only from within that experience of suffering.

New Testament Christians did not expect to be free of suffering themselves, but Jesus had set them an example of relieving the sufferings of others, so they accepted the double role of both fighting suffering and accepting it.

That remains the recommended course: to relieve suffering and yet to live with it—even to expose oneself to it for love's sake. As with stress, so with suffering generally: it is to be neither cultivated nor evaded. The psychological sickness of those who cultivate suffering is known as masochism. The spiritual sickness of those who seek to have nothing to do with it has no one name but is probably more common. One feature of this latter condition is lovelessness, because love certainly makes men and women more vulnerable to pain.

We have no business holding a view of God or a theory of life that can be subsequently challenged by the fact of suffering. Suffering is there from the start. A realistic faith builds itself into a world view that takes account from the beginning of both suffering and joy. Perhaps a capacity for joy is inevitably a capacity for suffering.

SUFFERING

OLD TESTAMENT

Job 3:20, 24; 21:7; 30:25–27;
34:1, 5, 10–11; 38:1–4; 42:7

Wherefore is light given to him that is in misery,
And life unto the bitter in soul;
For my sighing cometh before I eat,
And my roarings are poured out like the waters.
Wherefore do the wicked live,
Become old, yea, are mighty in power?
Did not I weep for him that was in trouble?
Was not my soul grieved for the poor?
When I looked for good, then evil came unto me:
And when I waited for light, there came darkness.
My bowels boiled, and rested not:
The days of affliction prevented me.

Furthermore Elihu answered and said,

For Job hath said, I am righteous:
And God hath taken away my judgment.
Therefore hearken unto me, ye men of understanding:
Far be it from God, that he should do wickedness;
And from the Almighty, that he should commit iniquity.
For the work of a man shall he render unto him,

And cause every man to find according to his ways.

Then the Lord answered Job out of the whirlwind, and said,

Who is this that darkeneth counsel
By words without knowledge?
Gird up now thy loins like a man;
For I will demand of thee, and answer thou me.
Where wast thou when I laid the foundations of the earth?
Declare, if thou hast understanding.

And it was so, that after the Lord had spoken these words unto Job, the Lord said to Eliphaz the Temanite, My wrath is kindled against thee, and against thy two friends: for ye have not spoken of me the thing that is right, as my servant Job hath.

Isaiah 53:4–5, 10

4 Surely he hath borne our griefs, and carried our sorrows: yet we did esteem him stricken, smitten of God, and afflicted.
5 But he was wounded for our transgressions, he was bruised for our iniquities: the chastisement of our peace was upon him; and with his stripes we are healed.

10 Yet it pleased the Lord to bruise him; he hath put him to grief.

NEW TESTAMENT

Matthew 8:16–17

16 When the even was come, they brought unto him many that were possessed with devils: and he cast out the spirits with his word, and healed all that were sick:

17 That it might be fulfilled which was spoken by Esaias the prophet, saying, Himself took our infirmities, and bare our sicknesses.

Mark 8:31–34

31 And he began to teach them, that the Son of man must suffer many things, and be rejected of the elders, and of the chief priests, and scribes, and be killed, and after three days rise again.

32 And he spake that saying openly. And Peter took him, and began to rebuke him.

33 But when he had turned about and looked on his disciples, he rebuked Peter, saying, Get thee behind me, Satan: for thou savourest not the things that be of God, but the things that be of men.

34 And when he had called the people unto him with his disciples also, he said unto them, Whosoever will come after me, let him deny himself, and take up his cross, and follow me.

Mark 15:25, 29–32

25 And it was the third hour, and they crucified him.

29 And they that passed by railed on him, wagging their heads, and saying, Ah, thou that destroyest the temple, and buildest it in three days,

30 Save thyself, and come down from the cross.

31 Likewise also the chief priests mocking said among themselves with the scribes, He saved others; himself he cannot save.

32 Let Christ the King of Israel descend now from the cross, that we may see and believe.

Hebrews 2:10–11

10 For it became him, for whom are all things, and by whom are all things, in bringing many sons unto glory, to make the captain of their salvation perfect through sufferings.

11 For both he that sanctifieth and they who are sanctified are all of one: for which cause he is not ashamed to call them brethren.

SYMPATHY

The Old Testament prophets made what now seems a conventional distinction between religious rites and human sympathy, but they were probably not being at all conventional at the time. They addressed people who could well have imagined (though it was not official doctrine) that their standing with God had more to do with fasting than with a concern for other people's troubles. Moreover, the prophets insisted that it had to be an active concern. *Feelings* of sympathy were not enough.

Not that sympathetic feelings have no place. Job's friends showed true sympathy when they sat with him in silence for a week. Only when they started lecturing him on the theology of suffering did they become "Job's comforters" in the derogatory sense.

The trouble is that those who feel sympathy and even give active help are inclined to look for gratitude and admiration in return. As the psalmist learned, thanks are not always forthcoming. The importance of sympathy is in no way reduced by that fact. Sympathy is essentially disinterested love, not a way of bringing pressure to bear. It is identification with those in need.

The Gospel parable about the sheep and the goats reveals the deep levels at which sympathy moves. The story uses as furniture a very conventional and stylized picture of the last judgment, but the story is clearly aimed at the present rather than the future. It is a parable about sympathy rather than an allegory of the end of time. And it says not only that sympathy must be active in the form of feeding and clothing and visiting, but also that it is the prime element in our relationship with heaven. The Lord himself identifies with those in need. Our dealings with them are not just influenced by our relationship with God, they *are* our relationship with God.

The prophets had good reason to look simultaneously at religious observance and sympathetic action. Sympathy has the mystic power to join humanity and God as feasts and fasts and sacrifices aim to do. In sympathy we can identify with those with whom God is identified. Thus the service of the needy becomes a sacrament of communion.

Modern communications have exposed humanity's sympathetic nerve endings to the sorrows and troubles of people all around the world. If feelings were what mattered most, the sheer quantity of the pain to be shared might overwhelm anyone. But what matters is to feel enough to make one act, and to act in a way that is designed simply to help—not to be a form of self-interest or self-promotion dressed in the clothing of benevolence. Much overseas aid has been undertaken by the West with an expectation of dividends. Some have expected trade in return, and some have expected to be loved in return, but neither attitude reflects pure sympathy.

One of the things that pure sympathy has always had to learn to do is to help without humiliating. The old-style Lady Bountiful finds it hard to see that her basket of goodies so graciously bestowed on the humble peasantry is an additional burden she has laid on their backs. That they should covet her land so as to be able to do without her humiliating charity may be a human reaction rather than an ungrateful one. She herself would see things differently and act differently if she learned the New Testament way of seeing in the needy not her dependents but her Lord.

Sympathy is above all a way of seeing the world, a form of vision. It is the view of those who look at every situation not from a secure distance but through the eyes of the people subjected to it.

It is not all pain, either. Paul said, "Rejoice with them that do rejoice, and weep with them that weep" (Romans 12:15).

SYMPATHY

OLD TESTAMENT

Isaiah 58:5–7

5 Is it such a fast that I have chosen? a day for a man to afflict his soul? is it to bow down his head as a bulrush, and to spread sackcloth and ashes under him? wilt thou call this a fast, and an acceptable day to the Lord?

6 Is not this the fast that I have chosen? to loose the bands of wickedness, to undo the heavy burdens, and to let the oppressed go free, and that ye break every yoke?

7 Is it not to deal thy bread to the hungry, and that thou bring the poor that are cast out to thy house? when thou seest the naked, that thou cover him; and that thou hide not thyself from thine own flesh?

Job 2:11–13

11 Now when Job's three friends heard of all this evil that was come upon him, they came every one from his own place; Eliphaz the Temanite, and Bildad the Shuhite, and Zophar the Naamathite: for they had made an appointment together to come to mourn with him and to comfort him.

12 And when they lifted up their eyes afar off, and knew him not, they lifted up their voice, and wept; and they rent every one his mantle, and sprinkled dust upon their heads toward heaven.

13 So they sat down with him upon the ground seven days and seven nights, and none spake a word unto him: for they saw that his grief was very great.

Psalm 35:11–14

False witnesses did rise up;
They laid to my charge things that I knew not.
They rewarded me evil for good
To the spoiling of my soul.
But as for me, when they were sick, my clothing was sackcloth:
I humbled my soul with fasting;
And my prayer returned into mine own bosom.
I behaved myself as though he had been my friend or brother:
I bowed down heavily, as one that mourneth for his mother.

NEW TESTAMENT

Matthew 25:31–45

31 When the Son of man shall come in his glory, and all the holy

angels with him, then shall he sit upon the throne of his glory:

32 And before him shall be gathered all nations: and he shall separate them one from another, as a shepherd divideth his sheep from the goats:

33 And he shall set the sheep on his right hand, but the goats on the left.

34 Then shall the King say unto them on his right hand, Come, ye blessed of my Father, inherit the kingdom prepared for you from the foundation of the world:

35 For I was an hungered, and ye gave me meat: I was thirsty, and ye gave me drink: I was a stranger, and ye took me in:

36 Naked, and ye clothed me: I was sick, and ye visited me: I was in prison, and ye came unto me.

37 Then shall the righteous answer him, saying, Lord, when saw we thee an hungered, and fed thee? or thirsty, and gave thee drink?

38 When saw we thee a stranger, and took thee in? or naked, and clothed thee?

39 Or when saw we thee sick, or in prison, and came unto thee?

40 And the King shall answer and say unto them, Verily I say unto you, Inasmuch as ye have done it unto one of the least of these my brethren, ye have done it unto me.

41 Then shall he say also unto them on the left hand, Depart from me, ye cursed, into everlasting fire, prepared for the devil and his angels:

42 For I was an hungered, and ye gave me no meat: I was thirsty, and ye gave me no drink:

43 I was a stranger, and ye took me not in: naked, and ye clothed me not: sick, and in prison, and ye visited me not.

44 Then shall they also answer him, saying, Lord, when saw we thee an hungered, or athirst, or a stranger, or naked, or sick, or in prison, and did not minister unto thee?

45 Then shall he answer them, saying, Verily I say unto you, Inasmuch as ye did it not to one of the least of these, ye did it not to me.

Hebrews 13:3

3 Remember them that are in bonds, as bound with them; and them which suffer adversity, as being yourselves also in the body.

TEACHING

The Old Testament regards all truth as residing in God, so all sound teaching is from him. Some of his lessons are taught through the natural world and learned by practical experience. Many lessons are given by fathers to sons, and provision was made to stimulate a child's curiosity so that teaching could be given as a response to his own questions. The Passover ceremonies, for instance, were designed to provoke a child into asking, "What mean ye by this?" (Exodus 12:26). In answer to this question the history of Israel was to be taught.

Special skills—artistic craftsmanship, for instance—sometimes required special teachers. Bezalel and Oholiab were not only inspired workmen, but inspired teachers, who recognized God as the source both of the content of their lessons and of their ability to impart knowledge.

Above all, however, the priestly tribe of Levi bore the responsibility of seeing that each generation understood God's law. Exiles returning to Jerusalem in the time of Nehemiah had been cut off from this formal teaching, so a big effort of popular education was mounted under the leadership of Ezra. It became a sort of teaching festival, notable for its enthusiasm and for the fact that women and young people were among those taught. It was hoped that eventually even Gentile nations would be included.

The New Testament Gospels report that the teaching style of Jesus was regarded as unusual. He taught as one with direct access to truth (that is, to God) rather than as an interpreter of traditional authorities. All the same, he was commonly addressed as Rabbi, or Teacher—sometimes by sincere and educated enquirers such as Nicodemus, sometimes by flattering enemies about to spring a trick question. All parties accepted that teaching could be done through dialogue, in the form of questions and responses.

The followers of Jesus believed that through him, and through the gift of the Spirit, they too had a new and more direct access to the truth. Nevertheless, the office of teacher became a recognized function within the economy of the early church: "first apostles, secondarily prophets, thirdly teachers" (1 Corinthians 12:28). Apostles might kindle faith, and prophets might reveal new insights, but there was need for teachers to perform the continuing and less dramatic task of seeing that converts understood what was to be believed and what way of life followed from believing it.

The word "academic" is often used now in a derogatory sense to indicate teaching that is detached from any relationship to life. The term could well be rescued from this usage, but there does exist a kind of teaching that appears to be an end in itself. The lessons learned acquire significance only in examination rooms and quiz games. The biblical idea of teaching is something very different.

Teaching, in the Bible's view, is always a life-enhancing opening up of the connection between ultimate truth and immediate circumstances. The lessons taught are not necessarily job-related, but they are related to life and to the questions that life provokes in those who are ready to learn. True teaching is essentially a dialogue—between an individual and the environment, if not between individuals. And understanding was always expected to result in action. A typical teaching pattern would run this way: "That being the case, this is what you should do."

Such a view does allow for specialized subjects and specialist teachers. Since all truth has a single transcendent source, however, it is even more important to understand the connection between different branches of knowledge than it is to understand some particular branch in minute detail. Given the complexity of modern knowledge, it may be too much to ask that a specialist should look far beyond the boundaries of his or her narrow field, but if the specialist does not do so, then somebody else must. The coordination of knowledge is essential to the work of teaching as the Bible understands it, and that coordination has to be in terms of the questions raised by living as a human being.

TEACHING

OLD TESTAMENT

Isaiah 28:24–26

24 Doth the plowman plow all day to sow? doth he open and break the clods of his ground?

25 When he hath made plain the face thereof, doth he not cast abroad the fitches, and scatter the cummin, and cast in the principal wheat and the appointed barley and the rie in their place?

26 For his God doth instruct him to discretion, and doth teach him.

Exodus 35:34 (on God's gifts to a craftsman)

34 And he hath put in his heart that he may teach.

Proverbs 4:1–2

Hear, ye children, the instruction of a father,
And attend to know understanding.
For I give you good doctrine,
Forsake ye not my law.

Nehemiah 8:1–3, 7–8, 12

1 And all the people gathered themselves together as one man into the street that was before the water gate; and they spake unto Ezra the scribe to bring the book of the law of Moses, which the Lord had commanded to Israel.

2 And Ezra the priest brought the law before the congregation both of men and women, and all that could hear with understanding, upon the first day of the seventh month.

3 And he read therein before the street that was before the water gate from the morning until midday, before the men and the women, and those that could understand; and the ears of all the people were attentive unto the book of the law.

7 The Levites, caused the people to understand the law: and the people stood in their place.

8 So they read in the book in the law of God distinctly, and gave the sense, and caused them to understand the reading.

12 And all the people went their way to eat, and to drink, and to send portions, and to make great mirth, because they had understood the words that were declared unto them.

Micah 4:2

2 And many nations shall come, and say, Come, and let us go up to the mountain of the Lord, and to the house

of the God of Jacob; and he will teach us of his ways, and we will walk in his paths.

NEW TESTAMENT

Matthew 7:28–29

28 And it came to pass, when Jesus had ended these sayings, the people were astonished at his doctrine:

29 For he taught them as one having authority, and not as the scribes.

Matthew 22:16–17

16 And they sent out unto him their disciples with the Herodians saying, Master, we know that thou art true, and teachest the way of God in truth, neither carest thou for any man: for thou regardest not the person of men.

17 Tell us therefore, What thinkest thou? Is it lawful to give tribute unto Cæsar, or not?

John 3:1–2

1 There was a man of the Pharisees, named Nicodemus, a ruler of the Jews:

2 The same came to Jesus by night, and said unto him, Rabbi, we know that thou art a teacher come from God: for no man can do these miracles that thou doest, except God be with him.

John 14:25–26

25 These things have I spoken unto you, being yet present with you.

26 But the Comforter, which is the Holy Ghost, whom the Father will send in my name, he shall teach you all things, and bring all things to your remembrance, whatsoever I have said unto you.

1 Corinthians 2:12–13

12 Now we have received, not the spirit of the world, but the spirit which is of God; that we might know the things that are freely given to us of God.

13 Which things also we speak, not in the words which man's wisdom teacheth, but which the Holy Ghost teacheth; comparing spiritual things with spiritual.

TEMPERANCE

Temperance is obviously something different from abstinence, and neither applies exclusively to alcoholic drink. In the general sense of the word, the Old Testament shows no particular enthusiasm for striking a careful balance between having and doing without. Possibly the Greeks thought more than did the Hebrews about the virtue of moderation. Biblical writers tended to have a greater respect for absolute commitment or total self-denial. So, on the narrower subject of alcohol, it is not surprising to find passages in praise of wine and other passages saluting as especially holy a group of men who did not touch as much as a grape skin.

On one occasion Jeremiah used a group of abstainers in order to make a point in a way that would gain attention. Some Rechabites were taking shelter in Jerusalem in spite of the fact that they were sworn to a nomadic life without wine or fixed housing. Jeremiah took them to the temple and offered them wine. When he met with the expected refusal, he said to the rest of the crowd, "See how these people have kept the command of their ancestor, yet you have disregarded the command of God." As so often happens, the small group taking an extreme position presented a challenge to the majority and to its conscience, although there was no suggestion that the life-style of the minority was in itself superior (see Jeremiah 35).

The New Testament makes very clear that, although self-indulgence and excess are abuses, abstinence from the good things of life is never an end in itself. It may be good to abstain in order to concentrate on some other activity that will bring one closer to God, but it is not the abstinence itself that has that effect. Abstaining is merely a way of making room in life for other things. This attitude allowed different patterns of life to be considered equally valid. So John the Baptist followed one life-style and Jesus another, even though it resulted in his being accused (unjustly, no doubt) of being a glutton and a drunkard.

Paul disciplined his body not because he despised it but in order to be fit for his job. In line with this, he said that married couples might reasonably deny themselves sexual satisfaction, but only so long as it was for a special purpose and a limited time (1 Corinthians 7:55). He had trouble enough with those who believed that bodily deprivations were in themselves pleasing to God, though he was always prepared to adjust his own behavior in order to avoid troubling another Christian's conscience: "if meat make my brother to offend, I will eat no flesh while the world standeth" (1 Corinthians 8:13).

As the churches became increasingly organized, it began to be worth saying that their leaders should be chosen from among those who had shown themselves to be temperate. This meant that the leaders should be in control of their appetites, weakened by neither indulgence nor deprivation. Timothy himself was urged to "drink no longer water, but use a little wine for thy stomach's sake" (1 Timothy 5:23).

On the subject of temperance the Bible is really quite temperate. One wonders, in fact, how later generations of Christians came either to reconcile themselves to the luxuries of court life (as some did) or to see hair shirts and scourges as proper ways of making life uncomfortable for themselves (as others did). Crippling the body, whether by self-punishment or by self-indulgence, was a poor way of coordinating body and spirit in the service of one who was said to have come "that they might have life, and that they might have it more abundantly" (John 10:10).

In a modern setting the biblical understanding of temperance could well be extended socially, politically, and economically. Personal temperance writ large might look very like a concern for ecological balance. A civilization that does not control its appetite for fuel and food and alcohol (in industrial as well as potable form) is certainly liable to collapse—and to do so as a direct result of excess. A society focused on consumption may need the discipline of temperance. The back-to-nature freaks could be the Rechabites of our day.

TEMPERANCE

OLD TESTAMENT

Leviticus 10:8–9; Numbers 6:1–4

8 And the Lord spake unto Aaron, saying,

9 Do not drink wine nor strong drink, thou, nor thy sons with thee, when ye go into the tabernacle of the congregation, lest ye die.

1 And the Lord spake unto Moses, saying,

2 Speak unto the children of Israel, and say unto them, When either man or woman shall separate themselves to vow a vow of a Nazarite, to separate themselves unto the Lord:

3 He shall separate himself from wine and strong drink, and shall drink no vinegar of wine, or vinegar of strong drink, neither shall he drink any liquor of grapes, nor eat moist grapes, or dried.

4 All the days of his separation shall he eat nothing that is made of the vine tree, from the kernels even to the husk.

Psalm 104:1, 14–15

Bless the Lord, O my soul.
He causeth the grass to grow for the cattle,
And herb for the service of man:
That he may bring forth food out of the earth;

And wine that maketh glad the heart of man.

Isaiah 28:7

7 But they also have erred through wine, and through strong drink are out of the way; the priest and the prophet have erred through strong drink, they are swallowed up of wine, they are out of the way through strong drink; they err in vision, they stumble in judgment.

Proverbs 23:20–21

Be not among winebibbers;
Among riotous eaters of flesh:
For the drunkard and the glutton shall
    come to poverty:
And drowsiness shall clothe a man with
    rags.

Ecclesiastes 5:10; 6:9

10 He that loveth silver shall not be satisfied with silver; nor he that loveth abundance with increase: this is also vanity.

9 Better is the sight of the eyes than the wandering of the desire: this is also vanity and vexation of spirit.

NEW TESTAMENT

Luke 1:13–15

13 But the angel said unto him, Fear not, Zacharias: for thy prayer is

heard; and thy wife Elisabeth shall bear thee a son, and thou shalt call his name John.

14 And thou shalt have joy and gladness; and many shall rejoice at his birth.

15 For he shall be great in the sight of the Lord, and shall drink neither wine nor strong drink; and he shall be filled with the Holy Ghost, even from his mother's womb.

Luke 7:33–34

33 For John the Baptist came neither eating bread nor drinking wine; and ye say, He hath a devil.

34 The Son of man is come eating and drinking; and ye say, Behold a gluttonous man, and a winebibber, a friend of publicans and sinners!

1 Corinthians 9:25–27

25 And every man that striveth for the mastery is temperate in all things. Now they do it to obtain a corruptible crown; but we an incorruptible.

26 I therefore so run, not as uncertainly; so fight I, not as one that beateth the air:

27 But I keep under my body, and bring it into subjection: lest that by any means, when I have preached to others, I myself should be a castaway.

Colossians 2:16, 20–23

16 Let no man therefore judge you in meat, or in drink.

20 Wherefore if ye be dead with Christ from the rudiments of the world, why, as though living in the world, are ye subject to ordinances,

21 (Touch not; taste not; handle not;

22 Which all are to perish with the using;) after the commandments and doctrines of men?

23 Which things have indeed a shew of wisdom in will-worship, and humility, and neglecting of the body; not in any honour to the satisfying of the flesh.

1 Timothy 3:8; Titus 1:7–8

8 Likewise must the deacons be grave, not double-tongued, not given to much wine, not greedy of filthy lucre.

7 For a bishop must be blameless, as the steward of God; not selfwilled, not soon angry, not given to wine, no striker, not given to filthy lucre;

8 But a lover of hospitality, a lover of good men, sober, just, holy, temperate.

TEMPTATION

However it got here, there is in the world such a thing as evil. Whatever we call it, we do sometimes find it enticing. That enticement is temptation. The biblical word used for it can also mean testing or proving, and can therefore be used with no reference to evil, but the possibility of giving way to what is wrong constitutes temptation as we now understand it. There is indeed an element of testing in our flirtations with evil, and some regard this as the justification for evil's existence, but for practical purposes it is more important to know how to cope with temptation than to consider its hidden purpose or its mysterious origins.

The Bible recommends unmasking evil, praying about it, teaming up with those who are good at defeating it, and contemplating the good alternative to the tempting evil. The Bible's recommendations are sometimes expressed as stories in which evil is personalized in some way, but they remain practical stories for the tempted rather than metaphysical speculations for the philosophical.

The Adam and Eve story in the Old Testament makes it clear that giving way to temptation produces a whole chain of consequences. Even what is innocent (nakedness) is felt to be shameful, and in the rush to shift the blame, all relationships are damaged. Adam blames Eve—with a broad hint that God himself is not altogether free of responsibility ("the woman whom thou gavest to be with me"). Eve blames the serpent and claims to have been deceived—as she had (but there is a voluntary side even to being deceived).

Choosing to face the fact that temptation is temptation—instead of allowing yourself to think of it as an enlargement of life experience—is one of the Old Testament's recommended approaches to defeating it.

New Testament writers believed that Jesus was perfect but that his perfection by no means placed him above temptation. Indeed, they were glad to know that he was indeed not above being tempted. As one writer says, "In that he himself hath suffered being tempted, he is able to succor them that are tempted" (Hebrews 2:18). The emphasis here may be on temptation as testing, but Jesus himself spoke of his being tempted to do wrong. After all, the story of his temptations in the desert could have come from no one else, and in it he is tempted by self-interest (bread), by power (all the kingdoms of the world), and by publicity stunts for furthering the work of the kingdom (leaping from the temple). Such trials, he said, are inevitable, but that is no excuse for bringing them on other people.

A world in which men and women had no inclination to choose evil would be a world in which choosing good carried no significance. If they were kept from evil by its being made so unattractive as to be repulsive, then they would be merely bribed into goodness. If goodness were accomplished by making evil simply unattainable, then human beings would be deprived of freedom and turned into automata. The evolution of a moral being must surely include at least a stage when badness is a real option and when the only thing to be said for goodness is that it is good. But while the Bible throws some light on such speculations, it does not work them out.

The biblical approach is a practical one: face the fact that you are going to be tempted; see temptation for what it is and turn to transcendent goodness for help. To appreciate the good is the best way to blunt your appetite for evil. The moral taste buds can be educated (see Conscience). The truly life-enhancing experiences are the ones that reveal how shoddy and deceptive the alternatives are. And the Bible insists that there is that in our environment which is supportive of the right choices.

So there is no need to be as defeatist (and little hope of being as witty) as the Oscar Wilde character who said, "I can resist everything except temptation."

TEMPTATION

OLD TESTAMENT

Genesis 3:1–13

1 Now the serpent was more subtil than any beast of the field which the Lord God had made. And he said unto the woman, Yea, hath God said, Ye shall not eat of every tree of the garden?

2 And the woman said unto the serpent, We may eat of the fruit of the trees of the garden:

3 But of the fruit of the tree which is in the midst of the garden, God hath said, Ye shall not eat of it, neither shall ye touch it, lest ye die.

4 And the serpent said unto the woman, Ye shall not surely die:

5 For God doth know that in the day ye eat thereof, then your eyes shall be opened, and ye shall be as gods, knowing good and evil.

6 And when the woman saw that the tree was good for food, and that it was pleasant to the eyes, and a tree to be desired to make one wise, she took of the fruit thereof, and did eat, and gave also unto her husband with her; and he did eat.

7 And the eyes of them both were opened, and they knew that they were naked; and they sewed fig leaves together, and made themselves aprons.

8 And they heard the voice of the Lord God walking in the garden in the cool of the day: and Adam and his wife hid themselves from the presence of the Lord God amongst the trees of the garden.

9 And the Lord God called unto Adam, and said unto him, Where art thou?

10 And he said, I heard thy voice in the garden, and I was afraid, because I was naked; and I hid myself.

11 And he said, Who told thee that thou wast naked? Hast thou eaten of the tree, whereof I commanded thee that thou shouldest not eat?

12 And the man said, The woman whom thou gavest to be with me, she gave me of the tree, and I did eat.

13 And the Lord God said unto the woman, What is this that thou hast done? and the woman said, The serpent beguiled me, and I did eat.

NEW TESTAMENT

Luke 4:1–13

1 And Jesus being full of the Holy Ghost returned from Jordan, and was led by the Spirit into the wilderness,

2 Being forty days tempted of the devil. And in those days he did eat

nothing: and when they were ended, he afterward hungered.

3 And the devil said unto him, If thou be the Son of God, command this stone that it be made bread.

4 And Jesus answered him, saying, It is written, That man shall not live by bread alone, but by every word of God.

5 And the devil, taking him up into an high mountain, shewed unto him all the kingdoms of the world in a moment of time.

6 And the devil said unto him, All this power will I give thee, and the glory of them: for that is delivered unto me; and to whomsoever I will I give it.

7 If thou therefore wilt worship me, all shall be thine.

8 And Jesus answered and said unto him, Get thee behind me, Satan: for it is written, Thou shalt worship the Lord thy God, and him only shalt thou serve.

9 And he brought him to Jerusalem, and set him on a pinnacle of the temple, and said unto him, If thou be the Son of God, cast thyself down from hence:

10 For it is written, He shall give his angels charge over thee, to keep thee:

11 And in their hands they shall

bear thee up, lest at any time thou dash thy foot against a stone.

12 And Jesus answering said unto him, It is said, Thou shalt not tempt the Lord thy God.

13 And when the devil had ended all the temptation, he departed from him for a season

Luke 11:2, 4

2 And he said unto them, When ye pray, say . . .

4 And lead us not into temptation. . . .

Luke 17:1–2

1 Then said he unto the disciples, It is impossible but that offences will come: but woe unto him, through whom they come!

2 It were better for him that a millstone were hanged about his neck, and he cast into the sea, than that he should offend one of these little ones.

1 Corinthians 10:13

13 There hath no temptation taken you but such as is common to man: but God is faithful, who will not suffer you to be tempted above that ye are able; but will with the temptation also make a way to escape, that ye may be able to bear it.

TRUST

The entry for Faith explains that the biblical concept of faith is indistinguishable from that of trust (see also Confidence). But when we, with our larger vocabulary, ask the Bible about trust we are presumably asking to what extent we should put ourselves or our possessions into the hands of others. The man who invites a surgeon to operate on him is a typical example of trust in our sense of the word, because he puts his life in another's hands.

The first thing the Old Testament says is that in relation to God this kind of trust must be absolute. Even if it seems likely to cost you your life, you must be true to your allegiance and leave the consequences in God's hands. The stories in the Book of Daniel only dramatize the Old Testament's constant assurances of the trustworthiness of God.

So preoccupied is the Old Testament with this thought that it usually mentions trust in connection with human beings only to speak of their relative untrustworthiness: "Cursed be the man that trusteth in man" (Jeremiah 17:5). However, it was said of the men carrying out temple repairs for King Joseph that "There was no reckoning made with them of the money that was delivered into their hand because they dealt faithfully" (2 Kings 22:7). And many prophets looked forward to a time when people would be able to depend utterly on one another: "A man shall be as an hiding place from the wind" (Isaiah 32:2).

The New Testament in some ways reverses the angle. It takes for granted that men should trust God, but speaks more particularly about God's trusting his interests into the hands of men. Jesus' parable suggests that this is a cumulative process: the more trustworthiness men show, the more is entrusted to them.

Superficially there might seem to be some conflict between self-reliance on the one hand and trust on the other—especially trust in a transcendent power strong enough to cancel out all human effort. Humanists sometimes claim to be better motivated to do what needs doing in the world because they do not trust in God to do it. But the Bible sees no such conflict. We rely on ourselves and trust one another within and as part of our trust in God. The larger trust embraces the smaller without diminishing its significance. "Trust in God and keep your powder dry," said Cromwell to his troops, combining self-reliance and religious trust in a memorable order of the day.

What trust *is* opposed to is our insistence on guarantees. Some people will not even go on holiday except to places to which they have been recommended by a neighbor who has already been there. Others will not venture into any experience without demanding foreknowledge of its outcome. Still others will not enter into any new relationship for fear it will impose unexpected demands on them. And yet others will not take on a new job for fear of what it may require of them. No guarantees can be given for such enterprises. We have to go forward in trust. If we do not, life will be a narrow experience—and one that is more likely to shrink than to grow.

A certain confidence that the universe is to be trusted is a prerequisite for an expanding life. Particularly useful is the two-way confidence that the Bible encourages: a readiness to trust and to be trusted; a belief that what is outside us will prove the more trustworthy the more we trust it; a belief that what is within us will grow to meet the responsibilities entrusted to it. The Bible offers no guarantee that this course will be free of danger. Jesus dies, and does so to the sound of men jeering: "He trusted in God!" Trust does not always stop the fire from burning, but the fire need not extinguish the trust. Jesus responds to the jeers by saying as he dies, "Father, into thy hands I commend my spirit."

TRUST

OLD TESTAMENT

Daniel 3:15–28

15 Now if ye be ready that at what time ye hear the sound of the cornet, flute, harp, sackbut, psaltery, and dulcimer, and all kinds of music, ye fall down and worship the image which I have made; well: but if ye worship not, ye shall be cast the same hour into the midst of a burning fiery furnace; and who is that God that shall deliver you out of my hands?

16 Shadrach, Meshach, and Abednego, answered and said to the king, O Nebuchadnezzar, we are not careful to answer thee in this matter.

17 If it be so, our God whom we serve is able to deliver us from the burning fiery furnace, and he will deliver us out of thine hand, O king.

18 But if not, be it known unto thee, O king, that we will not serve thy gods, nor worship the golden image which thou hast set up.

19 Then was Nebuchadnezzar full of fury, and the form of his visage was changed against Shadrach, Meshach, and Abednego: therefore he spake, and commanded that they should heat the furnace one seven times more than it was wont to be heated.

20 And he commanded the most mighty men that were in his army to bind Shadrach, Meshach, and Abednego, and to cast them into the burning fiery furnace.

21 Then these men were bound in their coats, their hosen, and their hats, and their other garments, and were cast into the midst of the burning fiery furnace.

22 Therefore because the king's commandment was urgent, and the furnace exceeding hot, the flame of the fire slew those men that took up Shadrach, Meshach, and Abednego.

23 And these three men, Shadrach, Meshach, and Abednego, fell down bound into the midst of the burning fiery furnace.

24 Then Nebuchadnezzar the king was astonied, and rose up in haste, and spake, and said unto his counsellors, Did not we cast three men bound into the midst of the fire? They answered and said unto the king, True, O king.

25 He answered and said, Lo, I see four men loose, walking in the midst of the fire, and they have no hurt; and the form of the fourth is like the Son of God.

26 Then Nebuchadnezzar came near to the mouth of the burning fiery furnace, and spake, and said, Shad-

rach, Meshach, and Abednego, ye servants of the most high God, come forth, and come hither. Then Shadrach, Meshach, and Abednego, came forth of the midst of the fire.

27 And the princes, governors, and captains, and the king's counsellors, being gathered together, saw these men, upon whose bodies the fire had no power, nor was an hair of their head singed, neither were their coats changed, nor the smell of fire had passed on them.

28 Then Nebuchadnezzar spake, and said, Blessed be the God of Shadrach, Meshach, and Abednego, who hath sent his angel, and delivered his servants that trusted in him, and have changed the king's word, and yielded their bodies, that they might not serve nor worship any god, except their own God.

NEW TESTAMENT

Luke 19:12–26

12 He said therefore, A certain nobleman went into a far country to receive for himself a kingdom, and to return.

13 And he called his ten servants, and delivered them ten pounds, and said unto them, Occupy till I come.

14 But his citizens hated him, and sent a message after him, saying, We will not have this man to reign over us.

15 And it came to pass, that when he was returned, having received the kingdom, then he commanded these servants to be called unto him, to whom he had given the money, that he might know how much every man had gained by trading.

16 Then came the first, saying, Lord, thy pound hath gained ten pounds.

17 And he said unto him, Well, thou good servant: because thou hast been faithful in a very little, have thou authority over ten cities.

18 And the second came, saying Lord, thy pound hath gained five pounds.

19 And he said likewise to him, Be thou also over five cities.

20 And another came, saying, Lord, behold, here is thy pound, which I have kept laid up in a napkin:

21 For I feared thee, because thou art an austere man: thou takest up that thou layedst not down, and reapest that thou didst not sow.

22 And he said unto him, Out of thine own mouth will I judge thee, thou wicked servant. Thou knewest that I was an austere man, taking up that I laid not down, and reaping that I did not sow:

23 Wherefore then gavest not thou my money into the bank, that at my coming I might have required mine own with usury?

24 And he said unto them that stood by, Take from him the pound, and give it to him that hath ten pounds.

25 (And they said unto him, Lord, he hath ten pounds.)

26 For I say unto you, That unto every one which hath shall be given; and from him that hath not, even that he hath shall be taken away from him.

Luke 16:10–11

10 He that is faithful in that which is least is faithful also in much: and he that is unjust in the least is unjust also in much.

11 If therefore ye have not been faithful in the unrighteous mammon, who will commit to your trust the true riches?

TRUTH

The Old Testament word for truth can equally well mean faithfulness. It is now often translated that way. Truth in this sense is not thought of as an intellectual thing: it is an attitude of consistency expressed in word and deed. It is supremely an attribute of God. In Old Testament times, a right relationship with God was certainly thought to involve a commitment to veracity, but that was only the tip of the iceberg. Truth had to be supported by inward integrity and all-round dependability.

In fact the tip of the iceberg sometimes got chipped a bit. Abraham was said to have deceived people about his relationship to Sarah, and to have told her to do the same. His subsequent explanation to Abimelech ("Well, she is my *half* sister . . .") does not help much. Yet the story is not regarded as revealing a serious blemish on the character of the great patriarch, any more than, say, the deceptions practiced by Jacob are regarded as sufficient reason to be ashamed of him as an ancestor. Such men were certainly not praised for the discrepancy between their word and fact, but as a measure of a man's truthfulness his verbal accuracy was not to be compared with his consistency in pursuing the purposes of God.

The language of the Old Testament is, in any event, so full of poetic images and symbols that a prosaic correspondence between words and events is not particularly sought after.

The New Testament was written not in Hebrew but in Greek, so the word "truth" was open to the more Hellenistic and modern association with what is thought or believed. In spite of that, truth in the New Testament is something that can be done as well as understood. Jesus does not merely communicate the truth, he *is* the truth. And when he says to God in prayer, "Thy word is truth," he means more than "Thy word is true." The true word of God is active and powerful, not just notional. The truth makes us holy.

In the letter to the Ephesians "truth" is actually a verb, and "to truth it in love" has been suggested as a fairly literal translation.

The biblical emphasis on truth as something to be done and not just thought or spoken obviously issues no license to lies, half-truths, prevarication, or wishful thinking. The idea of truth as a consistent relationship with eternal reality broadens and deepens the modern idea but does not detract from it.

Adding the biblical idea to the modern one gives rise to no problems. Reading the modern idea of truth back into the Bible does. For instance, the first chapter of the Bible describes the creation of man and woman by the word of God. The second chapter gives a rather different account of the making of the first man, and, some time later, of the first woman. If these chapters were read in the way in which scientific reports are read, doubts would be raised about their truth. But such a notion of truth is just not relevant. The truth of the passages lies in their picture of the relationship between humanity and God. The accounts are consistent with God's purpose and humanity's experience. They point toward the right actions and the right attitudes. That is their truth.

Again, in the Gospels of Mark and Luke the triumphal entry of Jesus into Jerusalem involves the use of just one animal. In Matthew's account there are two. If the Gospels were read in the way newspapers are read, the discrepancy might be serious. But Matthew is not concerned with journalistic truth. He is eager to bring out the significance of the event rather than to report what a mere film camera could have observed. So he tells the story in a way that underlines its significance as the fulfillment of an Old Testament prophecy about the coming of the king of peace. His concern is for the truth, but not for journalistic accuracy.

Truth is sacred, but takes many forms. Understanding its breadth helps us to live in its depth. Too narrow an approach to it can cut out the transcendent dimensions of reality, leaving us with a few crumbs of desiccated fact to store in our heads and little with which to nourish our lives.

TRUTH

OLD TESTAMENT

Exodus 20:16

16 Thou shalt not bear false witness against thy neighbour.

Isaiah 65:16

16 That he who blesseth himself in the earth shall bless himself in the God of truth; and he that sweareth in the earth shall swear by the God of truth.

Psalm 43:3

O send out thy light and thy truth:
Let them lead me; let them bring me
   unto thy holy hill,
And to thy tabernacles.

Genesis 20:1–7, 10–13

1 And Abraham journeyed from thence toward the south country, and dwelled between Kadesh and Shur, and sojourned in Gerar.

2 And Abraham said of Sarah his wife, She is my sister: and Abimelech king of Gerar sent, and took Sarah.

3 But God came to Abimelech in a dream by night, and said to him, Behold, thou art but a dead man, for the woman which thou hast taken; for she is a man's wife.

4 But Abimelech had not come near her: and he said, Lord, wilt thou slay also a righteous nation?

5 Said he not unto me, She is my sister? and she, even she herself said, He is my brother: in the integrity of my heart and innocency of my hands have I done this.

6 And God said unto him in a dream, Yea, I know that thou didst this in the integrity of thy heart; for I also withheld thee from sinning against me: therefore suffered I thee not to touch her.

7 Now therefore restore the man his wife; for he is a prophet, and he shall pray for thee, and thou shalt live.

10 And Abimelech said unto Abraham, What sawest thou, that thou hast done this thing?

11 And Abraham said, Because I thought, Surely the fear of God is not in this place; and they will slay me for my wife's sake.

12 And yet indeed she is my sister; she is the daughter of my father, but not the daughter of my mother; and she became my wife.

13 And it came to pass, when God caused me to wander from my father's house, that I said unto her, This is thy kindness which thou shalt shew unto me; at every place whither we shall come, say of me, He is my brother.

Proverbs 12:19; 23:23

The lip of truth shall be established for
   ever:
But a lying tongue is but for a moment.
Buy the truth, and sell it not;
Also wisdom, and instruction, and un-
   derstanding.

NEW TESTAMENT

John 1:17; 3:21; 4:24; 14:6; 16:13; 17:17; 18:38

17 The law was given by Moses, but grace and truth came by Jesus Christ.

21 He that doeth truth cometh to the light, that his deeds may be made manifest, that they are wrought in God.

24 God is a Spirit: and they that worship him must worship him in spirit and in truth.

6 I am the way, the truth, and the life: no man cometh unto the Father, but by me.

13 When he, the Spirit of truth, is come, he will guide you into all truth.

17 Sanctify them through thy truth: thy word is truth.

38 Pilate said unto him, What is truth?

1 John 1:5–6; 3:18

5 This then is the message which we have heard of him, and declare unto you, that God is light, and in him is no darkness at all.

6 If we say that we have fellowship with him, and walk in darkness, we lie, and do not the truth.

18 My little children, let us not love in word, neither in tongue; but in deed and in truth.

Ephesians 4:14–15, 25

14 That we henceforth be no more children, tossed to and fro, and carried about with every wind of doctrine, by the sleight of men, and cunning craftiness, whereby they lie in wait to deceive;

15 But speaking the truth in love, may grow up into him in all things, which is the head, even Christ.

25 Wherefore putting away lying, speak every man truth with his neighbour: for we are members one of another.

UNITY

The Bible is not *all* about unity. It reports a movement of separation as well as a movement of union. Yet even in the Old Testament the impression is given that the demand for separation is temporary and the demand for unity final. Unity is an end; separation is a means to that end. Israel is required to separate itself from other nations and other influences so that it may become the depository of truth for all. The objective is a unity based on truth, not falsehood.

So some Old Testament passages sing the praises of unity, and other passages report with horror that Israelites have united themselves with aliens. At the close of a period of exile, Ezra and Nehemiah purged the nation of such alien influences. They were concerned only with the unity of Israel. The prophets, however, looked beyond this to a wider unity that these measures would eventually serve.

In fact the Old Testament speaks of an underlying unity that not only will follow the period of separation but that also preceded it. A special covenant exists between God and Israel, but prior to this is the covenant made with all mankind in the person of Noah. To the Hebrews the rainbow was the enduring symbol of the unity of all men and all creatures under the providence of God.

The New Testament covers the end of a process of separating and the beginning of a process of drawing in. The unity celebrated in the New Testament is that of a new Israel, the Christian church, but membership in that church is open to all who embrace its truth: "There is neither Jew nor Greek, there is neither bond nor free, there is neither male nor female: for ye are all one in Christ Jesus" (Galatians 3:28).

Such unity is the gift of God, the fruit of his Spirit, but men still have to work at it.

Probably one of the most misused texts in the Bible is the one that says, "Come out from among them, and be ye separate." It had its origin at a critical time in the life of Israel (Isaiah 52:11) and was quoted afresh at a critical time in the life of the young Christian church (2 Corinthians 6:17), but it has been used at other times to justify the self-righteous separatism of those who fancy themselves a spiritual elite. It has divided churches, families, and nations. It has masked all kinds of intolerance and spiritual snobbery.

Admittedly the Bible gives no encouragement to the kinds of unity that are achieved by papering over cracks. It calls for unity in the truth. But that is not the same thing as unanimity of opinions. To be one with each other, people do not have to be carbon copies of each other. Indeed, their differences are essential to the fullness of the union—as in the case of men and women who were pronounced by Paul to be one though still biologically different.

Nor do people need to be united in all respects before being united in some respects. If that were so, there could be no union of nations or cultures, no brotherhood of man.

What is needed is that each union should be based on a true understanding of such values and purposes as are common to those uniting—and the Bible suggests that there are many. There is a unity of the creation that transcends even humanity. Human beings are just one element in a larger harmony which they should express in a common attitude toward the environment. And within humanity there is an intrinsic humanness (see Man) that provides another basis for unity in truth.

Over all achieved unities the Bible holds up a vision of unity yet to be attained—a mystical unity embracing earth and heaven, human beings and God. That wars of religion should have divided humanity in the name of this higher unity is a monstrous perversion. All lesser unity points beyond itself to the greater unity beneath it and beyond it, and the connection can be stated the other way around: the greater unity is to be served in all the lesser unities and communities that mirror it.

UNITY

OLD TESTAMENT

Genesis 9:14–16 (the rainbow covenant)

14 And it shall come to pass, when I bring a cloud over the earth, that the bow shall be seen in the cloud:

15 And I will remember my covenant, which is between me and you and every living creature of all flesh; and the waters shall no more become a flood to destroy all flesh.

16 And the bow shall be in the cloud; and I will look upon it, that I may remember the everlasting covenant between God and every living creature of all flesh that is upon the earth.

Psalm 133:1

Behold, how good and how pleasant it is
For brethren to dwell together in unity!

Ecclesiastes 4:12

12 And if one prevail against him, two shall withstand him; and a threefold cord is not quickly broken.

Nehemiah 13:23–26

23 In those days also saw I Jews that had married wives of Ashdod, of Ammon, and of Moab:

24 And their children spake half in the speech of Ashdod, and could not speak in the Jews' language, but according to the language of each people.

25 And I contended with them, and cursed them, and smote certain of them, and plucked off their hair, and made them swear by God, saying, Ye shall not give your daughters unto their sons, nor take their daughters unto your sons, or for yourselves.

26 Did not Solomon king of Israel sin by these things?

Zechariah 14:9

9 And the Lord shall be king over all the earth: in that day shall there be one Lord, and his name one.

NEW TESTAMENT

John 17:1, 6, 11, 20–23

1 These words spake Jesus and lifted up his eyes to heaven, and said, Father, the hour is come; glorify thy Son, that thy Son also may glorify thee:

6 I have manifested thy name unto the men which thou gavest me out of the world:

11 And now I am no more in the world, but these are in the world, and I come to thee. Holy Father, keep through thine own name those whom thou hast given me, that they may be one, as we are.

20 Neither pray I for these alone, but for them also which shall believe on me through their word;

21 That they all may be one; as thou, Father, art in me, and I in thee, that they also may be one in us: that the world may believe that thou hast sent me.

22 And the glory which thou gavest me I have given them; that they may be one, even as we are one:

23 I in them, and thou in me, that they may be made perfect in one; and that the world may know that thou hast sent me, and hast loved them, as thou hast loved me.

Acts 10:34–35 (Peter visits a Gentile home)

34 Then Peter opened his mouth, and said, Of a truth I perceive that God is no respecter of persons:

35 But in every nation he that feareth him, and worketh righteousness, is accepted with him.

Ephesians 4:2–6

2 With all lowliness and meekness, with longsuffering, forbearing one another in love;

3 Endeavouring to keep the unity of the Spirit in the bond of peace.

4 There is one body, and one Spirit, even as ye are called in one hope of your calling;

5 One Lord, one faith, one baptism,

6 One God and Father of all, who is above all, and through all, and in you all.

Romans 15:5–9

5 Now the God of patience and consolation grant you to be likeminded one toward another according to Christ Jesus.

6 That ye may with one mind and one mouth glorify God, even the Father of our Lord Jesus Christ.

7 Wherefore receive ye one another, as Christ also received us to the glory of God.

8 Now I say that Jesus Christ was a minister of the circumcision for the truth of God, to confirm the promises made unto the fathers:

9 And that the Gentiles might glo-rify God for his mercy; as it is written, For this cause I will confess to thee among the Gentiles, and sing unto thy name.

1 John 3:2

2 Beloved, now are we the sons of God, and it doth not yet appear what we shall be: but we know that, when he shall appear, we shall be like him; for we shall see him as he is.

UNIVERSE

What the men of the Old Testament had to say about the universe tney said in Hebrew and in terms of a conventional model. The model was no more an essential part of their message than was the language, but both conditioned the way in which that message was expressed. And the model was a three-decker. The earth on which the Old Testament writers lived and spoke and wrote was the middle deck. Under their feet was the shadowy region of sheol, the home of the dead. Over their heads was a bright layer of sky that was to them the floor ot heaven. It had windows in it. Through these the rain and snow were at times poured down, having been stored in large containers. Supremely, however (and here they were beginning to deliver their message), heaven was the home of God.

In the developed form of the message two points stood out. One was that the universe, having but one God, was a *uni*verse. A single consistent rule of law operated throughout. This was a lesson that had to be learned. In the earlier parts of the Old Testament one can see a belief that Israel's God was just one god among many—the one with authority over the Israelite people and their land, but with limited jurisdiction elsewhere. This notion was gradually banished with the help of the three-tier model. Israel's God was seen to rule over the entire universe.

The second point—also a lesson to be learned over a period of time—was that the consistency that made the universe a single system was a consistency of purpose rather than a mechanical one. The system was flexible in God's hands, responsive to his will. Since the Hebrew mind was not dominated by machines, this was in one sense an easier lesson, but what needed working on was the notion that the ever-present purpose was a moral one. The universal laws operated in favor of right living rather than right ritual or sheer blind favoritism and power.

The New Testament takes all this as understood and speaks of sun, stars, and

365

moon chiefly as symbols of God's sovereignty in the lives of men and women. The star of Bethlehem is a theological rather than an astrological phenomenon. The furniture of the story is provided by the lore of the period, but its significance is better understood in the light of Old Testament prophecies than of astrological calculations.

As in the opening chapters of the New Testament, so in the closing ones: Jesus, "the bright and morning star" of the Book of Revelation (22:16), is indeed portrayed as the Lord and destiny of the universe, but the galactic phenomena described in that book are not astronomical predictions so much as poetic symbols.

In a quite matter-of-fact sense, however, the Old Testament writers treated the universe as a phenomenon of limited duration. As it had been created, so too it could and would be ended—but only in the fulfillment of its purpose.

The astronomy of Galileo and the physics of Newton have changed the appearance of our mental models of the universe. By now the physics of Einstein should have changed them again, but for practical purposes we do not find it necessary to update our picture of the universe with each discovery. The Bible is a practical book, too. Its business is with questions that arise from our need to know how to live in the universe rather than with fascinating but less urgent questions about its mechanisms.

The biblical answer to the first group of questions is something like this: Live in the universe as an orderly system but not as a soul-less mechanism; see it as consistently responsive to the moral purpose that it serves and that will be found to transcend even the existence of the mysterious and beautiful apparatus we rightly call a *universe*.

UNIVERSE

OLD TESTAMENT

Genesis 1:3–8

3 And God said, Let there be light: and there was light.

4 And God saw the light, that it was good: and God divided the light from the darkness.

5 And God called the light Day, and the darkness he called Night. And the evening and the morning were the first day.

6 And God said, Let there be a firmament in the midst of the waters, and let it divide the waters from the waters.

7 And God made the firmament, and divided the waters which were under the firmament from the waters which were above the firmament: and it was so.

8 And God called the firmament Heaven. And the evening and the morning were the second day.

366

Job 38:31–33

Canst thou bind the sweet influences of Pleiades,
Or loose the bands of Orion?
Canst thou bring forth Mazzaroth in his season?
Or canst thou guide Arcturus with his sons?
Knowest thou the ordinances of heaven?
Canst thou set the dominion thereof in the earth?

Isaiah 40:21–23, 26

21 Have ye not known? have ye not heard? hath it not been told you from the beginning? have ye not understood from the foundations of the earth?
22 It is he that sitteth upon the circle of the earth, and the inhabitants thereof 'are as grasshoppers; that stretcheth out the heavens as a curtain, and spreadeth them out as a tent to dwell in:
23 That bringeth the princes to nothing; he maketh the judges of the earth as vanity.
26 Lift up your eyes on high, and behold who hath created these things, that bringeth out their host by number: he calleth them all by names by the greatness of his might, for that he is strong in power; not one faileth.

Psalm 147:4–6

He telleth the number of the stars;
He calleth them all by their names.
Great is our Lord, and of great power:
His understanding is infinite.
The Lord lifteth up the meek:
He casteth the wicked down to the ground.

NEW TESTAMENT

Matthew 2:1–2, 9

1 Now when Jesus was born in Bethlehem of Judæa in the days of Herod the king, behold, there came wise men from the east to Jerusalem,
2 Saying, Where is he that is born King of the Jews? for we have seen his star in the east, and are come to worship him.
9 When they had heard the king, they departed; and, lo, the star, which they saw in the east, went before them, till it came and stood over where the young child was.

Philippians 2:10–11

10 That at the name of Jesus every knee should bow, of things in heaven, and things in earth, and things under the earth;
11 And that every tongue should confess that Jesus Christ is Lord, to the glory of God the Father.

2 Peter 3:10–13

10 But the day of the Lord will come as a thief in the night; in the which the heavens shall pass away with a great noise, and the elements shall melt with fervent heat, the earth also and the works that are therein shall be burned up.
11 Seeing then that all these things shall be dissolved, what manner of persons ought ye to be in all holy conversation and godliness,
12 Looking for and hasting unto the

coming of the day of God, wherein the heavens being on fire shall be dissolved, and the elements shall melt with fervent heat?

13 Nevertheless we, according to his promise, look for new heavens and a new earth, wherein dwelleth righteousness.

Revelation 12:1–5

1 And there appeared a great wonder in heaven; a woman clothed with the sun, and the moon under her feet, and upon her head a crown of twelve stars:

2 And she being with child cried, .

travailing in birth, and pained to be delivered.

3 And there appeared another wonder in heaven; and behold a great red dragon, having seven heads and ten horns, and seven crowns upon his heads.

4 And his tail drew the third part of the stars of heaven, and did cast them to the earth: and the dragon stood before the woman which was ready to be delivered, for to devour her child as soon as it was born.

5 And she brought forth a man child, who was to rule all nations with a rod of iron: and her child was caught up unto God, and to his throne.

VALUES

A character in one of Oscar Wilde's plays defined a cynic as "a man who knows the price of everything and the value of nothing." The Old Testament is an antidote to that condition. It regards "the law" (the revealed value system of God) as the supreme therapy, but another of its medicines is the moral tale. When Elisha's God cured Naaman the Syrian of leprosy, the man of God declined to accept any gift. To Elisha it was just not that kind of transaction. Elisha's servant, however, thought otherwise—until by trading on Naaman's gratitude he found he had also acquired Naaman's leprosy. It is a grim story, but designed to teach values of a nonmaterial kind and to warn that those who adopt material standards take on the defects as well as the advantages of that value system.

The writer of Ecclesiastes tells no grim story but offers poetic reflections on his own extensive experience in the search for true values. He, too, says that monetary values only confuse the issue. Like others in this part of the Bible ("the Writings"), he identifies wisdom as the supreme value (see Wisdom). This wisdom, however, is very comprehensive. It involves being aligned to all the values God has built into life, so it manifests itself not as a headful of bright ideas, but as a life well adjusted to work, to people, to the environment. The Teacher in Ecclesiastes rejects pleasure as a goal to be aimed at, but commends the happiness to be found in doing what has to be done and in enjoying what there is to enjoy. The wise man, he says, will value more highly the satisfaction to be had from doing his work than he does the financial reward that comes from it.

The New Testament shares this concern for humanity's total orientation toward all that is truly valuable. "Whatsoever things are true, whatsoever things are honest, whatsoever things are just, whatsoever things are pure, whatsoever things are lovely, whatsoever things are of good report . . . think on these things" (Philippians 4:8; see Goodness). Jesus says that monetary values may get in the way of eternal ones (see Wealth).

The New Testament also reverses the angle of view: it says not only that human beings are to find their true values in the nature of God, but that God himself values the true nature of humanity. This itself affects human value judgments. To be of value to God makes it ridiculous to regard anything else as being of supreme worth. All merely social, material, hedonistic values are cut down to size, while the simple interpersonal values summed up in the word "love" are exalted.

To give notional assent to such a system of priorities is not difficult. To live by it is. What a great painting is worth is clearly not the same thing as what it will sell for, but the second measurement is a good deal easier to arrive at. Values of this more measurable kind are built into us by a society that is at best a merit system, and frequently less generous even than that. The New Testament may say that God's value system is one of unconditional giving and that ours should be the same, but we are kept alive by a trading and price-tagging society. And just in case we are not sufficiently enamored of the system, a good deal of propaganda for the materialist cause is deliberately and skillfully aimed at us. It is easy enough to say sentimentally that the best things in life are free (though in fact the best things are personal relationships and can be very demanding), but even that simplified gospel does not really get hold of us down at the roots of our behavior.

There is no simple remedy for this state of affairs. The Bible uses the language of miracle to describe the process of change. But perhaps the beginning of the process can be triggered by a deliberate act of imagination. It is (as so often is the case) a matter of *seeing* life the way the Bible portrays it. If the imagination is allowed—or encouraged—to play on the true values where they have been embodied in human living, then there is a chance of falling in love with them and of seeing through their tawdry substitutes. It is down there where the heart is that the effective values are enthroned.

VALUES

OLD TESTAMENT

2 Kings 5:20–27

20 But Gehazi, the servant of Elisha the man of God, said, Behold, my master hath spared Naaman this Syrian, in not receiving at his hands that which he brought: but, as the Lord liveth, I will run after him, and take somewhat of him.

369

21 So Gehazi followed after Naaman. And when Naaman saw him running after him, he lighted down from the chariot to meet him, and said, Is all well?

22 And he said, All is well. My master hath sent me, saying, Behold, even now there be come to me from mount Ephraim two young men of the sons of the prophets: give them, I pray thee, a talent of silver, and two changes of garments.

23 And Naaman said, Be content, take two talents. And he urged him, and bound two talents of silver in two bags, with two changes of garments, and laid them upon two of his servants; and they bare them before him.

24 And when he came to the tower, he took them from their hand, and bestowed them in the house: and he let the men go, and they departed.

25 But he went in, and stood before his master. And Elisha said unto him, Whence comest thou, Gehazi? And he said, Thy servant went no whither.

26 And he said unto him, Went not mine heart with thee, when the man turned again from his chariot to meet thee? Is it a time to receive money, and to receive garments, and olive-yards, and vineyards, and sheep, and oxen, and menservants, and maid-servants?

27 The leprosy therefore of Naaman shall cleave unto thee, and unto thy seed for ever. And he went out from his presence a leper as white as snow.

Ecclesiastes 2:1–3, 13; 3:12–13

1 I said in mine heart, Go to now, I will prove thee with mirth, therefore enjoy pleasure: and, behold, this also is vanity.

2 I said of laughter, It is mad: and of mirth, What doeth it?

3 I sought in mine heart to give myself unto wine, yet acquainting mine heart with wisdom; and to lay hold on folly, till I might see what was that good for the sons of men, which they should do under the heaven all the days of their life.

13 Then I saw that wisdom excelleth folly, as far as light excelleth darkness.

12 I know that there is no good . . . but for a man to rejoice, and to do good in his life.

13 And also that every man should eat and drink, and enjoy the good of all his labour, it is the gift of God.

NEW TESTAMENT

Matthew 6:19–21; Luke 12:6–7; Mark 9:36–37; Matthew 10:42

19 Lay not up for yourselves treasures upon earth, where moth and rust doth corrupt, and where thieves break through and steal:

20 But lay up for yourselves treasures in heaven, where neither moth nor rust doth corrupt, and where thieves do not break through nor steal:

21 For where your treasure is, there will your heart be also.

6 Are not five sparrows sold for two farthings, and not one of them is forgotten before God?

7 But even the very hairs of your head are all numbered. Fear not therefore: ye are of more value than many sparrows.

36 And he took a child, and set him in the midst of them: and when he had taken him in his arms, he said unto them,

37 Whosoever shall receive one of such children in my name, receiveth me: and whosoever shall receive me, receiveth not me, but him that sent me.

42 And whosoever shall give to drink unto one of these little ones a cup of cold water only in the name of a disciple, verily I say unto you, he shall in no wise lose his reward.

Galatians 5:22–23

22 But the fruit of the Spirit is love, joy, peace, longsuffering, gentleness, goodness, faith,

23 Meekness, temperance: against such there is no law.

1 Corinthians 13:10–13

10 But when that which is perfect is come, then that which is in part shall be done away.

11 When I was a child, I spake as a child, I understood as a child, I thought as a child: but when I became a man, I put away childish things.

12 For now we see through a glass, darkly; but then face to face: now I know in part; but then shall I know even as also I am known.

13 And now abideth faith, hope, charity, these three; but the greatest of these is charity.

VIOLENCE

The Old Testament is strongly opposed to violence, but has few qualms about the use of force. Force can be allied with justice; violence only with injustice. So the victims of violence have God on their side, while its perpetrators can expect only to stir up violence against themselves. In this sense violence—even the violence of the godless Babylonians—becomes an instrument of divine justice. A subtle providence turns their unjust action to the service of God's rule. They continue to do wrong, but it is used to do right.

For the future, however, there is the hope of a city and nation from which violence has been totally excluded. And, strangely, the door to this future is to be opened by a victim of violence—one who will be prepared to absorb the violence in his own suffering rather than reciprocate in kind.

In the New Testament Jesus takes up this role, preaching nonviolence but expecting to suffer violence and ready to absorb it. Violence destroys only its perpetrators. The peaceable kingdom advances not merely in spite of it but through it.

His later followers had in New Testament times little chance of adopting any other policy. If they had used violence or had even replied to it in kind, they would have been crushed and their cause extinguished. Under the leadership of such men as Paul (see Enemies), they adopted the policy of absorbing it. Against all the odds, it worked. If it had not, the New Testament would never have come down to us. The Gospels not only *say* that the meek will inherit the earth: their continued existence shows that there is something in it.

One cause of violence is violence. Another is the absence of force. Power is bound to play a part in human life. The real issue concerns whether power will be present as disciplined force serving justice or as undisciplined violence serving injustice. Power used by an unjust regime can be regarded as violence, however outwardly legal it may be.

The connection between violent causes and violent outcomes is concealed at times. For one thing, violence feeds on itself. It creates an appetite for more violence. Terrorists can become more interested in the violence they use than in the political end they profess to serve, so that they may go on using violence when it is doing more harm than good to the political objective. Then again, violence may provoke a counterviolence very different in form and appearance from its cause. What goes in as a rough childhood may come out as political terrorism. Or what goes in as political terrorism may come out as roughness toward children. It is never easy to read the connections in the right order. Violent crime, for instance, may be provoked by violent punishment as well as the other way around. The Bible suggests that so long as the cauldron of violence is kept on the boil, it will find some way to erupt.

Not only violence engenders violence, however. So does the absence of just force. The terrorist could be the product of an indulgent childhood rather than a rough one. The pointless warfare of youth gangs could spring from the absence of early restraints rather than from a history of baby bashing. Dodging the issue of compulsion is no way to avoid the development of violence.

The true alternative to violence is not a mere absence of violence, but the presence of something else. Nonviolence itself needs to be such a positive presence—a powerful and purposeful spirit of peace, disciplined by justice and love and totally rejecting the gratification of hatred, anger, and self-interest. Much is at stake. Martin Luther King said that "the modern choice is between nonviolence and nonexistence."

VIOLENCE

OLD TESTAMENT

Proverbs 16:29

A violent man enticeth his neighbour,
And leadeth him into the way that is not
good.

Psalm 72:12–14

For he shall deliver the needy when he
crieth;
The poor also, and him that hath no
helper.
He shall spare the poor and needy,
And shall save the souls of the needy.
He shall redeem their soul from deceit
and violence:
And precious shall their blood be in his
sight.

Ezekiel 7:23, 27

23 Make a chain: for the land is
full of bloody crimes, and the city is
full of violence.

27 The king shall mourn, and the
prince shall be clothed with desolation, and the hands of the people of
the land shall be troubled: I will do
unto them after their way, and according to their deserts will I judge them;
and they shall know that I am the Lord.

Habakkuk 1:5–7, 9

5 Behold ye among the heathen,
and regard, and wonder marvellously:
for I will work a work in your days,
which ye will not believe, though it be
told you.

6 For, lo, I raise up the Chaldeans,
that bitter and hasty nation, which shall
march through the breadth of the land,

to possess the dwellingplaces that are
not theirs.

7 They are terrible and dreadful.

9 They shall come all for violence.

Isaiah 53:8–9, 11; 60:18 (a song of the suffering servant)

8 He was taken from prison and
from judgment: and who shall declare
his generation? for he was cut off out
of the land of the living: for the
transgression of my people was he
stricken.

9 And he made his grave with the
wicked, and with the rich in his death;
because he had done no violence,
neither was any deceit in his mouth.

11 He shall see of the travail of his
soul, and shall be satisfied.

18 Violence shall no more be heard
in thy land, wasting nor destruction
within thy borders; but thou shalt call
thy walls Salvation, and thy gates
Praise.

NEW TESTAMENT

Luke 6:29

29 And unto him that smiteth thee
on the one cheek offer also the other;
and him that taketh away thy cloak
forbid not to take thy coat also.

Matthew 21:33–41

33 Hear another parable: There was
a certain householder, which planted
a vineyard, and hedged it around about,
and digged a winepress in it, and built
a tower, and let it out to husbandmen,
and went into a far country:

34 And when the time of the fruit

drew near, he sent his servants to the husbandmen, that they might receive the fruits of it.

35 And the husbandmen took his servants, and beat one, and killed another, and stoned another.

36 Again, he sent other servants more than the first: and they did unto them likewise.

37 But last of all he sent unto them his son, saying, They will reverence my son.

38 But when the husbandmen saw the son, they said among themselves, This is the heir; come, let us kill him, and let us seize on his inheritance.

39 And they caught him, and cast him out of the vineyard, and slew him.

40 When the lord therefore of the vineyard cometh, what will he do unto those husbandmen?

41 They say unto him, He will miserably destroy those wicked men, and will let out his vineyard unto other husbandmen, which shall render him the fruits in their seasons.

Matthew 26:52, 55–56

52 Then said Jesus unto him [Peter], Put up again thy sword into his place: for all they that take the sword shall perish with the sword.

55 In that same hour said Jesus to the multitudes, Are ye come out as against a thief with swords and staves for to take me? I sat daily with you teaching in the temple, and ye laid no hold on me.

56 But all this was done, that the scriptures of the prophets might be fulfilled.

WAR

The Old Testament is by no means pacifist. Its ultimate hope is for the beating of swords into plowshares, but it recognizes interim conditions in which the exact reverse may be the right thing to do. The divine title Lord of hosts indicates a God of battle. The struggle that liberated Israel from Egypt was naturally spoken of as war, but it was said to have been a war that God won single-handed. In other conflicts the Israelites themselves were less passive, but they still believed that God was fighting for them and teaching them to fight for themselves.

Yet it could not be assumed that the enemies of Israel were the enemies of God. When Israel forsook God, the prophets saw him fighting for Israel's enemies and against his own chosen people. In such experiences the people learned the horror of war and nourished the hope of peace. They also learned that God's struggle was not just the same thing as the national one.

If the Old Testament starts bellicose and ends peace-loving, the New Testament could almost be said to reverse that pattern: the Gospels are pacifist, but the closing book of the Bible speaks fiercely of battles fought in heavenly places finally to establish God's sovereignty. The pattern is not quite as simple as that, however.

The New Testament recognizes two kinds of warfare. There are the ordinary conflicts between armies, and there is an underlying spiritual conflict between the forces of good and the forces of evil. These two forms of warfare are in some respects quite distant from each other and yet in other respects may be related.

They are distinct in that final victory in the spiritual war can be gained, according to the New Testament, only with spiritual weapons. The Christian cause needs no swords. Loving acts and believing prayers and patiently accepted sufferings are weapons better suited to its terrain. Similarly, the individual Christian, so far as his or her personal interests are concerned, is committed to the pacifism of the Gospels.

Yet there is also a connection between spiritual and military warfare. The Gospels speak of international wars as a sign of the new spiritual order struggling to be born. Paul sees the church militant as the true inheritor of the cause in which the armies of Israel had once been used. Different as were the weapons which he recommended, his use of martial imagery was not just a poetic fancy. It was the appropriate language for him to use.

Nor is it certain that Paul altogether renounced using the physical equivalents of his spiritual weapons. New Testament Christians were never in command of armies, so they did not discuss the uses of the blunter kind of weaponry, but Paul believed in supporting civil government, so he may have thought it quite right that armed force should be used in the maintenance of order. He respected the sword of the magistrate as well as the sword of the Spirit.

The Bible sets a question mark against all military action. It sees the connection between military force and the spiritual forces of good as being at best tenuous and fragile. But it is a question mark rather than an absolute prohibition. Military conflict is not irrelevant to the spiritual one. International war exists because spiritual war exists. It is unlikely that the forces of good and evil are ever lined up in a way that exactly coincides with the lineup of opposed armies, but the cause of good may be advanced or retarded by the course of battle. The exercise of armed force, like every other human activity, has to be done with a responsible eye on its potentiality and its limitations. It has to be made to yield such good as it can and be restrained from doing the harm it can.

Withdrawal from conflict is the one option we are not given, but it seems clear that as martial weapons become more destructive and conflicts more ideological, warfare in the military sense becomes less viable and the spiritual struggle more openly relevant than ever.

WAR

OLD TESTAMENT

Joel 3:9–10

9 Proclaim ye this among the Gentiles; Prepare war, wake up the mighty men, let all the men of war draw near; let them come up:

10 Beat your ploughshares into swords, and your pruninghooks into spears.

Exodus 15:3–5

3 The Lord is a man of war: the Lord is his name.

4 Pharaoh's chariots and his host hath he cast into the sea: his chosen captains also are drowned in the Red sea.

5 The depths have covered them: they sank into the bottom as a stone.

2 Samuel 22:33–35

33 God is my strength and power: And he maketh my way perfect.

34 He maketh my feet like hinds' feet: and setteth me upon my high places.

35 He teacheth my hands to war; so that a bow of steel is broken by mine arms.

Jeremiah 21:4–5

4 Thus saith the Lord God of Israel; Behold, I will turn back the weapons of war that are in your hands, wherewith ye fight against the king of Babylon, and against the Chaldeans, which besiege you without the walls,
and I will assemble them into the midst of this city.

5 And I myself will fight against you with an outstretched hand and with a strong arm.

Isaiah 2:3–4

3 Out of Zion shall go forth the law, and the word of the Lord from Jerusalem.

4 And he shall judge among the nations, and shall rebuke many people: and they shall beat their swords into ploughshares, and their spears into pruninghooks: nation shall not lift up sword against nation, neither shall they learn war any more.

NEW TESTAMENT

Matthew 5:38–39

38 Ye have heard that it hath been said, An eye for an eye, and a tooth for a tooth:

39 But I say unto you, That ye resist not evil: but whosoever shall smite thee on thy right cheek, turn to him the other also.

Mark 13:5–8

5 And Jesus answering them began to say, Take heed lest any man deceive you:

6 For many shall come in my name, saying, I am Christ; and shall deceive many.

7 And when ye shall hear of wars and rumours of wars, be ye not troubled: for such things must needs be; but the end shall not be yet.

8 For nation shall rise against nation, and kingdom against kingdom: and there shall be earthquakes in divers places, and there shall be famines and troubles: these are the beginnings of sorrows.

Ephesians 6:10–15

10 Be strong in the Lord, and in the power of his might.

11 Put on the whole armour of God, that ye may be able to stand against the wiles of the devil.

12 For we wrestle not against flesh and blood, but against principalities, against powers, against the rulers of the darkness of this world, against spiritual wickedness in high places.

13 Wherefore take unto you the whole armour of God, that ye may be able to withstand in the evil day, and having done all, to stand.

14 Stand therefore, having your loins girt about with truth, and having on the breastplate of righteousness;

15 And your feet shod with the preparation of the gospel of peace.

Revelation 12:7–9

7 And there was war in heaven: Michael and his angels fought against the dragon; and the dragon fought and his angels,

8 And prevailed not; neither was their place found any more in heaven.

9 And the great dragon was cast out, that old serpent, called the Devil, and Satan, which deceiveth the whole world: he was cast out into the earth, and his angels were cast out with him.

WEAKNESS

"Only be strong," says the God of the Old Testament to one of its heroes (Joshua 1:6), but that same God is described as well aware that most people are not strong. Far from blaming them on that account, he offers his own strength as the remedy for their weakness. Israel itself owes its special role as a nation, says the Old Testament, to its weakness rather than to its strength. It is to achieve its final triumph through one who is "a tender plant . . . despised and rejected" (Isaiah 53:2–3). Considered as saga, the Old Testament is strangely unheroic. It has a weakness for the weak. "Not by might, nor by power, but by my Spirit, saith the Lord of hosts" (Zechariah 4:6).

The New Testament heightens the paradox of strength through weakness. A child was the living symbol of weakness and dependence, but Jesus said that it was in that spirit of a child rather than in a spirit of strength and confidence that the kingdom was to be entered. He, as its king, was the defenseless wearer of a crown of thorns. Soldiers mocked him, authorities dismissed him, and the crowds were easily persuaded to prefer Barabbas—a man who put some muscle into messianism.

Even the resurrection of Jesus from death did not change him from a weak figure to a strong one in the ordinary sense of the word. His enemies remained in power, and his cause was left in the hands of the few weak men to whom he revealed himself. They were, however, men who were now sufficiently aware of their weakness not to depend on their own strength. The later parts of the New Testament say over and over again that a Christian's weakness is to be acknowledged and accepted so that he can be used as an instrument of divine power. Paul spoke for others in saying, "When I am weak, then am I strong" (2 Corinthians 12:10).

There are two wrong ways of handling our human fragility. The fact that they are opposite ways does not seem to stop most of us from following both of them. Inconsistency is just another human weakness.

One wrong way is to be ashamed of weakness and to hide it. There are many different forms of concealment. One is to bluster and pretend that the weakness is not there. Another is to retreat from every situation in which the weakness may be revealed. Many a defective child has been virtually hidden by its parents, and many adults who find life too demanding have lost themselves in a fantasy world of trivialities—via television, quite often. On the other hand, many a little man has talked big in hope of being accorded a stature he does not really possess. All these people, and many like them, have declined to accept and acknowledge weakness as a constant factor in the human condition.

The opposite (yet sometimes simultaneous) way is to use weakness as an excuse for evading responsibility: "I couldn't help it. . . . I was under orders.   . It's no good asking me to do a thing like that; I haven't the nerve/the ability/the courage/the education/the experience/the patience. You name what it takes, and I can claim I haven't got it." In other words (which can be addressed to humanity, to God, or to conscience), "I am weak, so don't ask me to do good deeds, or think deep thoughts or hold high hopes. Leave me to my mediocrity."

The biblical view is that weakness is understandable and can be dealt with, but mediocrity is intolerable. You may be a great saint or a great sinner. You may even be a great saint *and* a great sinner. But you do have to be something significant. The self-made strong man or woman and the self-satisfied weakling are not significant.

WEAKNESS

OLD TESTAMENT

Deuteronomy 7:7–8

7 The Lord did not set his love upon you, nor choose you, because ye were more in number than any people; for ye were the fewest of all people:

8 But because the Lord loved you, and because he would keep the oath which he had sworn unto your fathers.

Psalm 18:4–6, 16–18

The sorrows of death compassed me,
And the floods of ungodly men made me
  afraid.

The sorrows of hell compassed me about:
The snares of death prevented me.
In my distress I called upon the Lord,
And cried unto my God:
He heard my voice out of his temple,
And my cry came before him, even into
  his ears.
He sent from above, he took me,
He drew me out of many waters.
He delivered me from my strong enemy,
And from them which hated me: for they
  were too strong for me.
They prevented me in the day of my
  calamity:
But the Lord was my stay.

Isaiah 35:3–6

3 Strengthen ye the weak hands, and confirm the feeble knees.

4 Say to them that are of a fearful heart, Be strong, fear not: behold, your God will come with vengeance, even God with a recompence; he will come and save you.

5 Then the eyes of the blind shall be opened, and the ears of the deaf shall be unstopped.

6 Then shall the lame man leap as an hart, and the tongue of the dumb sing.

NEW TESTAMENT

Luke 18:15–17

15 And they brought unto him also infants, that he would touch them: but when his disciples saw it, they rebuked them.

16 But Jesus called them unto him, and said, Suffer little children to come unto me, and forbid them not: for of such is the kingdom of God.

17 Verily I say unto you, Whosoever shall not receive the kingdom of God as a little child shall in no wise enter therein.

Mark 15:6–20

6 Now at that feast he [Pilate] released unto them one prisoner, whomsoever they desired.

7 And there was one named Barabbas, which lay bound with them that had made insurrection with him, who had committed murder in the insurrection.

8 And the multitude crying aloud began to desire him to do as he had ever done unto them.

9 But Pilate answered them, saying, Will ye that I release unto you the King of the Jews?

10 For he knew that the chief priests had delivered him for envy.

11 But the chief priests moved the people, that he should rather release Barabbas unto them.

12 And Pilate answered and said again unto them, What will ye then that I shall do unto him whom ye call the King of the Jews?

13 And they cried out again, Crucify him.

14 Then Pilate said unto them, Why, what evil hath he done? And they cried out the more exceedingly, Crucify him.

15 And so Pilate, willing to content the people, released Barabbas unto them, and delivered Jesus, when he had scourged him, to be crucified.

16 And the soldiers led him away into the hall, called Prætorium; and they called together the whole band.

17 And they clothed him with purple, and platted a crown of thorns, and put it about his head,

18 And began to salute him, Hail, King of the Jews!

19 And they smote him on the head with a reed, and did spit upon him, and bowing their knees worshipped him.

20 And when they had mocked him, they took off the purple from him, and put his own clothes on him, and led him out to crucify him.

2 Corinthians 13:3–4

3 Ye seek a proof of Christ speaking in me, which to youward is not weak, but is mighty in you.

4 For though he was crucified through weakness, yet he liveth by the power of God. For we also are weak in him, but we shall live with him by the power of God toward you.

Revelation 3:14–18

14 And unto the angel of the church of the Laodiceans write; These things saith the Amen, the faithful and true witness, the beginning of the creation of God;

15 I know thy works, that thou art neither cold nor hot: I would thou wert cold or hot.

16 So then because thou art lukewarm, and neither cold nor hot, I will spue thee out of my mouth.

17 Because thou sayest, I am rich, and increased with goods, and have need of nothing; and knowest not that thou art wretched, and miserable, and poor, and blind, and naked:

18 I counsel thee to buy of me gold tried in the fire, that thou mayest be rich; and white raiment, that thou mayest be clothed, and that the shame of thy nakedness do not appear; and anoint thine eyes with eye-salve, that thou mayest see.

WEALTH

The Old Testament is not hostile to riches. It has a special concern for the poor, but is prepared to admire the wealthy, such as Solomon. It does object, however, to unjust methods of acquiring wealth, uncharitable ways of spending it, and the folly of letting it destroy your sense of proportion and of true values. Realism is the thing. What money does is make you wealthy: not happy, not good, not important, and certainly not immortal—just wealthy (and probably sleepless).

Jesus in the Gospels sees wealth as a positive hindrance to the gaining of true riches (see Values). His first disciples, men with an inherited respect for wealth, found this attitude hard to accept. Most of his later disciples (but still within the period of the New Testament) were poor enough to be clear of temptation, but they still found some difficulty in taking a rich man at his true value—a value that had much to do with what he *was* and nothing at all to do with what he was "worth." "Is it not the rich who are exploiting you?" asks James (2:6), evidently thinking that the wealthy might still be getting too much respect—though they were not likely to be left with much *self*-respect after reading the diatribe in Chapter 5 of James's letter.

The verdict of the New Testament is harsh enough without making it harder by misquotation or mistranslation. In the original, money is *not* said to be the root of all evil: the *love* of money is *a* root of all *kinds* of evil, as a modern version correctly translates it.

One real use for wealth is to provide an image of the spiritual condition that the New Testament believes Christ has opened to all. The true riches are those that he freely shares, but Christ's sharing has by reflex an effect on the use of material riches. Those too must be shared.

During the centuries since the New Testament was written, the view that wealth is a sign of God's blessing has probably been more influential (in spite of Saint Francis) than the doctrine of the camel and the kingdom. That being so, it ill behooves the beneficiaries of wealth to profess a belated conversion to the virtues of poverty when addressing those who have been relatively poor and are now making a bid to join the relatively wealthy.

For instance, it ill behooves the advanced nations to tell the underdeveloped countries that they are happier as they are than they will be if they demand Western standards of material welfare. The sermon, even if true, is made particularly unfitting if it includes threats of ecological death and hell as the wages of working for wealth.

Similarly, it ill behooves bosses who have done nicely under the (then) sacred laws of supply and demand to denounce as greedy those workers who acquire some muscle and use it to play under the same rules.

And yet wealth *is* something of a snare. The biblical belief that it tends to become a master rather than a servant is not ill-founded. All too easily wealth becomes a measure of value rather than a mere possession. When that happens, not only do people lose their true significance, but the wealth itself loses its true significance as well. For wealth to be valued correctly it has to be assessed in terms of how it can be used as a source of shared enjoyment.

The Bible is a very materialist book. It values highly the good things of the earth. But it values them by standards that transcend the material. It does not allow them to become the measure of their own significance. Those who practice a life of Christian simplicity render a particular service to wealth: they show riches in perspective and make it possible for wealth to be appreciated at its true worth.

WEALTH

OLD TESTAMENT

2 Chronicles 9:13, 22

13 Now the weight of gold that came to Solomon in one year was six hundred and threescore and six talents of gold.

22 And king Solomon passed all the kings of the earth in riches and wisdom.

Psalm 62:10

Trust not in oppression,
And become not vain in robbery:
If riches increase, set not your heart upon
them.

Amos 8:4–7

4 Hear this, O ye that swallow up the needy, even to make the poor of the land to fail,

5 Saying, When will the new moon be gone, that we may sell corn? and the sabbath, that we may set forth wheat, making the ephah small, and the shekel great, and falsifying the balances by deceit?

6 That we may buy the poor for silver, and the needy for a pair of shoes; yea, and sell the refuse of the wheat?

7 The Lord hath sworn by the excellency of Jacob, Surely I will never forget any of their works.

Proverbs 1:18–19

And they lay wait for their own blood;
They lurk privily for their own lives.
So are the ways of every one that is greedy
of gain;

Which taketh away the life of the owners
thereof.

Ecclesiastes 5:12

12 The sleep of a labouring man is sweet, whether he eat little or much: but the abundance of the rich will not suffer him to sleep.

NEW TESTAMENT

Luke 18:22–27 (conversation with a young ruler)

22 Now when Jesus heard these things, he said unto him, Yet lackest thou one thing: sell all that thou hast, and distribute unto the poor, and thou shalt have treasure in heaven: and come, follow me.

23 And when he heard this, he was very sorrowful: for he was very rich.

24 And when Jesus saw that he was very sorrowful, he said, How hardly shall they that have riches enter into the kingdom of God!

25 For it is easier for a camel to go through a needle's eye, than for a rich man to enter into the kingdom of God.

26 And they that heard it said, Who then can be saved?

27 And he said, The things which are impossible with men are possible with God.

Luke 16:13

13 No servant can serve two masters: for either he will hate the one, and love the other; or else he will hold

to the one, and despise the other. Ye cannot serve God and mammon.

1 Timothy 6:6–10, 17–18

6 But godliness with contentment is great gain.

7 For we brought nothing into this world, and it is certain we can carry nothing out.

8 And having food and raiment let us be therewith content.

9 But they that will be rich fall into temptation and a snare, and into many foolish and hurtful lusts, which drown men in destruction and perdition.

10 For the love of money is the root of all evil: which while some coveted after, they have erred from the faith, and pierced themselves through with many sorrows.

17 Charge them that are rich in this world, that they be not high-minded, nor trust in uncertain riches, but in the living God, who giveth us richly all things to enjoy;

18 That they do good, that they be rich in good works, ready to distribute, willing to communicate.

2 Corinthians 8:9

9 For ye know the grace of our Lord Jesus Christ, that, though he was rich, yet for your sakes he became poor, that ye through his poverty might be rich.

WISDOM

Wisdom is a major theme of the Old Testament, but rarely does it mean speculative thought, as in the Greek view of wisdom. Frequently it means the practical ability to make thought effective in action. Certainly wisdom is said to be available only from God and on condition of good behavior: a wise bad man would be a contradiction in Hebrew terms. Occasionally wisdom is said to be a transcendent being, created before the world and instrumental in its making.

That idea was further developed in Israel before New Testament times. The Book of Wisdom, though written in Greek and outside the canon of the Old Testament as Protestants generally understand it, is true to the Hebrew tradition when it says (in the New English Bible translation):

Wisdom moves more easily than motion itself, she pervades and permeates all things because she is so pure. Like a fine mist she rises from the power of God, a pure effluence from the glory of the Almighty; so nothing defiled can enter into her by stealth. She is the brightness that streams from everlasting light, the flawless mirror of the active power of God and the image of his goodness. She is but one, yet can do everything; herself unchanging, she makes all things new; age after age she enters into holy souls, and makes them God's friends and prophets, for nothing is acceptable to God but the man who makes his home with wisdom. She is more radiant than the sun, and surpasses every constellation; compared with the light of day, she is found to excel; for day gives place to night, but against wisdom no evil can prevail. She spans the world in power from end to end, and orders all things benignly (7:24–8:1).

By the time the New Testament was written, the Christian church had moved out into the Greek world. There the word "wisdom" not only meant something more academic than it had in Hebrew but was the special theme of all kinds of Gnostic sects claiming to possess some esoteric wisdom that made their members superior to ordinary mortals. New Testament writers therefore used the word with care.

Sometimes they avoided it. The theme of personified Wisdom as God's agent in creation was taken up at the beginning of John's Gospel, but with the word "Logos" ("Word") substituted: "all things were made by him; and without him was not anything made that was made" (John 1:3). It is this Word that becomes flesh in Jesus.

Paul also speaks of Jesus as "the wisdom of God" and says that in him "are hid all the treasures of wisdom and knowledge" (Colossians 2:3), but Paul and other New Testament writers have to guard against being thought to speak of the knowledge claimed by philosophers and Gnostics. To such people the wisdom of Christ, found not in a classroom but on a cross, was sheer folly, but to the Christians this folly was that wisdom from above of which the Old Testament had spoken.

Academic knowledge, intellectual insight, technical skill, and ordinary cleverness are not the same thing as wisdom in the biblical sense, but they are not irrelevant to it. All can have their place under wisdom—but very definitely *under* it. Biblical wisdom claims the authority to direct science and technology, defining the ends that they are to serve. Wisdom would not, for instance, allow science to do as it pleased with the world just because scientists had discovered how it could be done.

Wisdom is no excuse for ignorance and no substitute for thinking, but it is available to all. It provides a sort of map on which all knowledge and experience can be located. The truly wise man may have to answer "Don't know" to many a profound question, but when he meets with trivia he will know that they are trivial, and when he meets with something serious he will know that it is serious. He will have a sense of balance and proportion that will enable him to accept a fact as a fact—and that is not the commonest of gifts.

WISDOM

OLD TESTAMENT

Job 28:12–16, 21–28

But where shall wisdom be found?
And where is the place of understanding?

Man knoweth not the price thereof;
Neither is it found in the land of the living.
The depth saith, It is not in me:
And the sea saith, It is not with me.

It cannot be gotten for gold,
Neither shall silver be weighed for the
price thereof.
It cannot be valued with the gold of Ophir,
With the precious onyx, or the sapphire.
Seeing it is hid from the eyes of all living,
And kept close from the fowls of the air.
Destruction and death say,
We have heard the fame thereof with our
ears.
God understandeth the way thereof,
And he knoweth the place thereof.
For he looketh to the ends of the earth,
And seeth under the whole heaven;
To make the weight for the winds;
And he weigheth the waters by measure.
When he made a decree for the rain,
And a way for the lightning of the thunder:
Then did he see it, and declare it;
He prepared it, yea, and searched it out.
And unto man he said,
Behold, the fear of the Lord, that is
wisdom;
And to depart from evil is understanding.

Proverbs 8:12, 14–22, 27–31

I wisdom dwell with prudence,
And find out knowledge of witty in-
ventions.
Counsel is mine, and sound wisdom:
I am understanding; I have strength.
By me kings reign,
And princes decree justice.
By me princes rule,
And nobles, even all the judges of the
earth.
I love them that love me;
And those that seek me early shall find
me.
Riches and honour are with me;
Yea, durable riches and righteousness.
My fruit is better than gold, yea, than
fine gold;
And my revenue than choice silver.
I lead in the way of righteousness,
In the midst of the paths of judgment:

That I may cause those that love me to
inherit substance;
And I will fill their treasures.
The Lord possessed me in the beginning
of his way,
Before his works of old.
When he prepared the heavens, I was
there:
When he set a compass upon the face of
the depth:
When he established the clouds above:
When he strengthened the fountains of
the deep:
When he gave to the sea his decree,
That the waters should not pass his
commandment:
When he appointed the foundations of
the earth:
Then I was by him, as one brought up
with him:
And I was daily his delight,
Rejoicing always before him;
Rejoicing in the habitable part of his earth;
And my delights were with the sons of
men.

NEW TESTAMENT

1 Corinthians 1:20–25

20 Where is the wise? where is the
scribe? where is the disputer of this
world? hath not God made foolish the
wisdom of this world?

21 For after that in the wisdom of
God the world by wisdom knew not
God, it pleased God by the foolishness
of preaching to save them that believe.

22 For the Jews require a sign, and
the Greeks seek after wisdom:

23 But we preach Christ crucified,
unto the Jews a stumblingblock, and
unto the Greeks foolishness;

24 But unto them which are called,

both Jews and Greeks, Christ the power of God, and the wisdom of God.

25 Because the foolishness of God is wiser than men; and the weakness of God is stronger than men.

James 3:14–15, 17

14 But if ye have bitter envying and strife in your hearts, glory not, and lie not against the truth.

15 This wisdom descendeth not from above, but is earthly, sensual, devilish.

17 But the wisdom that is from above is first pure, then peaceable, gentle, and easy to be entreated, full of mercy and good fruits.

WORK

The Old Testament does *not* say (as some have alleged on the basis of Genesis 3:17–19) that work is a curse, a punishment for sin. That must be a misinterpretation of Genesis, since Adam has already been set by God in the Garden of Eden to work it, and indeed God himself has been described as a creative worker. What the passage does say, in its pictorial way, is that all this creative activity is spoiled and made burdensome by Adam and Eve's departure from the divine purpose.

Even so, work remains an honorable activity—even an inspired one—in the Old Testament. The psalmists see work as part of the rhythm of nature, joyful when God blesses it (65:13), futile when he does not (127:1–2). Ecclesiastes seems to say that work is futile if you look on it as a means of accumulating wealth: only the satisfaction to be had in the work itself is of real value.

In John's Gospel, Jesus develops the thought of God as a continuously active worker, and he justifies his own Sabbath healings as equally valid work. In his hometown Jesus was referred to as "the carpenter," but this did not hinder his manifesting divine wisdom and power. In many of his parables he allowed the daily trades of his neighbors to mirror the divine. He chose as the symbol for himself the hardworking shepherd. In fact, he even implied that it is possible to see into the nature of God by studying the attitude of a shepherd to his work, the argument being that if a shepherd will do this, will God do less?

Paul was a tentmaker and did not abandon that trade when he became a missionary (Acts 18:1–4). The first generation of Christians seems to have been largely composed of manual workers, and all were taught to treat their work as an expression of their faith—even if it was the work of a slave.

Literature from many periods and places provides an apt commentary on the biblical view of work. From Israel between the Testaments came the Book of Ecclesiasticus with its vivid account of the way in which various crafts preoccupy people's attention so that they never become scholars, and yet (to quote one of the two translations offered by the New English Bible), "Without them a city would have no inhabitants; no settlers or travellers would come to it . . . they maintain the fabric of this world, and their daily work is their prayer."

Nearly two thousand years later in the country rectory of Bemerton, George Herbert considers how every task can be purified by doing it "For Thy sake": "A servant with this clause Makes drudgery divine."

Three hundred years later in Paris, Charles Péguy remembers his peasant mother who supported her family by mending chairs: "During all my childhood I saw chairs being caned exactly in the same spirit, with the same hand and heart as those with which the same people fashioned its cathedrals. . . . It was the innate being of work which needed to be well done."*

In none of these examples does work acquire significance only if its products can be marketed. Work needs to be well done because of its "innate being." Should the time come when all marketable goods are produced under the direction of microprocessors so that little human labor is required, there is no reason why creative activities with no marketable outcome should not be regarded (and rewarded) as work. Growing flowers for your husband or your wife, going swimming with your children, reciting poetry for your friends—these things may at present be the sort of leisure activities that we contrast with real work, but in a biblical view they could be included among the occupations man was first set in the Garden of Eden to follow.

WORK

OLD TESTAMENT

Genesis 3:17–19

17 And unto Adam he said, Because thou hast hearkened unto the voice of thy wife, and hast eaten of the tree, of which I commanded thee, saying, Thou shalt not eat of it: cursed is the ground for thy sake; in sorrow shalt thou eat of it all the days of thy life;

18 Thorns also and thistles shall it bring forth to thee; and thou shalt eat the herb of the field;

19 In the sweat of thy face shalt thou eat bread, till thou return unto the ground; for out of it wast thou taken: for dust thou art, and unto dust shalt thou return.

Exodus 35:35

35 Them hath he filled with wisdom of heart, to work all manner of work, of the engraver, and of the cunning workman, and of the embroiderer, in blue, and in purple, in scarlet, and in fine linen, and of the weaver, even of them that do any work, and of those that devise cunning work.

*Charles Péguy, "The Honor of Work," in *Basic Verities*, tr. Ann Green and Julian Green (London: Kegan Paul, 1943).

Psalm 104:21–23

The young lions roar after their prey,
And seek their meat from God.
The sun ariseth, they gather themselves together,
And lay them down in their dens.
Man goeth forth unto his work
And to his labour until the evening.·

Ecclesiastes 2:17–24

17 Therefore I hated life; because the work that is wrought under the sun is grievous unto me: for all is vanity and vexation of spirit.

18 Yea, I hated all my labour which I had taken under the sun: because I should leave it unto the man that shall be after me.

19 And who knoweth whether he shall be a wise man or a fool? yet shall he have rule over all my labour wherein I have laboured, and wherein I have shewed myself wise under the sun. This is also vanity.

20 Therefore I went about to cause my heart to despair of all the labour which I took under the sun.

21 For there is a man whose labour is in wisdom, and in knowledge, and in equity; yet to a man that hath not laboured therein shall he leave it for his portion. This also is vanity and a great evil.

22 For what hath man of all his labour, and of the vexation of his heart, wherein he hath laboured under the sun?

23 For all his days are sorrows, and his travail grief; yea, his heart taketh not rest in the night.

24 There is nothing better for a man,

than that he should eat and drink, and that he should make his soul enjoy good in his labour. This also I saw, that it was from the hand of God.

NEW TESTAMENT

John 5:16–18

16 And therefore did the Jews persecute Jesus, and sought to slay him, because he had done these things on the sabbath day.

17 But Jesus answered them, My Father worketh hitherto, and I work.

18 Therefore the Jews sought the more to kill him, because he not only had broken the sabbath, but said also that God was his Father, making himself equal with God.

Mark 6:1–3

1 And he went out from thence, and came into his own country; and his disciples follow him.

2 And when the sabbath day was come, he began to teach in the synagogue: and many hearing him were astonished, saying, From whence hath this man these things? and what wisdom is this which is given unto him, that even such mighty works are wrought by his hands?

3 Is not this the carpenter? . . .

Matthew 18:12–14

12 How think ye? if a man have an hundred sheep, and one of them be gone astray, doth he not leave the ninety and nine, and goeth into the mountains, and seeketh that which is gone astray?

13 And if so be that he find it, verily I say unto you, he rejoiceth more of that sheep, than of the ninety and nine which went not astray.

14 Even so it is not the will of your Father which is in heaven, that one of these little ones should perish.

Ephesians 6:5–8

5 Servants, be obedient to them that are your masters according to the flesh, with fear and trembling, in singleness of your heart, as unto Christ;

6 Not with eye-service, as men-pleasers; but as the servants of Christ, doing the will of God from the heart;

7 With good will doing service, as to the Lord, and not to men:

8 Knowing that whatsoever good thing any man doeth, the same shall he receive of the Lord, whether he be bond or free.

WORLD

The Old Testament writers had no more scientific knowledge of the world than other men of their time, but they observed the world accurately—without sentimentality and without prejudice. They came to believe that their God made it all, a belief stated pictorially in the opening chapters of the Bible and celebrated joyfully in many a Psalm. But this did not cloud their observation. Far from letting their idea of God distort their picture of the world, they read off from their knowledge of the world something of their idea of God.

Job agonized over the problem of unjust suffering. Instead of being answered, he was given a precise account of various natural phenomena and zoological specimens. He had to learn to live in the world as it is and to worship God from a base in reality, not from the idealized, unreal world that his friends described as existing—and that he himself had felt ought to exist.

Not that this realism made the world religiously of no significance. On the contrary. Many a religious idea—such as the popular notion that God's favor could be bought by sacrifices—could be corrected just by taking account of the fact that the world as it is belongs wholly to God.

The New Testament is equally realistic, but it recognizes that the world as we know it is a spoiled one. Even natural forces can be rebuked and corrected. The world contains not only birds and flowers that express the abundance of divine provision, but also destructive forces and diseases and evil spirits to be challenged and expelled in God's name. It is a world to be received with gratitude as God's gift, yet a world to be redeemed by God's grace (see Nature, Environment, and Evil).

Particularly in John's Gospel and epistles the word "world" is used in two quite different senses. In one sense it is the created order that God loves; in another sense it is the "worldly" order that is organized against him. Either way, the word covers the same area of space, since the real world is simultaneously both the good creation of God and the corrupt instrument of evil. The New Testament does not speak as if the world were one of these before the Fall and the other after: creation is continuous, and the Fall is always, so the double nature of the world is ever-present.

In the biblical view we inhabit a world to be both loved and fought against. It is a gift to be accepted; it is a rebellious force to be subdued. Just as it can be said of a man that he is his own worst enemy and needs to be saved from himself, so we can say of the world that it needs to be saved from its worldliness in order to be its true self.

The tools of this trade include everything from prayer to nuclear science. No distinct line separates the religious from the secular. How could such a line exist if the whole world is God's? But the human being is the key figure, the gateway through which both corruption and redemption invade the world. Until humanity is aligned with the underlying purpose of the world's existence, not only will men and women be out of harmony with the world around them, but that world will be thrown off course, too. The human race is so integral a part of the world that there is no salvation for men and women or for the world apart from each other.

This is the verdict not only of zoologists, who increasingly see humanity embedded in nature, but also of Christian mystics such as Thomas Traherne who see redeemed humanity as one with nature spiritually. "You never enjoy the World aright," says Traherne in *Centuries of Meditations*, "till the sea itself floweth in your veins, till you are clothed with the heavens, and crowned with the stars: and perceive yourself to be the sole heir of the whole world, and more than so, because men are in it who are every one sole heirs as well as you."

WORLD

OLD TESTAMENT

Genesis 1:9–13

9 And God said, Let the waters under the heaven be gathered together unto one place, and let the dry land appear: and it was so.

10 And God called the dry land Earth; and the gathering together of the waters called he Seas: and God saw that it was good.

11 And God said, Let the earth bring forth grass, the herb yielding seed, and the fruit tree yielding fruit after his kind, whose seed is in itself, upon the earth: and it was so.

12 And the earth brought forth grass, and herb yielding seed after his kind, and the tree yielding fruit, whose seed was in itself, after his kind: and God saw that it was good.

13 And the evening and the morning were the third day.

Job 41:1–2, 7, 10–11 (God challenges Job to consider one of his creatures—perhaps the crocodile)

Canst thou draw out leviathan with an
    hook?
Or his tongue with a cord which thou
    lettest down?
Canst thou put an hook into his nose?
Or bore his jaw through with a thorn?
Canst thou fill his skin with barbed irons?
Or his head with fish spears?
None is so fierce that dare stir him up:
Who then is able to stand before me?
Who hath prevented me, that I should
    repay him?
Whatsoever is under the whole heaven is
    mine.

Psalm 50:1, 7–11

The mighty God, even the Lord, hath
    spoken,
And called the earth from the rising of
    the sun unto the going down thereof.
Hear, O my people, and I will speak;
O Israel, and I will testify against thee:
I am God, even thy God.
I will not reprove thee for thy sacrifices
Or thy burnt offerings, to have been con-
    tinually before me.
I will take no bullock out of thy house,
Nor he goats out of thy folds.
For every beast of the forest is mine,
And the cattle upon a thousand hills.
I know all the fowls of the mountains:
And the wild beasts of the field are mine.

NEW TESTAMENT

Matthew 6:9–10

9 After this manner therefore pray
ye: Our Father which art in heaven,
Hallowed be thy name.

10 Thy kingdom come. Thy will
be done in earth, as it is in heaven.

Luke 8:22–25

22 Now it came to pass on a certain day, that he went into a ship with
his disciples: and he said unto them,
Let us go over unto the other side of
the lake. And they launched forth.
23 But as they sailed he fell asleep:
and there came down a storm of wind
on the lake; and they were filled with
water, and were in jeopardy.
24 And they came to him, and
awoke him, saying, Master, master, we
perish. Then he arose, and rebuked
the wind and the raging of the water:
and they ceased, and there was a calm.
25 And he said unto them, Where
is your faith?

John 3:16; 15:18 (two senses of "world")

16 For God so loved the world, that
he gave his only begotten Son.

18 If the world hate you, ye know
that it hated me before it hated you.

Acts 14:15–17 (Barnabas and Paul on the "world" in the first of two senses)

15 We also are men of like passions
with you, and preach unto you that ye
should turn from these vanities unto
the living God, which made heaven,
and earth, and the sea, and all things
that are therein:
16 Who in times past suffered all
nations to walk in their own ways.
17 Nevertheless he left not himself
without witness, in that he did good,
and gave us rain from heaven, and

fruitful seasons, filling our hearts with food and gladness.

1 John 2:15–16 (on the "world" in the second of the two senses)

15 Love not the world, neither the things that are in the world. If any man love the world, the love of the Father is not in him.

16 For all that is in the world, the lust of the flesh, and the lust of the eyes, and the pride of life, is not of the Father, but is of the world.

WORSHIP

The Old Testament hardly bothers to say that human beings *ought* to worship God. The merest glimpse or the least sign of his presence will produce that effect quite involuntarily. Some have even suggested that the root of the Hebrew name for God ("Yah") was simply the sound of breath caught or expelled in wonder and awe. The question of why God should want to be worshiped does not arise. He just cannot *not* be. And the worship that goes out to him is not mere admiration. Just as it arises irresistibly, so it leads inevitably to obedience. Moses at the burning bush, Elijah at the cave's mouth, Isaiah in the temple—all were both overawed and summoned.

All the same, Old Testament worship needed to be organized. Worship is easily misdirected, and the worship of false gods (invariably more accessible and less demanding ones) will falsify all the rest of life, too. The temple at Jerusalem was designed as a focus of disciplined worship, less vulnerable to the temptations of idolatry than local sanctuaries had proved to be. When the temple was destroyed, the prophets spoke of its restoration as central to all the hopes of the nation. The glory of God in the temple was inseparable from the peace of Israel in the world.

The New Testament opens with the Jerusalem temple restored as the center of Israel's worship, but local synagogues were now an accepted part of Jewish life. In addition the half-Jewish, heretical Samaritans looked a little wistfully at the ruins of their temple on Mount Gerizim, destroyed in 129 B.C. In John's Gospel, Jesus' attention is called to disputes about the correct forms and places of worship, but he points to a level at which such distinctions are transcended.

In A.D. 70 the Jerusalem temple was again destroyed, but already Christian worship was organized on the lines of synagogue worship, though with significant additions such as the sacramental reenacting of Jesus' last supper with his disciples.

The link between worship and conduct was so well maintained that the New Testament letter writers seem quite unaware of changing the subject when they pass from life to worship, or from worship to life. Peace and thanksgiving were characteristics of both.

Worship, it has often been said, is essentially the acknowledgment of worth. A community that knew nothing of worship would know nothing of any absolute standards of worth. There is something in this argument, but one could easily draw the wrong conclusions from it. It invites a simplistic conclusion: We need standards of worth, and we need a basis for them; therefore let us attend to worship.

The difficulty with this simplistic course is that it does more to invite than to avoid the perils of idolatry. To take our own standards of worth, to project them on some infinitely distant screen called God, and then to worship that projection is to bow down to an extension of ourselves. It is idolatry as surely as bowing down to a graven image would be; it is the worship of a mental image instead of a metal image.

The Bible in its attack on idolatry insists that only God is to be worshiped. Of course, it will not be God as he truly is, without error or distortion. We cannot know God like that even if we believe in the incarnation. But one characteristic of true worship is that it is offered to a God who reveals himself in ways that are both surprising and demanding. Another characteristic is that he is acknowledged to be far greater than has been understood even through this revelation.

Some of the early biblical pictures of God are extremely crude, but they are a challenge to the worshiper and not just a projection of human wishes. The god who confirms our prejudices and ministers to our complacency is a man-made god. When the true God reveals himself with intrinsic and irresistible authority, he astonishes us by his grace and asks us to become what we are not—and perhaps didn't really want to be. *He* is to be adored.

WORSHIP

OLD TESTAMENT

Exodus 20:3–5

3 Thou shalt have no other gods before me.

4 Thou shalt not make unto thee any graven image or any likeness of any thing that is in heaven above, or that is in the earth beneath, or that is in the water under the earth:

5 Thou shalt not bow down thyself to them, nor serve them: for I the Lord thy God am a jealous God.

Exodus 33:18–23

18 And he [Moses] said, I beseech thee, shew me thy glory.

19 And he said, I will make all my goodness pass before thee, and I will proclaim the name of the Lord before thee; and will be gracious to whom I will be gracious, and will shew mercy on whom I will shew mercy.

20 And he said, Thou canst not see my face: for there shall no man see me, and live.

21 And the Lord said, Behold, there

is a place by me, and thou shalt stand upon a rock:

22 And it shall come to pass, while my glory passeth by, that I will put thee in a clift of the rock, and will cover thee with my hand while I pass by:

23 And I will take away mine hand, and thou shalt see my back parts: but my face shall not be seen.

1 Kings 19:11-13

11 And he said, Go forth, and stand upon the mount before the Lord. And, behold, the Lord passed by, and a great and strong wind rent the mountains, and brake in pieces the rocks before the Lord; but the Lord was not in the wind: and after the wind an earthquake; but the Lord was not in the earthquake:

12 And after the earthquake a fire; but the Lord was not in the fire: and after the fire a still small voice.

13 And it was so, when Elijah heard it that he wrapped his face in his mantle, and went out, and stood in the entering in of the cave.

Psalm 29:1-3, 9

Give unto the Lord, O ye mighty,
Give unto the Lord glory and strength.
Give unto the Lord the glory due unto his name;
Worship the Lord in the beauty of holiness.
The voice of the Lord is upon the waters:
The God of glory thundereth:
The Lord is upon many waters.
The voice of the Lord maketh the hinds to calve,
And discovereth the forests:

And in his temple doth every one speak of his glory.

NEW TESTAMENT

John 4:19-24 (Jesus and a woman of Samaria)

19 The woman saith unto him, Sir, I perceive that thou art a prophet.

20 Our fathers worshipped in this mountain; and ye say, that in Jerusalem is the place where men ought to worship.

21 Jesus saith unto her, Woman, believe me, the hour cometh, when ye shall neither in this mountain, nor yet at Jerusalem, worship the Father.

22 Ye worship ye know not what: we know what we worship: for salvation is of the Jews.

23 But the hour cometh, and now is, when the true worshippers shall worship the Father in spirit and in truth: for the Father seeketh such to worship him.

24 God is a Spirit: and they that worship him must worship him in spirit and in truth.

1 Corinthians 11:23-26

23 For I have received of the Lord that which also I delivered unto you, That the Lord Jesus the same night in which he was betrayed took bread:

24 And when he had given thanks, he brake it, and said, Take, eat: this is my body, which is broken for you: this do in remembrance of me.

25 After the same manner also he took the cup, when he had supped,

saying, This cup is the new testament in my blood: this do ye, as oft as ye drink it, in remembrance of me.

26 For as often as ye eat this bread, and drink this cup, ye do shew the Lord's death till he come

Colossians 3:15–17

15 And let the peace of God rule in your hearts, to the which also ye are called in one body; and be ye thankful.

16 Let the word of Christ dwell in you richly in all wisdom; teaching and admonishing one another in psalms and hymns and spiritual songs, sing-ing with grace in your hearts to the Lord.

17 And whatsoever ye do in word or deed, do all in the name of the Lord Jesus, giving thanks to God and the Father by him.

Ephesians 5:19–20

19 Speaking to yourselves in psalms and hymns and spiritual songs, sing-ing and making melody in your heart to the Lord;

20 Giving thanks always for all things unto God and the Father in the name of our Lord Jesus Christ.

YOUTH

The Old Testament regards youth as a time of energy, daring, and delight, but it qualifies this view in two ways.

First, it recognizes that although joy should be the dominant note of youth, events can tragically dictate otherwise. It laments as one of the saddest features of a period of defeat, such as is reflected in the Book of Lamentations, the ruin of that youthful experience.

The other qualification is that the loss of youth's vitality, whether by war or by age, can be accepted and redeemed. This vitality is not the product merely of having lived so many years and no more. There is in God a creative source of life capable of renewing at any time the zest and energy of youth. One prophet's vision was of a day when old and young would be equally inspired: "Your sons and your daughters shall prophesy, your old men shall dream dreams, your young men shall see visions" (Joel 2:28).

Youth in the New Testament betrays the usual mixture of characteristics. One young man in the Gospels misses his chance to follow Jesus precisely because he acts with the prudence of age rather than the impetuousness of youth. Another, in Mark's Gospel (possibly Mark himself), lets his curiosity take him so close to the arrest of Jesus that he gets away only by shedding the garment by which he has been caught. There is one young man in Acts whom Paul bores—almost literally to death. There is another, Paul's own nephew, who smells out a plot and flits dangerously from one person to another forestalling it. Paul himself was

395

once "a young man whose name was Saul" and who kept an eye on the clothes of the men stoning the first Christian martyr.

The psychological characteristics of youth, from fanaticism to excessive caution, were all present in the New Testament, but religiously they were treated as nothing special. The aged John addressed his message of love to all impartially, and with the rhythmic parallelism of Old Testament poetry:

> I write unto you, fathers,
> because ye have known him that is from the beginning.
> I write unto you, young men,
> because ye have overcome the wicked one.
> I write unto you, little children,
> because ye have known the Father.
>
> (1 John 2:13)

Youth both is and is not special. It has its own psychological patterns, but its special features are just variations on the theme of being human. Youth's deepest needs and highest aspirations transcend all generation gaps.

The youth culture of the mid-twentieth century has had at least two slightly ridiculous side effects. One is that throwing off the life-style of one's elders became too easy. It was not necessary to work out one's own alternative. A well-marketed and well-publicized pattern was there to conform to. The other embarrassing spectacle was that of an older generation some of whom lived out a pathetic pursuit of their own lost adolescence, feeling it unfair that they had been born too soon to taste the joys of liberated youth.

But the joys (and the sadnesses) of youth have little to do with liberation from mere conventions. The experience flows from deeper sources—sources that need not dry up with age. Both the realism and the idealism of the Bible are needed to see youth in perspective. To treat it as if it were itself the source of its own goodness, as if it were always good and the only good, is to invest in a wasting asset.

The youthful possibilities of vision, of openness to change, of resilience, of discovery—these are gifts to be discovered in youth and valued always. If need be, they can be discerned in someone else's experience of youth, but once recognized the heart must remain always open to them.

YOUTH

OLD TESTAMENT

1 Samuel 17:33-37

33 And Saul said to David, Thou art not able to go against this Philistine to fight with him: for thou art but a youth, and he a man of war from his youth.

34 And David said unto Saul, Thy servant kept his father's sheep, and there

came a lion, and a bear, and took a lamb out of the flock:

35 And I went out after him, and smote him, and delivered it out of his mouth: and when he arose against me, I caught him by his beard, and smote him, and slew him.

36 Thy servant slew both the lion and the bear: and this uncircumcised Philistine shall be as one of them, seeing he hath defied the armies of the living God.

37 David said moreover, The Lord that delivered me out of the paw of the lion, and out of the paw of the bear, he will deliver me out of the hand of this Philistine. And Saul said unto David, Go, and the Lord be with thee.

Lamentations 5:1–3, 11–15

Remember, O Lord, what is come upon us:
Consider, and behold our reproach.
Our inheritance is turned to strangers,
Our houses to aliens.
We are orphans and fatherless,
Our mothers are as widows.
They ravished the women in Zion,
And the maids in the cities of Judah.
Princes are hanged up by their hand:
The faces of elders were not honoured.
They took the young men to grind,
And the children fell under the wood.
The elders have ceased from the gate,
The young men from their musick.
The joy of our heart is ceased;
Our dance is turned into mourning.

Isaiah 40:30–31

30 Even the youths shall faint and be weary, and the young men shall utterly fall:

31 But they that wait upon the Lord shall renew their strength; they shall mount up with wings as eagles; they shall run, and not be weary; and they shall walk, and not faint.

NEW TESTAMENT

Matthew 19:21–22

21 Jesus said unto him, If thou wilt be perfect, go and sell that thou hast, and give to the poor, and thou shalt have treasure in heaven: and come and follow me.

22 But when the young man heard that saying, he went away sorrowful: for he had great possessions.

Mark 14:51–52 (at the arrest of Jesus)

51 And there followed him a certain young man, having a linen cloth cast about his naked body; and the young men laid hold on him:

52 And he left the linen cloth, and fled from them naked.

Acts 20:7–10

7 And upon the first day of the week, when the disciples came together to break bread, Paul preached unto them, ready to depart on the morrow; and continued his speech until midnight.

8 And there were many lights in the upper chamber, where they were gathered together.

9 And there sat in a window a certain young man named Eutychus, being fallen into a deep sleep: and as Paul was long preaching, he sunk down with sleep, and fell down from the third loft, and was taken up dead.

10 And Paul went down, and fell

on him, and embracing him said, Trouble not yourselves; for his life is in him.

Acts 23:16–17, 19–22 (Paul imprisoned in Jerusalem)

16 And when Paul's sister's son heard of their lying in wait, he went and entered into the castle, and told Paul.

17 Then Paul called one of the centurions unto him, and said, Bring this young man unto the chief captain: for he hath a certain thing to tell him.

19 Then the chief captain took him by the hand, and went with him aside privately, and asked him, What is that thou hast to tell me?

20 And he said, The Jews have agreed to desire thee that thou wouldest bring down Paul tomorrow into the council, as though they would inquire somewhat of him more perfectly.

21 But do not thou yield unto them: for there lie in wait for him of them more than forty men,

22 So the chief captain then let the young man depart, and charged him, See thou tell no man that thou hast shewed these things to me.

ZEAL

Zeal is tricky. Passionate enthusiasm for a cause is a fine quality so long as the cause is just, but things can easily go wrong. Blind enthusiasm can carry the cause in directions that are no longer just. Fanatical enthusiasm can use anger instead of love as its fuel. Overexpended enthusiasm can lead to despondent self-pity. All these perversions of zeal, as well as the true form, are represented in the Old Testament.

Elijah provides an example of the reaction that can follow a passionate campaign, especially if one remembers that the words "jealous" and "zealous" are essentially one (see Jealousy). Elijah's boast that he has been "very jealous for the Lord God Almighty" is amply justified. On Mount Carmel he had got the better of all the prophets serving Baal and Asherah—the male and female deities worshiped in defiance of Israelite law. Yet afterward Elijah is a spent force, overly proud of his unique contribution and overly sorry for himself. At Horeb he has to be put together again and recommissioned.

Even the most admired Old Testament examples of human zeal seem to involve bloodshed. The zealous act by which Phinehas was believed to have saved all Israel from the wrath of God consisted of going into a tent and putting a spear through a man and a woman whose marriage was illegal because of the wife's nationality and religion.

But God, too, is said to be zealous, and in a more compassionate way (at least in the later Old Testament books). Isaiah repeats the refrain, "the zeal of the Lord of hosts will perform this," and "this" is invariably a reference to justice and peace.

The prophecy of a child whose birth will mark the cessation of all war ends with this same refrain (see Isaiah 9 under Peace).

In the New Testament one of the apostles of Jesus is called "the zealot." It is characteristic of the ambiguities of zeal that scholars are not quite sure whether this is a favorable reference to his record as a disciple or a less favorable reference to his politics. Certainly there was, a few years later, a faction of extreme militants known as the Zealots.

Paul makes a useful distinction between zeal which is "based on knowledge" and that which is not. As an example of the latter he cites his own history as a persecutor of Christians. (In the final quotation "the affect" seems to mean "to be on the side of".)

As an example of the right kind of zeal the New Testament offers the story of Jesus chasing the tradesmen from the one part of the temple that was open to all. John attaches to this event a text about zeal from the Psalms.

The towering energy that El Greco put into his picture of the cleansing of the temple is a tribute to the power of true zeal, but the genuinely passionate and intense conviction that what one is doing is right is not in itself enough to justify the action. Such conviction may make the action right in terms of motive, but the act itself can still be objectively wrong. Zeal has to be judged not just by the sincerity behind it, but by the justice of its cause and the goodness of its effect as well.

The biblical treatment of zeal underlines the importance of being right in spirit and motive, and also points to an outer, public zone where one must be right both in fact and in action. Biblical standards are personal and interior, but they are also as public and objective as the laws of nature.

In a way this is hard on us, because we have two chances of being wrong to every one of being right: we can do the wrong thing for the right reason and be condemned for our action; we can do the right thing for the wrong reason and be condemned for our motive. Only when both the action and the motive are right is all well. But then, the religion of the Bible is a root-and-branch religion. Both its remedies and its condemnations penetrate to the inner heart and extend to the outer world.

ZEAL

OLD TESTAMENT

Numbers 25:10–13

10 And the Lord spake unto Moses, saying,

11 Phinehas the son of Eleazar, the son of Aaron the priest, hath turned my wrath away from the children of Israel, while he was zealous for my sake among them, that I consumed not the children of Israel in my jealousy.

12 Wherefore say, Behold, I give unto him my covenant of peace:

13 And he shall have it, and his seed after him, even the covenant of an everlasting priesthood; because he was zealous for his God, and made an atonement for the children of Israel.

1 Kings 19:4–10

4 But he himself went a day's journey into the wilderness, and came and sat down under a juniper tree: and he requested for himself that he might die; and said, It is enough; now, O Lord, take away my life; for I am not better than my fathers.

5 And as he lay and slept under a juniper tree, behold, then an angel touched him, and said unto him, Arise and eat.

6 And he looked, and, behold, there was a cake baken on the coals, and a cruse of water at his head. And he did eat and drink, and laid him down again.

7 And the angel of the Lord came again the second time, and touched him, and said, Arise and eat; because the journey is too great for thee.

8 And he arose, and did eat and drink, and went in the strength of that meat forty days and forty nights unto Horeb the mount of God.

9 And he came thither unto a cave, and lodged there; and, behold, the word of the Lord came to him, and he said unto him, What doest thou here, Elijah?

10 And he said, I have been very jealous for the Lord God of hosts: for the children of Israel have forsaken thy covenant, thrown down thine altars, and slain thy prophets with the sword; and I, even I only, am left; and they seek my life, to take it away.

Isaiah 59:15–17

15 The Lord saw it, and it displeased him that there was no judgment.

16 And he saw that there was no man, and wondered that there was no intercessor: therefore his arm brought salvation unto him; and his righteousness, it sustained him.

17 For he put on righteousness as a breastplate, and an helmet of salvation upon his head; and he put on the garments of vengeance for clothing, and was clad with zeal as a cloak.

NEW TESTAMENT

John 2:13–17

13 And the Jews' passover was at hand, and Jesus went up to Jerusalem,

14 And found in the temple those that sold oxen and sheep and doves, and the changers of money sitting:

15 And when he had made a scourge of small cords, he drove them all out of the temple, and the sheep, and the oxen; and poured out the changers' money, and overthrew the tables;

16 And said unto them that sold doves, Take these things hence; make not my Father's house an house of merchandise.

17 And his disciples remembered that it was written, The zeal of thine house hath eaten me up.

Philippians 3:4–6

4 If any other man thinketh that he hath whereof he might trust in the flesh, I more:

5 Circumcised the eighth day, of the stock of Israel, of the tribe of Benjamin, an Hebrew of the Hebrews; as touching the law, a Pharisee;

6 Concerning zeal, persecuting the church; touching the righteousness which is in the law, blameless.

Romans 10:1–4

1 Brethren, my heart's desire and prayer to God for Israel is, that they might be saved.

2 For I bear them record that they have zeal of God, but not according to knowledge.

3 For they being ignorant of God's righteousness, and going about to establish their own righteousness, have not submitted themselves unto the righteousness of God.

4 For Christ is the end of the law for righteousness to every one that believeth.

Galatians 4:17–18

17 They zealously affect you, but not well; yea, they would exclude you, that ye might affect them.

18 But it is good to be zealously affected always in a good thing, and not only when I am present with you.

INDEX

A

Abednego, 110
Abel, 4, 30, 234
Abimelech, 359
Abner, 86
Abraham, 33, 45, 122, 191, 197, 244, 359
Absalom, 107, 231
"Academic," 347
Adam, 27, 95, 140–41, 206, 234, 237, 270, 353, 386
Adultery, 1–4
Aggression, 4–6
Ahab, 54, 277
Alcohol, 349–50
Ambition, 6–9
Anger, 9–12
Anxiety, 12–15
Anxiety (Munch), 13
Ashe, Geoffrey, 219
Authority, 15–18

B

Barabbas, 129, 377
Bathsheba, 1, 231, 234
Beauty, 18–21
Belshazzar, 271
Benjamin, 30
Bezaleel, 33, 347
Birth, 21–23
Blake, William, 310
Blessing, 24–26
Boaz, 188
Body, 27–29
Bradford, John, 65
Brotherhood, 30–33
Buber, Martin, 241–42
Buonaparte, Napoleon, 216

C

Cain, 4–5, 30, 65, 234
Calling, 33–34
Carretto, Carlo, 198
Centuries of Meditation (Traherne), 390
Chesterton, G. K., 247
Commitment, 39–42
Communication, 42–45
Competition, 45–48
Confidence, 48–51
Conscience, 51–54
"Corban," 40
Corruption, 54–57
Courage, 58–61
Creation, 61–64
Crime, 64–67
Cromwell, Oliver, 356
Curran, John, 120
Cyrus, 92
Cyrus the Persian, 256

D

Daniel, 13, 177, 197, 271
David, 1, 58, 71, 86, 107, 122, 158, 189, 215, 231, 234, 255, 265, 289, 321
David Copperfield (Dickens), 168
Death, 67–70
Depression, 70–73
Desire, 73–76
Dickens, Charles, 165, 168
Disaster, 76–79
Discipline, 79–82
Divorce, 83–86
Dr. Faustus (Marlowe), 153
Duty, 86–89